Defying Gravity

DEFYING GRAVITY

THE CREATIVE CAREER OF STEPHEN SCHWARTZ

FROM
GODSPELL TO *WICKED*

Carol de Giere

THEATRE & CINEMA BOOKS

An Imprint of Hal Leonard Corporation

New York

Published in 2008 by Applause Theatre & Cinema Books
An Imprint of Hal Leonard Corporation
7777 West Bluemound Road
Milwaukee, WI 53213

Trade Book Division Editorial Offices
19 West 21st Street, New York, NY 10010

Printed in the United States of America

Book design: V. Paul Smith Jr.
Book website: defyinggravitythebook.com

Library of Congress Control Number: 2010291113

ISBN 978-1-55783-745-5

www.applausepub.com

CONTENTS

Wicked

EXTRAS

Dedicated to the creative spirit within each of us

The Musicals of Stephen Schwartz

Stage Musicals

1971: **Godspell** — (music and new lyrics)

1971: **Bernstein's Mass** — (additional lyrics)

1972: **Pippin** — (music and lyrics)

1974: **The Magic Show** — (music and lyrics)

1976: **The Baker's Wife** — (music and lyrics)

1978: **Working** — (four songs, direction and co-adaptation)

1985: **Personals** — (music for three songs)

1986: **Rags** — (lyrics)

1991: **Children of Eden** — (music and lyrics)

1999: **Der Glöckner von Notre Dame** — (lyrics)

2003: **Wicked** — (music and lyrics)

2005: **Captain Louie** — (music and lyrics)

2005: **Mit Eventyr** — (music and lyrics for eight songs)

2006: **Geppetto & Son** — (music and lyrics)

Movie Musicals

1973: **Godspell** — (music and new lyrics)

1995: **Pocahontas** — (lyrics)

1996: **The Hunchback of Notre Dame** — (lyrics)

1998: **The Prince of Egypt** — (music and lyrics)

2000: **Geppetto** — (music and lyrics)

2007: **Enchanted** — (lyrics)

Overture: Entry to Schwartz's Oz

'Cause getting your dreams
It's strange, but it seems
A little—well—complicated

WICKED

During a rewrite session late one May evening in 2003, Stephen Schwartz paced the hotel room floor behind Winnie Holzman, who sat at her computer tapping in script revisions. At San Francisco's Curran Theatre next door, billboards heralded their new musical, *Wicked*, as "The untold story of the witches of Oz." Ready or not, their loose adaptation of Gregory Maguire's novel, *Wicked: The Life and Times of the Wicked Witch of the West*, with songs by Schwartz and book by Holzman, would open in a few days for its pre-Broadway tryout. Glancing across Holzman's room, Schwartz noticed their half-eaten sandwiches on the coffee table and crumpled pages of script scattered on the floor beneath the desk.

"Oh my God! We're living the cliché!" he said, grinning at his collaborator. "I've seen this movie!" She laughed with him as they joked about classic Hollywood film scenes: the camera pans a messy room where frustrated writers tear reams of paper from a typewriter in an eleventh-hour attempt to save their work in progress. "But in the movies," Schwartz noted, "there's a little ripple dissolve and then you see a perfectly formed show."

In the real world, how do artistic people like Stephen Schwartz and his collaborators cross thresholds and bring their dream creations into being? How do they make musicals that appeal to millions of people? These were among the many questions I brought with me when I entered their world. I had no sense

To use the medium of musical theatre to tell stories, and to investigate certain philosophical ideas—that's what interested me as a writer.

STEPHEN SCHWARTZ

of how complex the answers would be. Now, eight years later, this first edition of *Defying Gravity: The Creative Career of Stephen Schwartz, from Godspell to Wicked* is going to press, with my hope that readers will gain insight into the development process for new musicals.

The main narrative of *Defying Gravity* covers musical-making creativity within the context of Stephen Schwartz's career. From his childhood dream of writing musicals through *Wicked*'s opening on Broadway, the book follows the peaks and crises of his artistic life—a storyline that is reminiscent of a three-act play. In Act I, Schwartz burst onto the New York City theatre scene with a succession of hits: *Godspell*, *Pippin*, and *The Magic Show*. With Act II, he faced a series of disheartening flops: *The Baker's Wife*, *Working, Rags,* and *Children of Eden* in London. For Act III, he bounced back with songs for award-winning films, and the mega-hit musical *Wicked*.

In many of the chapters I've inserted "Creativity Notes" in which I quote Schwartz and others sharing insights about the creative process.

I've included an "Extras" section that starts on page 433. Like the bonus featurettes often offered on DVDs, this section provides additional material beyond that found in the chronological narrative. I include chapters based on my experiences in Schwartz's world. (A first-person narrative seemed the best way to present the personality and teachings of a still-active writer.) I also describe Schwartz's newer projects since 2003.

I invite you to visit the book's website for updates or to contact me with your comments.

Carol de Giere
www.defyinggravitythebook.com

ACT I
1948–1974

PHOTO BY WILLIAM "POPSIE" RANDOLPH

~ Grammy Awards Dinner 1972 ~

Stephen Schwartz, age 7, practices his piano lessons on the family's Knabe upright.

Siblings Stephen and Marge perform one of Stephen's early songs. Ralph Sammis, who lived next door to the Schwartz family in Roslyn Heights, New York, remembers confident Stephen walking around the neighborhood recruiting an audience for a little show he'd written. "He played the piano and sang, and his sister danced and spoke some words. It was short, but it was a window on things to come."

CHAPTER I

A Focused Childhood

With a talent like yours, dear
There is a defin-ish chance
If you work as you should
You'll be making good

WICKED

On warm days in the Long Island suburb of Rosyln Heights, seven-year-old Stephen Schwartz could hear piano music coming through his open window. Neighbor George Kleinsinger worked at home while preparing a musical, *Shinbone Alley*, for Broadway. He sometimes allowed the young Schwartz boy to come over and sit at the piano. "Steve," as he was then called, would pick out the tunes he just heard. Kleinsinger encouraged him, and told his parents that the boy had talent.

In his own living room, Schwartz stretched his small fingers over the keys of the family's upright. Although he did learn classical pieces assigned by his neighborhood piano teacher, Mr. Harrel, he much preferred to improvise. "He was always fooling around at the piano," his mother Sheila recalls. "Every once in a while I'd realize what he was doing and I'd say, 'Let's practice first; do that later.'"

Stephen Lawrence Schwartz, the future award-winning composer-lyricist, had arrived at dawn on March 6, 1948, in New York City, where the Schwartz family lived until they moved to France fifteen months later. His father, Stanley ("Stan") Schwartz, a disabled World War II veteran, used GI Bill funds for college tuition to enroll in graduate school in Paris.

During the family's year and a half overseas, Sheila observed how quickly her son learned two languages. "He would speak to

I was the changeling child. Nobody in my family was ever in show business. Nobody knew about it. I just got bitten by the bug.

STEPHEN SCHWARTZ

his little French friends in French and then he'd turn and speak in English to me."

Even more noteworthy to his parents than his facility with language was Stephen's love of music. His favorite toy wasn't a stuffed animal or his little red wagon, but rather his phonograph on which he played yellow 78 rpm records. "There was always music in our house, since I'm a music lover," says Sheila, who had sung in shows in high school. "I remember we didn't have heat in our house. When Steve had an ear infection, we went to stay with our friend, Hilda, who had a nice warm apartment in Paris. She had a recording of *Boris Godunov* (the opera by Russian composer Modest Mussorgsky). Steve loved *Boris Godunov*. There was one aria that he referred to as 'The High Lady.' He just loved it. Kind of strange taste for a little boy."

Opera later became one of his favorite musical genres, another part of the storehouse of impressions from which he would draw for scores like those of *Children of Eden* and *Wicked*. Hilda also played on her grand piano with Stephen watching, collecting his earliest impressions related to his future career.

In mid-1951, the family moved back to New York in time for Sheila to give birth to a daughter, Marge.

Wherever the Schwartzes lived, Stephen absorbed the musical atmosphere mostly created by his mother. Stan was tone deaf, but Sheila sometimes sang as she worked around the house. She frequently played her growing LP collection of classical music and opera, Broadway and film musicals, and folk music.

Three years later Stan and Sheila purchased a small home for their family of four. The upper-middle-class suburb of Roslyn Heights was about twenty minutes from where Stan worked at the Naval Training Devices Center. (He later shifted into businesses of his own. At one point, Sheila began teaching preschool and continued this profession for many years.)

The Schwartz home at 140 Yale Street was part of a development that featured two-story, wood-shingled houses on flat quarter-acre lots, accented by a tree or two. In the backyard or basement playroom, Stephen and Marge commandeered their parents as the audience for their adventures into playmaking. "I was always writing songs and putting on little musicals," Schwartz recalls.

Marge and Stephen Schwartz in 1953.

He got started by staging puppet shows using a little theatre fashioned out of a cardboard box and resting it on the backyard picnic table. Stephen's musical *Hi Dog* was among the shows mounted in this petite venue. It starred Marge's stuffed animals and dolls in lieu of puppets. *Hi Dog* presented the tale of a runaway puppy, and included music and lyrics for one of his first original pieces, "Little Lullaby."

Because he loved so many kinds of music, Stephen hadn't yet set his heart on writing for the Broadway stage. Soon enough, the close proximity of an amiable Broadway composer swayed his career affections for good. Sheila describes her friend and neighbor, George Kleinsinger, as "fun to be with. He used to come over and play songs for us. He was a very good musician." Kleinsinger was best known for "Tubby the Tuba," a 1945 hit record performed by Danny Kaye. With Joe Darion he also wrote a musical narration of *archy and mehitabel*, based on the Don Marquis stories about archy the cockroach (who wrote his story by bouncing on the typewriter keys but couldn't depress the shift key to form capital letters) and mehitabel the cat. Kleinsinger and colleagues started converting it into a Broadway musical, *Shinbone Alley*.

As part of the pre-Broadway preparations for *Shinbone Alley*, Kleinsinger invited cast members to his home to rehearse for a backers' audition. The entire hubbub enthralled young Stephen, who could witness the excitement of a creative project underway, with strangers arriving to sing by the composer's piano, tunes dancing under swift piano hands, and score sheets stacking up.

⤜⤛

For Sheila and Stan, tickets for the glamorous opening of *Shinbone Alley* came compliments of George. They arranged for a babysitter for nine-year-old Steve and his younger sister and headed into the city to the Broadway Theatre on April 13, 1957. The audience found Kleinsinger's stage fantasy enchanting and the Schwartzes believed it would succeed. However, many critics panned the show. (Theatre writer Steven Suskin later quipped, "…how do you do a stage musical in which the main characters are cats?")

For Sheila's music-loving son, no review could have diminished his wide-eyed appreciation when she brought him to view the stylized *Shinbone Alley* during its brief 49-performance run. As the curtain rose, Eartha Kitt (mehitabel) crooned while nearly two dozen dancers moved across the stage. Throughout the night, performers paraded in and out in colorful animal costumes that would garner a Tony Award® nomination. Ms. Kitt sang "Toujours Gai" (French for "always cheery"), and as the story unfolded, Eddie Bracken (archy) sang numbers that seemed especially suited to young audiences, like "The Lightning Bug Song" and "The Moth Song."

By the time archy, mehitabel, and the ensemble poured their full song and dance power into a "Toujours Gai" reprise finale, Stephen Schwartz's new life passion had been aroused. "From then on," Schwartz reflected later, "that was my ambition and direction—to write for the Broadway musical theatre. I think a lot of us get smitten and fall in love with theatre the first time we see it; it certainly was true in my case."

While other parents encouraged their children to prepare for "practical" professions, Stan and Sheila never tried to dissuade their son from a career in the arts. "My parents were supportive," Schwartz affirms. "I didn't have to go through what Leonard Bernstein did; he encountered such enormous resistance from his family, particularly from his father, and I didn't feel that at all. They were quite encouraging." It was a fortunate convergence of nature and nurture: Stephen came equipped with perfect pitch and an acute sensitivity to music, and benefited from an environment that fostered an accelerated artistic development.

For Father's Day in 1957, Stephen "took" his dad to see *Damn Yankees* on Broadway. Over the next years while he lived at home, Stephen eagerly opened large, flat presents for birthdays and Christmas, finding new Broadway albums beneath the wrapping and ribbons. He attended the original productions of *My Fair Lady, Gypsy,* and *West Side Story,* and would continue to add to the list of Broadway experiences every year.

Sheila brought home books about Broadway that included charts of the longest-running shows, and these inspired her son's ambition for his future musicals. "I remember making up a fictitious list of long runs," Schwartz says when making light of his earlier behavior. "It would be like *Hi Dog* and I'd make up some number of performances like 873."

Schwartz's early music training included not only the weekly private piano lessons, but also group lessons in music theory. In 1960, Stan and Sheila heard about classes for children at the Juilliard School of Music Preparatory Division in Manhattan. They brought their son in to audition and he qualified for admission. Nearly every Saturday for four years, they either drove him into the city or he traveled alone by train to study performance, theory, and composition.

A portrait of Stephen Schwartz at age 14.

I used to go to the library and take out the scripts for musicals I hadn't seen. I would look at the lyrics and write tunes to them, then go listen to the cast album and hear what the composer had actually done.

STEPHEN SCHWARTZ

A Dramatic Lyricist in the Making

As Stephen's music skills flourished, so did his proficiency with language and academics. In mid spring of 1958, he and three other gifted students were advanced from fifth grade into sixth, with permission to enroll in seventh grade the following year. In the new sixth grade class at Meadow Drive School, he and his neighbor, Billy Gronfein, became close friends. After school they played at each other's houses, expanding their linguistic skills with puppet theatre, writing play scripts, and discussing intellectual topics, including foreign affairs.

Gronfein remembers that everyone in the Schwartz home loved to talk. "His parents were very intelligent, very verbal. So I think that's associated with why Steve loved words so much. It would be natural coming from his house."

Not only was he verbally proficient, Schwartz also evidenced a quality essential to the constrained craft of matching lyrics to music: the love of working puzzles. "He was very good at putting puzzles together," remembers Gronfein. "We had a puzzle called Hex, and it involved putting together variously-shaped pieces in such a way that the colors formed a particular pattern. It was very difficult, but Steve got it."

During his junior high school years, as Stephen launched his advanced musical studies at Juilliard, he also kept himself busy with movies and reading. Mystery novels attracted him. He especially enjoyed the "whodunit" puzzles of Agatha Christie mysteries. He and Billy even tried writing an Agatha Christie-style novel together, and made it through twenty pages before moving on to other pastimes.

He liked foreign films and watched as many Ingmar Bergman movies as he could. *The Seventh Seal* imagery influenced several of Schwartz's later musicals.

There was one language-based trait Schwartz seemed to be born with that sometimes got him in trouble: he spoke his mind. His mother reports on problems at school related to her son's willful expressions. "He would speak out of turn, and maybe want to talk without giving other people a turn. He didn't do anything seriously delinquent in any way, but he was not a docile little boy in class."

His behavior made some of his peers feel uneasy. "He had a little bit of a 'take no shit' attitude," says Gronfein, "and you weren't supposed to, if you were a nerd or geek in our position. He would speak his mind more than others of us would."

Schwartz suspects he was hyperactive as a child, and consequently difficult for some teachers to handle. He remembers bringing home a report card with all "A" grades except one. "When it came to Deportment it said 'D.' My parents were like, 'How could you get a 'D' in Deportment?'" He is grateful to Mrs. Green, his fifth grade teacher, who assigned extra homework to keep him busy. "It gave me interesting things to accomplish. It also allowed me to begin socially to relate better with kids."

High School Drama and Future Plans

At Mineola High School, Schwartz poured his extra energy into creative outlets such as the extracurricular Thespian Society. Although he never aspired to become a professional actor, he took to the stage with his characteristic bold flair and played several father roles, including one in *The Diary of Anne Frank*. "I did a lot of shows with white shoe polish in my hair," he remembers. He also accompanied shows on piano, and even drafted his first original musical.

Steve was a dominant figure in the high school drama scene.

BILL GRONFEIN

In spite of his enriched surroundings and the opportunities he was given, Stephen still felt like he'd been born on Mars and it would take a special effort to get comfortable. "It was not just his intelligence," Gronfein explains about the oddness his friend felt, "but where his intelligence put him in the distribution of people in Mineola; he was way out there."

Stephen Schwartz performs in a theatre camp production of *Spoon River Anthology* in the early 1960s.

Gronfein adds that his friend's disinclination toward team sports gave his peers further reason for disdain. "In our high school that made kids wonder what kind of weirdo he was. 'You're a boy and you don't like sports, what's wrong with you?'" His short stature didn't help, and he and Billy were sometimes bullied. In future musicals, especially *Pippin* and *Wicked*, he would write songs exploring themes of alienation and acceptance.

In order to adapt to his high school environment, he found kids with whom he could relate and adjusted his behavior. "My way of dealing with feeling out of place was to be chameleon-like and assume a great deal of protective coloration in order to fit in," he explains. "And I wound up having a very good time and having a lot of friends, but there was a sense inside myself of fraudulence, of wearing a mask, because if people knew who I really was, I would be completely isolated."

At least if he could get out on his own, he could determine his surroundings. He would be graduating from high school at age sixteen rather than the usual age of eighteen (because he had started kindergarten at four and skipped a grade). He felt ready to burst out of the gate for the race toward a more fulfilling future.

Stan Schwartz had high expectations for his smart son's future. For a while it didn't seem Stephen was having luck in the college entry arena. In 1963, they drove around to visit various colleges. The fifteen-year-old applied to Harvard, Yale, and Oberlin. He was rejected by all of them in spite of excellent scores on the Scholastic Aptitude Test and his high grades.

"It's better to be lucky than smart," Stan Schwartz used to repeat to his family. Luck had come Stan's way years earlier when a friend shared his invention of a process that polarized light. They formed a company called Technamation, manufacturing signs and training aids, and did very well with it, including a contract to supply signage at the 1964 World's Fair in New York.

During an exhibit hall installation for the fair, Stan found himself working alongside the renowned Broadway and film scenic designer, Jo Mielziner, who had graduated from Carnegie Institute of Technology. When Stan described his son's predicament, Mielziner said, "Well, if he's really interested in the theatre, he should check out Carnegie."

Stephen hadn't yet heard of this school that included the oldest college drama department in America and drew the cream of young acting and directing talent to the campus in Pittsburgh, Pennsylvania. It was Carnegie Institute of Technology at the time, and shortly thereafter merged with Mellon Institute to become Carnegie Mellon University. He applied there and was initially accepted as a playwriting major, after submitting a play he'd written.

That fall, Stan and Sheila Schwartz drove their sixteen-year-old freshman and his belongings across the mountains of Pennsylvania to his first home away from home—a shared room in a modern, concrete dormitory at the edge of the attractive college campus in a quiet area of Pittsburgh.

Carnegie was exactly the right school for me, and exactly the right environment. And so it was serendipitous, and it was the beginning of my belief that sometimes when things seem to be going wrong for you, if you wait long enough, they're actually going to turn out right.

STEPHEN SCHWARTZ
ABOUT GETTING REJECTED
FROM HARVARD AND YALE

Stephen Schwartz plays mandolin in *As You Like It*. For this Carnegie drama department production, Schwartz set Shakespeare's lyrics to his own music. The show was a main stage theatre production in the Frick Fine Arts Building during the 1966-1967 school year.

Frick Fine Arts Building at Carnegie Mellon University.

CHAPTER 2

MORNING GLOW: THE COLLEGE YEARS

Morning glow, morning glow,
Starts to glimmer when you know
Winds of change are set to blow
and sweep this whole land through

PIPPIN

From 1964 to 1968, Stephen Schwartz studied for his BFA in drama, while across America, the nonconforming youth culture blossomed. On the lawns of the Carnegie Mellon University campus, colorfully adorned arts students in jeans and fringed vests tossed Frisbees between classes as slide rule-toting engineering students walked past them in their button-down shirts.

Schwartz's own membership in the liberated 1960s was assured on many levels, from his casual dress to his antiwar sentiments. The school newspaper, *Carnegie Tech Tartan*, showed no photo of him, but his peers remember the wildly colored print shirts he often wore and his peroxide-lightened, chin-length hair—a kind of New York-hippie-meets-the-Beach Boys combo.

The social idealism reflected in much of his later lyrics awoke in his moral conscience during this period (as in "Someday" from *The Hunchback of Notre Dame* and "In the Beginning" from *Children of Eden*).

He didn't join peace marches until later, but was a proponent of the civil rights movement, and more than anything, responded to music from African-American artists, particularly the songs of the Holland-Dozier-Holland writing team.

During his first semester in Pittsburgh, he came back to his dorm room one day and found his roommate playing an album he'd never heard: *Where Did Our Love Go*, written by Holland-Dozier-

In terms of liberation and "doing your own thing," Carnegie was the sixties squared—it was very extreme in that way, and I found it very helpful.

STEPHEN SCHWARTZ

Holland and sung by the Supremes. It featured radio hit tunes such as the title song, "Baby Love," and "Come See About Me."

The energetic and heartfelt material captured Schwartz instantly. "We pretty well wore it out. I remember becoming so obsessed by the Supremes that I made my parents take me to see them perform at the Deauville Hotel in Miami Beach when we were on vacation there the following winter. The Motown sound became one of the kinds of music that changed my writing from more theatrically-oriented music to more pop, and one can hear Motown influences in many of my songs." Schwartz also listened to Martha & the Vandellas and The Four Tops, who had hit singles of Holland-Dozier-Holland songs. While he still would listen to and write songs in other genres, chart-topping pop music began seeding his musical soul.

Carnegie students majoring in the visual and performing arts walked to classrooms on the marble floors under vaulted ceilings in the magnificent Frick Fine Arts Building. Some of the drama department faculty members maintained a traditional approach to their classes and productions, staging Shakespearean dramas and shows like *Hedda Gabler* in the building's theatre or the neighboring Studio Theatre. Others explored newer, more experimental directions.

No one offered musical theatre training. "Musicals represented mainstream, and this was a very rebellious time," explains Leon Katz, who taught drama history there. "When you mentioned *My Fair Lady* you had to frown and turn up your nose—'Oh, one of those mainstream musicals.'"

Sitting in playwriting classes, Schwartz, already a loner in his dedication to musical theatre, felt isolated from the lively actors' world. He persuaded the dean to let him switch to a directing major so that he could broaden his experience and be more involved with other

"Dramats," as the students in the drama program were called.

He wrote songs during his free time. Among Schwartz's early companions at school was an attractive blonde Dramat named Colette Bablon, who listened to his newly composed works. "There was a tiny cubicle of a rehearsal room in the fine arts building with a piano," Bablon recalls. "That's where he would play me his songs. I was amazed at what was coming from this kid. And the lyrics were really clever. He was very precocious."

Her friend stood out from the crowd by the strength of his dream. "It never occurred to him that he wouldn't be successful. That was quite unusual. The actors were like, 'I hope we make it. Wouldn't it be great?' Stephen was just, 'When I'm famous...'"

On September 22, 1964, Schwartz attended the Broadway opening of *Fiddler on the Roof* as guest of a star's daughter, whom he had befriended the previous summer. Had he been told he'd one day collaborate with the show's bookwriter, Joseph Stein, it wouldn't have surprised him, for that was the level of his unequivocal dream.

Taking Creativity Public — The Scotch 'n' Soda Club Musicals

With the force of his ambition to write for the musical theatre, Schwartz identified the extracurricular "Scotch 'n' Soda Club" as the best outlet for his creativity. The club, funded by student activities fees and ticket sales, mounted original musicals each spring in a theatre in the Skibo Student Center.

Designed to promote cooperation between students with different majors, the club's activities brought together students from a range of departments. It served as a testing ground for budding talents in a similar way that the University of Miami's Dramatics Club had for Jerry Herman. For Schwartz, the next four years of work for Scotch 'n' Soda proved "instrumental in training me for my career that followed."

Katherine Morgan (left) and Rebecca Smith (right) perform roles in the 1965 Scotch 'n' Soda production of *Whatserface*.

There was an aura of knowing around Stephen. He was trying to get everything just perfect, and he did.

KATHERINE MORGAN

Before the end of each academic school year, the club's governing board (composed of students and one faculty advisor) held auditions for ideas for the following year's musical. In the spring of 1964, Iris Rainer Dart (the future author of *Beaches* and other novels) won the committee over with the funny story of *Whatserface,* a show about a cleaning lady who becomes a spokesmodel for a cosmetics firm. However, the show's songs weren't in good shape. Board members were delighted when a real composer showed up the following fall. Schwartz transformed *Whatserface* into a full musical.

"He was a whirlwind," says Katherine ("Kay") Morgan, who acted in *Whatserface* in 1965. She watched the then-seventeen-year-old whip a group of assorted singers into shape as if he had been doing it for years. Morgan remembers his charisma. "He had a respect for talent, and everyone was happy to do things his way."

After weeks of preparation using a makeshift stage in the ballroom of the Skibo Student Center, *Whatserface* opened. "The audience went crazy for it," Morgan recalls. The comic musical's financial success at the box office refilled the club's coffers, which had been depleted by the previous year's over-budget extravaganza.

For Schwartz, it was his first experience working with an orchestrator, and there were lessons to learn about how to mix the sound: too heavy on the saxophone here, too little piano there; it was hard to get it right. In years to come, he would always give orchestrators specific suggestions.

With the popular and financial response to *Whatserface,* the Scotch 'n' Soda committee was pleased to receive a proposal from Stephen and Iris for the following year. *Nouveau* would be based on the art scene, and would feature a jubilant score in the mode of Jule Styne with hints of a pop-music sound.

With the 1966 production of *Nouveau*, Schwartz could add another campus box office hit to his résumé. The musical included an intricate four-part fugue called "A New Society," which the composer revised eight years later for *The Magic Show* (with new lyrics and renamed "The Goldfarb Variations").

The Drama of Drama Studies

Nina Faso

In the fall of 1966, two students joined the directing program who would become key collaborators in Schwartz's musical theatre career. One was John-Michael Tebelak, who, several years later, would conceive *Godspell*. The other was Nina Faso, a petite, raven-haired girl from an Italian family in Syracuse, New York, who grew up loving opera, musicals, and popular music. Faso eventually would share more of Stephen Schwartz's career journey than just about anyone (in her roles as the future stage manager for *Godspell* in New York, director of several regional companies of *Godspell*, co-adaptor of *Working*, and original co-director of *Rags*). Faso and Schwartz quickly became friends when she started dating one of Schwartz's roommates.

Not that Dramats had abundant time to socialize. The directing program required students to train in every area of theatre, from acting through the complete range of technical production procedures. Faso reports, "We were carrying double loads: the acting program *and* the directing program. It was a very exhausting regimen."

In spite of the intense focus, she and Schwartz occasionally relaxed over Italian food and listened to opera recordings. "We used to go out to dinner and to all the main stage productions at the Pittsburgh Playhouse. We always sat together and ate opera mints and he would make snide remarks. He just cracked me up."

To keep music as a centerpiece of his existence, Schwartz took a part-time job accompanying silent films shown on campus, and remembers playing at screenings of *Birth of a Nation* until his fingers were sore.

During this period he moved off campus and tested his freedom to make choices, though not with recreational drugs. ("I'm relieved to say that I missed the drug thing by a year—the class after me started that," he once commented.) He explored the use of different names. For his first college musical playbill he had listed himself as "Stephen Sandford" just because he liked the name. Colette Bablon recalls, "Stephen had a notion that when he became famous he was going to change his name to Lawrence Stephens, because his name is Stephen Lawrence. He used to joke about the fact that 'only my real friends would know to call me Stephen and that's how you would know that you were really my friend.'"

Schwartz would later describe his next musical—*Pippin, Pippin*—as full of "bitchy, sarcastic dialogue," which Colette says represented the way they talked. They would sit in the back of a theatre or movie dissing people. "We were very judgmental in the way that eighteen-year-olds who don't know anything about anything can be judgmental. We thought we were cooler and better and funnier and smarter."

Schwartz's untamed roguishness at least allowed him to move into the center of things creatively.

Pippin, Pippin in Pittsburgh

I was in my very serious and pretentious phase.

STEPHEN SCHWARTZ

For Schwartz in 1967, the approach of spring signaled an opportunity to stage his next Scotch 'n' Soda show. On his nineteenth birthday, as director, choreographer, and co-writer of *Pippin Pippin*, he whirled fellow students into the fast-paced rehearsal period for the musical.

The Tartan reporters had been chatting up preparations for this new musical with news and feature articles, as if the show had every reason to be taken seriously. As reported in the paper, the idea of making this piece of history into a musical came from Ron Strauss, a music major. "[Strauss] was reading through his history book when he came upon the idea for this year's Scotch 'n' Soda show. Eliminating several historical figures and reviving others, he and junior director Lawrence Stephens (Steve Schwartz) wrote the Charlemagne succession drama into a musical they called 'Pippin, Pippin.'"

What Strauss considered stageworthy was the real-life quagmire of family issues relating to the sons of Charlemagne, especially his illegitimate son, Prince Pepin, born around 770 AD. According to historical records, discontented nobles encouraged the prince to stage an uprising and assassinate King Charles. When that insurrection failed, Charles sent Pepin to live out the rest of his life as a monk in a monastery. "Pippin," Strauss knew, was the anglicized spelling of Pepin, and he used the name in the title. (Neither he nor Schwartz remembers why their college version became *Pippin, Pippin* instead of just *Pippin*.)

The collaborative effort began one day when Schwartz heard music coming from a practice room in the fine arts building. He entered the room where Strauss was playing the piano.

"That sounds wonderful! What are you doing?" Schwartz inquired. Strauss replied that he was writing a musical for Scotch 'n' Soda. He explained the story concept, which instantly appealed to Schwartz.

"Do you want some help? I'd like to help you do this!"

Strauss agreed, initially pleased to share the process of completing such a huge task, even though he eventually wanted to write a full opera from this material on his own. With the draft of a script and partial score already completed, Strauss had focused on Prince Pippin's life immediately preceding his attempt to overthrow his father, and the strong emotions that seemed

appropriate for opera—the father-son relationship, court intrigue, jealousy, and betrayal.

Schwartz had in mind more traditional musical fare, which
meant adding humorous songs (to Strauss' consternation) and
developing an elaborate story structure. He wasn't yet sensitive
to the nuances of collaboration and wanted to test his ideas.

By the time the two writers completed a score, Schwartz had
added lyrics to most of the twenty musical numbers and written
music for nearly half of them. As a vanity record pressed for the
cast attests, the work was uneven but mature for teenagers. This
early score was not pop-music-inspired, but rather attempted a
medieval sound blended with a musical theatre style.

Schwartz contributed several angry rants: one between Pippin
and his girlfriend, followed by another between Queen Fastrada and
her mother, Berthe. He triumphed with several pieces, including
"Victorious," a number that anticipated "Glory" for his Broadway
version. He revealed his greatest virtuosity with a five-part piece
called "Preparations," inspired musically and conceptually by the
"Tonight" quintet from Bernstein's *West Side Story*.

With casting completed at the end of 1966, preparations began
in earnest the next spring. "Since March 6 the 33-member cast
has been meeting six days a week in order to learn the staging
and choreography," reported the *Tartan*.

"Keeping with the show's medieval milieu, director/choreog-
rapher Lawrence Stephens has staged such events as a country
dance, coronation and sword battle. Chorus members portray
courtiers in one scene, peasants in another and monks in still
another scene—all in the same act." As with any Scotch 'n' Soda
show, the college students approached it with ambition, not only
performing in the shows, but also creating the music, lyrics, book,
lighting, set design and construction, costumes, orchestrations
and orchestral performance.

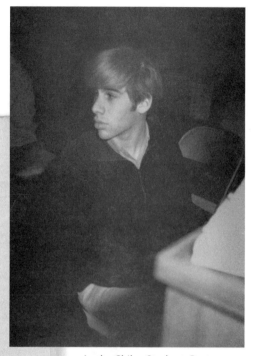

In the Skibo Student Center, Stephen Schwartz accompanies an early work session for *Pippin, Pippin,* in December 1966.

SCOTCH 'N' SODA

PRESENTS

pippin, pippin

A MUSICAL PLAY BY

RON STRAUSS AND LAWRENCE STEPHENS

———————

SETTINGS BY STANLEY THOMAS

COSTUMES BY RICHARD ARAM KESHISHIAN

LIGHTING BY DON EARL

TECHNICAL DIRECTOR LEN ALEXANDER

MUSICAL DIRECTOR DAVID GERWIG

———————

DIRECTED AND CHOREOGRAPHED BY

LAWRENCE STEPHENS

FACULTY ADVISOR JEWEL WALKER

PRESENTED APRIL 28, 29, MAY 1, 2, 3, 4

SCOTCH 'N' SODA THEATER

SKIBO

For the *Pippin, Pippin* program, Stephen Schwartz used his briefly adopted pen name, Lawrence Stephens.

SCENES

The action of the play alternates between King Charles' palace at Aix-la-Chapelle and the province of Prum in the late Ninth Century.

ACT I

Scene 1. The Throne Room at
           Aix-la-Chapelle
Scene 2. The Courtyard
Scene 3. Fastrada's Bedchamber
Scene 4. The Courtyard
Scene 5. Country House at Prum
Scene 6. Fastrada's Bedchamber
Scene 7. A Country Fair
Scene 8. The Courtyard
Scene 9. The Throne Room
Scene 10. Country House

ACT II

Scene 1. The Throne Room
Scene 2. A Corridor
Scene 3. The Tavern
Scene 4. The Courtyard
Scene 5. The Tavern
Scene 6. Fastrada's Bedchamber
Scene 7. The Chapel
Scene 8. The Throne Room
Scene 9. The Monastery at Prum

MUSICAL SYNOPSIS

ACT I

OVERTURE
To Be A King ....Charles and Court
Goodbye, Yesterday ....Pippin
Run Into Your Arms ....Fastrada
Father Said ....Pippin
Victorious ....Charles, Pippin and Court
They Will Listen To You....................Pippin and Berthe
I Don't Owe You A Thing ....Adrienne
Begging Milady's Pardon ....Fastrada and Berthe
A Simple Dance ....Adrienne, Pippin, Dancers, Peasants
While You Were Away ....Gisela, Carloman, Charles, Fastrada
                                                              and Court
Easy To Be Happy ....Pippin and Adrienne
Pippin, Pippin ....Pippin and Adrienne

ACT II

ENTR'ACTE
The Next King ....Carloman, Fastrada and Court
The Next King (Reprise) ....Pippin
Come With Me ....Nobles, Simone, Dancers, Peasants
Somebody Loves You ....Adrienne
Preparations ....Pippin, Fastrada, Simone, Nobles
                                                             and Adrienne
My Son ....Berthe and Charles
Kyrie ....Monks
Soliliquy ....Pippin
Finale ....Adrienne and Pippin

The program for *Pippin, Pippin* reveals the level of ambition of its creators. Scotch 'n' Soda productions were full-scale original musicals.

Charlemagne (Bob Calvert), Fastrada (Rebecca Smith), and Charlemagne's mother, Berthe (Peggy North), argue over family matters in in the 1967 Scotch 'n' Soda production of *Pippin, Pippin*.

Nancy Swartz dances during the "Come With Me" number in *Pippin, Pippin* while several of the 34 other cast members look on.

Pippin, Pippin **On Stage**

Pippin, Pippin opened April 28, 1967, with Stan and Sheila Schwartz in attendance. The show rewarded the audience with its ambition as much as its content. This original musical offered a varied score, an involved story, elaborate costumes, sets, and dances.

Billy Gronfein flew in from Chicago for the show. "I remember being blown away that my friend, this person I knew, actually did something as gigantic as this, whether it was *West Side Story* or not." Gronfein remembers that after the *Pippin, Pippin* performance that night, Schwartz seemed tremendously exhilarated, and joined an opening celebration with the hardworking cast and orchestra. This was the morning glow—the glimmer of good things to come.

The climax of the story came later when the vanity album pressed for the cast became important to the show's future. Sometime in 1967 or early 1968, Schwartz returned to his apartment after class and found a letter with a New York City return address. In the letter, a stranger named Harry Lynn wrote that he'd heard the recording of *Pippin, Pippin* and believed it had potential. He inquired as to whether the writers would like to take it further.

Schwartz remembers waving the letter in front of *Pippin, Pippin*'s co-writer to discuss further development. Strauss didn't really believe in the letter and said he was moving to Oregon, but wished him luck.

Interestingly enough, the new musical involved the unequivocal dreams of a college-age young man (Pippin), who pursued his dream. Strauss had been uncomfortable with the way Schwartz pursued his dreams by moving in on a work in progress.

Lawrence Miller, a Scotch 'n' Soda board member, admits that Schwartz "glommed onto" Strauss' project and eventually took it over. But the board had encouraged it, especially after the financial success of *Whatserface* and *Nouveau*. "Steve had been so wonderful that it was worth it to have him write the score, as long as Ron was willing. It ended up as a collaboration."

Schwartz felt justified in claiming the piece of history as source material for his Broadway-bound efforts and believed the show's first conceiver could still write his own version for an opera anytime—no one was stopping him. Schwartz had worked hard on *Pippin, Pippin* for six months and wanted to move ahead.

When he started rewriting the show, it became simply *Pippin*, and over the coming years changed completely. Even so, because Strauss had conceived the original version, an arrangement was made so that he would have some continuing financial interest in the show when a fully revised version opened on Broadway.

A BFA and New Life

In the spring of 1968, Schwartz was ready to graduate with a Bachelor of Fine Arts degree after directing Bock and Harnick's *The Diary of Adam and Eve* as his senior project. During that final semester, he had also collaborated with friend David Spangler for a Scotch 'n' Soda production of *Twice Upon a Time*. Schwartz created a one-act opera, *Voltaire and the Witches*. He describes Spangler's half of the show, *Shakespeare in London*, as being a charming musical that was better than his own.

As Schwartz switched over from student to alumnus, he joined the ranks of his peers who would eventually land television, stage, and film roles in *Hill Street Blues, L.A. Law, Sesame Street, Godspell, Grease, 1776,* and others.

He would always count his training in the dramatic arts as essential for his future artistic efforts. "I decided to go to drama

Stephen was the only person I knew at Carnegie who wanted a musical theatre department. Music was always his first love.

NINA FASO

school when I went to college, rather than majoring in music," Schwartz explained to an interviewer later in his career. "I think everybody writing for theatre should take acting, because the processes are so similar. A lot of writers don't understand how to get that internal process going, so they write songs that are nice but not really actable."

He continually relies on lessons from the drama world for his work and teaching. "For me, when I am working on a musical number for a show, the story I am trying to tell comes first. It is a little like an acting exercise—I try to become the character, think about what the character's action is (what he or she is trying to 'do' at that moment), and then express myself as that character would."

It was at Carnegie, also, that he decided to focus on lyrics as well as music. "I had always wanted to be a composer, and then I began being my own lyricist in college because I couldn't find people to write lyrics for my songs whose work I felt strongly enough about."

Thus he became that rarity in the world of musicals—a "composer-lyricist."

CREATIVITY NOTES

A Working Process That Connects With Feeling

While writing songs for his Scotch 'n' Soda Club musicals, Stephen Schwartz established his compositional process. He later contrasted his process with that of composers such as Leonard Bernstein, who sometimes wrote out music without first playing the notes. "I understand the logic of writing away from the piano," Schwartz comments. "But for me, the emotion comes out through my fingers on the keyboard. A lot of times, I don't know what something is going to be, musically. I sit there and think, 'What's the story I'm telling?' and 'Who's the character?' and 'What is he or she feeling?' and I kind of let my fingers tell me. Then I'll hear things and select them. There is this automatic, unconscious process going on, and part of me is just trying to stay conscious and alert to it and say, 'Oh, it seems like that would be good,' as opposed to sitting at a drafting table with music paper and writing from there. It's just a different way of working."

His gift for mellifluous accompaniments comes in part by way of his ability to sing a separate melody as he plays something far more complex. "My process is that I sing the songs as I'm writing them," he explains. "I'm playing something at the piano and I'm singing to it. I'm not writing out the melody, I'm singing the melody either to words or 'la la's. I don't have the greatest voice in the world so sometimes they are written for better voices than mine, but my songs are written to be sung."

While Schwartz likes to work at the piano, other artists find their own route for connecting to a core emotion or idea. In *Wild Mind: Living the Writer's Life* (p. 73), author Natalie Goldberg advises writers to warm up with regular writing practice. If they feel they are treading water, they can stop mid sentence, add a dash, and write— "What I really want to say is" and then proceed. Says Goldberg, "It allows you to drop to a deeper level or to make a one-hundred-and-eighty-degree turn in what you are writing. It's a device to help you connect with what is going on inside."

Stephen Schwartz and friends formed The Pipe Dream rock 'n' roll group. Left to right: Tom Ellis, Chris Murphy, David Spangler, Melon Roos, Stephen Schwartz, John Harrison.

CHAPTER 3

TRANSITIONS: KEEP DANCING THROUGH...

Let's go down to the Ozdust Ballroom
We'll meet there later tonight
We can dance till it's light
Find the prettiest girl
Give 'er a whirl
WICKED

In the summer of 1968, with so many steps to master in the real world of theatre, Schwartz headed to the green hills of New Hampshire for the New London Barn Playhouse, just as he had for the previous two summer stock seasons. Had the twenty-year-old gone straight to New York to work in theatre, his lack of experience might have been more of an obstacle. At the New London Barn Playhouse he could rise to as many occasions as his natural talent would allow. After starting as assistant musical director, he advanced to musical direction, musical staging, and directing, expanding his backstage experiences with shows like *How to Succeed in Business Without Really Trying, Oliver!*, and *Camelot*. Occasionally he appeared in a show, as in the chorus for *Kiss Me, Kate*.

When the Playhouse lost its contracted choreographer, the director drafted Schwartz to fill in. "I had a bit of a flair for it (though Messrs. Robbins, Fosse, and Champion need have had no worries)," Schwartz comments. "I have absolutely no dance training, so I worked out musical numbers by figuring out stage movement patterns and flow rather than by specific steps. When I needed actual steps, I would rely on some of the dancers in the company to help come up with them."

One of those dancers was Joanne Jonas, whom he later invited to audition for the cast of his first off-Broadway show.

Show business is a difficult entry-level profession; there's no clearcut route into it. If you want to be a lawyer or a doctor, we all know what steps you need to go through. With show business, it's all sort of haphazard, which is why parents don't want their children to go into it. It is a struggle to get started.

STEPHEN SCHWARTZ

Another performer would help with the dance in his broader life drama. Twenty-one-year-old actress Carole Piasecki (stage name Carole Prandis) played the role of Gladys Bumps in *Pal Joey*, which Schwartz ended up directing. Carole brought a bold, powerful energy to her stage performance and a down-to-earth practicality to her perspective on musical theatre. She had "gold hair with a gentle curl," as he would later write in a *Wicked* song. "That's the girl he chose" to receive the roses, pearls, and the house in the country one day. With her unassuming pragmatism, Carole would serve as an essential sounding board for his creative outpourings in years to come.

In the fall of 1968, the two continued seeing each other. Carole had moved to Manhattan and was singing in clubs, and Stephen resided with a friend on 72nd Street. Through Carole's contacts, he got a job playing piano for a tour of *Young Abe Lincoln* put on by the TheaterWorks children's theatre company, while Carole performed in the show.

His parents knew that Carole, with her Polish Catholic background, would celebrate Christmas. As the gift-giving season approached, his mother asked, "What are you giving Carole for Christmas?"

"I think I'll give her an engagement ring," he answered.

"We were rather surprised," Sheila Schwartz remembers, "because he was only twenty."

Carole and Stephen married on June 6, 1969. Stephen moved into Carole's apartment at 155 West 81st Street, a relatively quiet section of Manhattan's Upper West Side, and had movers bring up a used piano on which he would write much of the music for *Godspell* and *Pippin*. *(See photo on page 41.)*

Carole had the talent for a professional acting career but was already experiencing the downside of the uncertainties it entailed. She had been chosen for a small part in *1776* and had looked forward to her Broadway debut until the entire role was cut during the out-of-town tryout. In February of 1970, she understudied the lead role in a new Broadway musical and found the experience disillusioning. "When I got into a Broadway show—a flop called 'Georgy'—I discovered that once you attain it, you find that it's really not what it's cracked up to be."

Her desires shifted toward a starring role at home, raising a family, and letting Stephen step into the limelight.

Carole Piasecki Schwartz

CREATIVITY NOTES

Subterranean Ways

In the early days of their marriage, Carole Schwartz learned that a songwriter playing solitaire is a songwriter creating. She tried conversing while he pored silently over card arrangements with his blank writing pad beside him. He'd be polite for a while and then ask her "pleeezze" not to disturb him. "You're just playing solitaire," she used to say. "No, I'm working!" he'd insist.

Playing solitaire is one of several types of activities artists use to access subtler intuitive processes. Schwartz says that if he gets stuck while working out a lyric or a song idea, he'll stop and engage his attention in something that requires "extremely shallow consciousness, like driving, or playing solitaire, or hitting tennis balls against a ball machine, or even taking a shower."

These activities become a kind of meditation—a way of detaching and getting into a different space. He comments, "You're engaging in just a little bit of mental activity. You're thinking about watching the road, or watching the ball or something, but it's not very deep thinking, and I find that frees up my subconscious and suddenly *whissst*—all this stuff comes from my unconscious into my consciousness. It feels like channeling because you're not in control of it at all."

Carole Piasecki (stage name Carol Prandis) plays the lead in *South Pacific* in a production in Flint, Michigan, and Anna in *The King and I* in a New Hampshire summer stock production.

Career Connections

Meanwhile, Schwartz followed up on his only lead for New York's entertainment industry, beginning a convoluted journey which proved that "making it" in show business is not a paint-by-numbers process.

He looked at the address on the letter he'd received his senior year of college from prospective producer Harry Lynn, who wanted to produce *Pippin*, and made an appointment to see him. For many years afterward he would remember the climb to Lynn's tiny sixth-floor walk-up apartment, and his surprise in finding a space so small that the bathtub, covered with a piece of plywood, doubled as the dining room table. Sitting at the bathtub table, he and Lynn, another young man with aspirations, planned a backers' audition in an effort to get seed money for further work.

By the time of the audition, Lynn had dropped out, but an agent wannabe who worked in the mailroom at a large talent agency, Ashley Famous, invited writer's agent Bridget Aschenberg to attend with him. Aschenberg was impressed.

"I don't know anything about music at all," she said to Schwartz, "but I think that you are talented. I'm going to go back to my agency, and I'm going to tell a friend of mine about you."

About two weeks later, Schwartz received a call. "Bridget Aschenberg keeps haranguing me to call you, so come in and meet with me," Shirley Bernstein said.

Leonard Bernstein's dark-haired, sophisticated sister knew her way around the entertainment world.

As if to foreshadow the family connection, one morning during Schwartz's high school days, his clock radio, tuned to classical station WQXR, woke him with the overture for Leonard Bernstein's *Candide*. "They must have announced what it was right before it started, so then I spent months trying to find out what it was," he recalls. Entranced by its beauty, he asked anyone who might know of it, humming a little passage until finally a friend's mother identified it. The great maestro's works became a source of inspiration for the young composer.

Some weeks before his twenty-first birthday, Schwartz entered into an agent-client relationship with Shirley Bernstein. She agreed to represent him after listening to him perform songs from *Pippin* in the small audition room at the Manhattan agency office. (Stan Schwartz had to sign the agency contract for his underage son.)

Among other suggestions, Shirley asked "Steve" to use his full real name, and "Stephen Schwartz" officially became his professional moniker.

Shirley would be Stephen's key to unlocking doors of the show business world for the next twenty-five years. She invested time in an untested client, and he would make them both a fortune.

Butterflies Are Free opened in October of 1969 with the title song by Stephen Schwartz.

Musical Futures

Like the young man in Leonard Gershe's play, *Butterflies Are Free*, Stephen Schwartz had moved to a big city not knowing how he would make his way as a musician. Bernstein's client Keir Dullea needed a song to sing in that play in which he was cast as a blind folk singer. Shirley made a deal with the producers to allow Schwartz to submit a song "on spec."

After reading the script, Schwartz wrote the song "Butterflies Are Free." "I tried to write something that sounded a little like an amateur folk singer (only a few guitar chords) and lyrics that were devoid of visual imagery because he was blind." It worked well and he earned his first Broadway credit when the show opened October 21, 1969.

The play ran on Broadway at the Booth Theatre for 1,128 performances. However, a one-song credit seemed only a first step to the ambitious composer-lyricist, and certainly didn't offer financial security at $25 a week in royalty income.

His pathway to greater prosperity came as a result of youthfulness, talent, and good timing. One day Bernstein brought her client to a meeting at RCA to talk to them about a music publishing deal. He played his *Pippin* score on a piano and gave them a demo recording of two pop songs. To his astonishment, they offered him a job in their A&R (Artists and Repertoire) department. Much of the job would entail going to clubs to listen to new acts and recommending to RCA those he thought had potential. He was to bring the most promising in to the studio and record demos with them. He cautioned them, "I don't know anything about recording studios." But they responded that he would learn. "It was at a time," he remembers, "when older people who had been in the music industry a long time weren't trusting their judgment anymore as to what the record-buying kids wanted, so they were willing to hire young people without a lot of experience."

It turned out that because of his theatre background, he would also advise RCA on what shows they might record. (Among those he recommended was the cast album of *Follies*, but RCA declined; ironically, two years later, *Godspell* would win the cast album Grammy Award over *Follies*.)

One of the most fortunate parts of the job was producing demo recordings and some full albums. While at RCA he learned through experience, and, as he admits, a lot of mistakes, about the recording studio. He became acquainted with technical details about sound equipment and seemed to have an ear for what would work, so that in later years he could produce his own cast recordings. Among the albums that Schwartz produced for RCA was the 1970 original cast album of Gretchen Cryer and Nancy Ford's *The Last Sweet Days of Isaac*.

Musical Transitions

In the late 1960s and early 1970s, Schwartz often listened to other people's recordings, a habit that helped him cultivate the kind of blended sound in his own songwriting that would later make his work so popular with theatre crowds.

Among the record album covers near Stephen and Carole's turntable at the 81st Street apartment was one with a painted self-portrait—a Canadian singer whose blonde hair hung straight and long. Stephen would listen as Joni Mitchell's voice slid through poetical songs on her album *Clouds,* like "Chelsea Morning." The final track, "Both Sides Now," was the most breathtaking for him, and would remain his favorite song of all time.

"Both Sides Now" expressed how he looked at things. Joni Mitchell sang about life's illusions and seeing things from multiple points of view. The topic of illusions and reality would remain a major theme in Schwartz's work for his entire career.

Regarding his job with RCA:
I was 21 years old and making what seemed to me an enormous salary, and learning about the studio. Synthesizers were just coming out, so to me it was like being paid for going to recording school.

STEPHEN SCHWARTZ

"What Laura Nyro used that I hadn't heard before in pop music was her poly-chords and tempo changes within songs. She did really radical things."

STEPHEN SCHWARTZ

He had not faced the hardships that others of his favorite artists encountered, like James Taylor with his drug problems. Still, he had his share of challenges. "I came to New York not knowing anybody, or how to break into the business, and I just sat in my apartment on 72nd Street looking out at the people on the street, thinking 'I'm just going to die up here, not having done anything, not even knowing how to try to do anything, while all these people down there seem to be going on with their busy lives.'"

But as he absorbed the music of his favorite pop artists, he unknowingly moved himself closer to his goal. Another artist whose work impacted his style significantly was Laura Nyro. Her album *New York Tendaberry* would frequent the front of the stack beside the turntable. The cover featured Nyro with her eyes closed, head tilted back as if she were soaring through an inner universe of feeling. A *New York Times* reporter once described her as having "a three-octave range of emotions." Schwartz loved how she let the tempo flow and change as suited the mood of her songs. He learned from her style—how she'd combine a chord with an unusual bass note—and that became part of his sound.

Schwartz's musical vocabulary expanded further as he listened to the rich harmonies of The Mamas and the Papas and The Beach Boys, the passionate music of Jefferson Airplane, the mellow sounds of *Sweet Baby James*, with James Taylor classics like "Fire and Rain" and the title song. Although Stephen would be writing for musical theatre, he felt liberated listening to pop artists like these, as if they gave him permission to explore new possibilities.

"I think that everybody is influenced by things that particularly speak to them," Schwartz says. "I just feel like my style is a big mishmash of all the things I've seen and heard that I really liked and I just recycle them in some way."

Of course he was also influenced by Broadway composers whose work he loved: Richard Rodgers, Jerome Kern, Irving Berlin, Jule Styne, Leonard Bernstein, and Jerry Bock. And he maintained his constant appreciation for the "serious" music training he'd received in his piano studies when he explored the works of Handel, Bach, Beethoven, and others. Later composers also suited his taste, including Mussorgsky, Rachmaninoff, Puccini, and Copland. (He was unknowingly so fond of Copland that, as a child, he used to turn on the television to watch CBS Reports because of the "amazing theme music," which someone eventually told him was from *Appalachian Spring*.)

All of this music poured into Stephen Schwartz's musical melting pot and somehow helped meld the styles that fans came to love. As musical historian Stanley Green would later write, "What the composer has brought to the theater is a modern, youthful, crisp sound, primarily influenced by rock but also endowed with sensitivity and melodic grace."

He drew from an amalgamation of influences as he revised the score for *Pippin*, moving it away from the medieval music pastiche of some of his college efforts into a blended pop/rock score.

Schwartz also followed the young musicians' urge of the day and joined a rock band. He and college buddy David Spangler, along with others, formed "The Pipe Dream," sharing songwriting efforts in the "classical rock" style, as Spangler describes it, with multi-part harmonies. Their success remained a pipe dream, but it was good practice in songwriting.

A First Music Team Member

Schwartz was certainly not alone as a young musician in the process of making and remaking himself in the early 1970s. New York was a mecca for aspiring songwriters and performers looking for that big break by being offered a recording contract or by winning stage roles.

The closing of *Minnie's Boys* on Broadway in May of 1970 had left one such seeker, Stephen Reinhardt, asking himself, "What do I want to do with the rest of my life?" He'd been a dancer in the show but now drew from his natural rhythmic and musical talents to become a singer-songwriter. Reinhardt, with his long hair falling into his face, became a wandering troubadour auditioning at record companies.

On the afternoon of Reinhardt's appointment at RCA, a then-unfamiliar Schwartz entered the waiting room where several wannabes had gathered.

"Who's my three o'clock?" Schwartz said.

Reinhardt raised his hand.

"Uh, okay, come on in." As the two walked toward the audition room, Schwartz sighed and remarked, "Boy, it hasn't been a good day. I hope you're good."

Reinhardt sang a few pieces, accompanying himself on piano. Schwartz said, "I want to record you!" They felt at ease with each other and became friends as they worked on demos.

Not long afterward, Reinhardt got a call from Schwartz. "I'm writing this show called *Pippin*," he said. "You have kind of a similar style of playing as I do. Would you like to work with me on it? I need to get some arrangements together."

Despite his lack of experience, Reinhardt, in a "What the heck?" mood said, "I'd love to."

Yet the breakthrough would not come with *Pippin*. Something remarkable was brewing in Greenwich Village.

The upright Sohmer piano used by Stephen Schwartz when he composed songs for *Godspell* and *Pippin*.

My piano in New York was a very good-sounding upright—an old Sohmer with a metal frame, incredibly heavy, that I think pre-dates the twentieth century. It's shamefully out-of-tune now and I don't really play it anymore; I just can't bring myself to get rid of it. I might roll it out the basement door into the pond one day.

STEPHEN SCHWARTZ

Cast members in the pre-Schwartz version of *Godspell* at La MaMa bring cheer to their audience. Left to right: Robin Lamont, Prudence Holmes, Jeffrey Mylett, Peggy Gordon, Herb Braha, and James Canada.

CHAPTER 4
GODSPELL OFF-OFF-BROADWAY

You are the light of the world!
But if that light's under a bushel,
It's lost something kind of crucial
You've got to stay bright to be the light of the world

GODSPELL

When Shirley Bernstein's efforts to get *Pippin* produced yielded nothing in terms of percentage income for her agency, her superiors pressured her about "the kid." But she continued shepherding New York producers into her office to show off Stephen Schwartz. Edgar Lansbury (Angela Lansbury's brother) and his business partner, Joe Beruh, were on her long list of people to invite. "She had a young man with a musical that she wanted very much for us to hear," Lansbury recalls.

Lansbury, a former scenic designer, and Beruh, a Carnegie Mellon graduate, were on the lookout for new shows to mount at the Promenade Theatre on the Upper West Side, which they owned. They also booked shows at the Cherry Lane Theatre in Greenwich Village and had a certain amount of control over its offerings. To satisfy changing tastes of the early 1970s, they sought something unusual in theatrical style. Also, if they could find it, they wanted a piece with a spiritual bent.

When Stephen Schwartz played and sang *Pippin* for them, they didn't feel the show was ready for serious consideration, but they were enthused about the songwriter. "We were very, very impressed with this talented young guy who seemed to be fluent in all kinds of ideas and styles," Lansbury says.

Shirley Bernstein was entirely responsible for my career. She believed in me and killed herself on my behalf.

STEPHEN SCHWARTZ

John-Michael was truly religious. But he was also of the 1960s. So the two things were there in an odd combination.

LEON KATZ

⟨⟩

Unbeknownst to any of them, an early version of *Godspell* had recently hatched at Carnegie Mellon and was about to play off-off-Broadway. The brainchild of John-Michael Tebelak, "*The Godspell*," as it was first called, was supposed to 'weave God's spell over the audience'—or so Tebelak told one of the actors he recruited for the cast.

Godspell would ideally match the producing team's wish list for innovation and spirituality. In fact, Tebelak's idea of linking clown characters with Biblical parables was so unprecedented that even the student actors in the first cast couldn't grasp the concept for the first few weeks of rehearsal.

The impetus for *Godspell* originated from Tebelak's master's degree thesis requirements for directing a show. As an undergraduate he'd been interested in Greek drama and mythology, but for his final work he decided to adapt something from a Judeo-Christian source. He read miracle plays and passion plays, but felt them to be "very heavy." One afternoon he read the four Gospels in one sitting.

Then Tebelak, who was raised Episcopalian, decided to attend a church service and it was there that a spiritual experience, or rather lack thereof, completed the inspiration for the new musical.

On a snowy Easter morning in 1970, Tebelak arrived at the Anglican Cathedral in Pittsburgh wearing his standard overalls and scraggly Afro haircut. The people sitting near him were complaining about the snowfall upsetting their plans.

He explained later to *Dramatics Magazine*, "...an old priest came out and mumbled into a microphone, and people mumbled things back, and then everyone got up and left. Instead of 'healing' the burden, or resurrecting the Christ, it seems those people had pushed Him back into the tomb. They had refused to let Him come out that day."

As Tebelak left the service, a policeman who had been sitting a few pews in front of him wanted to frisk him for drugs. "Apparently he had thought I was ducking into the church to escape the snowstorm. At that moment—I think because of the absurd situation—it angered me so much that I went home and realized what I wanted to do with the Gospels: I wanted to make it the simple, joyful message that I felt the first time I read them and re-create the sense of community, which I did not share when I went to that service."

John-Michael Tebelak

The 1960s peace-love spirit supported *Godspell*'s gestation, as did trends in the dramatic arts. Viola Spolin's improvisational techniques had inspired new styles that led to *Second City* and later *Saturday Night Live*. These were in vogue among the less traditionally-minded faculty members and students in Carnegie's drama department. The approach that led to *Godspell* involved an ensemble of actors as the creative team. Without prewritten scripts or precise instructions from a director, a show's storyline and content evolved through group participation.

In 1968, Leon Katz invited the Living Theatre group to campus, allowing Tebelak and friends to be exposed to the extremes of experimentation. "We all went crazy when the Living Theatre was there," Nina Faso recalls. "They were absolutely the wildest group of people we had ever seen. They were guerilla theatre—all very dramatic people who just went overboard with everything."

Tebelak revered stage and film director Peter Brook, and adapted some specific ideas from his *Marat/Sade*. In Brook's stageplay and film, a group of mental patients performed a play for the aristocracy of France. Some of them wore clown outfits. A wire fence surrounded their stage. These images became central to *Godspell*.

Nina Faso remembers Tebelak's fascination with Jerzy Grotowski's work. "Grotowski was a revolutionary Polish theatre

The Living Theatre set John-Michael on fire. His entire working process changed after that experience.

PEGGY GORDON

director whose theatre would look almost like a boxing arena, with benches on both sides. Actors would sit on benches in sight of the audience, and when they had to do something, they just got up and became that character."

To help justify the show's style academically, Tebelak read and referred to Harvard Professor Harvey Cox's treatise, *The Feast of Fools*, describing the concept of Christ as a clown—a bringer of joy.

By the summer of 1970, Tebelak had collected the ingredients: Biblical parables, clowns, a fenced-in arena, cast members leaping up to act out a scene, and actors creating some kind of in-the-moment happening. But the recipe wouldn't work without a group of cooperative chefs.

As a directing major working on a project, Tebelak could select actors from the casting pool made up of sophomores and upperclassmen. He posted a list on the casting board for clowns 1-10. But when he tried communicating his intentions for reverent comedy to his recruits, they resisted. "I held a rehearsal with the cast, reading the Bible, saying this is a funny show, and by the end, eight of the ten performers were crying, trying to quit," he later revealed. "They thought I had finally flipped!"

Andy Rohrer, who played Jesus, says it took the cast several weeks of rehearsal meetings before they grasped John-Michael's approach. "The clown concept, though it was on paper, didn't penetrate the rehearsal process until late. John-Michael was an idea guy, living in his intellect. You'd listen to him and just think, 'What is he talking about?' You couldn't relate it to any practical reality."

Then one night he brought in grease pencils to a rehearsal. Tebelak said to the cast, "All right, tonight everybody's going to paint everybody else." They started drawing crazy pictures on each other's faces as their mood shifted from worried to light and playful. When they realized he expected them to wear clown faces for the show, they suddenly understood the theatrical context for performing Bible parables. The room exploded with creativity, and the earliest *Godspell* sprang to life.

"Everybody would take the stage and act out a story," recalls Sonia Manzano. "We eventually called it 'Mickey Mousing' the parables, like if you said, 'A sower sowed a seed,' you might mime someone sowing or even sewing for that matter!"

They experimented with reverse engineering scenes based on Bible phrases. Knowing how Jesus completed a parable, actors invented a charade or game or other goofy behavior to give him a reason to teach that lesson. As the ten clowned around, Tebelak either approved or nixed their antics for use in the show. Meanwhile, his friend Duane Bolick wrote some rock music to go with lyrics from hymns or psalms. These became the songs for Tebelak's thesis project.

The tiny cinderblock Studio Theatre at Carnegie Mellon University only held about fifty people. *The Godspell* played for a few days in December of 1970, with more people attending each night as word of mouth spread. By the final night of the sold-out show, people were crowding into the standing room at the back.

Audiences savored the theatrical feast: parable vignettes with a sprinkling of hymns set to rock tunes accompanied by actors playing kazoo or guitar, or by a three-piece band. Actors with grease-painted clown faces performed charades, slapstick, and send-ups of movie stars. They served wine at intermission, depicted the betrayal and crucifixion of Jesus, and carried their Jesus through the audience and out the front door. Then the room exploded with wild cheers. This piece simply had to go further.

Next, Tebelak ventured into New York City to meet with Ellen Stewart, founder of the experimental theatre called Café La MaMa. She could fit the show into a two-week opening in her calendar in late February, 1971.

John-Michael was a genuine eccentric. He came by it honestly. That's really who he was but he also cultivated it a little bit. It was studied eccentricity...he was very multidimensional, very creative, almost free-associative sometimes.

COLETTE BABLON

Around that same time, Stephen Schwartz quit his job at RCA. "I just let it end," he says about the two-year contract he chose not to renew. He'd already been moonlighting as music director for *The Survival of St. Joan*. But the rock musical might fail in the face of lackluster winter attendance at its off-off-Broadway venue. "I said to Carole, 'I won't have the courage to quit my RCA job if *St. Joan* closes, so I think I'll do it now.'"

On Saturday, March 6th, the telephone rang at Stephen's parents' home on Long Island. He and Carole were visiting to celebrate his twenty-third birthday. Stephen picked up the phone and listened to the enthusiastic voice of his college friend Charlie Haid (later known for playing Andy Renko on *Hill Street Blues*), who invited him to see *The Godspell* the next day in Manhattan's East Village. It was the final performance, explained Haid, who was becoming an associate of the show's prospective producers, Beruh and Lansbury. They had hopes that the piece was right for the Cherry Lane Theatre if someone could write a contemporary theatrical score. Stephen was reticent about schlepping into the city in the spring rain, but spoke with his agent and with Carole. They both encouraged him to check it out.

The next day, Stephen and Carole arrived at La MaMa on East 4th Street and entered a new world. To Stephen's surprise, on stage he saw mostly familiar faces from Carnegie "Dramats." He enjoyed the cheery clowning-around by his peers. The show was Woodstock made Biblical. "My first impression of the show was that it was messy but inspired," Schwartz said later.

Producers Beruh and Lansbury attended as well. They believed that the show, now dubbed "*Godspell*," would succeed commercially if it had a new score. There was a slot to be filled at the Cherry Lane in mid May, which meant relying on a composer for a fast transformation.

On Monday, Schwartz walked into the producer's office at West 51st Street and Broadway feeling a little more optimistic about his future. When asked if he could turn *Godspell* into a full-scale musical, complete with new song and dance numbers, he felt ready.

"Sure, I'd be happy to," he told them without hesitation.

"Great. We go into rehearsals April 11th."

And that was that. About the absurd deadline Schwartz later remarked, "I was so young and stupid, I had no idea that you couldn't do this. I didn't say to them, 'But that's impossible.' I just said, 'Uh, okay.'"

Beruh and Lansbury brought him back to La MaMa with the intention of delicately introducing to the cast a stranger who would be altering their show. Instead of an awkward hush, the place filled with shrieks of delight over the "small world" serendipity. "They had accidentally hired one of our friends to do our music," recalls Nina Faso, who had become the show's stage manager. For her it was like, "You're introducing me to Stephen Schwartz? Why don't you just introduce me to my mother?"

Creative Team

They made an odd-looking creative pair: athletic and trim Stephen Schwartz at 5'8," and ultra hippie John-Michael Tebelak, whose bushy hair accentuated his height of 6'1". Yet there was a comfortable feeling between them; they worked together smoothly and symbiotically.

When they held their first meeting, Tebelak handed over a mimeographed script that included psalms, hymns, and parables for Schwartz to work with. New song placement and tunes were now up for grabs, though the show's basic structure remained intact.

When Stephen saw Godspell, *he understood it immediately, which is why he could do it quickly, especially since he already knew all of us.*

NINA FASO

It's a lot easier to write something when you see it, and you know what it is, and it works. It wasn't like it had to be fixed—it just had to be musicalized in a way that was more accessible or emotional, and had more variety.

STEPHEN SCHWARTZ

For most of the rest of his career, Schwartz would become involved with shows from their inception. In this case, he had the luxury of being an audience member of a fully formulated version before beginning his score. And since lyrics take Schwartz much longer to write than music, the idea of using lyrics already adapted from hymns and psalms seemed ideal. He readily entered into the spirit of the piece, sprinting to complete the assignment in the fastest possible way.

Neither he nor his casually Jewish parents saw a problem with him working on *Godspell*. He hoped his ignorance would prove an advantage in terms of a novel perception. "I don't come from a Christian upbringing and therefore I really didn't know the New Testament," he once explained. "I was reading some of these parables for the first time, and the hymns that I set with new music for the show are all from the Episcopal Hymnal. I basically was responding to the material fresh."

As Schwartz composed at the piano, he found ways to express the themes of love and joy, as well as the exuberantly expansive flavor of the production. The gravity-defying act here would be to convert both the show and the cast's opinion of it from pure wildness into a more definitive structure. His view of the La MaMa *Godspell* as "messy" was not a compliment. It was up to him to make it a little more straightforward, while still preserving the playful thrust. His experience taught him that musical theatre had a structure, with things like an opening number, a character singing about what he or she wants, a big production number, a first act climax, and a big finale. There had to be a balance of ballads and uptempo numbers. Could this approach be imposed upon such a sprawling hodgepodge of material? Could the talky prologue be the opening? Could he invent a finale with power? He was eager to try.

For Schwartz's version, his credit would read "Music and New Lyrics," for he only slightly amended hymn or psalm lyrics, but wrote all new music.

He and Tebelak discussed ways of making the show appeal to people of various faiths by making it dramatically compelling. For example, if Jesus and Judas had a conflict at the end with the betrayal, then earlier in the show they needed to develop a caring relationship of some kind. And so he wrote "All For the Best" as a vaudevillian soft-shoe duet number to demonstrate their friendship.

To add conceptual strength and drama to the end, Schwartz converted a long (and dramatically dull) monologue into the song, "Alas for You."

Unlike the original music, which had been largely group numbers, Schwartz's score revolved around a lead singer for each song. "Bless the Lord," for example, seemed ideal for a lead vocalist accompanied by a lively group backup. At his piano, Schwartz followed the lyric he'd been given for "Bless the Lord." He wrote a flashy new two-speed tune in Laura Nyro style.

Casting for *Godspell*

While Schwartz tinkered with songs, eight of the ten La MaMa *Godspell* players reassembled (two with weak singing voices departed).

Carnegie *Godspell* cast members Robin Lamont, Sonia Manzano, and David Haskell, all college juniors, had previously accepted Tebelak's call after petitioning their academic dean for time off. However, the dean had declined permission to senior Andy Rohrer. Several other students decided to continue their studies rather than run off to New York.

To fill out the New York cast, Tebelak enlisted Carnegie graduates he'd directed in a summer stock program in Ohio: Jeffrey

Everybody had a musical number that began with him or her and became his or her signature tune, so that each of the eight disciples had a moment where he or she declared themselves.

STEPHEN SCHWARTZ

Mylett, Gilmer McCormick, and Stephen Nathan. Soon their clowning would be preserved in the script as the dialogue of characters "Jeffrey," "Gilmer," and "Stephen" (Jesus).

Tebelak remembered Herbie Braha (sometimes listed by his stage name Herb Simon) from some offbeat comedic performances at Carnegie, and phoned him. Another college friend, Peggy Gordon, came to help with music, and then decided to join the adventure as a cast member at La MaMa.

Schwartz sought out Joanne Jonas, whom he remembered from summer stock in New Hampshire, where he'd admired her vocal and dance talents. He'd written the song "Bless the Lord" with her voice in mind, and wanted her in the show. That made her audition pretty easy. She came into a rehearsal hall, learned "Bless the Lord" on the spot, and then debuted the song for the producers an hour later. They loved both the song and Joanne, so she was in.

Lamar Alford, a well-trained singer, had performed in another Café La MaMa show, and Tebelak recommended him. Schwartz wrote "All Good Gifts" with him in mind.

Thus, ten clowns for the Cherry Lane production were more or less ready to reinvent a musical filled with joy and love, once it had a new score.

Schwartz decided to keep "By My Side," a song he'd heard at La MaMa. In his meetings with John-Michael he said, "I could try to write a new song for this spot, and maybe I would write a song as good as this, but why bother if we have this wonderful song?" Peggy Gordon, the song's composer, and Gilmer McCormick, who wrote the song's harmony, had performed it in New York. (Lyrics are by their college friend, Jay Hamburger.)

Before proceeding further, Schwartz phoned Stephen Reinhardt to ask if he would be music director and keyboard player for *Godspell* rehearsals and performances. Although Reinhardt

I was delighted to have a song written for me, as was I to work with Stephen again. He's so talented and we had so much fun in summer stock. The concept for Godspell *was awesome and I was very happy to do it.*

JOANNE JONAS

replied, "I've never been a musical director for anything in my life," Schwartz just said, "I know you can do it"—a gesture of faith that he would give many aspiring musicians in the coming years.

Reinhardt was one of the first to hear the new *Godspell* songs and remembers, "They were really wonderful, very clever and very heartfelt." From that point on they started preparing for the production together. Schwartz gave him handwritten lead sheets. "All we had were notes, words, and chords and my idea of how it went," Reinhardt recalled later. "There were no recordings or demo tapes or anything like that. I learned the songs off these pieces of paper."

Once the producers heard and approved the music, it was time for an in-house debut. The cast, who had been working up a new version of the script, assembled at the New York City apartment of one of the producers. Stephen Schwartz, Steve Reinhardt, Joanne Jonas, and Lamar Alford performed the new score.

Until that moment, the show had been freewheeling and eccentrically nontraditional. No one in the cast was quite prepared for it to sound like a professional musical, except, of course, Joanne and Lamar. Schwartz accompanied at the piano, with Joanne debuting "Day by Day," he and Steve Reinhardt singing some of the others, Joanne belting "Bless the Lord," and Lamar singing "All Good Gifts." It was a *tour de force* beyond anything that anyone had imagined.

When they finished, the room settled into a fidgety silence. There was no warm applause or congratulations. Without saying anything, two cast members pulled out their guitars. Not knowing how else to respond, they began singing the familiar old songs.

The original *Godspell* cast for the Cherry Lane Theatre production encircles director John-Michael Tebelak. Clockwise from top: Stephen Nathan, Gilmer McCormick, David Haskell, Herb Braha, Jeffrey Mylett, Peggy Gordon, Sonia Manzano (with the feather), Robin Lamont, Lamar Alford, and Joanne Jonas.

The Cherry Lane Theatre in Greenwich Village.

CHAPTER 5

GODSPELL AT CHERRY LANE

You guessed! It's all for the best
GODSPELL

"We were stunned when we first heard this music," says Peggy Gordon about Schwartz's *Godspell* score. "It was not only different, but there was so much more of it. We were protective of the old and a little reserved toward the new."

Edgar Lansbury believed Schwartz was on the right track, even if the cast "balked a little bit" when asked to let go of their previous songs. "Actors are like that. They become very possessive of the way things are done." Soon enough, the cast adjusted to the new material and began to love it.

Raising about $50,000 to launch an oddball off-Broadway musical required a substantial effort by Beruh and Lansbury. They brought in investor Stuart Duncan as a co-producer. Schwartz and a few cast members drove to Duncan's house in New Jersey for a backers' audition. "They sang Stephen's score that the kids had just learned seconds before," Lansbury remembers. "It was all very new. Stephen had hardly even played the songs more than once or twice." Sonia Manzano recalls being asked to work the room by walking around and interacting with the potential backers. It went well and they raised the initial cash, although additional financial arrangements would be needed to continue through the summer.

With an opening scheduled for May 17th, rehearsals began in mid April at the historic 99-seat Cherry Lane Theatre, nestled in a quiet corner of Greenwich Village, where streets followed 17th-century cow paths and farm fencerows rather than the formal grid imposed north of 14th Street. Playwrights whose work

We were all very anti-showbiz at the time, and Stephen wanted to turn Godspell *into a musical comedy. He managed to do it successfully, but it took a little while to get into the spirit of what he wrote.*

NINA FASO

was presented behind the brick façade of the Cherry Lane—Albee, Beckett, Ionesco, among others—were often those who eschewed dramatic grids passed along by previous generations. *Godspell* would continue that legacy. The new musical embodied the dynamic relationship between tradition and innovation, and streamed toward full production amidst these two riverbanks of creativity.

Finding *Godspell* Again

I was a minister's daughter. There were six generations of Anglican bishops in my family. When we started poring over the Bible for Godspell, *I said to John-Michael, 'I'm so offended. I feel like lightning is going to strike.' Yet in the course of rehearsals I found what a reverence he had for whom he called God. He wanted to take Jesus down off the cross and exemplify the joy of the Gospel.*

GILMER MCCORMICK

In rehearsing for Cherry Lane, the cast, now with Joanne and Lamar, returned to the improvisation process used for the earlier incarnations of the show. As before, they worked primarily with the Gospel According to St. Matthew, and made new choices about who would bring to life each parable.

"When we got the script, it was just the Bible," Gilmer McCormick recalls about the process. John-Michael asked them to consider what would be their personal experience if they met Jesus. He'd say, "If this kind of person came into your life for a period of a day, this kind of perfect soul, what kind of person would you become?" From that they were to derive their character. McCormick told the director, "I would become like a small child. I'm a real daddy's girl, and I kind of want him to pick me up and carry me away at the end of the show." So all her clowning was based on her childlike character.

Peggy Gordon remembers, "We fashioned ourselves after the seven dwarves [from *Snow White and the Seven Dwarfs*]—the shy one, the bold one, the showy one. My concept of my character was she was the shy one." Gordon knew she would be singing "By My Side," which includes a line about daring to walk with Jesus. Becoming a shy character "gave credence to the whole thing of putting the pebble in the shoe, daring herself to go with him."

Stephen Nathan's developments for the show included rhythmic echo talk as a kind of sonic game. He would say a word and others echoed it as if they were in a cave. (He'd say "The lamp" and the others echoed "lamp, lamp, lamp…").

Although Tebelak appreciated the innovative contributions, he sometimes cautioned actors against wandering too far. Peggy Gordon recalls, "John-Michael wanted the humor to serve the innocence and never to sacrifice the innocence, because that's what was going to enable audiences to open up and have an extraordinary experience. And he was right."

Stephen Schwartz helped bring structure to the spontaneity. While planning the score, he and John-Michael discussed the overall flow of the show and appropriate spots for musical numbers. They evaluated the event of each song, so that the actors wouldn't just be stopping the story to sing. In most instances, songs suggested characters' moments of revelation or conversion. "They are pledging their loyalty, their belief, their faith to become a member of this community that's being formed," Schwartz explains. Accordingly, he wrote songs for a featured cast member to lead.

To insert "Day by Day," they had to find the moment that Robin (the first character to sign on) has a breakthrough. This occurs after she listens to a parable about a man who doesn't forgive his brother's debts and is condemned. The Jesus character then explains the parable's meaning in terms of the importance of forgiveness, inspiring Robin's epiphany and reason to sing "Day by Day."

Joanne Jonas remembers that they based the song spot for "Bless the Lord" on a moment during the rehearsal that she personally experienced a revelation. "In *Godspell*, the Jesus clown inspired the other clowns to listen and try to understand some very profound concepts about love, care, integrity, humility,

The Three Stooges probably inspired us as much as anybody. Everything was a goof. It was whatever each actor had in their bag of nutsyness that became these characters.

NINA FASO

Top: Stephen, Robin, Herb, and Jeffrey act out the Pharisees parable early in Act II.

Bottom: The mood dampens as the group prepares for the finale in Act II.

sacrifice, and so on. One day while we were rehearsing the 'rich man' parable, I had a revelation about the power of love that was coming through Jesus. A lightbulb went off inside me, the actress, and I said, 'Oh, I get it!!' out loud. John-Michael and Stephen said, 'Right there—that's when you should sing 'Bless the Lord'.'"

Sonia Manzano's clown manner was replete with comic sexual innuendos. Schwartz thought it would be fun for her to perform a Mae West-style musical number. The words to "Turn Back, O Man," a cautionary Episcopal hymn sung by Robin Lamont in the La MaMa *Godspell*, seemed perfect for a send-up.

When discussing the song's placement with the director, Schwartz concluded that it should open the second act to establish a contrast between the "slightly ribald and innocent fun" of the other nine players and Jesus' mood when looking ahead to the challenge of his betrayal. "Thus he sings a more serious third verse of the song, then gets caught up in a little of the fun. But as soon as the song finishes, he quiets the rest of the celebrating cast members and tells them, 'This is the beginning.' And we are into the second act."

Act II included the only part of the show with a straightforward storyline: the Last Supper and the final moments of Jesus' life. This, in combination with the community-building aspect of Act I, gave the show something of a musical structure from opening to finale.

Their plans for bringing in color after the "Prologue" presaged Schwartz's theatrical connection to *The Wizard of Oz* three decades later. "John-Michael and I viewed the "Prologue" as being like the black-and-white opening of *The Wizard of Oz*. [The "Prologue"] is interrupted by the arrival of John the Baptist and then the whole band comes in and all the colored lights bang on," relates Schwartz, "corresponding to the switch in the movie from black-and-white to Technicolor."

As preparations continued, Schwartz, who handles details well, found himself running rehearsals. Tebelak had trouble coping with the fast-paced development pressure. Experiencing inner turmoil over his art and his personal relationships, he often turned to alcohol and drugs, and wasn't functioning well as a director. But by then his ideas had taken root in the imagination of his cast members, who would bring them to fruition.

This last part of the process of creating a commercial musical was mostly Schwartz's territory anyway. As Nina Faso explains, "Stephen had been writing musicals and studying musical theatre for so long. He knew things that we didn't know, like how to get applause on a number."

His involvement also coincided with the script's evolution to final form. For the La MaMa production, Nina Faso wrote out a minimal version of a script in longhand, but as the show moved closer to opening at Cherry Lane, the producers began to panic about copyright. Faso says, "There was no script and you can't copyright something that isn't on paper, or add lighting cues. And the musicians couldn't play music that wasn't written down. So when Stephen came along everything had to be written down—codified. The characters had to have names—they had just been clowns one through ten."

Although the music was still mostly in his head or on lead sheets, Schwartz wrote out the lyrics. The actors finalized their formerly improvised parts, memorized their songs, and gathered for rehearsals. The petite theatre had no extra rehearsal spaces, so when not on the stage as a group, they found places to practice their parts outdoors or in corners of the hall.

Steve Reinhardt remembers the first day the cast rehearsed the "Prologue." Schwartz brought index cards with the music solos written out for each cast member. He'd play a part on the piano for one actor and then send Reinhardt outside with the actor to rehearse it *a cappella*.

Fortunately, by then the actors were sold on Schwartz's new tunes. "It was heaven," says Peggy Gordon, "pure, blissful, joyful, exuberant heaven to learn these songs, to learn our individual harmony parts and then sing them in the context of the show."

With no official choreographer (it wasn't supposed to look slick anyway), Stephen Schwartz, Stephen Reinhardt, and Joanne Jonas served as ringleaders for staging *Godspell*. Jonas had been hired, in part, because of her years of experience as a dancer, and she developed movements for some of the major numbers. Reinhardt knew how to stage a softshoe, so he choreographed "All For the Best" and others.

Schwartz managed it all and explained the kind of thing he wanted, while Tebelak said things like, "I don't know how to make it feel like this, but here's the way I want it to feel…"

The actors were all involved in their own moves, so it truly was "choreography by committee." Jonas remembers how "Stephen would say to the girls, 'Peggy, you take Robin and Sonia out in the other room and see what you can come up with for this.' Then one of the guys would say, 'I'm going to take the guys over here and we'll work out something.'"

Since La MaMa, Nina Faso had been scrounging for props and set material. When Tebelak first conceived *Godspell*, he wanted to enclose the action within a chain link fence suggesting an abandoned inner-city playground. The actors arranged three unfinished wooden planks on a couple of sawhorses providing the remainder of the scenery. Props and costume add-ons used in the show came out of garbage bags on stage or were hung on the fence at the top of the show. As Schwartz later explained, "In lieu of area lighting, illumination was often provided by one or more of the nine PAR lights that were hung in three rows over the stage and which actors could turn on and off when they needed to be lit. The emphasis was on simplicity, on 'Theatre of Poverty,' on theatrical magic created by the actors with minimal production values."

Simple it may have been, but the group was ready to have fun with it. Faso, as stage manager at La MaMa, added props to the metal fence backdrop. "When Stephen saw the show, he loved that, and so he kept giving me more stuff to put on the fence."

Playful mayhem seemed to be the general tenor of rehearsals. "Everyone was laughing all the time," Faso recalls. "It was always like, 'Well, who could do the stupider stuff?' Especially for 'We Beseech Thee.' It was ridiculous. We laughed so hard!"

To add color and movement for this song, Schwartz asked Faso to collect some batons and colored banners or posters. He suggested one with the song's often-repeated lyric "Hear Us." Nina went off and returned with banners that spelled out the words in separate letters: H-E-A-R U-S. Chaos reigned as the cast began using them. Says Faso, "Stephen thought it was hysterically funny when they got it mixed up and they would have H-E in the middle, then they'd change it back. So the cast's attempts to flash the spelling for the audience became a standard part of the antics."

Schwartz stopped laughing during technical rehearsals, as there was so much to finish before the opening. He didn't have time to worry about reviews. The producers hired press agents, Michael and Edwin Gifford, who invited critics to the opening and proved invaluable for getting the word out.

"We never really thought past opening night," Schwartz remarks. "It was just like, 'Oh, well we're doing a show.' As we got close to the opening, all of a sudden it began to occur to us that people were going to come and look at the show and write

The original program for
Godspell at Cherry Lane.

things about it."

Before the first preview, Joe Beruh invited the young composer to dinner at the Blue Mill Tavern next door to Cherry Lane. That night Beruh made a prediction.

Schwartz says, "I guess I was pretty terrified and Joe said, 'Look. I just want to let you know that this is going to be okay. You guys are going to be okay with the show, I can tell you right now—I've been around. But if you really work hard these next few days and you guys really pull this together, you and John-Michael and the cast, if you really do your work, you're not going to believe what's going to happen.'"

Opening Night and Beyond

Godspell's run at the Cherry Lane Theatre started with three previews. According to Reinhardt, the group worried that although the show seemed perfect for Greenwich Village, "the mentally overwrought critics were going to come down and tear it apart. You have to have your heart on your sleeve when you come to see *Godspell* in order to receive the full experience that it has to offer."

On Sunday night, May 16, 1971, critics started attending the show. More came on Monday, the official opening. That night reviews would be published in newspapers or presented on the three local network television stations.

Their opening night party was to be at Sardi's restaurant on 44th Street, where theatre producers and others traditionally gathered to wait for reviews. After the May 17th show, Schwartz joined his fellow *Godspell*ians at the party, but he was worried because he didn't believe it was the best performance. "I was quite trepidatious," Schwartz recalls, "as one would expect from my first major show in New York." His agent stayed beside him and reassured him in a way he would remember for many years.

"Well, maybe tonight's performance wasn't that strong," Shirley Bernstein began, in an effort to calm her client. "But you said that Sunday's performance was your best yet, and that was the performance the *New York Times* came to. This is off-Broadway and the only thing that matters off-Broadway is the *Times*. No one really cares about anything that anybody else says."

A moment later, the press agent came up and told Schwartz, "I feel I have to tell you that we've heard that the *Times* review is not very good. They just didn't go for the show."

Shirley overheard that and said, "Well, the *Times* doesn't matter off-Broadway! It's all about a consensus. The *Times* is very important on Broadway, but off-Broadway the people just read all different things. It's all going to be a big consensus."

Schwartz says, "Of course by this time I was completely hysterical. And we get into the elevator to go upstairs because they used to show the three television reviews, which were very important at that time. Shirley is saying to me, 'Look, this isn't really your show the way that *Pippin* is your show. I mean, that was a show that started with you, that's really your show, this is a show you came in on and worked on, it's not like this is really your show. You'll have a chance with your show.'

"The doors of the elevator open, there are three televisions, Channel Two comes on, and Channel Four comes on, and Channel Seven comes on, and they're unqualified raves. And then we start to find out that everything but the *Times* has been a rave. We're watching the television reviews and Shirley turns to me and she says, 'This is *your* show, darling,' and she hugged me delightedly.

"I thought, at that point, I'm staying with this woman for the rest of my life. This is what you want in an agent. You want someone that's going to try to make you feel good about things no matter what."

After the party at Sardi's, Carole and Stephen drove out to Long Island to Stephen's parents' home, reviewing the thrilling experiences of the evening along the way. "Our life is never going to be the same," Stephen commented. He also expressed his gratitude for what had transpired. "No matter what else happens, no one can take this night away from me."

With a chain link fence as a backdrop, *Godspell* cast members act out parables. The actor playing Jesus sits in front wearing his Superman shirt (Stephen Nathan); Judas is on the right. In *Godspell*, the characters of John the Baptist and Judas are combined into one role, that of Jesus' right-hand man who ultimately betrays him (here played by David Haskell).

CREATIVITY NOTES

The Playfulness Factor

"The creation of something new is not accomplished by the intellect but by the play instinct acting from inner necessity. The creative mind plays with the objects it loves."
—Carl Jung

"Godspell was really all based on play, the innocence of children who see the world uncorrupted—that is how the whole piece evolved. Through improvisations we found what worked and what didn't work. Ultimately, in the rehearsal process, we solidified those moments that seemed alive and true, and suited the structure of the piece. It was a very transformative process."
—Stephen Nathan, original *Godspell* cast member

Godspell's success is a testament to the value of play for the creative process and the attractiveness of exuberant enthusiasm. *The Artist's Way*, written by Julia Cameron with Mark Bryan, connects enthusiasm, play, and the needs of artists. "Enthusiasm (from the Greek, 'filled with God') is an ongoing energy supply tapped into the flow of life itself. Enthusiasm is grounded in play, not work. Far from being a brain-numbed soldier, our artist is actually our child within, our inner playmate. As with all playmates, it is joy, not duty, that makes for a lasting bond."

In theatre work, directors sometimes use improvisational games to initiate spontaneous play. Theatre game developer Viola Spolin once commented, "Through spontaneity we are re-formed into ourselves. It creates an explosion that for the moment frees us from handed-down frames of reference, memory choked with old facts and information and undigested theories and techniques of other people's findings."

Another value of play is the balance it provides the mind. Stephen Schwartz has always involved himself with recreational activities: he plays tennis, works word puzzles or Sudoku, sees shows, dines at interesting ethnic restaurants with friends, and travels to out-of-the-way places. Recharged and back at the piano, his inner child romps with renewed enthusiasm.

Stephen Schwartz sings "With You" from his forthcoming musical *Pippin* at a very special wedding in February of 1972. Original *Godspell* cast member Gilmer McCormick (under the hat) and music director Stephen Reinhardt (standing) were the first of many couples who met during a production of *Godspell*.

Larry Uttal, President of Bell Records, speaks with Stephen Schwartz at the Grammy Awards dinner party March 15, 1972, after *Godspell* won two Grammys. Schwartz recalls, "This was the night when I said to Larry, 'Listen, if the 5th Dimension is never going to release a single of 'Day by Day,' why don't we release the recording off the cast album?'" The "Day by Day" single quickly rose to the top 40 chart where it remained for nine weeks. The album earned a gold record.

CHAPTER 6

GODSPELL MEETS MASS AND PIPPIN

So let your light so shine before men
Let your light so shine
So that they might know some kindness again
We all need help to feel fine (let's have some wine!)
GODSPELL

Godspell absorbed all of Stephen Schwartz's attention from March through May 1971, as he transformed his own restless quest for success into a surge of enthusiasm for this new off-Broadway production. When the show opened, no one knew how long it would last. The first few weeks at the Cherry Lane Theatre were "very iffy," a cast member recalls, but the publicity team made every effort to contact clergy as well as the media, helping spread the word about the show.

Once the cast sang "Day by Day" on *The Today Show* and spoke with anchors Barbara Walters and Hugh Downs, everything shifted. Robin Lamont recalls, "When we came to the theatre that night, the producers were jumping all around. They said, 'The phones are ringing off the hook!' From that moment, we were sold out almost every night, as a result of that appearance and word of mouth. It was delightful."

Celebrities, too, began to flock to Cherry Lane Theatre. When people like Paul Newman and Joanne Woodward came, the cast would peek out at the audience before the show. "They're here!" they would shout to each other, and then rev themselves up for an energetic performance.

Schwartz often attended performances, standing in the back of the theatre. "It was so amazing to watch the audience, and there were all these celebrities coming down. I was twenty-three-years

Godspell was like a fire lit in a cold neighborhood and people came and warmed themselves by it.

GILMER MCCORMICK

PLAYBILL, INC.

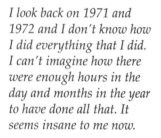

I look back on 1971 and 1972 and I don't know how I did everything that I did. I can't imagine how there were enough hours in the day and months in the year to have done all that. It seems insane to me now.

STEPHEN SCHWARTZ

old—I went a lot."

Godspell quickly outgrew the 99-seat Cherry Lane Theatre in Greenwich Village and moved to the Promenade Theatre in August. Though the building is actually on Broadway at 76th Street on the Upper West Side, it was considered "off-Broadway" because its seating is limited to 399. (The show would run for 2,123 performances at the Promenade, setting a record at that time as the fourth longest-running off-Broadway musical.)

Both the *Godspell* cast album and the single, "Day by Day," crossed over as popular music hits, with "Day by Day" reaching number 11 on the top 40 charts in the summer of 1972. Of course, the album's success boosted ticket sales for performances.

Over the next few years, insanity ruled for the producing team of Beruh and Lansbury and the *Godspell* company manager, Marvin Krauss. They had started with a small office space on the 10th floor at 1650 Broadway, but the success of the show required them to expand down the hall, adding rooms to house more administrators and accountants. At one point, as many as seven resident companies of *Godspell* operated simultaneously in North America: New York City, Boston, Washington, Los Angeles, San Francisco, Chicago, and Toronto, in addition to the ongoing tours. Many of the companies had extended runs lasting one to two years. "We really had to hustle in order to get enough casts together," Lansbury recalls.

In his native London, Lansbury scheduled a West End house for *Godspell*, but the theatre owner reneged on the arrangement. "We ended up going into the Roundhouse, an off-West End theatre, which turned out to be the luckiest thing that ever happened because it set the show in the right kind of atmosphere." For the first two months of the run, the audience for the more intimate Roundhouse Theatre greeted the show with enthusiasm and spread the word. The musical then moved to the West End, where it ran for several years.

The show's breakaway success kept a core group of Godspellers busy. Experienced cast members like Dean Pitchford, Andy Rohrer, Lynne Thigpen, and Nina's brother Laurie Faso shifted between productions where they were needed. Nina Faso directed five USA productions, including two national tours, and set up the Paris production, arranging for translations. Schwartz and Reinhardt traveled to every location to hire musicians. In Toronto they cast the stellar first company that featured Martin Short, Victor Garber, Gilda Radner, Andrea Martin, Eugene Levy and others, with Paul Shaffer as music director. Tebelak and Schwartz also helped develop the movie version of *Godspell* that was filmed in the summer of 1972.

Shirley Bernstein

During this period, the ongoing client-agent relationship between Stephen Schwartz and Shirley Bernstein proved so mutually supportive that they became like family to each other. Shirley even traveled with Stephen and his wife on a Caribbean vacation one year.

In previous years, when Shirley had fielded complaints from her bosses at the agency about Schwartz not making them any money, she stood firm, believing that he would eventually make them a lot of money. But in January or early February of 1971, they let her go. She decided to form her own company, taking Schwartz with her. "A month later we got the call about *Godspell*," Schwartz recalls, "and after it opened, suddenly her agency was flush."

Godspell quickly became a substantial hit and huge money-maker. Bernstein's former employers appealed to her to get some of the agent's royalty percentage, but she was able to demonstrate that the contract came through after she was booted out.

TOP: Nina Faso and company manager Marvin Krauss discuss *Godspell* productions. BOTTOM: Nina Faso, Edgar Lansbury, Carole Schwartz, and Stephen Schwartz attend the opening of *Godspell* in London.

"They didn't get a cent," Schwartz says with glee. "It hardly ever happens, something as just as that."

Schwartz's relationship with Ms. Bernstein afforded him many new opportunities, one of which would allow him to collaborate with a major force in American music who happened to be Shirley's brother, Leonard.

The Bernstein Mass

Lyric writing for Leonard Bernstein's *Mass* slipped into Schwartz's agenda shortly after *Godspell* opened. The project, eventually titled *Mass: A Theatre Piece for Singers, Players, and Dancers,* had been in the works for many years.

Back in 1966, the press announced that the great composer-conductor had accepted Jacqueline Kennedy's invitation to write an opening piece for the new arts complex in the nation's capital, the Kennedy Center, which was to open in 1971. Bernstein, never one to finish projects early, got behind schedule.

According to Bernstein biographer Humphrey Burton, the composer renewed his efforts in the autumn of 1970, after Roger Stevens, director of the Kennedy Center, suffered a heart attack.

After illegally penetrating the hospital ICU, Bernstein approached the director's bedside and asked, "Is there anything I can do to help?"

"Lenny, one thing I'd like to have you do for me is finish *Mass*," Stevens replied.

Stevens' request re-inspired Bernstein to finish *Mass* in time for the opening. Much of the work had been composed or adapted "from existing bottom-drawer compositions" during a retreat that December. He left for other conducting work in Europe, fully aware of the looming deadline, but eased by his knowledge that shows are often completed by artists working in a creative panic.

He returned in May of 1971 to face *Mass* full on, including writing English lyrics for songs he would intersperse with elements of the Catholic Mass in Latin. Bernstein wanted *Mass* to express an enduring interest of his: the difficulty of sustaining religious faith in seemingly inhumane times.

In June, Shirley Bernstein paid a visit to her brother, finding him "…terribly depressed and searching desperately for a collaborator to work on lyrics for the songs." In her mind, Stephen Schwartz was the obvious best choice. She decided her brother should see Schwartz's newly opened musical, *Godspell*. "Lenny was almost docile," Shirley remembers; "I took him by the hand and led him into the show."

Having enjoyed it and duly noted Schwartz's clever lyrics for songs, "All For the Best" and "Learn Your Lessons Well," Leonard Bernstein invited *Godspell*'s young songwriter to assist with English lyrics for *Mass*. The two met in Bernstein's Park Avenue studio and they clicked. Delighted, the elder composer called his sister to say, "Oh my God, this is it. Now I can finish *Mass*."

Stephen Schwartz stepped into the rush to finish the piece that summer. "The Kennedy Center was set to open at the beginning of September," he once commented, "and *something* had to be up on the stage! Therefore, many of the lyrics were first draft, without time to go back and polish."

When Schwartz entered the scene, *Mass* wasn't fully shaped. Even though it was more of a concert piece, "Lenny wanted there to be a dramatic arc," Schwartz recalls. "I mostly worked with him on shaping the dramatic structure." He feels that "some of the youthful spirit of *Godspell* influenced the content of the piece and the character of the Celebrant that Lenny and I devised."

Once the show's structure crystallized, Schwartz and Bernstein hurried forward with the songs, sometimes starting with music, sometimes with lyrics. When *Godspell* moved to the Promenade

Theatre in early August, Stephen often sat at the piano during rehearsal breaks, working out lyrics for *Mass*.

Carole Schwartz had turned down an opportunity to be cast in *Mass* at the upcoming Kennedy Center opening because she had already committed to perform the title role in *Hello, Dolly!* in New Hampshire. In September one of the singers in *Mass* became ill, and Carole was asked to step in. Stephen was pleased because it meant the couple could be together in Washington, D.C. for the big event.

I learned a lot from the mistakes I made on Mass, *and I did make a lot of mistakes. But there's much in the piece that I'm very proud of, and I think the structure is pretty successful. In any event, it got done!*

STEPHEN SCHWARTZ

Schwartz admits the work could have been better. "Though Lenny and I collaborated in more or less the usual way, I didn't really know enough about collaboration at that point to do as good a job as I like to think I would now. For instance, if I provided a lyric first and then Lenny set it to music, I didn't know enough then to go back and rewrite the lyric to help it sit on the music better."

On September 8th, the premiere of *Mass* inaugurated the John F. Kennedy Center for the Performing Arts. The show received mixed reviews but continued to play to enthusiastic audiences. Most important for Schwartz's career was Bernstein's influence. He later commented, "Even before working with Lenny, his music had been an enormous influence on me. After spending those brief months working with him, that influence became a permanent part of how I thought about music. One need only listen to the first two measures of *Wicked*, written thirty-plus years later, to know that."

A comment made to a reporter in 1971:
As for the critical reactions, I think they've been good but, you know, we can't write for the critics.... We just have to write for ourselves.

STEPHEN SCHWARTZ

An original cast recording, including The Norman Scribner Choir and The Berkshire Boys Choir, came out on the Sony Music label in 1971. (In 2004, Kultur Video released a DVD of a production for the Vatican's Jubilee 2000 celebration. Schwartz revised the lyrics in 2005.)

At the curtain call for *Mass* in previews at the Kennedy Center in 1971, director Gordon Davidson (left), Leonard Bernstein (center), Stephen Schwartz (right), and the cast accept audience applause. Note Schwartz's "mod" garb, which now really embarrasses him.

Shirley Bernstein relaxes at the home of Stephen and Carole Schwartz several years after she became Stephen's agent.

CREATIVITY NOTES

Comparison—A Creative Block to Avoid

Artists who achieve success often face new creative blocks related to fame and their reputations. Stephen Schwartz once wrote about a lesson he learned while working with Leonard Bernstein on *Mass*: "One day when I was waiting for him to start working, I was working on a song for *Pippin*. He came in, listened for a bit, and said, 'I remember when I used to do that: just sit down at the piano and knock out a tune. Now it's so hard for me to put two notes together. I think—are these two notes worthy of Leonard Bernstein?' I never forgot that. It was a great lesson when I was twenty-three, to hear that and think to myself, 'No matter what, don't let that happen to you.'"

Many years later, a fan raised the topic of living up to his reputation: "I can't think of anything that would be as destructive to creativity as the fear of failure. So how do you silence these kinds of thoughts, if you have them, so that you'll be free to do the most creative work you can?"

Schwartz answered, "I never worry about trying to compete with past accomplishments. To the contrary, I always see past work as flawed and hope to do better next time. Far from being intimidated, I tend to feel goaded to try to improve. I've never done anything I thought was so perfect that I was worried about living up to it."

Pippin Connections

Even though *Godspell* absorbed much of his time, Schwartz kept pushing forward with *Pippin*. It had been *Pippin*, after all, that started the journey, and Schwartz wasn't abandoning his dream of writing for Broadway. But the musical-in-progress was about to shift focus away from its original *Lion in Winter*-style of intrigue to a contemporary quest for meaning, even while remaining set in the 8th century.

[*See Chapter 2, pages 20–27, for a description of the original college version of* Pippin, *then called* Pippin, Pippin.]

In the spring of 1969, Ms. Bernstein's efforts had yielded a special, if somewhat daunting, meeting for her twenty-year-old client. In an 8th-floor office of the St. James Building on 44th Street, they sat with mustachioed Broadway impresario David Merrick. In his late fifties, Merrick was known for producing successful Broadway shows with an "ends justifies the means" philosophy.

Around that time, Merrick was seeking ways to bridge the growing generation gap and entice a younger audience to the theatre. He listened to the young man before him play some songs from *Pippin* as he silently calculated the economic promise of the show. He signed an option contract presuming a suitable book for the musical could be prepared. However, a Merrick-Schwartz agreement was not to yield a musical until *The Baker's Wife,* five years later. *Pippin*'s early book by recent Harvard graduate James Dickson was disappointing, and Merrick released the option. (It was a decision he later regretted.)

When it came time to write a new version of *Pippin* for the 1970s, Schwartz was in the middle of his own quest to find his place in a world that wasn't turning out to be as storybook-like as he'd expected. He and his peers felt at odds with the older generation's values and their government's politics (exemplified by the war in Vietnam). News reports were filled with stories of student activism and antiwar demonstrations, like Columbia University sit-ins and the "March on Washington" in November of 1969, that brought together hundreds of thousands of dissenters.

Although Schwartz participated in some of the New York candlelight vigils and other anti-Vietnam protests, his primary march was more private. Through his songwriting he could criticize war efforts and comment on other social issues about which he felt strongly.

He wasn't alone in wanting to reflect the changing times in his music. In his Manhattan apartment, he listened to songwriters like Joni Mitchell, who described his generation's quest for meaning in her song, "Woodstock." Paul Simon, another of Schwartz's favorite pop chart singer-songwriters, voiced the mood of the day in his song "America" (another of Schwartz's favorites, recorded on Simon and Garfunkel's 1968 album, *Bookends*):

> *Kathy, I'm lost, I said,*
> *Though I knew she was sleeping.*
> *I'm empty and aching and*
> *I don't know why.*
> *Counting the cars*
> *On the New Jersey Turnpike.*
> *They've all come*
> *To look for America,*
> *All come to look for America.*

I feel an emptiness my words cannot express Is my life a total mess?

Pippin singing to Bertha in an early version of *Pippin*

That "empty and aching and I don't know why" experience filtered its way into the new script and score of *Pippin*. Schwartz needed to reveal Pippin's angst and restlessness.

While conceptualizing the musical in 1969 and 1970, Schwartz discovered the heart of *Pippin* in the things that occupied his attention at the time—primarily his personal journey. "I write about what interests me, what concerns me," he says. "*Pippin* became a semi-autobiographical quest or story about a young man in search of himself, and that got grafted onto this medieval setting." His show's fictional hero, too, felt restless and out of place. How could that be conveyed in song?

Nights and weekends, Schwartz settled in at his old metal upright piano, notepad resting on top, rewriting songs for *Pippin*. "No Time At All" and "With You" were already done. His latest song, then called "Maybe You'll Show Me," would introduce Pippin's youthful quest for his life's purpose and meaning. Schwartz liked the tune he came up with but couldn't work out the lyrics even after several weeks of struggle. He realized he had to scrap it and start over.

While Stephen worked at the piano, Carole Schwartz memorized lines for her upcoming leading role in *Last Sweet Days of Isaac*. The rock musical had done well enough off-Broadway to spawn a regional production in Washington, D.C., in which Carole would perform. When the show opened on November 12, 1970, Stephen made several car trips to the nation's capital during Carole's rehearsal or performance days.

The Schwartzes remember one trip during which Carole was driving while Stephen pored over his notes about *Pippin*. By then he had a new notion that the naïve character Pippin would be searching for something that didn't exist in reality. So the songwriter was on the lookout for images that were poetic yet didn't actually exist. As if stepping into Pippin's head, he came up with a title, "Corner of the Sky." A sky doesn't have corners but the expression worked to symbolize something he wanted. Pippin could say something on the order of, "This fits here, that fits there, why do I feel I don't fit anywhere?"

Over the hum of the car engine, he explained to Carole what he needed:

"What are things that fit places?"

"Well, cats fit on a windowsill," she replied readily.

The image settled in his imagination, and from there he was on a roll, penciling lyrics that sprang to mind.

> Cats fit on the windowsill,
> Children fit in the snow.
> Why do I feel I don't fit in anywhere I go?

Back home, once he wrote new music to go with it, "Corner of the Sky" emerged, a song that would help establish a sizable corner for him in the hearts of Broadway music fans around the world.

CREATIVITY NOTES

Knowing When To Quit

Persistence for reaching one's goals is essential for creative success, but giving up and letting go of a particular effort sometimes opens an artist's creativity. Early in his career, Schwartz noted that when he gave up "Maybe You'll Show Me," a much better song, "Corner of the Sky," emerged. After a few more experiences like this, he recognized a pattern.

"We always feel like we need to work hard on things," Schwartz reflects. "But one thing I've learned about the songwriting craft is that if something is too difficult, usually there is something wrong with it. You have to throw it out and start again. That's not to say it doesn't always take you time to write a song, and you don't have moments when you come up against a wall and have to break through. But if you're really, really struggling, there's something misbegotten about it. It's hard to give up but there's a certain point where I think you have to say, 'You know what? This is not working. I just have to start again.'"

Roger O. Hirson

For *Pippin* to continue its journey toward Broadway, a new bookwriter had to be found. Among writers Bernstein recommended was Roger O. Hirson, who had written prolifically for television during its "golden age" and had playwriting credits as well. In addition to penning plays for off-Broadway and London's West End, he'd developed an original book for the 1966 Broadway musical, *Walking Happy*.

Schwartz was cautious about agreeing to a new writer. "I read a lot of plays and talked to a lot of people who were recommended to me for *Pippin* before I finally found a writer who understood the property, who understood what I was trying to do with it." Hirson seemed a wise choice and the two formed a compatible team.

The musical that emerged from Schwartz's piano and Hirson's typewriter was entirely distinct from the 1967 college version of *Pippin, Pippin*. "Not a note or lyric remained the same," the songwriter would often say in future interviews. Contrary to reports of later years, he wasn't clinging to the college version, for that was long gone anyway.

My relationship with Stephen, both working and personal, has been warm and exceedingly pleasant, from the beginning and to this day.

Roger O. Hirson

Ben Vereen and *Pippin*'s Players. Costumes are by Patricia Zipprodt.

The creative team of *Pippin* meets to read through the script before rehearsals for the pre-Broadway tryout. Bob Fosse is leaning back in his chair (upper left). Seated at the table: Stephen Schwartz, Roger O. Hirson, Stuart Ostrow, and others. Broadway Arts Building, New York, August 1972.

CHAPTER 7

Pippin Comes to Broadway

I wanted magic shows and miracles
Mirages to touch
I wanted such a little thing in life
I wanted so much

PIPPIN

It would ultimately help Stephen Schwartz's career that in 1971, Broadway producer Stuart Ostrow wanted something distinctly new for his next show. His *1776*, with a traditional musical the-atre score, had been running strong at the 46th Street Theatre for two years, but times were changing. The thirty-eight-year-old im-presario believed that musicals ought to reflect cultural shifts in order to attract new generations of theatregoers. Unfortunately, his first effort in this direction failed.

Ostrow had commissioned Archibald MacLeish and Bob Dylan to write *Scratch*, a new musical based on *The Devil and Daniel Webster*. Dylan finished a few songs, including "New Morning," but the collaboration didn't gel. Instead, Dylan recorded the songs on the *New Morning* album for Columbia Records. Ostrow felt betrayed and stuck. He mounted a nonmusical version of *Scratch* on May 6, 1971, and closed it after four performances.

As he explains in one of his memoirs, "That's when Stephen Schwartz, recently graduated from Carnegie Mellon University, came to my Broadway office to play his score for *Pippin*. Dressed in the hippie uniform of the day (stained glass print shirt tails over chinos) and sporting a shoulder length hairdo, Stephen was the embodiment of self-confidence bordering on arrogance. He reminded me of when I was twenty, nose and all, and from the moment he played 'Corner of the Sky' I knew Stephen was the new voice I was looking for. The rest of the score was just as fresh...and I agreed to produce it on the spot."

To get *Pippin* on its path toward Broadway, Stuart Ostrow, Roger Hirson, and Stephen Schwartz began meeting regularly in Ostrow's home, a rural retreat in Pound Ridge, New York. As the script unfolded in Hirson's hands, it grew to about 108 pages of dialogue and song—more than twenty pages longer than the spare final version.

The writers also assisted in the search for a director. Michael Bennett and Joseph Hardy were considered, but both rejected the project. Hal Prince also passed.

Bob Fosse as Director - Choreographer

Stuart Ostrow especially admired Bob Fosse's work in *The Pajama Game* and *Damn Yankees*. He had been aspiring to produce a Fosse show and therefore approached him about helming a new Stephen Schwartz musical. Fosse agreed to hear the score; he had been a fan of *Godspell*, and was intrigued about coming back to Broadway.

The next time Schwartz flew to L.A. to work on a *Godspell* production there, he met with forty-four-year-old Fosse, who was in Hollywood completing the movie version of *Cabaret*. Upon hearing the *Pippin* score performed by its composer, Fosse signed on, and agreed to begin work after he finished *Cabaret*.

Schwartz called Hirson, eager to share his elation that the musical had attracted such a big name in the business. Hirson replied, "This is our last happy day on this show." The prophecy would play out pretty accurately.

Bob Fosse with ever-present cigarette

MARTHA SWOPE

CREATIVITY NOTES

Compression and Expansion

Shortly after *Godspell* opened, Shirley Bernstein gave her client what seemed like good news: Hal Prince agreed to listen to a pitch for *Pippin*. On the appointed day, Stephen Schwartz and Roger Hirson headed over to Prince's office in Rockefeller Center. Schwartz was awed by the huge roulette wheel mounted on one wall, with images of Prince's shows around the rim. Would the great producer/director gamble on *Pippin*? Schwartz performed his songs and explained the story. Although Prince declined, he suggested a way to restructure the show.

"He didn't want to direct it," Schwartz explains, "but he said, 'I'm more intrigued by what happens after your show ends. You should take the entire show [which ended shortly after Pippin's assassination attempt on his father, Charlemagne] and make it the first act, then tell the rest of the story.' Because he was Harold Prince, naturally we took his advice. Years later, I told this story to the writer Joseph Stein, and he said, 'But everyone knows that when you go to Hal Prince and he turns down your show, he tells you to make your whole show the first act.' Roger and I were the only ones who had actually taken him seriously—fortunately for us, because in the case of *Pippin*, he was right!"

Prince's remark may have been a brush-off, but it suggests a useful creative strategy—story compression to heighten drama and sustain audience attention. Tightening a story also leaves room for fresh additional content, and inspires further creativity.

Fosse's reputation for collaboration issues had preceded him. In social settings he enjoyed the company of certain writers, like his friends E.L. Doctorow, Paddy Chayevsky, and Herb Gardner. Within a creative team, he seemed to have a difficult time communicating with writers who had visions of their own.

For Schwartz, this first Broadway gig would prove "as different from what I had been doing as becoming a professional athlete is different from playing sandlot baseball." *Godspell* had floated into his life as an idyllic bubble. When he guided rehearsals, he felt respected and included in the playfulness as youthful actors shifted around sawhorses and planks in the rough-hewn off-Broadway show. With an imperious choreographer-director in charge of *Pippin*, Schwartz's ease and influence diminished while highly trained dancers slinked into Fosse-style poses in the stylized musical-in-progress.

Schwartz did have an influence on the script, and that was the first order of business.

Prince Pippin and the Players

Prior to Bob Fosse's involvement, *Pippin* included dark plot elements. A group of players in medieval France invite Charlemagne's innocent son, Prince Pippin, to join them, luring him to an act of self-destruction that will fulfill his quest for the ultimate extraordinary experience.

The idea for the troupe slipped in by way of Stephen Schwartz's cinematic affections. He loved foreign films, including pictures by Swedish director Ingmar Bergman. Bergman's existential film about a medieval knight returning home from the Crusades, *The Seventh Seal* (1957), included scenes with actors who travel around with their caravan. Calling to mind the players in the movie, Schwartz wrote lyrics for the song "Magic to Do." (It was a different tune from the one he ultimately used in the show.)

Join us—leave your fields to flower
Join us—leave your cheese to sour

After Hirson, Schwartz, and Ostrow met over a second version of the script, the Players, led by "Old Man," introduced the story, as well as ended it.

In Scene 1, Players introduce "our most mysterious and miraculous tale" about an unsatisfied youth from ancient Greece named Peregrinus. A "Young Man" plays the central character, whose chief trait is his "insatiable hunger for life."

The true story of Cynic philosopher Peregrinus Proteus (100-165 A.D.) inspired the "Young Man" role and the fire imagery. Peregrinus threw himself into a flaming pyre at the Olympic games in 165 A.D. as a way of affirming his beliefs.

In *Pippin*, a Player called Peregrinus performs a magic trick, swallowing fire and blowing it from his mouth. Only he doesn't succeed and burns himself. The troupe sings part of "Magic to Do" as they close up their caravan and move on.

In Scene 2, the story of Prince Pippin commences with his return home from college and discovery that nothing in ordinary life is particularly fulfilling—certainly not his interactions with his father, King Charles (Charlemagne), his half-brother, Lewis, or his stepmother, Fastrada.

He launches his quest for an extraordinary experience. After going to battle with his father, a felled soldier confirms Pippin's suspicions that one battle is like another. Pippin laments, "I thought there'd be more plumes"—a Roger Hirson line that remained in place through all future drafts of the show and that is Schwartz's favorite in the musical.

Pippin plots to overthrow the king and stabs him to death, but discovers he doesn't like making royal decisions. Charles obligingly comes back to life and takes back the throne.

Pippin sets out again in search of fulfillment and meets Catherine, a widow with a small boy and a large estate, who wants to marry him. He runs away from the prospect of an ordinary life as a husband.

That's when Pippin meets up with the Players (whom the audience has met in Scene 1). They coax him to perform the role of Peregrinus in their play, showing him the flashy costumes he would wear. They also hint that in his performance he would actually consume fire and perish in a spectacular display. Hearing this, Pippin wakes up to their sinister intentions and life's realities.

He sings:

> *You showed me crimson, gold and lavender*
> *A shining parade*
> *But there's no color I can have on earth*
> *That won't finally fade…*

He returns to Catherine, ready to compromise his ideals and settle down. He sings of his realization:

> *I'm not a river or a giant bird*
> *That soars to the sea*
> *And if I'm never tied to anything*
> *I'll never be free…*

On one level, the show's ending reflected transitions in Schwartz's own life as he and Carole settled into the first home of their own in rural western Connecticut. The New England setting on a winding, heavily wooded road about an eighty-minute drive northeast of Broadway provided the peace the songwriter needed for his work, even though it tied him down to mortgage payments.

Stuart Ostrow visited one day and praised it as "a really nice first house," to the chagrin of the young couple, but it worked well for them for three years, until they had the funds to pay up front for a large estate built according to their specifications. The buffer of positive experiences in quiet Connecticut proved essential for preserving Schwartz's sanity while he worked in the intense commercial world of Broadway.

At one point during *Pippin*'s development, Schwartz's friend, David Spangler, was staying with Stephen and Carole. When Spangler drove into the city for his own work, Schwartz rode along so that he could be dropped off at Bob Fosse's apartment building for meetings. "Stephen had to take pills to calm himself down because he got so very upset," Spangler reveals. "Fosse treated him like dirt."

Bob Fosse may have believed he was doing Broadway beginner Schwartz a favor by directing his show. Spangler suggests, "Fosse was truly interested in keeping current with trends that were beginning to happen, like rock music, which was starting to enter the vocabulary of Broadway. He just thought he'd whip Stephen into shape."

Pippin Cast and Conflicts

By the time Stephen Schwartz turned twenty-four on March 6, 1972, *Pippin* had found its Pippin. The director's pick for the title role was pianist Arthur Rubinstein's son, the slender twenty-five-year-old actor John Rubinstein. Schwartz was pleased, especially after watching hundreds of others audition. He and Rubinstein soon became friends, and counted on each other for moral support in the months to come.

The role of Pippin's love interest, Catherine, was promised to Katie Hanley, who charmed Fosse in auditions and was about to appear in the *Godspell* movie. However, at the last minute Fosse opted for Jill Clayburgh. "We all liked Jill," Schwartz recalls. "Jill was someone that Bob felt very strongly about. He felt that she had movie star quality and it turned out he was right. With Catherine's entrance coming late in the show, he needed someone who would really make an impression, who would stand out from the rest of the cast, and Jill did."

Irene Ryan, famous for her role as the grandmother in the TV show *Beverly Hillbillies*, accepted the part of Pippin's grandmother, Bertha, and would soon enthrall audiences with her rendition of Schwartz's jaunty sing-along number "No Time At All."

The role called Old Man seemed the most challenging to cast. It wasn't until a "triple threat" actor-singer-dancer came for auditions that something clicked and catalyzed a revamping of the entire musical.

"We need someone vivid for the part," Fosse told casting director Michael Shurtleff, "and I'd love to have a dancer." Shurtleff, who later reported the process in his book about auditioning, contacted seasoned character actors in the city, but few had kept up their dancing.

Then Shurtleff mentioned twenty-five-year-old Ben Vereen. Fosse was delighted to consider him, having worked with him as a dancer in the film *Sweet Charity*. Vereen had been stunning critics and audiences with his power-packed Broadway performance as Judas in *Jesus Christ Superstar*.

Shurtleff remembers Vereen's audition: "For the first time, our 'Old Man' came to life in the person of a young, sexy, humorous black actor who was an irresistible singer and dancer."

Schwartz remarks, "Bob brought him in and said, 'I don't know what we can do with this guy but he's just amazingly talented.' Ben gave this fantastic audition. We met afterward. Bob said, 'Maybe he could be the Old Man but there's not enough to do.' And Roger said he thought he could combine a bunch of

I remember seeing The Weavers in concert when I was a kid and the audience singing along with 'Goodnight, Irene.' That experience led directly to my wanting to do an audience sing-along with "No Time At All" in Pippin.

Stephen Schwartz

parts to make one good role."

Hirson headed back to his typewriter and began combining dialogue for a "Leading Player" based on a Balladeer (a narrator character who sang to the audience in earlier versions), the Old Man, and several lines previously delivered in unison by the ensemble. He thereby crafted the new role specifically for Ben Vereen.

Schwartz wrote "Magic to Do" for Vereen's character in one weekend, setting his existing lyrics to a fresh tune—a bluesy vamp to suit the new cast member.

Ben Vereen performs "Glory." Stephen Schwartz wrote "Glory," "Magic to Do," "Simple Joys," and "On the Right Track" with Vereen's singing skills in mind.

Where Does the Leading Player Lead?

As the expanded creative team focused the musical, they explored ways the new Leading Player role and the show's fire theme would fit together. They cut all references to Peregrinus and let the Players attempt to influence Pippin more directly. They decided that the Leading Player could be a companion for Pippin throughout the show, seductively luring him toward his demise.

Schwartz then revised his earlier versions of "Simple Joys" and "Glory" for Vereen to sing. (For the tone and rhythmic feel of "Glory," Schwartz used the "O Fortuna" section from Carl Orff's popular choral work *Carmina Burana* as an inspiration.)

Schwartz wrote the solo "I Guess I'll Miss the Man" for the moment toward the end of the show when the restless hero leaves Catherine. Upset about the situation, Catherine turns to the audience to sing, disregarding the Leading Player's protestations about the song not being in the script. She and Pippin have to overcome the influence of the Players in order to live a meaningful life.

The magic trick with fire had to be replaced with something larger and more dramatic. The creative team decided the Players should motivate Pippin to leap through a special gateway into the flames. They promise a most extraordinary experience for Pippin and a spectacular finale for the audience. Schwartz wrote the rousing "Finale" (Think About the Sun) for that moment.

Pippin realizes he has to turn back, stop running, and settle down.

The Collaboration of Fosse and Schwartz

Intrigue, plots to bring disaster

"Magic to Do" lyric by Stephen Schwartz

On June 17, 1972, the *Washington Post* announced a break-in at the Democratic National Headquarters located in the Watergate Hotel and office complex. A subsequent cover-up investigation led to President Nixon's resignation. Ironically, Schwartz, who used much of his antipathy toward Nixon and the Vietnam War to inform the writing of *Pippin*, would stay at the same hotel later that summer while preparing the musical's out-of-town tryout.

During the final months of work on *Pippin*, Schwartz tried to hold his own against Bob Fosse's authority. Animosity burst open between them over casting of the ensemble. Fosse, like other director-choreographers of his day, wasn't casting for vocal prowess, but rather for dancing ability. Schwartz protested when his choices for ensemble singers were all vetoed. Fosse turned to Stuart Ostrow and said, "Either I get my dancers or I quit." Ostrow sided with his director and remained closed to his younger team member in a way that twenty-four-year-old Schwartz hadn't experienced before.

When Fosse began demonstrating his ideas for staging to the dancers, Schwartz squirmed again. As reported by Fosse biographer Martin Gottfried, when dancers finished demonstrating a draft of the opening number to Schwartz, the songwriter explained that he'd pictured it more like Jerry Robbins' choreography in *West Side Story*. Then he rose from his chair to give a little demonstration.

Had this been the group of twenty-somethings working on *Godspell* together, no problem. But Bob Fosse was the forty-five-year-old God of Dance. In the eyes of the dancers, Schwartz had just sinned big time.

Ongoing interactions with the intense, chain-smoking artist would constantly startle the show's young composer, who had never worked with anyone so autocratic. Bob Fosse had been working in film, a director's medium, and would dominate the *Pippin* company in the same manner to which he was accustomed. Then there was his emphasis on dance. Fosse's roots from childhood were in vaudeville revue-style shows and burlesque, where storylines weren't the key to success. Some of his most renowned pieces were dance numbers set off from the storyline, like "Steam Heat" from *The Pajama Game* and "Who's Got the Pain?" from *Damn Yankees*. People around Fosse guessed that he saw *Pippin* as a show where the story could serve the dance and not the other way around. This often meant that creative decisions for the visual impact of *Pippin* took precedence over writers' concerns.

Los Angeles Times reporter Paul Rosenfield once asked Fosse for six adjectives he'd use to describe himself. "Fosse didn't miss a beat: 'Eager, pushy, needy, scared, hungry, confident.'" This combination of qualities made for challenging collaborations. Mel Gussow commented in the *New York Times*, "In a profession not known for its even temperaments, Fosse was especially outspoken. He probably quit more shows than he directed. There were problems with writers and composers...."

The director, who enjoyed bashing the piece when he spoke to friends and journalists, freely suggested that Prince Pippin's journey was his own—the journey of a restless man who tries out an array of potentially enticing experiences, finds them all wanting, then settles for family life. Fosse's restlessness played out in

About Bob Fosse's changes in *Pippin*:

At the time, Stephen was devastated. I've never seen him have a confrontation with anybody that seemed to upset him more than with Bob Fosse.

NINA FASO

his extramarital relationships and art, although he had stayed married to Gwen Verdon since 1960, and they had a daughter, Nicole Fosse.

In any case, the *Pippin* script seemed incomplete in his eyes. When a New York reporter asked him what material he had been given to work with from Schwartz, Hirson, and Ostrow, Fosse claimed, "Very little of what you see now. It was small-scaled… and fey," even though most of the central story was in place in advance of his arrival on the scene.

Songwriter Schwartz lived and wrote close to his emotions. He might be brash on the surface when confronted, but he was vulnerable and sensitive—a guy who wept upon hearing the beautiful Leonard Cohen ballad "Suzanne" for the first time, who loved watching people leave *Godspell* with beaming faces, who had regularly chummed around with his Carnegie friends while they were working on the show. He and Fosse would never be chums.

"Because my career got off to an astonishingly and bewilderingly quick start," Schwartz remarks, "I still had enormously romantic illusions about what working in the professional theatre was going to be like. And those illusions were, for both better and worse, bolstered by the experience that I had on *Godspell*. It was my first experience and it turns out it was a totally anomalous one. It had nothing really to do with working in professional musical theatre. It had much more to do with sort of amateur community theatre: getting together and putting on a show in a barn [as in the Judy Garland and Mickey Rooney movie, *Babes in Arms*], which is all I had done up to that time. So when I went to work on *Pippin* and suddenly confronted the reality of working in the professional theatre on Broadway, it was a huge shock."

It seemed that the closer the show moved toward a full physical production, the more it became a divisive nightmare. With

Godspell there had been a spirit of openness. Suddenly, with *Pippin*, Schwartz was being told to shut up and stay in his corner: don't talk about casting, dance, costumes, or even orchestrations.

It wasn't that rehearsals were all bad. "There were moments," Schwartz would later reveal, "when I would come in and see a number that Bob had staged and it would be 'Magic to Do' and I thought it was absolutely amazing, or the whole war sequence, and I thought it was brilliant and did exactly what I had hoped for, but in a way that was so much more imaginative and visually inventive than I could ever have envisioned on my own." But he found other aspects infuriating, like all the "yuk yuk" interruptions in "War is a Science," Fastrada's thinly disguised Gwen Verdon impersonation, the campy backup vocal staging of "Kind of Woman," or, most significantly, the way the Leading Player was becoming more of a primary character than Pippin. "There were times I would see things that Bob did that I thought were vulgar and stupid and crass and simplistic and completely at odds with what I wanted the show to be. And it was very hard to make my case in those instances, to ask him to change them or adjust them."

As rehearsals proceeded, Fosse drew the cast he was working hard closer to him. When Schwartz expressed discontent, he was shut out.

He didn't know how to handle the frustration of not being heard or heeded in any way. John Rubinstein remembers about Stephen, "He was thrown out of an early rehearsal…when, in front of the cast, he argued with Fosse over a song by stating, 'I'm the one who has a record in the top ten!' He was out from then on. Too bad, because he had written a marvelous show, and his continued collaboration with Fosse could have made the result even better."

Schwartz held out some hope that the out-of-town trial in Washington, D.C. would be a better experience. Fosse wanted

Schwartz around for rewrites but still kept him completely away from the cast and the actual daily process, which meant the songwriter had plenty of time to pace and brood. There wasn't anything he could do; his darling was out of his hands. He was not cool about being told to clam up and couldn't understand why he couldn't play on the team. "I'd worked on that show for seven years," he told a reporter. "I know I'm tactless. I just wanted somebody to ask what I think, and if they give me a good reason, I'll back down."

Out-of-Town Tryout in Washington, D.C.

People mistake that the difference between me and Fosse was about content. But it wasn't. It was about style.

STEPHEN SCHWARTZ

In September 1972, the Kennedy Center's stately white marble, with contrasting international and state flags hanging in the sweeping tall hallways, seemed ready for ceremonial gatherings of ambassadors or presidents. The year before, when *Mass* was staged at this living memorial to John F. Kennedy, Stephen Schwartz had been hailed as Leonard Bernstein's hero for helping a great maestro meet his deadline. Now he was Bob Fosse's irritant and an outcast from his own musical. *Pippin* would open September 20th.

In a rehearsal hall of the Kennedy Center, Bob Fosse shuffled the cast of *Pippin* across the open space. Over a table in his Watergate Hotel room next door, Stephen Schwartz shuffled playing cards with percussive assertiveness, then dealt another hand for a game of bridge. Conversations between fellow card players Roger Hirson, Shirley Bernstein, and Arthur Laurents were supposed to help transport Schwartz from his worries. (Bernstein's client, Laurents, was present out of curiosity and to keep them company.)

Schwartz's quibble about the latest version of the show now being prepared to open in a month's time at the Imperial Theatre was over style. "My issue with Bob Fosse was not the darkness of his vision," he later explained, "but the tawdriness and the emphasis on bumps and grinds and cheap jokes. I also felt that the Leading Player was undercutting the focus on Pippin in some cases and forcing Pippin to become a relatively one-dimensional character."

At one point, Schwartz and Fosse quarreled over "Kind of Woman," in which Catherine introduces herself to Pippin and to the audience in a self-satisfied manner. Fosse couldn't work it into his staging and insisted on cutting it. Schwartz gave in on other occasions, writing new songs at the director's bidding, but this time he balked and invoked the Dramatist Guild contract that protected librettists and lyricists from having their work altered without their permission. Fosse acquiesced and found a way to stage it to his satisfaction, though he wasn't exactly pleased.

Pippin's composer-lyricist felt trapped and only intermittently happy in his room in the Watergate Hotel. Hirson had been right about Fosse—this was no fun. If Fosse's game was upsetting, it was up to Schwartz to find a more enjoyable one. He found it at Ford's Theatre, less than a two-mile walk past the White House and over to Tenth Avenue. *Godspell* had opened there the previous spring, starring Dean Pitchford as Jesus.

At Ford's he was more than welcome. The *Godspell* cast reveled in the rare opportunity to have the composer on hand. While they donned their kneepads and warmed up their voices in the vintage building where President Abraham Lincoln attended shows, Stephen sat holding his pencil and legal pad, taking notes. It was heartening to hear his songs, "Day by Day," "Bless the Lord," "On the Willows," and all the others lift toward the balcony.

He could relax with this group of *Godspell* actors who, like him, were at the beginning of their careers. At the end of the rehearsal, they gathered around him and listened to his suggestions for improving the performance.

For after-hours chumming around, Stephen was especially drawn to Hawaii native, twenty-year-old Dean Pitchford. Pitchford would take over for Rubinstein as Pippin for a series of Monday night performances the following summer, and so he got to know and understand Bob Fosse from an actor's perspective. Pitchford had already collected literary and drama degrees from Yale, and would later write lyrics for *Fame* as well as the screenplay and stage play for *Footloose*. In his acting, Dean displayed both sweetness and star-power strength.

It was probably their mutual affection for word-smithery and puzzle working that drew him and Stephen into a deep friendship that bolstered their careers in years to come. To help fill the time out-of-town, the two new buddies worked through tough crossword puzzles and played Scrabble®.

On opening night at the Kennedy Center, creative influences from years of work flowed together to please audiences and critics alike. "This one looks like a winner—could be a big winner," declared *Variety*'s reviewer. "There is an abundance of energy and flashiness, theatricality that is always self-aware and funny." *The Washington Post*'s critic wrote on September 21st, "Last night's premiere at the Kennedy Center Opera House proves that the innovative spirit yet lives in the American musical theatre."

Back in his hotel room, Stephen Schwartz phoned *Pippin, Pippin* originator Ron Strauss so they could share the pleasing prospect of a commercially successful show. It seemed the years of effort and collaboration had worked after all.

New York

The buzz from the out-of-town trial of *Pippin* in September 1972 was that it might be the first hit of the 1972-73 season. Fosse had doubts. He was known for his inner war. Often anxious about his work, he attracted turmoil into his life through drugs (uppers and downers) and lifestyle choices that disregarded common boundaries. As E.L. Doctorow later wrote, "The Bob Fosse I knew was insecure, self-doubting, tormented, tense in his victories, angry in his defeats—everything I trust in an artist." But for *Pippin*, he didn't trust the material or his audience.

John Rubinstein remembers Fosse's panic about what New Yorkers would think of him. He insisted on adding more jokes to the script, and asked Rubinstein to end the show with "Trapped," leaving off "but happy." That decision later wound up in arbitration, with Schwartz and Hirson winning, allowing them to add the words back for the licensed version of the show.

Rubinstein recalls, "As we approached New York, Fosse became more and more afraid that the show was too sentimental, not crisp and mean enough. He worried that the New York critics would label him soft. So during the two weeks of previews at the Imperial Theatre, he (with the help of Roger Hirson as well as other 'play doctor' friends of his) added some off-color joke lines ('the fornicating I'm getting . . .' and 'Lewis is an asshole,' etc.) and removed some of the more sentimental lines (most notably, 'but happy')."

Although many theatergoers liked the crude jokes, Rubinstein and others who had witnessed the show's development believed they weakened the show. "One effect was to make the whole sense of the evening less heartfelt," says Rubinstein. "It heightened the appeal of the Leading Player, it made the show snappy and hip, it definitely avoided the pitfalls of sentiment and self-pity that the authors had allowed to seep in here and there; but by contrast with all the show-biz glitter and show-stopping numbers, the rather simple and pure story of Pippin himself became a bit dull and predictable, and many of my own efforts to overcome this with my own personality and levity were held firmly in check

The general impression about the show was 'Dazzling, but cold.' I spent the next two years working like crazy eight times a week to make Pippin himself a character more worthy of the audience's attention and identification.

JOHN RUBINSTEIN

by Fosse. He wanted the Players to dominate the evening. Not a wrong concept, unless you really want the audience to root for Pippin, to care what happens to him, to identify with his plight, and to feel his joy and pain at the end of the evening."

When *Pippin* opened on October 23rd at the Imperial Theatre, critics lavished praise on Fosse's work and largely dimissed Schwartz's contribution. Clive Barnes, writing the *New York Times* review, raved about everything but the "feeble" book and the "bland" music, while his *Times* colleague Walter Kerr wrote, "*Pippin* is almost entirely an exercise in style, an opening of the theatre's box of toys without tearing the wrappings, deliberate as dance, disarming as sleight-of-hand. As such, recommended." *Variety*'s New York review called the songs "passable." John Simon in *New York* described Schwartz's music and lyrics as having "awkward and amateurish charm."

If young Mr. Schwartz began feeling misunderstood at this point, it is not surprising. He had believed in this work and pushed it forward, beginning in the fall of 1966 and working through the fall of 1972. Many critics made fun of the slight book, which Fosse had made all the slighter through extensive cuts. They ridiculed the seeker story and the troupe of players approach. They belittled the conclusion about Pippin settling into a domestic life. It would have been hard not to take it all personally.

But it was also hard to complain about success. When the album came out (UNI/Motown 1972), it too became a hit, especially among college-age music enthusiasts, and helped overcome some of the mediocre reviews for the score. Performer and writer V.J. Gillespie (founder of Talkinbroadway.com) was among the early audience members who attended the show many times. He later commented about *Pippin*: "Who cared what Clive Barnes had to say about the score in his *New York Times* review? Theatregoers were mad about the score. It was the staging and number after

The response to the show was very annoying and hurtful to me because some of the things we got blamed for were things we had no control over; they were things that Bob Fosse did.

STEPHEN SCHWARTZ

number of rich songs that kept *Pippin* running for five years. I didn't know a soul back then who did not own the Original Cast Recording, or couldn't sing every word to the score. *Pippin* was indeed so infectious that when our drama coach asked us to do a musical number for the yearly review, there was only one number brought to the table, and that was 'Magic to Do.'"

Theatre critic Peter Filichia comments: "[Schwartz's] score was one of the most influential to those who were young actors, young composer-lyricists, and young theatergoers in the 1970s .... There is no question that Bob Fosse's contributions to *Pippin* were invaluable, but more to the point, if he had not had the songs to work with, he wouldn't have had any magic to do."

Pippin played on Broadway from October 23, 1972 to June 12, 1977, for a total of 1,944 performances.

Pippin was a success before the now-famous television commercial—the first for a Broadway musical. The commercial helped sustain the run, as did the talents of replacement cast members like Betty Buckley, who stepped into the role of Catherine in June of 1973.

Since 1977, Music Theatre International has licensed the show for many thousands of stock and amateur productions.

Whether Pippin *would have succeeded without Bob, who can say? If Hal Prince had directed it or Michael Bennett had directed it, I think the script would have been better because I think Bob undercut things in the script. But be that as it may, the show worked.*

STEPHEN SCHWARTZ

CREATIVITY NOTES

Communication Styles in a Collaboration

The following are comments from Dean Pitchford, who played Jesus in *Godspell* and the title role in *Pippin* on Broadway in the early 1970s. Pitchford went on to become an Academy Award-winning songwriter as well as a close friend of Stephen and Carole Schwartz.

Dean Pitchford:

I've found throughout my career that everybody in different aspects of this business communicates in their own way. Sometimes they speak with music and they can't find words. Sometimes they speak with movement. Sometimes a designer can't describe a design but they say let me have a piece of paper, and they can draw it. The challenge of any collaboration is to find that very narrow strip where your abilities to communicate and understand overlap. I think Stephen Schwartz is very smart and very verbal. As a matter of fact, Stephen taught me to do the *New York Magazine London Observer* crossword puzzle. When we get together, we end up playing Scrabble®. He's an amazing crossword puzzle addict, and he's written crossword puzzles.

I'm only saying this because I think Bob Fosse was a hoofer – hoofer is an old term for vaudeville dancer. Bob Fosse talked with his body. If you talk to his cast members, Bob is notorious for being loved by his cast members and loathed by his collaborators. That's a pretty broad statement, but across the board he had famous feuds with co-writers.

Bob was a gypsy. And what he did was a combination of language and body and presence. He would gesture. He'd get up and show you. Ultimately, what Bob needed to communicate was what the stage needed because it was physicalized. It took on shape.

Charlemagne (Eric Berry) and
Ensemble perform "War is a
Science," a parody of war.

Pippin tries pleasures of the
flesh as part of his quest for
an extraordinary experience.

Pippin and the ensemble sing "Morning Glow."

"Morning Glow"—A Lesson About Vocal Arrangements

Schwartz was naive when it came to teaching songs to the *Pippin* cast. He recalls, "I had never done a professional Broadway show before. I had just come from doing *Godspell*. There, the way we did the vocal arrangements was that the lead singer would sing the song and the cast would start to improvise harmonies. Musical director Steve Reinhardt and I would sit there and go, 'That. Keep that.' When it came time to do *Pippin*, the chorus came in to learn 'Morning Glow,' and John Rubinstein is singing, and I'm saying to the chorus, 'Okay, you've heard it a couple of times, start to sing some stuff.' They looked at me as if I was from Jupiter. In a Broadway rehearsal, I learned, singers are handed their parts and they sing them. So, abashed, I went home and wrote vocal arrangements."

"Marking Time" Becomes "Extraordinary"

Schwartz wrote "Extraordinary" in D.C. to express Pippin's determination to stay committed to his quest. "Marking Time," the previous song for that spot, was clearly not working for Rubinstein. The actor comments, "'Marking Time' was a perfectly good song, but that part of the show needed a punch, and that song was sort of an easygoing Laura Nyro-esque piece. Fosse asked Stephen to write another."

Players attempt to seduce Pippin into self-immolation as the ultimate extraordinary experience—one that would provide the most extraordinary ending to the show.

Finale and The Players

Schwartz comments: "I liked the malevolent subtext—the idea that this very seductive troupe of players you thought was so alluring and delightful, you gradually realize has some nefarious design. And the metaphor, of course, is that these self-destructive voices exist within all of us. The concept of self-destruction—the longing for death—was particularly personal to Bob, as one can see in *All That Jazz,* (The semi-autobiographical film featuring a Fosse-like character).

The Pippin Compromise

Pippin declines the Player's invitation when it becomes clear that the restless quest for fulfillment has to stop somewhere in order for him to actually find fulfillment. About this compromise with an ideal, Schwartz says: "This is a struggle all of us face in our lives: when to settle and what to settle for. On the one hand, you don't want to stop striving and experimenting, growing and trying to improve yourself. On the other hand, you don't want to spin your wheels so that ultimately you get nowhere."

Pippin (John Rubinstein) and Catherine (Jill Clayburgh) pause for a love song.

"Love Song"

The sweetest gift for the musical from the days in Washington was inspiration for "Love Song." In a meeting, Schwartz and Fosse discussed the Pippin-Catherine love duet, "Just Between the Two of Us," because it wasn't coming across well enough to the audience. Back at the piano, Schwartz suddenly found himself tapping into what the characters needed to say, drawing from memories and letting the music flow. "I remember that 'Love Song' felt like a writing breakthrough to me, particularly in its shifting time signatures. It felt like one of those moments of really getting in touch with an inner flow, and just riding that."

Shortly thereafter, he invited Rubinstein and Clayburgh to hear it. "We loved it the first time he played it for us on the piano," Rubinstein recalls. "I thought, 'Oh, thank God! Now we have a shot at making that moment really work!' When you want to express an emotion and the song doesn't do it for you, or the line of dialogue doesn't do it for you, you struggle. That original love song, 'Just Between the Two of Us' was like that. Perfectly nice, but it didn't have that beautiful, 'I'm madly in love with you' dreaminess about it, which 'Love Song' did."

> "They say the whole is greater
> Than the sum of the parts it's made of.
> Well, if it's true of anything
> It's true of love."

Leading Player (Ben Vereen) and barefoot Pippin (John Rubinstein) step together in "On the Right Track."

"On the Right Track"

The song's development proved to be one of the most positive outcomes of the Bob Fosse/Stephen Schwartz collaboration. In August of 1972, rehearsals began in earnest for the musical that would open in late September for the out-of-town trial at the Kennedy Center. Bob Fosse had plenty to work on, getting all his dancers to perform the big "Glory" production number, the sex ballet, and so many others. He didn't prepare any major dance scene for the homespun hero, the barefoot Pippin played by John Rubinstein.

"After two weeks of rehearsals," Rubinstein reports, "I said to him with uncharacteristic chutzpah (and with a twinkle in my eye) that I refused to play the title role in a Bob Fosse musical without dancing! He liked that idea (even though he knew full well I was no dancer) and created 'On The Right Track' as a duo dance number for Ben and me! What fun that was, and how great for *Pippin*!"

The story continues with Fosse and Schwartz: "When I originally wrote the song, all the notes of the tune had corresponding words," Schwartz recalls. "It was Bob's suggestion, in order to provide interesting places for dance and make the song more unusual, that I cut every extraneous word of lyric I could. He would fill those beats with dance steps. This is what led to the idiosyncratic, jagged structure of the lyrics, which I like a lot. And that was a very cool way to write a song."

> *There's no trick to staying sensible*
> *Despite each cul-de-sac*
> *'Cause each step's indispensable*
> *When you're on the right track…*

MARTHA SWOPE

In Broadway's *The Magic Show*, Doug levitates his assistant Cal, balancing her on the tips of swords, and then pulls one out to leave her floating in air. Doug Henning and Dale Soules perform this magic act after Soules sings "Lion Tamer."

CHAPTER 8

THE *MAGIC SHOW* CONJURES UP A CROWD

'Cause there's one thing I know
turns a man of sixty
Back into a child of six:
Watching Dunninger, Houdini
Or Doug—the magic man
Up to his old tricks

THE MAGIC SHOW

At the very end of December in 1973, Stephen Schwartz was appreciating the warm shelter of his Connecticut home when a phone call came in from Joe Beruh and Edgar Lansbury at the *Godspell* office asking if he would please get on a plane for Toronto—there was a ticket waiting for him at the airport. "I was not particularly dying to go to Toronto in what was already a very cold winter," Schwartz later recalled, "but they wouldn't take no for an answer."

Godspell manager Marvin Krauss had been up in Toronto for another Beruh/Lansbury project and caught a performance of *Spellbound*, a rock musical that featured magician Doug Henning. Krauss watched, astonished, as Henning suspended a girl on the tip of a sword, flawlessly executed one of Houdini's escape illusions, and performed other amazing magic acts. When the show was over, he called Beruh and Lansbury and insisted they come to see it as it had potential for Broadway. They wanted to bring in Schwartz, as well as Nina Faso, who was working with Beruh/Lansbury on other projects. Reports vary as to who traveled together to Toronto, but in any case, once off the plane and in the theatre, the magic captured them. "I remember Joe being very excited because he loved magic," Nina Faso reports. Schwartz

The music [of Spellbound*] was terrible. Everything about the show was terrible except this young magician, Doug Henning.*

MARVIN KRAUS

Doug Henning. Nina Faso comments, "I thought Doug was brilliant. He had a psychology degree and he was the first one who looked at magic as a psychological thing instead of just tricks."

was as "dazzled and charmed" as anyone.

Edgar Lansbury recalls, "We'd actually been thinking of doing a show with magic. I hadn't seen any magic around [New York] for years and years and what I'd seen was top hat and tails type of thing. Here was this kid in blue jeans and T-shirt doing all these incredible illusions. We loved him." On the other hand, they didn't love *Spellbound.* Lansbury remembers insisting on being able to change the "very corny" story when they made rights arrangements with a then-little-known young man named Ivan Reitman, who was producing the show. (Reitman's involvement with *The Magic Show* on Broadway helped launch the career of the famed movie producer and director, later known for films *Ghostbusters, Kindergarten Cop,* and others.)

Although Schwartz was fascinated by the prospect of working with a real magician, he didn't believe the musical was worth years of effort. Besides which, he'd already been tapped for a score for *The Baker's Wife.* He'd consider writing songs for *The Magic Show* only if the show could be mounted in the coming spring Broadway season of 1974. That meant no out-of-town tryout. Just write it, cast it, rehearse it, and open by June. That suited the producers as well. "It didn't seem to us at the time that it was a terribly difficult undertaking," says Lansbury. "Really, with the magic, which was so extraordinary, that was what was important. And putting together a book and some songs shouldn't take much time."

Weighing on Schwartz's conscience as he made the decision to write a new musical was a potentially sticky situation regarding his friendship with David Spangler, with whom he had formed a rock band after college. Spangler's new Broadway-bound musical *Houdini* (score by Spangler, book by Muriel Rukeyser) had played at the Lenox Arts Center in Massachusetts in July of 1973, and Schwartz had attended.

After returning from Toronto he called Spangler. "Edgar and Joe want me to write a musical about magic," Stephen said. "I am friends with you and I will not touch this if it would upset you; if you would feel we would be stealing something from you."

"If you want to do it and you think you can make a good show out of it, then go ahead and do it," Spangler replied, pleased to have at least been asked. Schwartz later made him dance arranger for *The Magic Show*, so he'd get a Broadway credit and compensation.

Grover Dale, who had worked on *Houdini*, was tapped to direct and choreograph *The Magic Show*. *Houdini*'s producers cancelled efforts on Spangler's show when they learned of the new competition. Even so, Schwartz and Spangler remained friends.

Finishing a script in a hurry would not be an easy task. Lansbury and Beruh assigned the task to Bob Randall, a successful Broadway playwright, after letting go another writer who tried a first draft.

Doug Henning's inability to sing added to the challenge. He would have to play himself. As Schwartz describes it, "The notion was that, because Doug didn't sing, but had this very strong and distinctive personality, we would come up with a show built around a character very much like him." His onstage character became Doug the magician.

Schwartz continues, "We decided that the illusions would be his 'songs' and we would use these illusions to advance the plot in the way a traditional musical used songs, and songs could be written that lead up to and into specific magic acts. Doug gave us a list of illusions he wanted to perform, and Bob Randall, Grover Dale, and I tried to figure out how to incorporate as many as we could in the storytelling."

Henning's bag of tricks included the illusion for sawing a woman in half. He could also make objects, people, or wild animals appear or disappear. Worked into the show, this magic helped carry the story. "When Henning's character in the show became irritated with his assistant," Schwartz explains, "he made her disappear; when he wanted a beautiful new assistant, he conjured one up out of thin air; when he wanted to make amends to his old assistant, he turned the new one into a cougar; and so on."

Schwartz was amenable to working songs around Doug's magic. "The thing that was so appealing about Doug," he remarks, "was that, up until that time, magicians had been these sort of grandiose characters in top hat and tails, or these slick Las Vegas types, but Doug had this almost street kid, hippie-esque personality." From this, the team took their approach: "Therefore, we thought the tone of the show should be lower key. It wasn't about the Las Vegas thing, but sort of the anti-Las Vegas presentation."

We deliberately wanted to be low-key. Though we were a Broadway show, we wanted to try to have the feel of an off-Broadway show. We were kind of the scruffy alternative show as opposed to the big slick musical.

STEPHEN SCHWARTZ

Henning came to his passion for magic at age six, when he saw a magician levitate a woman on a television program. The Winnipeg native, born in 1947, studied magic both on his own and with master magicians. He dreamed of reviving magic as a grand theatrical art—not because he wanted to fool audiences, but out of a love for wonder and surprise.

The Magic Show team quickly discovered that the spry and playfully innocent image Henning had projected in *Spellbound* was his real personality. Schwartz said later, "I remember him coming up to me one day with a pencil tied to a string, whirling his hands, and my suddenly finding the string attached to my shirt button and impossible to remove. Another quick gesture from Doug and it was off again."

The writers could then set up a contrast between the character of an old-guard conjurer and the character of "Doug," the wonder-boy magician who was in love with his art. But working all the magic into a story seemed too extreme. "Doug was also extraordinarily deft with prestidigitation, sleight of hand,"

Schwartz affirms. "We thought it was very important to build into the show a section where he could come out and do magic that wasn't based on the giant illusions, but based on the deftness and skill of his close-up magic. So we incorporated some of the smaller magic into the section of the show called 'Doug's Act.'" They told Henning to do what he did naturally—for example, rolling a quarter across his knuckles—and they would try to highlight his talents.

For this "anti-Vegas" show that would highlight magic on both small and large scales, the producers wanted a more intimate setting than a large house would provide. They secured the Cort Theatre, a 1000-seat venue on 48th Street, a few blocks from the cluster of Broadway Theatres around Shubert Alley.

The creative team launched into a brisk development phase, working out scene concepts with input from Henning. "Bob Randall had the basic notion for the characters, the setting, and how he was going to put it all together," Schwartz explains. "From there, we made an outline—we figured out what illusions would go where. Then I started to write songs for the characters that Bob came up with, plus the specific illusions."

Schwartz headed for his piano while the audition and casting process went into full swing. He took time to watch a real magician in action "right before his very eyes," and even let some of it influence the beat of the music.

Auditions turned up actress/singer Dale Soules as Henning's flexible, fast-talking assistant. Dancer Anita Morris slid into the role of the magically conjured assistant Charmin. She was perfect for the part that called for an attractive, supple female—and she happened to be Grover Dale's wife.

For the role of a conceited old-guard magician, Nina Faso thought of David Ogden Stiers, whom she knew from her work in San Francisco. (Stiers later became known for his role as Major

The Mis-made Girl illusion.

Charles Emerson Winchester in the TV series *M*A*S*H*,
and worked again with Stephen Schwartz when voicing
roles for Disney's *Pocahontas* and *The Hunchback of Notre
Dame*).

Doug's onstage assistants in *Spellbound* were brought in
from Canada to assist him and to tutor the two dancers who
would play them on Broadway. Traditional Broadway musical dazzle would come from a total of nine singer/dancers
plus their non-singer star. Henning would train the cast in
a whole new set of skills to make magic acts look effortless
and wondrous.

A *Godspell*-like small band would form the "orchestra" at the Cort. Stephen Reinhardt came over from *Godspell* as
music director and keyboard player. Joining him in May in the
orchestra pit would be Paul Shaffer (the future sidekick of TV's
David Letterman) on keyboards and five others—a cozy group
who could play a score based on rock music, with theatre music
influences.

Refining the Story

Spellbound's story had been told almost exclusively through
song lyrics set to rock music. Henning played the part of a nightclub magician who was content to use hackneyed tricks of the
trade, like pulling a rabbit from a top hat, until he met his future
magic mentor, Maya. This Goddess of Magic showed Henning
how to use 'the magic within' to win the heart of Jenny, his love
interest in the show.

The Magic Show story would be worldlier. In eight days,
Randall completed a working draft of the script.

Manny is owner of the Top Hat nightclub in Passaic, New
Jersey, which has seen better days. He wants to ditch Feldman
the Magnificent, an aging and often drunk magician. Manny

recruits Doug to elevate the act, which already includes singers Dina and Donna. They learn that Goldfarb, a famous agent, is coming to see the show one night to hunt talent, and everybody wants to be discovered. For the romantic storyline, Doug is the love interest for his assistant, Cal. He ignores her, paying more attention to Charmin, a voluptuous second assistant he conjures up. Cal departs, Doug misses her, he turns Charmin into a cougar, and makes magic to get Cal back, transforming her into a lion (or cougar) tamer.

Dale Soules

While working on the musical, Schwartz would sometimes come down to the city from Connecticut to see what was happening at the Cort and then go to David Spangler's apartment in Chelsea where he'd take over the piano to do some writing. Meanwhile, Spangler was up at the Cort Theatre every day, working with Doug Henning to score illusion music, or at a dance studio with Grover Dale, carefully scoring dance arrangements to suit whatever the choreographer needed for his dancers. It all had to happen so quickly that he and Stephen barely had time to compare notes.

The illusions that were interwoven with or introduced by a song, such as "Lion Tamer," used Schwartz's music. Magic presentations in that era were accompanied by original music. Spangler and Schwartz created something that would truly enhance the suspense and drama of the performance.

Drawing from his pop/rock background, Schwartz wrote the speedy number "Solid Silver Platform Shoes." And he spun out another counterpoint melody piece (as he had with *Godspell*'s "All For the Best") for Dina and Donna's duet, "Two's Company." Another song was needed for the moment when Top Hat performers express their dream of being discovered by Goldfarb. Schwartz pulled a four-part fugue from his college musical *Nouveau* and wrote new lyrics to create "The Goldfarb Variations."

The show's writers included a magician's revenge story as part of the plot—a storyline that had a tradition in the magic world. Schwartz wrote "A Bit of Villainy"—a song that wasn't recorded on the cast album but was in the show.

During rehearsals Schwartz was constantly on hand to teach actors their songs and work through issues. During the day, the cast members who had solos would take time to work with either the musical director or the composer or both. Soules enjoyed rehearsing with the composer and says, "He was a wonderful teacher."

Schwartz's tour de force, "West End Avenue," emerged late but provided the Cal character, played by Soules, with a powerful song that suited her voice.

On With the Show

The production still had issues to resolve even as late as the final dress rehearsal. An illusion called "The Revenge of the Rabbits" bombed. Doug made a grand gesture toward the mezzanine where some magic with a giant mechanical rabbit was supposed to begin, but nothing happened. Schwartz, who had been watching from the audience, recalls, "The rabbit rattled down over the orchestra section where it dangled precariously, looking like it was going to fall any minute. The rabbit eventually got to the stage and then crashed. So that was the end of the rabbit, and another revenge against Feldman had to be devised."

When *The Magic Show* opened on May 28, 1974, the hastily assembled, homey musical won hearts. Even critics who knocked the score praised Doug. Martin Gottfried ended a litany of faults in his review by saying, "And still it has magic so fabulous I could watch the tricks all night." Aided by such publicity stunts as Doug Henning sawing Barbara Walters in half on the *Today Show*, the musical attracted sell-out crowds of every order, from theatre and magic buffs to busloads of kids from summer camps.

For *The Magic Show*'s songwriter, there were several disappointments. When the reviews came out, Stephen read them and felt attacked by the criticisms of his work. It was the last time he ever read reviews right after his New York openings. (He himself was not completely satisfied with his score—a trait that in the future inspired regular tinkering with his creations.)

Also, the magic had ceased to be magical. "As a kid, I always liked magic," he once wrote. "It was theatrical, and it was an intellectual challenge to try to figure out how seemingly impossible things were accomplished. I think maybe subconsciously I was hoping there would turn out to be such a thing as 'real' magic. When I was in high school and I wrote my first full-length musical, mercifully unproduced, the main character was a witch. This is probably all part of the ongoing theme in my work dealing with the tension between romantic ideals and facing reality. When I was first asked to write *The Magic Show*, I was very eager to learn how the illusions were done. But once I was in rehearsals and began to see, I felt so let down whenever I would actually find out that I stopped trying to."

Schwartz concluded later about *The Magic Show*: "Of necessity, it wasn't a show that went through a tremendous amount of rewriting and rethinking. To be perfectly honest, if we had been a little less slapdash from the book and lyrics aspect of it, it might have been a better show. But maybe not. There was something about it that just worked under those circumstances. It succeeded with the audience and it succeeded financially."

It ran long enough for Schwartz's son Scott, born in 1974, to attend a performance and become interested in magic. It certainly had a magical effect on the elder Schwartz's pocketbook, helping to pay for his new Tudor-styled dream house in Connecticut.

Wasn't that illusion fun? Not if you know how it's done!

Stephen Schwartz lyric from *The Magic Show*

Dina and Donna perform their nightclub act and sing "Before Your Very Eyes" in the show within the show. Pictured here are Lynne Thigpen as Dina, Lisa Raggio as Donna, and Doug Henning as Doug.

Doug conjures up a glamorous assistant (Louisa Flaningam) and saws her in half. While planning the musical, Schwartz and Randall had the idea of keeping the assistant's two halves separate for most of the show. "I remember talking to Doug and asking if that were possible without revealing the illusion or seriously injuring an actor," Schwartz says. "Doug thought it was a great idea."

The Magic Show — "West End Avenue"

"West End Avenue" has received extended interest outside the show as a cabaret or concert number and an audition piece. It is also featured on The Stephen Schwartz Album, a collection of his songs produced in 2002. As with "No Good Deed" from *Wicked* and "Meadowlark" from *The Baker's Wife*, the singer describes her internal tension over her situation while the driven rhythms of the music evoke a mood of frustration.

Given the short deadline he was on, Schwartz was pleased that "West End Avenue" came to him "more or less fully formed in a matter of hours." In one question-answer session, when asked why the unusual time signature, he explained more about how the song emerged: "In 'West End Avenue', the lyrics and music more or less came together, and the rhythms were determined by the natural flow of the words. I tend to write at the piano and then write the music out later. I was quite surprised when I wrote out 'West End Avenue' by all the changing time signatures! But since that was what I felt the lyrics demanded, I didn't try to 'neaten them up.' I don't really think about time signatures per se when I'm writing, except to be aware of something like: 'Well, every other song in this show has been in 4/4 so far, so maybe I ought to do something in 6/8.'"

To prepare for singing Cal's number, Dale Soules looked to her own younger years. "I felt like I knew what her emotional life was like. It was very different from my personal life, but I certainly experienced wanting someone who didn't necessarily notice me, and I certainly experienced wanting to change certain aspects of my life at home, which I think everyone does in adolescence.

"It's that period where no matter where you grew up you feel like a prisoner because you're on the cusp of becoming free. You are frightened by the freedom and yet very constricted. You have been protected, to a certain extent, by your parents or guardians. Now they want to know where are you going, what are you doing, why is the bathroom door shut, and what movie did you see? So there's that feeling of constriction or imprisonment, but in the moment of wanting to become free you also realize, 'Oh my God, now I'm responsible for all this.' And then suddenly you're out there on your own."

Cal (Dale Soules) sings "West End Avenue."

CREATIVITY NOTES

Artistic Ego

Are highly confident performers simply egomaniacal show-offs who need to be noticed? Maybe some are, but others, like the late Doug Henning, readily follow the beat of their inner drummer.

"My picture of Doug," Stephen Schwartz told Henning's biographer, "is that in talking to him, he would always be rolling a coin across his knuckles, or he would be fiddling with a piece of string that he broke into seven pieces and then suddenly made into one piece. He was always doing that kind of stuff—sort of like the comedian who's always on, but not as irritating. (I know a lot of comedians who are always on, and you just want to kill them.) That was not the case with Doug. It didn't seem to come from, 'I need everyone looking at me. I need to be the center of attention.' He was this sort of not-quite-of-this-world personality. When he floated into a situation, the world somewhat changed around him. I thought he was a gentle and pleasant soul who was just extremely good at what he did.

"Doug was incredibly easy to get along with. He had a strong work ethic. He was serious about what he did, but his personality really was very 'flower child.' He was a Transcendental Meditator, so he brought that kind of lightness of spirit and laid back quality to what he did."

In other situations, Schwartz has experienced ego conflicts with colleagues or performers. He advises, "When working in a collaborative medium like musical theatre, you have to learn to be ego-less about the work to the extent you can. If you're having a disagreement with a collaborator about something in a show, you need to look objectively at your own motivation: 'Am I just fighting for this because my ego needs to win the argument, or do I really think this is the best for the show?' Sometimes it's not so easy to know."

ACT II
1974–1991

~ Tennis Tournament 1988 ~

The Baker's Wife world premiere opens at the Dorothy Chandler Pavilion in Los Angeles on May 11, 1976, with set design by Jo Mielziner, costumes by Theoni V. Aldredge, direction by Joseph Hardy.

PREVIOUS PAGE: Stephen Schwartz (right) and Steven Boockvor (center) show off tennis trophies to friends gathered in Schwartz's backyard tennis area.

CHAPTER 9

THE BAKER'S WIFE: MIXED INGREDIENTS

And then one day, suddenly
Something can happen,
It may be quite simple,
It may be quite small

THE BAKER'S WIFE

Of Stephen Schwartz's early scores, his fourth commercial project, *The Baker's Wife*, offered the most robust emotionality as reflected in songs like "Meadowlark" and "Gifts of Love." Yet developing a version that worked to his satisfaction proved far more difficult than he could have imagined.

The journey began in an awkward moment over lunch with Neil Simon in a New York City restaurant in 1974. Stephen Schwartz realized he might have to decline collaboration with this world-famous playwright. No, he didn't want to musicalize *Mutiny on the Bounty,* or anything else being suggested. At the end of the meal Simon mentioned, "Well, I have this one other notion, but I don't think it's the sort of thing you'll respond to." And then he described the movie version of *The Baker's Wife,* which David Merrick had asked him to adapt for the stage.

Simon described the comedic 1938 black-and-white French film classic, Marcel Pagnol's *La Femme du Boulanger,* known in its English subtitled version as *The Baker's Wife,* which had charmed audiences with quirky characters and an odd community problem. A homely, middle-aged baker named Aimable moves to a rural village in the South of France with petite Aurelie, his young wife. She quickly attracts the local Marquis' hired hand, and they steal off at dawn on the Marquis' horse. Her husband, too distraught to bake, turns to drink. The normally quarrelsome

I lived in France as a young child, my parents both were Francophiles, and I had grown up hearing both French folk music and the music of the French Music Hall—Edith Piaf, Yves Montand, and Charles Aznavour.

STEPHEN SCHWARTZ

'Love is all very well but you've got to think about eating.'... What is a village without bread?

FROM *Blue Boy*
BY JEAN GIONO
SOURCE FOR THE FILM

villagers must set aside their differences and rally together for wife retrieval to restore their supply of daily fresh bread.

Schwartz's imagination fired up as Simon revealed the baker's behavior in the final scene of the movie. Early in the story, the couple's female cat disappears, presumably in pursuit of a tomcat, paralleling the way the baker's wife vanishes with an alluring young man. When the wife and the cat return home at the end of the film, the baker chides the cat instead of the wife, and accepts them both back.

"What hooked me immediately was the ending," says Schwartz. "I responded to the humanness of the baker's behavior in that last scene—the obliqueness and complexity of his behavior and how much of it was subtextual. It immediately appealed to me, and then as I thought more about it, I liked the idea of writing music with a French flavor."

(The young composer's involvement in a David Merrick production serendipitously would discharge a previous obligation—Merrick had released an option for Schwartz's *Pippin* under the provision that another option would be available for a future musical.)

When Neil Simon moved to Los Angeles in November and opted out of the project, Shirley Bernstein linked her veteran writer Joseph Stein (*Fiddler on the Roof, Zorba*) with her young client, creating an unlikely writing team. "Joe" Stein, born in 1912, was already sixty-two in 1974 when he began meeting with his twenty-six-year-old writing partner, whom he called "Steve." Stein's television background inclined him toward humorous quips and an open, casual writing style. His *Fiddler on the Roof* libretto represented the often-labeled "golden" era of traditional, book-based musical theatre. Stephen Schwartz had helped launch pop/rock musicals for the 1970s.

The two New York City natives were both short and trim. Stein's relaxed, unimposing personality contrasted with, but complemented, that of his driven young collaborator. The two were immediately friendly and believed they could write a seamless musical together despite their different ages and sensibilities.

To begin their adaptation, Schwartz and Stein sat together to watch *The Baker's Wife* film, noting the material's charm and limitations for the stage. Filmgoers benefited from a camera's tour through the old town and into the bakery, with its wood-burning oven built into the stucco wall. The cinematographer zoomed close to delighted faces of men and women crowded around the bakery counter to purchase—and sometimes affectionately pat—fresh loaves of bread. Audiences could chuckle over the depiction of an insular life that begs for a bit of scandal to go with the café's wine. And they could marvel at Raimu (Aimable), a French character actor who, as one reviewer commented, embodied the laughable pathos of the baker's experience in a touching, Chaplinesque performance.

Joseph Stein

I knew about Stephen's work and I guess he knew my work. We got along extremely well from the beginning.

JOSEPH STEIN

A stage version would need to reach further emotionally than the source material. In the film, Aurelie, the baker's wife, appears as a sluttish girl who unthinkingly slinks off with the first attractive man she meets. For a musical, Schwartz wanted to expand the film's meager portrayals of the wife and her lover, making them "more human and more believable."

As they outlined their show and began writing drafts, Stein and Schwartz preserved the basic architecture of the movie plot, with a few exceptions. "Aurelie," whom they renamed "Genevieve," would motor away in the Marquis' prized Peugeot automobile with Dominique, the chauffeur and assistant (instead of with the farmhand on a prized horse). They also dropped any reference to the baker's foiled suicide attempt.

*Each score should have its
own identity and should
make its own world.*

STEPHEN SCHWARTZ

Warming Up To a Score

For the research phase of *The Baker's Wife*, Schwartz immersed himself in a month-long French music piano-playing regime until the composers' styles became second nature. "I played Debussy and Ravel on the piano, just so my fingers would automatically go toward those chord structures, and I would have those sounds in my head," Schwartz recalls. "But when I started to write, I didn't pay attention to it, and what happened is what I'd hoped. I went instinctively to certain chords I wouldn't have gone to before I'd done that. It's like an actor's preparation, building up sense memory."

The French Impressionists' expressiveness, with their frequent use of dissonant, unresolved chords, flowed into Schwartz's sensibilities like a musical river. It would eventually overflow into his original opening song, "Welcome to Concorde," some of the chords for "Gifts of Love," and the mellifluous piano accompaniment to "Meadowlark."

He also listened exclusively to French recording artists like Edith Piaf and her one-time younger lover, Yves Montand. Schwartz explored folk music and planned for accordion and guitar sounds to be featured in the orchestrations.

His own heart being drawn to the interpersonal concerns of the love triangle, he first worked on emotionally pitched pieces for Aimable, Dominique, and Genevieve. He crafted a crowd-pleaser, "Proud Lady," for Dominique that allowed the young buck to strut his physique and display his youthful arrogance. He wrote "If I Have to Live Alone" (probably his saddest ballad ever) for the baker to sing after he is abandoned. He had yet to write a solo for Genevieve until his "Meadowlark" appeared, a song that provided a turning point not only for the character, but also for his development as a songwriter.

Although Schwartz had long been a fan of songwriters like Joni Mitchell, Paul Simon, and Laura Nyro, who could write directly from their emotions, he didn't normally compose songs influenced by his personal life. Rather, he mentally considered a character's experience in the context of a particular moment in a story, and tapped intuitively into that as best he could. "Meadowlark" would change his approach from then on, for he taught himself how to tie a character's feelings to his own.

He was writing *The Baker's Wife* at a junction in his life in which he was struggling with his responses to the realities of a Broadway-related career and with personal issues as well. Stymied creative efforts added to his discomfort. "I had written several songs for the musical, and I couldn't solve it at all. I just felt like there is a show here but I don't get it and I'm just not going to be able to write it."

While checking on *The Magic Show* tour in Boston, after a particularly difficult night that triggered strong emotional conflicts, he awoke early and headed over to the Wilbur Theatre and down into the orchestra pit, where he found comfort in playing the piano. A song flowed out of him for Genevieve to sing while she wrestles with her conflicting feelings about marriage and romance. "'Meadowlark' was one of those songs that sort of emerged just like *pffft*, there it was," Schwartz recalls. "I took the emotions that were going on in my life and superimposed them onto the character and situation. And that opened up the show and the score for me."

At first, Schwartz felt really awkward about sharing the evocative song with Joe Stein and his other colleagues. "After I finished the song I was very embarrassed about it and I thought, 'Oh, well, I could never actually have anyone hear this.' Even though I changed all the specific facts and everything, it was very close to the bone for me, and I thought no one can ever hear this because

The breakthrough moment was "Meadowlark." That was the first song written in this way, and the response to it (except from David Merrick) bolstered my courage about writing from such an exposed and personal place.

STEPHEN SCHWARTZ

everyone will know everything about me. And also I felt that therefore it wouldn't really work within the context of the show. I was wrong on both counts."

With the exception of David Merrick, Schwartz's colleagues readily accepted "Meadowlark" into the score as a dynamic and essential part of the storytelling.

For the next months (and as it would turn out, decades) of developing *The Baker's Wife*, Schwartz and Stein would ask themselves, "What is this about?" It was actually difficult to determine if it was Aimable's story of love and loss, or the villagers' story of longing and community-building, or a three-way story about the consequences of passions and infidelity. With the emotive power of songs like "Proud Lady," "If I Have to Live Alone," and "Meadowlark" for the three central characters, the villagers' story and songs would have to become very compelling to matter to the audience.

"The central story is about relationships," Schwartz reflected in later years. "For a relationship really to endure and be successful, whether it's a friendship or a marriage or whatever, each of the parties of the relationship has to face the truth about the other one, accept the other one's flaws as well as their strengths, and love them both in spite of and because of those things. It requires being clear-eyed and honest about who the other person is."

That didn't mean all the songs had to be romantic or angst-ridden. For comic moments in the show, Schwartz came up with boisterously funny songs like "Bread," the production number during which villagers could clamor over the first fragrant loaves to emerge from the new baker's oven, and "Luckiest Man in the World" for the village men to sing to comfort Aimable.

But it did mean that a second turning-point song and scene for Genevieve could provide a more clear-eyed view of her lover, herself, and her needs. The setting for "Where is the Warmth?"

in the musical is a small hotel room. Genevieve and Dominique are disenchanted with one another. While Dominique sleeps, Genevieve gathers her few things, preparing to leave, and sings the sensitive ballad:

> *Since I grow feverish*
> *With the flush that comes*
> *Every time he holds me*
> *Naturally you'd suppose I'd be warm*
> *When I'm hot / Well, I'm not…*

The musical concludes with its mature message: that a flash of passion, whether lingering or fading, is not sufficient for a lasting bond between two people. As Stein remarks, "One of the things the story clearly says is that there's an essential difference between superficial love and true love; between physical attraction and attraction of the heart. It's a rich kind of statement to make in musical form."

CREATIVITY NOTES

Emotional Truth as a Touchstone

Stephen Schwartz (after telling the "Meadowlark" story in 2003): What I've learned as a writer is that the more I can get to my own emotional truth, the more a song is actually about me, thinly disguised as an Indian princess or the hunchback of Notre Dame or other characters, oddly enough, the more it communicates universally. For the most personal songs I've ever written, I've had people come up to me and say, "How could you possibly have known that? I felt like you read my diary." It's really an interesting phenomenon, and of course it makes our job as songwriters a lot easier. I have this joke where people ask, "How do you write a song?" and I say, "Tell the truth and make it rhyme." But that's really it. The more you can tell your truth, the more it resonates for others. Of all the lessons about songwriting I've learned over time, that's been the most revelatory for me. I didn't actually go in knowing that. I had to learn it from experience.

The Long Pre-Broadway Tour

Merrick had booked a long out-of-town tour, expecting to warm up audiences, spread the word about the upcoming grand Broadway production, and give the writers an opportunity to work out any kinks. He thought in terms of a big production in large theatres with an elaborate set, substantial cast, and at least one familiar star. He no doubt expected to repeat the success he had with *Fanny*, a showy musical adapted from a trilogy of Marcel Pagnol films: *Fanny, Marius,* and *Cesar*. But the plot of *Fanny* on Broadway benefited from the complexities allowed in the multi-year storyline. The production ran for 888 performances, from 1954 to 1956, with much of its commercial success due to Merrick's marketing antics. The consummate guerrilla marketer once inspired the description: "Everything he touches turns to ink." His stunts for *Fanny* included his publicized attempts to get a hurricane named after the show, and hiring an airplane to fly over the heads of journalists during the wedding of American actress Grace Kelly and Prince Rainier in Monaco, skywriting the suggestion to see *Fanny* in New York.

But *Fanny* and *The Baker's Wife* were croissants from different batches of dough. *The Baker's Wife* was a thinly plotted story carried out over a short period of time. The show's chefs, Schwartz and Stein, had little interest in stirring up a showy and broadly entertaining piece. Instead, they pictured their musical as a modest production for one of the smaller Broadway theatres that would be appropriate for re-creating a cozy French town. Still, they had to follow Merrick's plan.

Unsuspecting about the arduous journey ahead, Stephen Schwartz welcomed Kurt Peterson ("Dominique"), Carole Demas ("Genevieve"), and other cast members into his spacious living room in Connecticut where he was about to play them *The Baker's Wife*'s score for the first time. Sitting near the grand piano, the cast watched the composer's fingers sweep busily over the ivories for the music of "Meadowlark." They listened while he accompanied himself, singing through the Italian aria-inspired "Serenade," the comedic "Proud Lady," and others. Peterson found himself in tears, and told Schwartz how beautiful it all sounded to him, and how pleased he was with the pieces he would sing in his role as a romantic lead.

The show's first director, Joseph Hardy, held a meeting at his home in Los Angeles with Teri Ralston (Denise), who would play the role of co-owner of a local café, and other West Coast cast members. Delighted with the upcoming prospects, Hardy spoke about his idea of piping the smell of baking bread into the theatre.

Cast member Darlene Conley (Hortense), who played the downtrodden wife of the village butcher, remembers being told that she and her cohorts were not ensemble members, but were featured players. Each had a name and a character. The implication was that their roles would be expanded over time, as the show evolved. (Unfortunately, it would take another twenty-five years for that to happen.)

On April 8, 1976, the *New York Times* announced the upcoming show, explaining that Topol, star of the film version of *Fiddler on the Roof*, would make his American stage debut with co-star Carole Demas, recently seen in *Grease*. The new musical would first try out on May 11th in Los Angeles as part of the Civic Light Opera company's season.

"American debut of an international star"—that was how Merrick wanted to sell his show. Joe Stein had wanted to cast Zero Mostel, Broadway's first Tevye in *Fiddler*, to be his baker. When Zero turned down the role, it seemed natural to consider Topol, who had starred as Tevye in London.

The cracks in the plaster began to show about two or three weeks into rehearsal. And they started with Topol. They started with the fact that he was very unhappy with Joe Hardy; he was very unhappy with the things he was doing.

STEPHEN SCHWARTZ

The feeling was that Topol was just too attractive. He's a very sexy, sexy man.

TERI RALSTON

As the cast began rehearsals, it appeared that forty-one-year-old Chaim Topol, a native of Israel, might not have carefully examined the script before signing his contract. His colleagues assumed he could adjust from playing the life-weary peasant, Tevye, in Russia to the optimistic, gentle baker in France. But the debonair actor apparently found playing a fat, unattractive Frenchman distasteful and resisted his role. "He was both woefully wrong for the show," Schwartz asserts, "and stubbornly unwilling to attempt to actually play the character."

By the time the show moved into tech rehearsals in Los Angeles, physical problems started factoring in. "The set was a total disaster," Stephen Schwartz recalls. "As David Merrick said when he

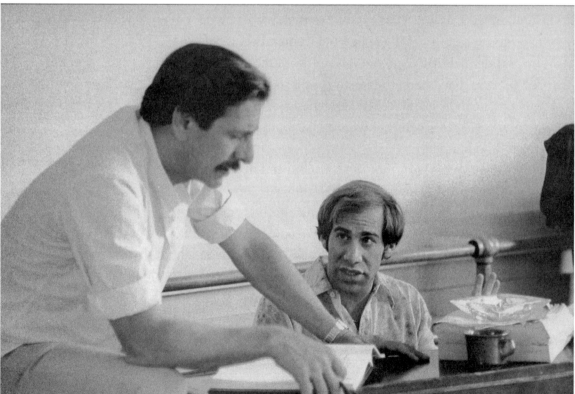

Topol and Stephen Schwartz in "a typically difficult rehearsal" (Schwartz's phrase).

came in and saw it in Los Angeles, it looked like a Welsh mining town. It looked like we were doing *How Green Was My Valley*. It was just a totally wrong choice. But there it was."

Merrick had contracted with seventy-five-year-old scenic designer Jo Mielziner, whose Broadway credits included such shows as *Finian's Rainbow, South Pacific,* and *The King and I*. (It had been Mielziner, a Carnegie Mellon graduate, who had recommended that Schwartz enroll in their drama program.) The Paris-born designer was familiar with the French landscape, was a technical innovator, and had a painterly, non-realistic style that might suit the romantic show. Then on March 16, 1976, Mielziner died unexpectedly. His associates took over. However, knowing they couldn't speak to the artist, they did not feel empowered to change his last set. Once it was built for the tour, it was too late for substantial modification.

May 11, 1976, was the world premiere for *The Baker's Wife* on its first tour stop in Los Angeles. Twenty-eight-year-old Stephen Schwartz entered the lobby of the Dorothy Chandler Pavilion beneath crystal chandeliers, stepping into the plush theatre. (Twenty years later he would be honored with an Academy Award in this same elegant space.)

The curtain rose, exposing the set meant to resemble a bakery and outdoor café area in a tiny French village in 1935. Two shingled cottages topped with dormer windows sat on their bulky turntables. The cast of sixteen offered a romantic musical tale, with fifteen songs orchestrated in a "Puccini-esque" grand style at the composer's request. Cast member Darlene Conley commented later about that night: "It was joyous. I remember standing there, and the opening music started. It was so ravishingly beautiful."

Critics made their notes and went home to write their reviews.

Reviews and Changes

The following day, one critic wrote that there might be a musical somewhere in the 1938 Marcel Pagnol–Jean Giono film, *The Baker's Wife*, but the creative team for the musical adaptation hadn't yet found it. The show needed a "delicate, bittersweet approach" that it wasn't getting, as well as more humor.

Merrick was so volatile. He loved firing and rehiring people. He loved power.

JOSEPH STEIN

Merrick knew the show had problems and began firing people in an effort to salvage it. Over the course of the tour, Patti LuPone replaced Carole Demas, John Berry replaced director Joseph Hardy, and associate musical director Robert ("Bob") Billig took over for music director Don Jenning. The choreographer changed twice—Dan Siretta was dropped and Rob Iscove filled in until Robert Tucker joined the company. Changes in choreographer meant changes in the "Bread" number. Ralston recalled later, "If I could tell you the hours we spent re-choreographing the 'Bread' number!"

These external changes could not reduce the discordance within the musical writing or between Merrick's ideas and the writers' vision. After Los Angeles, the tour limped through San Francisco, St. Louis, Boston, and on to Washington, D.C., but never succeeded. Schwartz says, "You can fix shows on the road if all you have to do is more tap dancing. If you've got a real story, it's very hard to fix it when you've gone off."

I tried to get myself fired. Now I'm glad I wasn't.

STEPHEN SCHWARTZ

The touring company was leaderless for about six weeks while Stein invited director friends to come see the show and consider helming it.

While they were in Los Angeles, he had encouraged the famous choreographer/director Jerome Robbins to come out and look at the show. "Jerry was not a man of many words," Stein reports about his friend and former collaborator. "He said, 'You haven't got an opening that's right.' I think he was very unhappy about the whole show, as we were by that time."

Schwartz recalls how a comment from Robbins inspired a new opening number. "Robbins suggested the larger-scaled chorus opening number be replaced by something folk-like. 'What about that girl who plays the café owner's wife? She's good. What about opening with her?" He was referring to Teri Ralston, an accomplished young actress who had already been featured in the Broadway productions of *Company* and *A Little Night Music*.

The story continued when *The Baker's Wife* moved to San Francisco. Ralston received an invitation from a professor friend to stay in one of the large, old Victorian homes in the hilly city. In the meantime, Schwartz had gone home for a reprieve from the madness. He decided to return with his wife and two-year-old son, and Ralston offered to share the house, which also had a piano in one of the downstairs rooms.

"We were all in this house together," Ralston recounts. "And Stephen said, 'Okay, I've written a song for you.' And I do remember so clearly him sitting down and playing 'Chanson' for me."

Schwartz had been able to draw from his fond memories of France to write this new opening that lures audiences into the imagery and mood of the place and time. From that point on, as the lights went up on subsequent productions of *The Baker's Wife*, audiences saw an outdoor café where a few guests are being served while the waitress/café-owner's wife, Denise, sings a verse of the opening number, "Chanson," in French and then continues in English. It is an enchanting solo folk-like piece with a slow waltz tempo. It's "Oh, What a Beautiful Morning," in a more folksy and petite French style that served as a better opening for a show set in rural France.

My part kept getting bigger because they decided to have the narrator telling more of the story than having the villagers. The cast was not real pleased with me.

TERI RALSTON

One Day Suddenly...

Although the introduction of "Chanson" into *The Baker's Wife* was a highlight, Schwartz remained discouraged and almost never attended the show during the seven-week run in San Francisco. "That's how distanced I was from the show. I was so disgusted with the whole thing." As an author of the show, he was contractually required to stay in town in case changes needed to be made, but he remained in the rented house much of the time. Meanwhile Carole, four months pregnant but there to lend support during this difficult time, ended up carrying Scott around, or pushing him in a stroller up and down the hills. Her extensive exertion may have influenced the ensuing events, and her husband's stress levels, too, could have impacted her. "It was a very stressful time for me and I'm sure that she internalized it," he comments. As badly as things were going with the show, the drama would pale in comparison with the family drama about to unfold in a life-changing situation that shifted Schwartz's focus from then on.

One day after Carole had returned home to Connecticut, she phoned with an urgent message for him to return home. Her water had broken in her fifth month of pregnancy and she didn't know what would happen with the baby. Schwartz called Merrick and received a completely sympathetic response. "There was not even a question," Schwartz remembers. "Absolutely, he said I should go home."

Carole was able to delay the birth through constant bed rest. Several weeks later, Stephen drove her to Yale University's medical center where the doctors delivered the tiny, premature baby Jessica, who weighed two pounds, eleven ounces. She would remain in Yale's special infant care unit incubator until she was four pounds. Stephen will always remember looking at his daughter in the fishtank-like incubator as she struggled to breathe. "You could see what a fighter she was. She was going to fight to live."

The life lesson seemed pretty clear. Several years earlier, as Schwartz fretted over production details for another show, the director had reminded him, "It's only a play." He'd lost that perspective during the arduous efforts for *The Baker's Wife*. But he could at last say with conviction, "This is not life or death here—it's only a show." This marked a turning point in his career. He never reentered the fray in quite the same way.

It Wasn't Getting Better

Eventually, Joe Stein invited his film director friend, John Berry, to help fix the show that was continuing on tour. Berry had been living in the South of France, so he had personal experience with regard to the setting.

Bob Billig recalls him reflecting about the show, saying something like, "This is not the South of France. The South of France is very light and transparent and bubbly. Everything you have here is very heavy." Indeed, the two huge turntables of the set were very heavy and cumbersome. Topol's performance dragged and the music was big and operatic. To orient *The Baker's Wife* toward the simplicity of the film, he suggested dropping the rich orchestrations, changing the script, and altering staging as well as character portrayals.

Teri Ralston felt sorry for the man she describes as being volatile. "He came in with great energy and ideas and then it just didn't get fixed, and that's got to be so hard for the director because it's all in your hands, and when it's not getting better you kind of lose confidence."

Berry didn't get along with Topol either. That situation was not improving. In rehearsals for the final leg of the tour, Topol was overheard saying something on the order of, "I'm only doing it for the money." Finally, Merrick got serious about replacing

There were a lot of chefs in the kitchen when we needed one. It's often said that in musical theatre you need a really talented dictator with a single vision.

Kurt Peterson

MARTHA SWOPE

Lovers Genevieve (Patti LuPone) and Dominique (Kurt Peterson) share a romantic though fleeting moment in *The Baker's Wife* pre-Broadway tour production.

We got Paul Sorvino, who was a great idea for the show, even though he was a little too young. He would have been wonderful if he had started at the beginning.

STEPHEN SCHWARTZ

him. The first four weeks of the engagement at the Kennedy Center Opera House in Washington, D.C., were part of their subscription series. The show was booked for six weeks and Merrick figured he could bring in Paul Sorvino as Topol's replacement for the final two weeks of the relatively long run.

Paul Sorvino's entrance temporarily heartened some members of the tour group, though they could not relate to his enthusiasm. Says Ralston, "Poor Paul comes in with all of this energy. 'Hi everybody, we're going to fix this show.' And at this point this is eight months (including rehearsals) of a very unhappy group on the road, and we're all saying, 'Grrrrrrrrrr. Don't try to cheer us up.'"

David Merrick's propensity toward power plays, combined with his genuine dislike of certain songs, impelled him to request changes throughout the tour. There was never a single performance of the show where all the songs that later appeared on the cast album were in the show at the same time. As Schwartz explains, "'Proud Lady' was cut very early in the Broadway tryout. It was something David Merrick felt strongly about. And it was gone before 'Chanson' came into the show so there was never a performance when 'Chanson' and 'Proud Lady' were in the show at the same time in the pre-Broadway trial."

Merrick especially despised "Meadowlark"and wanted it removed. Schwartz resisted. In Washington, D.C., the producer tried another tack. Reports differ on what actually happened. Bob Billig remembers a matinee when, after Patti Lupone sang the piece and the first act curtain went down, he got a call on his headset in the orchestra pit. It was the stage manager saying, "Mr. Merrick is here. He would like you to collect the orchestra parts for 'Meadowlark' and bring them up here right now."

Billig collected the music from the musicians and walked up to the stage manager's desk. "I handed the parts to the stage manager, he handed them to Mr. Merrick who put them in his briefcase, locked it, and walked out the door. I said, 'Oh, God. What the hell are we going to do? How are we going to make the dramatic high point of the act happen?' We had a show to do that night."

Billig called Schwartz. "You have to know what just happened," and explained the situation, upon which Schwartz said he would pull the score and close the show if it wasn't restored, again invoking the Dramatists Guild contract he had used to save "Kind of Woman" in *Pippin*.

Publicity director Josh Ellis remembers being in the stage manager's office backstage when someone stormed in regarding the pilfered music. He believed it was Schwartz (although Schwartz claims not to have been in Washington, D.C. at the time). Merrick told whoever was there fussing over the removed music, "…don't worry, we're in Washington, D.C., home of the FBI. They will find our little Meadowlark. It's clear it wasn't stolen. The Meadowlark just flew away." By the next performance, the music was back in Billig's hands and the song remained in the show.

On November 13th, audiences at the Kennedy Center Opera House in Washington, D.C. watched the last performance of the tour. Although *The Baker's Wife* was scheduled for a November 21st opening in Broadway's Martin Beck Theatre, Schwartz and Stein had been so dissatisfied with the seemingly unfixable show that they requested it be shut down before reaching Broadway. Merrick resisted because of his promises to Motown Record investors. Shirley Bernstein intervened on Schwartz's and Stein's behalf. According to a Merrick biographer, Bernstein flew to Detroit to meet with a Motown executive she knew, and persuaded him that Broadway critics would undo any benefit that might be achieved by opening in New York. Merrick and Motown

Kurt Peterson in chauffeur costume sings "Proud Lady," a song that Merrick cut from the show early in the pre-Broadway tour.

Just about everything that could go wrong with a show went wrong.

Stephen Schwartz

MARTHA SWOPE

Paul Sorvino (in the bread dough mixing trough, center) plays Aimable, the baker, at the Kennedy Center in Washington, D.C. In this scene villagers try to console Aimable, who is despondent after his wife has left him.

relented and canned the show. The half-year tour lost $1 million.

Aftermath

"There was no unanimity," Schwartz concludes about the failed development process. "There was no meeting of the minds as to what the show should be, what kind of show we were doing. Joe Hardy had a whole different picture of what it should be from David Merrick, who had a different picture, it turned out, from Joe and myself. There was just no unity of vision."

The story does have a happy ending, because Stein and Schwartz were eventually able to "catch the personality, the mix of comedy and emotional truth" that had eluded them, only it took many revisions and revivals to do it.

Cast Albums and Revivals

Schwartz was pleased when he received a phone call from Bruce Yeko expressing interest in recording *The Baker's Wife*. Yeko had always been a Broadway aficionado. When he heard that a new Stephen Schwartz musical, *The Baker's Wife*, was playing out of town, he drove from his Georgetown, Connecticut, home to Boston to attend. At the time, he and his wife, Doris Chu, had developed a record label they called "Take Home Tunes." They created partial albums for musicals during their pre-cast album days to be sold in theatres so audiences could take home the tunes.

They loved the score for *The Baker's Wife* and called Schwartz, who suggested they produce a full cast album. Yeko balked, but the two of them negotiated possibilities and, in early 1977, drove into New York City for a series of recording sessions in a tiny apartment studio in the Greenwich Village. Schwartz put together what he thought were the best songs. There wasn't room in the studio for the full cast. Schwartz said, "I'll save you money. All we need are the principals." The actors came in one by one to record their tracks, which Schwartz later helped mix.

The album caught on with Broadway aficionados. Schwartz received frequent requests for the sheet music. About a decade later, British director Trevor Nunn staged a revival. Schwartz came to believe: "The show got solved by Trevor Nunn. Trevor's production almost worked and got some quite good reviews, but more important, it pointed the way to finally fix the show."

A cast album of the complete score was produced, which kept interest in the show alive. However, it would take Stein and Schwartz several more rewrites and revivals before they found the exact mix of ingredients that allowed *The Baker's Wife* to rise to its fullest artistic heights.

Stephen is just the best in a studio! He's just amazing! He knows how to get the best performance out of you. Studio recording is a whole technique and he's great at it.

TERI RALSTON

Joseph Stein and Stephen Schwartz in 2006 after they finished revising *The Baker's Wife*.

TERENCE DE GIERE

CREATIVITY NOTES

Tonal Disparity and Finding the Right Mix

Schwartz is quick to defend his collaborator when anyone suggests that Stein's book was the weak element. "I think that's unfair and inaccurate. What I think is accurate is that there was a tonal disparity between the book and the score.

A different kind of writer doing the book with my score might have had more tonal consistency, but similarly, if Bock and Harnick had done the score it would have had a tonal consistency with Joe. We're different generationally; we're different in terms of sensibilities even though we like each other and get along well."

Twenty-nine years and many revisions later, Schwartz and Stein would finally find a unified tone for their work on *The Baker's Wife*. Schwartz comments, "I think it's important that for a musical to be successful, all the elements have to seem as if they belong in the same show. You can't have a book that's in one style and songs that are in another style, or even within songs, you can't have lyrics that have one kind of tone, with music that feels completely different. And I think that one of the things that happened to make *The Baker's Wife* become successful is that both Joe and I moved toward one another tonally so that now there seems to be more integrity of tone within the show."

See "Extras: Updates and New Projects," page 479 for the continuation of *The Baker's Wife* story.

OPPOSITE: Genevieve (Patti LuPone), her husband the baker (Topol), and the villagers of Concord celebrate the joys of fresh bread in the song "Bread."

MARTHA SWOPE

"Bread"

Fresh, warm bread
What is there like fresh, warm bread?
With a bit of butter spread…
Sheer ambrosia!
What is as luscious
As a brioche is?
When you're fed
Every day on fresh, warm bread
It's frightening how quick
You get addicted
Fresh, warm
Bread!

… Fresh, warm bread
You can keep your leg of lamb.
Who would ever hog a ham?
Not when there is
Something we want, like
Something croissant-like
Fresh warm bread

Maybe with a drop of jam…
There's no other food
Brightens your mood
Like fresh, warm…

Fresh, warm bread
Never take my fresh, warm bread.

Men
　　You can take my wife instead

Women
　　Take my husband!

All
　　I'll kiss the hand which
　　Hands me a sandwich
　　As we said
　　Til we're finally cold and dead
　　Dear Aimable Castagnet,
　　Our beloved boulanger,
　　Won't you give to us each day
　　Our daily bread!

"Chanson"

Chaque jour est un jour
Comme les autres doux jours
Le potage, l'ouvrage
Peut-etre l'amour
Le soleil, il voyage
Le monde fait un tour
Ainsi c'est toujours le meme...

Every day as you do
What you do every day
You see the same faces
Who fill the cafe
And if some of those faces
Have new things to say
Nothing is really different...

And the sheep dot the hill
Where the olive tree sways
And the world spins around
With the greens and the grays
And you never take time out
To think of the ways
Everything might be different...

And then one day, suddenly,
Something can happen,
It may be quite simple,
It may be quite small
But all of a sudden your stew tastes different
And you hear a gull cry in a different key,
And you see with new eyes,
And the faces you see
Are people you don't know at all...

And the someone who touches
Your hair every day,
Touches you now
In a different way,
And you may want to run
Or you may want to stay
Forever
And since life is the cry of the gull
And the taste of your stew
And the way that you feel
When he touches you
Now your whole life is different
Now your whole life is new...

LYRICS BY STEPHEN SCHWARTZ. USED WITH PERMISSION

Runaway lovers Dominique (Kurt Peterson) and Genevieve (Carole Demas) consider their future.

Demas remembers comments from the director or writers when she was cast as the wandering wife of the baker: "They said they wanted to cast someone who could be forgiven and they felt that was my essence."

Her impression from the show's description was that the baker would be a lovable older man and that the two young people, Genevieve and Dominique, would break his heart. The audience would feel the pull of relationship conflict because they would care about the charming baker and his wife, but also want the young lovers to be happy together, and therefore feel just as torn over the situation as Genevieve does when she sings "Meadowlark."

When Topol joined the cast mix, Demas was surprised by his qualities. "Topol was an extremely charismatic, virile man. I thought I must not have understood about the baker, because he's not just a kindly old man. He seems ever so much younger and far more lusty."

When Demas was injured in Los Angeles, Merrick tried to claim she was unfit to perform in order not to fulfill her contract. Actors' Equity Association provided Demas with a lawyer. She was out of the show but did get paid.

Years later, as Schwartz assessed the switch in cast, he said, "Carole Demas was unfairly scapegoated. There were major problems with the show and the major problem with the cast was Topol. And what Merrick chose to do was to fire everybody around Topol but not actually deal with the problem."

Legendary Chicagoan Studs Terkel, author of the nonfiction interview book *Working,* visits the set for the musical at the Goodman Theatre in Chicago, Illinois.

CHAPTER 10

WORKING: HELP WANTED

Hey somebody, won' cha turn your head
Take a look my way?

WORKING

In 1977, the disparity between Stephen Schwartz's own dreams and reality became essential fodder for his fifth major musical. Like many of the characters portrayed in his next musical, he'd survived disappointments, rejection, and failure. Even so, he preserved enough ambition and imagination to punch his own time clock for his latest venture—Broadway's *Working*—a show that would eventually employ a cast of seventeen plus dozens of behind-the-scenes personnel and orchestra musicians, at least temporarily.

Unlike most of the workers of his musical, the twenty-nine-year-old prospered materially at an enviable level. His piece of the American Dream included a beautiful country estate in Connecticut, complete with private tennis court and pool, plenty of travel money, a supportive wife, lively three-year-old son with whom he could be playful, and growing infant daughter. With the help of his wife's cooking, he gained ten pounds over his college weight, reaching around 145—still trim for a 5'8" man. From his earlier hippie phase of wearing floral or patterned shirts, he passed into Mr. Tennis with sporty casuals that dominated his wardrobe from then on. He grew a beard, scraggly and dark.

He might never have become so passionate about his next show if he hadn't suddenly awakened from his naiveté about the working world. This son of an entrepreneur had rarely been employed outside the entertainment industry or examined what "regular" jobs might be like. As a boy growing up on Long Island,

You'll never feel the same about your job again!

BROADWAY ADVERTISEMENT FOR WORKING

Schwartz flung newspapers from a bicycle while on his route (although not into the bushes as he suggests in his "Neat To Be a Newsboy" song that he'd soon write for *Working*). As a teenager, he guided kids in his role as camp counselor. Using his piano-playing skills, he accompanied silent films in college, and later picked up a few jobs accompanying singers at auditions and concerts. But that was about it. The rest of the time Schwartz earned his living off-Broadway, on Broadway, or in his relatively cushy position at RCA. He hadn't cultivated any particular empathy for people who were not involved with theatre or music.

Then, one day in 1974, as he sifted through his mail at home in Connecticut, he opened a Book-of-the-Month Club flier and spotted a sales pitch for Studs Terkel's latest interview collection, *Working: People Talk About What They Do All Day and How They Feel About What They Do*. He read an excerpt from an interview with a phone operator named Heather. The interview finished with a quote: "It's something to run into somebody who says, 'It's a nice day out, Operator. How's your day, busy? Has it been a rough day?' You're so thankful for these people...'"

In that moment, Schwartz suddenly became aware of Heather as an individual with her own dreams and goals, and he envisioned the inherent theatricality of making otherwise anonymous workers into dramatic characters. As he later confessed, "I was someone who tended to be abusive to operators. They were just some disembodied voice. I would be like the guy we put in the show who curses the phone company, and I would complain about it being a monopoly. Suddenly, I realized that there was a person sitting in some location that I'd never pictured in my mind, and he or she had a whole life and a series of dreams and disappointments and expectations and wearinesses that I had never thought about, and that I was connected to this person through this transaction. I had never given it an instant's thought.

Some people might find that obvious and not particularly compelling. To me it was enormously compelling, and I wanted to write about it."

Reading about Heather offered the kind of "Aha!" experience that he uses as a signal. "Something starts to reverberate," he explains about the way he decides what projects to commit to. "The first thing is just an instinct that says, 'That's mine. That's my territory.'"

He bought Terkel's book, and about halfway through reading it, decided he wanted to adapt it to the stage. He telephoned his agent about obtaining the stage rights, and called his friend Nina Faso to say, "I want you to read this book and we can talk about it." He described the collection of interviews and his excitement over this idea for a new musical.

To persuade Studs Terkel to release the stage rights, Schwartz flew to Chicago to meet with him. Terkel says he was astonished by the adaptation idea, but Schwartz's enthusiasm assuaged his doubts. "I was attracted to his vision. Something told me he had something; it was more than just a musical. It was a celebration of the 'ordinary' people, whose daily lives are unsung. He would sing about them, the anonymous many, whose lives touch ours every day without our realizing it. 'Go ahead,' I said. And he did."

The inspiration for *Working* had illuminated a path rarely traveled by musical writers. Of the hundreds of musicals and plays Schwartz had attended, he'd only seen one musical that was completely nonfiction. *The Me Nobody Knows* included ghetto children's commentaries and ran for about a year on Broadway, 1970 – 1971.

He also loved what Michael Bennett, Marvin Hamlisch, and their colleagues had created for their Broadway hit musical *A Chorus Line*, which had opened in the summer of 1975. All the

Studs' talent that is God-given and one-of-a-kind is that he is a key to your door. There's something about his eyes, his voice, and the safety you feel in his presence that opens those doors. He will ask a big question in a gentle way that will simply get one talking.

CRAIG CARNELIA

dancer characters in *A Chorus Line* had been suggested by real lives, including Schwartz's soon-to-be close friends, Steven Boockvor, who would join the *Working* cast, and his wife Denise Pence Boockvor.

"We took a dance class at midnight," remembers Denise about the night Michael Bennett collected the authentic audition-woes material for *A Chorus Line*. "Then Michael had the tape recorder and sandwiches and he started saying a little about himself, and that led all of us to talk about ourselves." From those tapes and their imaginations, the writers pieced together a musical that included a song called "Sing!" based on Denise's singing problems and her communication style. "I was really young, and Michael's reputation and creativity totally intimidated me. I would constantly lose my train of thought, and my husband Steve would help me figure out what I was trying to say to Michael. That's what they put in that song 'Sing!' What's really wonderful about *A Chorus Line* is that it isn't fictionalized." Boockvor clarifies, "You can say that the truth was extended into a theatrical musical."

One thing that immediately appealed to me about Working *was the fact that this was* true, *that you were going to be hearing from people in their own words.*

STEPHEN SCHWARTZ

Extending literal truth into emotional truth on stage—that's what Schwartz believed he could now do. The everyman's *A Chorus Line* would later become a publicity angle for *Working*. Even so, this type of musical based on interviews was exceedingly unusual for Broadway fare. As producer Irwin Meyer discovered the following year, "This show was so unique to Broadway and so special in its concept and in its design and production, that when you went to see it, you loved it, but trying to get you into the theatre, we just couldn't seem to build word of mouth."

Schwartz's belief in the concept was so strong that he didn't dwell on the likelihood of resistance. "The idea immediately spoke to me as something theatrical," he affirms, "and thematically something I was interested in." That's what mattered.

Irwin Meyer

During the three years that elapsed between inspiration and readiness, Schwartz waited for rights arrangements for *Working* to come through, and endured touring traumas for *The Baker's Wife*.

Finally, he could begin serious work on his next show. He yearned for *Working* to redeem what he thought was the anomalous failure of *The Baker's Wife* and gain him approval from the New York critics and intelligentsia. He decided to keep as much control as he could, having been burned by his experiences with the directors of *Pippin* and *The Baker's Wife*. For this new work, he'd direct the production, develop the book, and take responsibility for the score. If he had known that book problems would linger right up through opening night, he might have relinquished the countless directorial decisions to someone else.

Although he wanted control, he also wanted to develop the show in a workshop, with the cast helping to build it as a group rather than imposing a pre-written script. That meant he and Nina Faso (who was sharing in the adaptation effort) needed to do their homework and bring in some chosen monologues from Terkel's text as a starting point. The two buddies spent hours in Nina's Upper East Side condo paging through the published interviews.

Terkel had filled his book *Working* with over 130 transcribed interviews from a full range of professions, many with a raw, almost poetic power. A fireman tells why his work was truly real to him: "I worked in a bank. You know, it's just paper. It's not real. Nine to five and it's shit. You're looking at numbers. But I can look back and say, 'I helped put out a fire. I helped save somebody.' It shows something I did on this earth." That was one of the paragraphs that could be lifted directly to a stage monologue.

"I read every single one of those interviews a million times," Nina recounts. Naturally, they wanted the play to represent Terkel's range of occupations: migrant worker, supermarket checker, corporate executive, salesman, interstate trucker, teacher, and so on. They considered including as many as fifty examples in a two- to three-hour show.

Schwartz approached his newfound mission with zeal. "I don't really care what makes it theatre," he said when someone questioned the theatricality of a nonfiction adaptation. He felt very much at home with the honesty of the material. He often explains in interviews, "I'm not a big fan of people in glitzy costumes tap dancing." Here he could work out ways for a waitress to sing and dance with her plate of food, or for a fireman to express how he felt about saving someone's life. "I find it really moving."

He called friends and colleagues to set up an informal workshop. "I'm going to rent a space in New York two or three days a week and I'll provide lunch there and pay your carfare. Would you come and play?"

We thought we were doing something pretty wonderful to make it dramatic. But we had to teach the actors how to do this technique. It wasn't 'Isn't this a noble person?' We didn't gussy it up at all. Later we cleaned up a little bit of language because the producers wanted us to.

NINA FASO

As many as seventeen actors met in a rented rehearsal space. *Godspell*'s Robin Lamont, Gilmer McCormick, and Jeffrey Mylett joined the group. Faso recruited her brother Laurie and friend Bobo Lewis. Among others, Matt Landers and Steven Boockvor came in as friends. Lynne Thigpen contributed to the workshop by day and left early enough to dress for her evening performance as a nightclub singer in *The Magic Show*.

At the first gathering, Schwartz and Faso handed out monologues they had selected, as a place to start. Each actor received a copy of Terkel's *Working* as well, with the suggestion that they check for passages that sparked their interest. In a free-form, experimental way, the workshop group honed potentially stage-worthy material and watched each other improvise physical movements for particular jobs so that a vision of staging could emerge. "Every idea anyone came up with had to be tried, no matter how dumb or impractical it sounded to the rest of us," Schwartz says.

During one brainstorming session, Nina Faso came up with the idea of various telephone workers speaking contrapuntally and simultaneously. "It was one of those ideas that seemed impractical," says Schwartz. "How could the audience comprehend what was being said by two or three people speaking at once? But it worked surprisingly well when we tried it."

To add another layer of reality-based inspiration, Schwartz organized outings for the actors related to the character they were all focusing on for a day (a practice he now recommends for groups that license the musical). When discussing the Fireman, they visited a fire station. Later they went to a city parking lot to watch and speak with the staff who park cars. Some went to the phone company. When the whole group dined together in a restaurant, they would be especially attentive to the waitresses who were serving them. "We got embedded into the real behavioral understanding of each one of those characters," Boockvor recalls. "Stephen Schwartz is very organic that way."

Stephen Schwartz (left) meets with a fireman to test his range of motion wearing gear so that his staging of a fire station scene for *Working* would attain the "verisimilitude" he was seeking.

He and Nina were also aiming for a kind of consciousness-raising influence. "One of the reasons we picked many of the specific jobs that we did," Schwartz explains, "was that I wanted the next experience you had with a working person after leaving the theatre to be transformed by your experience of seeing the show. So consequently, there's a waitress and there's a parking lot attendant; when you go to get your car or you go to a restaurant after the show, you think about them and you're suddenly aware of this interconnectedness."

Still, it was hard for the group to completely trust in something so unusual. Matt Landers, who played the Fireman, remembers facing the odd structure of a long theatrical piece full of monologues. "One of the huge problems with the show is that nobody talks to each other. In the workshop we went crazy trying to figure out, 'Let's try to get a scene here,' and we couldn't do it."

For cohesion, the songs themselves would have to create unifying nodes along the network of workers' experiences and dreams expressed in the monologues.

Who would write the songs? At first Schwartz thought it was his show, but he was open to new possibilities.

Songwriter Quest

"I read *Working* and it changed my way of looking at the world," Schwartz told Micki Grant, as he sat near the piano in her wood-paneled apartment studio on Manhattan's Upper West Side. She had soundproofed her dining room to create the studio several years earlier when her Broadway show, *Don't Bother Me, I Can't Cope,* was about to open. Her score was one that Schwartz enjoyed, and now he could check his hunch that Grant would be right to help with some songs for *Working*.

He was so gung-ho and so enthusiastic about it, your doubts were just erased.

MICKI GRANT

Schwartz had brought a copy of Terkel's book for the prospective collaborator to review, pointing out the interview with parking lot attendant Alfred Pommier. Schwartz had already attempted a bluesy musical number for the character. He slid onto the piano bench to demonstrate a couple of musical ideas. When he'd worked on a Pommier song at home, he kept referencing Grant's style of writing. "I said to myself, 'This is silly. Why am I sitting here trying to do a Micki Grant song? Why don't I just call Micki Grant?'"

They laughed. Grant said she didn't realize she had a distinct sound, but was open to the venture. Next, she began strumming her guitar. Their conversation about themes from Terkel's book had stirred her memory about another song. She started singing "If I Could've Been," a piece about abandoned dreams that she had started for another project but never used.

Schwartz grinned. "I *knew* I made the right decision," he said about including Grant in his project. "That's a number I've been looking for!"

It was a bonus night for Schwartz. As he left Grant's studio, he carried with him the security that a blues solo and an ensemble number were almost in hand, and that the whole concept of sharing songwriting duties was going to work.

More enthused about contacting others, Schwartz mailed out letters to songwriters, including Joni Mitchell and Paul Simon, who replied that they were unavailable. He collected commitments from James Taylor and Richard Rodgers' daughter, composer Mary Rodgers. Lyricist Susan Birkenhead joined the team when "Mary Rodgers plucked me out of obscurity" to collaborate. (Schwartz regrets not reaching Billy Joel and says, "The saddest thing was that, after the show was practically finished, Billy Joel contacted me and said he was interested. He would have been brilliant at this material, but it was too late.")

Buzz about Schwartz's quest spread among Broadway followers, including writer (and future musical film producer) Craig Zadan. One night Zadan invited Schwartz to attend a cabaret act his college friend, Craig Carnelia, was performing in Soho. Schwartz was impressed enough to stop by the dressing room in the basement afterward to discuss *Working* with this relatively unknown writer. "He asked me that night to take a look at the book," Carnelia remembers. "About a week later we met and I told him what interested me and then he told me what he would

I give Stephen a lot of credit for choosing composers he admired, and whom he thought would do a better job than he would (on some songs). I think it's 'so Stephen' – it's why he accepted Peggy Gordon's "By My Side" in Godspell *instead of rewriting it.*

NINA FASO

Since the show Working *is essentially a documentary, and all the monologues are edited directly from the words of the interviewees in Studs Terkel's book, the songwriters tried to use as much of the words and locution of the characters they were writing about as possible.*

STEPHEN SCHWARTZ

James Taylor came in to oversee some of the orchestration, and I remember him turning to the band [that was playing "Brother Trucker"] and he said, 'Guys, guys, do you think we could kind of funk it up here?' Everyone cracked up. He wanted to get a little more raw edge."

ROBIN LAMONT

like me to look at." Carnelia's sensitive songwriting talents would prove invaluable.

In an unusual strategy for a musical's development, Schwartz divvied up interviews to be adapted, met individually with songwriters, and collected tapes of completed songs. He didn't want the artists to feel supervised from on high, so the group never sat together to discuss the show. (They only met for a photo shoot.) This independent approach added to the show's montage feeling.

Schwartz appreciated the privilege of working with James Taylor. He'd listened to *Sweet Baby James* and other albums countless times and had absorbed some of Taylor's folk aesthetic into his own songwriting style. One day he sat in Taylor's Manhattan apartment listening to him play "Millwork" while reading lyrics scrawled on a couple of yellow legal pads. Schwartz says, "I remember sitting there trying to remain 'directorial' and businesslike as I listened to the voice that always seems to have the power to bring tears to my eyes, and thinking, 'Oh, my God, he sounds just like James Taylor!'"

Robin Lamont, who was to sing "Millwork," felt similarly thrilled the moment Taylor came to a rehearsal. Stephen Reinhardt had been playing the song on piano as Lamont practiced. "James showed up with this guitar and mismatched socks and watched for a little while. We spoke. And when it came time to do it, he said, 'Why don't I play it on the guitar, you sing it, and I'll do backups.' So he did. We worked out a key and he did background vocals. It was one of the more exciting moments of my career. He is a lovely man: very nice, very down to earth, and very supportive. It was really an honor and treat to work with him."

Of course, one songwriter Stephen Schwartz had to recruit was himself, and he succeeded in writing four songs for the show.

CREATIVITY NOTES

Creating Character Through Realistic Detail

After seeing Craig Carnelia perform in a cabaret one night, Schwartz asked him to try writing a song based on Terkel's interview with a retired man. "Joe" was one of the first pieces written for the new musical. As a keen study in character-appropriate material, it evoked creative discoveries for both Carnelia and Schwartz.

"My favorite thing about *Working* in my life as a writer," Carnelia explains, "is that it taught me a great deal about how to write. One of the things it taught me is that people reveal their biggest truths in small ways. People are speaking about what they had for breakfast; 'And then I went to see my wife's grave, and I had some peanut brittle.' The whole book is full of the biggest and the littlest juxtaposed in the most innocent way and in the way that people actually do, as opposed to a kind of musical theatre that lives in overstatement or that lives in declaration, and says, 'I went to my wife's grave and I thought of all the beautiful things we did together, and I sat down and I wept, and I saw her come to life again.' No. That's not what happens. What happens is, 'I went to my wife's grave and I brought along some peanut brittle and then I saw a bird over there and the bird made me think of something.'"

Stephen Schwartz tuned into Craig's realism in his musical phrasing—the repetitive piano accompaniment and melody skillfully depicting the routine of retired life. "All of Craig's songs for *Working*, but most particularly 'Joe,' taught me something about writing for characters, and thus about writing for musical theatre," Schwartz reveals. "What Craig did, more vividly than other musical theatre composers I had heard, was to capture the essence of the character, not just in the lyric but in the music as well. The music was not just a tune with an appropriate mood, but a tonal portrait of the character's soul and circumstances. Even if you don't speak English, you can hear 'Joe' and the music will tell you about the character. Since working with Craig on *Working*, I've tried to emulate that aspect of his writing in my own."

In an interview, Lynne Thigpen recalled a day in the New York rehearsal hall when the songwriters first presented their pieces. By then, sheet music had been written up for the singers, who would sightread their new numbers. "I was delighted," Thigpen said about the first act closing number, "If I Could've Been." She and David Patrick Kelly were to sing it in duet, although it later turned into an anthem about the show that she sang with the company.

In rehearsals, after the script came together, choreographer Graciela Daniele helped actors spin dances from working-world movements. She understood the show's concept and had no problem creating a dance number out of supermarket checkers' movements or expressing the daydreams of a mill worker.

Out of my whole theatrical career, the staging concept for "Millwork" remains one of the things of which I'm most proud.

STEPHEN SCHWARTZ
IN 2008

Schwartz worked with her on potential staging, especially for the "Millwork" number. He drove to a working mill to observe the repetitive movements employees would make. The scene that became one of the more visually and emotionally arresting moments of the show included three mill workers upstage, moving to the beats that Schwartz researched so they could authentically mimic work at the mill. Terry Treas danced a ballet choreographed by Daniele that represented the workers' daydreams, and Robin Lamont sat downstage facing the audience, pouring her folk-singer voice into James Taylor's lament for routine work.

Of all the waitresses in Chicago, Terkel discovered Dolores Dante, who had worked at the same restaurant for twenty-three years. "To be a waitress, it's an art," Dante told Terkel. To Stephen Schwartz, her words leapt off the page as being suited to song. At his piano, he worked on music and lyrics for a piece based on her interview. He'd call it, "It's an Art."

"I feel like a ballerina," Dante continued. "I have to go between those tables, between those chairs…. If I drop a fork, there is a certain way I pick it up. I know they can see how delicately I pick it up. I'm on stage."

Schwartz was also struck by her comment that she speaks "*sotto voce*" — an Italian expression used in opera for soft voice. That triggered a musical notion. Schwartz says, "Having learned from Craig Carnelia the idea of having the characters' music strongly evoke them, I decided to make Dolores' song very Italian and so theatrical it's practically operatic. So for the music, I used Verdi — specifically, 'Sempre libera' from *La Traviata* — as a jumping-off point."

In the opera, the perky aria is character Violetta's ode to the joyous life of champagne, fun, and many male admirers. In *Working*, the waltz-time music underscores the waitress's observation that what she does is elegant and theatrical. She even hums a bit of *Swan Lake* that becomes part of the music. Tempo changes indicate shifts of mood as the waitress describes her day.

From Dante's text: "Some don't care. When the plate is down you can hear the sound. I try not to have that sound. I want my hands to be right when I serve. I pick up a glass, I want it to be just right. I get to be almost Oriental in the serving. I like it to look nice all the way."

From Schwartz's lyric:

> There's some as don't care
> When they put down the plate, there's a sound
> Not with me
> When they move a chair
> It will scrape with a grate on the ground
> Not with me
> I will have my hand right when I place a glass
> Notice how I stand right as customers pass

Serve a demi-tasse
With a gesture so gentle
Or do it again till
It's near Oriental…
It's an art, it's an art
To be a fine waitress….

In addition to writing "It's an Art," Schwartz claimed the opening number slot and composed "All the Live Long Day." *Working*'s score also featured his "Neat to Be a Newsboy" and "Fathers and Sons."

"'Fathers and Sons' is an extremely personal song," Schwartz says. "I almost didn't put it in the show because of its autobiographical nature, but then everybody liked the song a lot. Nina and Stephen Reinhardt said, 'I'll kill you if you don't put the song in the show.' It took a while actually to find out how to make it work in the show. Everybody used to cry. We'd sit there in rehearsal and everybody would cry trying to play it and perform it."

Working – Workshop Production in Chicago

The best way to get a grip on the work in progress was to test it on stage in front of an audience somewhere away from New York City. America's largest Midwest city, Chicago, where Terkel conducted most of his interviews, seemed the ideal spot for an initial staged workshop. Schwartz's agent Shirley Bernstein arranged with producers Irwin Meyer and Stephen R. Friedman to back the development and final production phases. Their musical *Annie* opened in April as a smash hit. Emboldened, they agreed to co-produce *Working* in association with Joseph Harris. A Chicago Loop venue, the not-for-profit Goodman Theatre, worked it into its calendar for December 30, 1977 (previews) through February 5, 1978. *Working* would breeze into the "Windy City" with an official opening on the fifth of January, in a small theatre at one edge of Grant Park that overlooks Lake Michigan.

Meyer later asserted that, although the Goodman Theatre's official rules did not allow for productions to be pre-Broadway trials, he intended to move the show to Broadway quickly. Schwartz and Faso requested an additional pre-Broadway production, and made arrangements with Zelda Fichandler, artistic director at Arena Stage in Washington, D.C., whom they knew from the time *Godspell* played in that city. An avid fan of Terkel's text, Fichandler scheduled *Working* into Arena Stage's spring season.

Studs Terkel and Stephen Schwartz confer about the musical.

The Clothesline

The biggest challenge Schwartz faced in mid 1977 was compensating for the ways *Working* varied from a traditional book musical. *A Chorus Line*'s emotional drive came from dancers all striving to make it into a show from an audition. *Working* had no natural storyline and at that point he believed a montage was not sufficient. He decided to create a storyline based on an interview toward the end of the *Working* book with Fred Ringley, a printing salesman, who lived in suburban Chicago with his wife and son. They decided to quit the Chicago rat race, sell their home, move to Arkansas, and start a mom-and-pop restaurant while developing some farmland. During *Working*'s development, Schwartz flew to Blaine, Arkansas, and spent a couple of days with them.

For a long time he clung to the Ringley story as an essential answer to the show's need for a dramatic emotional arc. "Stephen especially liked them," Faso recalls. "He kept calling their story the clothesline that we hang all the other characters on."

The audience would meet Fred and Kate Ringley soon after the opening number. James Taylor wrote a song called "American Dreaming" that described their aspirations. Mary Rodgers wrote a song for Kate about her work as a housewife, a piece that was later replaced by Carnelia's "Just a Housewife." Schwartz wrote "Neat to Be a Newsboy" for the son, John, to sing about his paper route. As the last solo in Act II, Schwartz created his pensive "Fathers and Sons" for the Fred Ringley character.

The idea could be tested in the upcoming tryout. As rehearsals for the Goodman production were due to begin, Schwartz sent out the script to his cast along with some notes about practicing their multiple roles. He asked the actors to select someone specific to talk to at all times. "The monologues must be personalized. Are you telling your story to a stranger? A group of strangers? A friend? A family member? A boss? A psychiatrist? What is your relationship to the person(s) you're talking to? How comfortable are you speaking to them?"

It was the worst winter I've ever experienced. I would just cry incessantly. Chicago is so windy and I was a lightweight in those days so I kept getting blown all over the place. Stephen would just laugh because I'd get blown down the street into a fence or something.

NINA FASO

As he continued his written notes to the cast, he asked them to be honing their characters. "In the preface to the book, Studs talks about the telling gesture that illuminates character. See if you can find one or two for each of your people, a gesture or physical habit that grows out of their work or environment. Think about how they stand, how they sit, how they move, where their center of balance seems to be. Do they speak rapidly or haltingly? Are they shy or aggressive in speaking? How has their work affected them physically? I expect you to begin rehearsal with very definite choices made. If you want to discuss a choice or have me see something before Chicago, please call me."

In November, with three-and-a-half-year-old Scott Schwartz in tow, Stephen traveled to Chicago for a few days of preproduction madness, meeting with the costume designer and auditioning local boys for a role. He knew previews were coming up too quickly. Schwartz called Terkel and asked him to go over the script. "I'm just sitting here being nervous and thinking I'm not ready," he told Terkel.

When Schwartz paused to sit with a visiting reporter, he spoke about his recent experiences with *The Baker's Wife*. Developing Broadway shows, he suggested, tends not to be about what's on stage but about money and power plays. That's not why he went into the theater in the first place. "Taking pride in yourself and what you do now seems to be the only worthwhile goal in terms of work itself." Realizing his comments pertained to *Working*, he added, "I suppose that's what the show is about."

Schwartz and company arrived for rehearsals in December to face what he described as "a ton of technical details." In addition, they needed to adjust the script and songs. Micki Grant recalls, "When we were in Chicago, I said to Stephen Schwartz, 'You know you have a whole class of workers that's not mentioned in your show anywhere and that's the domestic worker and I would like to do something with that.' He said, 'Go right ahead.' And that's when I came up with 'Cleaning Women.'"

Micki Grant comments about her song "Cleaning Women": "My compulsion to write the song stemmed from Stud's interview with Maggie Holmes. Everything I talk about, lyrically, in that song is directly influenced by Maggie's description of her and her antecedents' lives as domestics, and her hopes for her children. After reading it, I couldn't get her out of my mind. I think Stephen was happy that I made the choice to deal with it on my own, without his having suggested it. I was utterly floored by Lynne Thigpen's rendition. It was awesome."

It was a good song that added energy. That left the problem of fitting everything in. Even after previews, they had a running time of three hours and ten minutes—too long for comfort.

Schwartz and Faso, determined to make the show work, met before breakfast every morning for an extra hour or two. Faso remembers "…wracking our brains to make things work, making plotting decisions."

For newcomer Susan Birkenhead, the trials and traumas were more acute. She and Mary Rodgers had worked hard on a song for the Ringley family. Then there was a difference of opinion between Schwartz and Rodgers. "Mary said, 'We're going to pull this song,' and I remember sitting in the hotel and moaning, 'Don't pull the song, Mary!'"

Schwartz's inner game was perfectionism—something he found hard to release even in those stressful times. When the fussing over changes got out of hand, it could drive cast members a little crazy. "For the most part, we all respected Stephen a great deal," says Robin Lamont. "And if we worked hard, he worked three times as hard. We would leave at midnight, come in the next day at nine in the morning to rehearse after having done a show the night before. And he would have been up half the night. He was always, always, always working.

"We had terrible fights. I remember feelings running very high. There was frustration. We'd ask ourselves, 'Why isn't this playing as well as it should?' We'd come in and Stephen would say, 'I want to try this; I want to try that.' I think sometimes there was the feeling that, 'We're sick of this, we don't want to try it one more way. We want to go home and sleep.'"

During previews, rewrites continued in the rehearsal space located near the Art Institute's Impressionist collection. One day, Schwartz took a break to tour the museum. He admired George Seurat's *Afternoon on the Island of La Grande Jatte*, which would later

Choreographer Graciela Daniele leads dancers in rehearsal.

NINA FASO

become associated with another musical (Sondheim's *Sunday in the Park with George*). From a distance, the painting made a lovely scene with picnickers and boaters. Viewing the giant canvas up close, Stephen saw what seemed like meaningless dots of color.

In his own creative venture, he sometimes lost his vision in the dots and wasn't able to step back to view the scene he wanted. Perhaps feedback from others would help him.

Chicago Reviews and Rewrites

Opening night arrived as a bright spot on the development timeline. Terkel's interviewees, whose stories made up the show, were invited to watch and come backstage afterward for a party. "The waitress was thrilled," Schwartz recalls. Craig Carnelia remembers meeting the daughter of "Joe," whom he had immortalized in a song by the same name. "She came backstage and put her arms around me and said, 'Thank you for making my father a hero.'"

Lynne Thigpen, herself a substantially built African-American actress and dancer who had performed the role of the telephone operator, met her petite Caucasian counterpart that night. "She came up and said, 'You answered the phone just like I did,' and there she was, ten years older than I was, thirty pounds thinner, a small white woman. It was great! For them it was life validation. How could they not have loved it?"

Micki Grant, whose song "Lovin' Al" was based on an interview with Alfred Pommier, brought her whole Chicago family to the opening where they all met Pommier and his wife. She also recalls the smile on Studs Terkel's face that night. "It was great for Studs to see that it worked. I'm sure he probably had no idea as to how it was going to turn out. He just seemed to be very, very happy."

Music director Stephen Reinhardt conducts the orchestra in Chicago.

Reviews came out showing that critics in Chicago were basically in favor of the idea of staging Terkel's book. *The Chicago Daily News* reviewer wrote, "It's a long evening (3 hours and 10 minutes) dotted with awkward bridges and dead spots and not yet sure of where it's heading…but the musical has some genuinely wonderful scenes, a true and talented cast, a well-crafted mounting, stretches of confident momentum and, above all, the honest talk garnered by Studs Terkel."

The *Chicago Sun-Times* thought the show a work in progress that would someday "work." Connectivity was the chief issue: "The most irritating difficulty at the moment is trying to connect 42 stories together. Every one of these characters has a story to tell and Schwartz's technique to bind them into a whole is to use a family as connective tissue—a man and his wife and their little boy… It is not a cohesive ploy. It divides, it interrupts, it bores." The reviewer suggested that the audience doesn't need to have everything spelled out. Why not simply use Terkel's biographical introductions? "And what's wrong with a spotlight, a downbeat and a declarative narrative?"

On To Broadway

It was too bloody long.

Stephen Reinhardt

As the creative team worked through script issues in preparation for Broadway, they cut the clothesline. Schwartz says, "When we abandoned the unifying family story, the purer revue format emerged with a touch of cohesion provided by one character, the Steelworker (later updated to Ironworker to reflect changes in the American workplace)." The actor playing the Steelworker would begin and end the evening, and he also appears a few times in ensemble sections. Schwartz came to believe that the audience would supply structure as their appreciation of the workers unfolded.

In a meeting with the cast, Stephen Schwartz discusses the latest adjustments to the script of *Working*. "Stephen had a way with the cast and with the people involved in the show behind the scenes. It really was a family." —Irwin Meyer

Stephen Schwartz participates in dance warm-ups in Chicago. (He is in the center, with his hands at his sides.)

PLAYBILL, INC.

Broadway is rather merciless; unfortunately, they don't give you much time to fix things.

MICKI GRANT

Through Chicago, Schwartz had gotten along well enough with his very hands-on producer, Irwin Meyer. They played tennis together, and Meyer shared his enthusiasm for the musical, offering support as he could.

After Chicago it got tough. Friedman and Meyer had recently acquired the 46th Street Theatre—a Broadway venue. They optimistically believed they could bring *Working* in there and that it would run for years.

Schwartz believes that Meyer and company rushed the show. They looked at other shows for the 1977-1978 season and concluded it was a weak year for potential Tony nominees. Thus, *Working* would receive more attention if they could bring it in by the end of the season rather than wait until the following fall. That meant that every fix had to be attempted in rehearsals and previews in the 46th Street Theatre.

Schwartz fought the decision to move to New York but eventually relented, a decision with lasting consequences he would always regret. It didn't thrill the people in Washington, D.C., either (although their costume designer, Marjorie Slaiman, was able to transfer her work to the Broadway production). "We had included *Working* as part of Arena Stage's upcoming season when the rights were pulled for a Broadway production," remembers Zelda Fichandler. "It was a big disappointment for us." When the New York rehearsals revealed the script problems, someone from the show called and asked if she could provide advice. "I had moved on to other projects and, I'm sorry to say, still had negative feelings about the way things had been handled."

Making the transition more difficult, *Working* lost its choreographer. Schwartz and Faso received news that Graciella Daniele had been offered another show that would conflict with their rushed schedule for *Working*. "We were devastated," says Faso. "She was so central to the way we had conceived everything."

Onna White was brought in to oversee the Broadway choreography, but, says Faso, she was "a very old-time choreographer" and didn't relate well to their approach.

About resisting a rush to Broadway, Faso admits they weren't looking at things from a money standpoint. "We really wanted *Working* to evolve and be organic. And because parts of it were so wonderful, like Matt Landers' monologue as the Fireman—breathtaking—that we couldn't stand it if we couldn't get all the moments to work."

Too soon for the co-adaptors' comfort, rehearsals and previews began. By then the number of characters for *Working* had been whittled down to thirty-nine, played by seventeen actors. The show still ran too long, yet it wasn't easy to trim.

"It was a different show every night," Faso recalls. "We took musical numbers out; we put numbers in. The actors and crew and the orchestra performed death-defying stunts every night."

Everyone thought they had a tremendous hit during previews; the audience response was overwhelming, with cheering and standing ovations most nights. Schwartz's waitress song, "It's an Art," sung by Lenora Nemetz and the company, stopped the show almost nightly. James Taylor's melancholy "Millwork" moved people to tears, as did Schwartz's "Fathers and Sons." The Rodgers/Birkenhead number about a teacher stirred sympathies, while group numbers by Grant and Carnelia touched hearts with their meaningful lyrics and exhilarating music.

Despite all the effort on the show, opening night had come too quickly. According to Meyer, the press wasn't patient in terms of waiting for a delayed opening. "The show was a little long, and Stephen wanted a little more time [to trim and polish]. And we said okay. And then he wanted a little more time. And we said okay again, but then we got to the point where the critics

The set design was one of the most unusual and critical aspects of the show, with the opening scaffold coming down, actors coming from below stage on elevator platforms, and sliding stage sections for the last scene. It was incredible.

IRWIN MEYER

I still believe that their drive to open Working *was based on a more commercial motive: qualifying for that year's Tony Awards®. It's one of the reasons I feel that the Tonys are so destructive to Broadway, because it's become the tail wagging the dog.*

STEPHEN SCHWARTZ
IN 2008

said if you don't open this show we're going to just come in and review it, because you can't run indefinitely for previews. You have to have an opening night. You cannot keep pushing it back. We were getting a lot of pressure through our press agent that if we didn't get our act together and open, the critics would come in anyway and that could have been a disaster. So we picked an opening night and we said, 'Stephen, we're just going to have to open. At some point in time the show must go on.'"

Meyer especially felt the urgency of opening because money wasn't coming in. "Advances were insignificant," he reports. Not so keen on losing money every single week, they made efforts to get groups in, but the show didn't sell well. "This was not their kind of show," Meyer came to believe, and the reviews wouldn't help.

Openings and Closings on Broadway

May 14, 1978. It rained on opening night, Schwartz recalls. He and Carole dressed up and drove into the city through the drizzle. He told her, "This is going to change our lives in one way or the other. If this works, that will be one path, and if it doesn't work, I'm through."

It seemed to be working for the audience. Micki Grant attended the opening with a colleague who told her afterward, "This is one of the best shows I've ever seen."

"I believed that the show was ready," Meyer states. "When the people came out and performed that opening night, they rose to the heights of their careers at that time. They couldn't have given a better performance. It couldn't have gone off better."

Few critics agreed. Clive Barnes: "Ambivalence here we come!" Martin Gottfried in the *Saturday Review* called *Working* "an intelligent musical," but concluded it had faults, such as "no dynamics or tension."

In any case, there were enough mixed or negative reviews to scare audiences and the producers.

"The biggest problem," Schwartz concludes, "was the cancellation of the Arena Stage run with Zelda Fichandler and the decision to come straight to New York. It would have been better to have more time to work on it because it wasn't right when it opened. I think particularly the Washington production would have helped because Zelda was so smart. She loved the concept of the show and many of the things that she had to say about the show turned out to be right in terms of changes that needed to be made. I think there's a possibility that if we had gone to the Arena Stage and she had been around (which she would have), certain things that we discovered late in the preparations for Broadway might have been discovered earlier, and so time wouldn't have been wasted.

"Here's the truth," Schwartz later asserted. "The truth is we were not ready to open when we opened. And we were forced to open, I think for the Tonys, but also because it turned out that those guys owned a theatre and there was another show trying to get into the theatre. It turned out to be economically a good decision from their point of view, but was kind of a betrayal, since they were both producers of our show and the owners of a theatre that *The Best Little Whorehouse in Texas* wanted to come into."

Working closed after 12 previews and 24 performances. Two weeks later, *The Best Little Whorehouse in Texas* opened at the 46th Street Theatre, where it ran for three years.

Working and those connected with it received accolades in terms of Tony® nominations, and Schwartz won a Drama Desk award for direction.

We knew if we stopped after months of rehearsals as well as the Chicago production, we would lose momentum, the cast, and the creative energy that made Working *what it was. To sit around for another year would have been a much worse decision than going to Broadway.*

IRWIN MEYER

Scott and Stephen stretch together during a rehearsal for *Working*.

Working Resurrects

Mounted in smaller theatres, a finally revised *Working* proved popular. The initial inspiration came from Paul Lazarus, who asked permission from Schwartz to direct it at Dartmouth College in New Hampshire. When it worked there, others tried it, and after five or six successes, Music Theatre International decided to license it.

Schwartz believes that *Working*, unlike *The Baker's Wife*, was essentially fixed with some cuts, some reordering, and slight revisions. "With some shows, I think you can look at what didn't work and say, 'Oh, I can fix that,' and you can do it fairly easily, without tearing your hair out. That was true of *Working*."

CREATIVITY NOTES

Solving Problems of Placement

In the performing arts, because a work of art unfolds through time, decisions about sequence affect how each aspect will be received. Where will songs fit in the scheme of a musical? Sometimes a perfectly good piece fails because of its placement in the sequence.

In *Working*, a Gospel-Rock number, "Cleaning Women," added a burst of energy to the show while the ballad "Fathers and Sons" set audiences quietly reflecting about childhoods and parent/child relationships. For Stephen Schwartz, a song placement switch led to "one of the big lessons I learned about musical theatre structure."

When *Working* opened on Broadway, the songs were in the opposite order from what ended up succeeding. Schwartz recalls, "I thought 'Cleaning Women' had to be in the '11 o'clock' spot—the second to the last number. Neither of the songs really worked as well as I expected. When we did the first post-Broadway production, the director, Paul Lazarus, suggested we flip the order, and we tried it, so that 'Fathers and Sons' came later. And suddenly, without changing a single word or note of either song, they both worked! And I learned: sometimes the problem with a song is not the song itself, but where it comes in the show."

Matt Landers

Cast member Matt Landers comments: "I remember how powerful the show was. It made you notice how unappreciative people can be. That's the thing, the depersonalization of people by the jobs because they are defined by their jobs. You treat a waiter like a waiter, you treat a banker like a banker. You treat a cab driver like a cab driver. But they are all individual people underneath that, and that's the message of the show. That's what really made it work."

David Patrick Kelly

After performing in *Working*, actor David Patrick Kelly became involved in movies and television. His film credits include *Commando*, *K-PAX*, *The Longest Yard*, *Flags of Our Fathers* and others.

For his reflections on *Working* for this book, he writes: "Stephen Schwartz has always been high on my list of people I'm most grateful to. *Working* was my big break, my Broadway debut. The Charlie Blossom monologue was the funniest, scariest, most challenging material I had ever had. That speech was a personal breakthrough in terms of acting technique (specifically using emotion memory), and it got me my first film job in *The Warriors*.

Matt Landers and David Patrick Kelly

"The responsibilities Stephen entrusted us with (acting, singing, dancing, playing our own instruments, playing several different characters) was unheard of at that time and so empowering (we had to join the Musicians Union).

"I remember going out of town for the tryout at the Goodman Theatre in Chicago with two-foot snowdrifts, and how we really used that time to try so many different things. Using my background in mime and street performing, I made a triple-headed mask representing emotional confusion that was part of a monologue with ballet about an executive's nervous breakdown. It didn't make the show but it was such a creative time and gave me a new idea about artistic freedom.

"Not that Stephen wasn't a taskmaster with himself as well as us. I remember a night in Chicago when Matt and I were told to come up with stronger stuff for Charlie Blossom and Matt's tie salesman or they were out of the show. Another high point for me, coming from the downtown rock scene, was to play with James Taylor during those early workshops and have him compliment my guitar playing. I remember with joy Matt and I playing guitars and singing 'Millwork' with Robin."

Four generations of Schwartz men (1974): Stephen, baby Scott Schwartz, Stephen's father Stanley, and Stanley's father Sam. One hundred years separates the oldest from the youngest.

Future director Scott Schwartz looks over the poster for Broadway's *Working*.

Comments from Stephen Schwartz about his song "Fathers and Sons," written for *Working*:

"I think all boys have father issues. Working out my relationship to and with my father was central to my emotional and psychological development. And then becoming a father and how I related to my kids and the kind of parent I was, was also very important to me emotionally.

"It may be a common pattern of son-to-father relationships that when you're young you idealize your father and he's your hero. And then as you come into your teenage years and you become more realistic about who your father is, the fact that he has flaws is devastating in some way. So you have an unrealistic picture of him in the other way—he suddenly becomes this total failure and the negatives completely take over."

Other details in the song were true to life, like the "baseball games beneath the lights." Schwartz says, "When there was no National League team in the New York area my dad and I would drive down to Philadelphia once a year to see the Phillies play a night game against the Giants. And that was always one of my favorite memories."

About "and sleeping in the car," Stephen says, "I loved my father to carry me into the house when I fell asleep in the car, so sometimes I would pretend to be asleep."

"Fathers and Sons"

I heard a lotta songs say, "Where you goin' my son?"
Now I know they're true
Boy, you never stop to think how fast the years run
Now they're takin' you
I remember you was three 'n' a half
Your ma and me, we'd sit there after things got quieted
We'd laugh at some new word you said
How tough you were to get to bed
And we'd plan the night away
Planning for our kid…

I was your hero then
I couldn't do no wrong, as far as you were concerned
You thought I was the best of men
The tables hadn't turned
You hadn't learned
How little time it takes
And daddies make mistakes…

Seems to me that lately I been thinkin' a lot
I think about my dad
Lots of funny things come back I thought I'd forgot
Now they make me sad
High school and it used to be
I didn't want him touchin' me, and I shuddered if he did
Further back to summer nights
Baseball games beneath the lights
And sleepin' in the car
My daddy and his kid…

He was my hero then
He couldn't do no wrong, as far as I was concerned
I thought he was the wisest and the strongest
And the best of men
The tables hadn't turned
I hadn't learned
How little time it takes
And everybody breaks
And daddies make mistakes….

I heard a lotta songs say, "Where you goin' my son?"
Now I know they're for real
Boy, you never stop to think how fast the years run
And the things they steal
Now it seems I always knew
Why I do the things I do
And the things I never did
Why I work my whole damn life
So's I could give a better life
Than the one my dad could give me
I give it
To my kid….

Stephen Schwartz plays with his young children Jessica (on his lap) and Scott during his "retirement" period after *Working* failed.

CHAPTER II
MID-JOURNEY REFLECTIONS

One more disaster I can add to my generous supply.
No good deed goes unpunished
WICKED

We expect accomplished people to steel up to misfortune. We expect those with extraordinary talent to cope with negative feedback. For Stephen Schwartz, after *Working*'s last performance, June 4, 1978, it was time to be ordinary. Hurt and exhausted, he quit. Staying home with his wife and children, he almost never left their property for three years.

Nina Faso explores the depth of the reaction when she says, "*Working* kind of traumatized a lot of us, but Stephen Schwartz was really wounded. If you haven't had the tremendous pressure of being responsible for a huge, expensive Broadway show, it's hard to know how bad it feels when it fails. So many years of work gone, so much sacrifice. It happens all the time to people who lose their businesses. What can I say? Human hearts are fragile and life is only what you can make of it."

The Baker's Wife had been "an excruciating experience," and now after a year and a half of work on a newly failed show, he needed time off. "I had started to burn out, really. It started with *Pippin*, that *Pippin* was such a difficult experience, and I felt such an outsider in the New York theatre community which at that point in my life, I had actually really wanted to be a part of."

In those pre-Internet days, he had no way of being bolstered by an audience who cared for his work. A trickle of letters came in from fans who wrote him in care of the theatre, which he appreciated. The harsh words overshadowed positive ones.

Failure in theatre is the most public form of embarrassment.

STEPHEN SCHWARTZ

I was catapulted into fame and prominence before I was ready emotionally. I was just this kid who came into New York with illusions about what it would be like to work on Broadway, how it's all going to be this glamorous, collegial, wonderful atmosphere, and 'the community of the theatre' and all that total bullshit that they say on the Tony Awards®.

Stephen Schwartz

His sense of rejection was not just a response to reviews. People would say unkind things to his face and he carried the memory for years. About six months after *Pippin* opened, he was standing in a music publisher's office in Manhattan. A stranger walked up to him and said, "I bet you're thanking Bob Fosse every day. He really saved your ass on that one, didn't he!" And that was not uncommon.

When *The Magic Show* became an overnight smash hit, he'd felt even more rejected when he read the reviews and heard people talk. It was as if they resented his success. "I had had these two enormous hits, during one of which I was in conflict with a Broadway darling, and then I had followed this up with another great big hit that people felt artistically did not deserve to be a hit. I felt like I had crashed this party that nobody wanted me to be at and that I had come in and had eaten too much of the food and had too much to drink."

A couple of years later he was asked to write a theme song for a television show that Bruce Paltrow (Gwyneth Paltrow's father) produced, which he did. When he attended the filming of the pilot in front of a studio audience, as part of the audience warm-up the host asked them if they wanted to ask Stephen Schwartz any questions. The songwriter recalls, "Some guy raised his hand and said, 'Why, after shows like *Godspell* and *Pippin*, did you write something as awful as *The Magic Show?*' That was his question to me. I guess that's being frank but it's so rude because what can you say? You can't defend yourself. I said, 'Well, it was a fun experience, what can I tell you? Some people seem to enjoy it.' But it was really embarrassing. This kind of thing happened to me all the time."

He believes such people don't realize that they are being cruel, because entertainment is not their business. They are probably not actors or singers or songwriters. "They're not putting themselves out there all the time. They don't understand that it actually is like stabbing someone in their flesh. They don't understand that it hurts, because that kind of thing wouldn't hurt them."

A "friend" of his sent him a terrible review for one of his shows that he would otherwise never have seen, and wrote a note saying, "I thought you'd be amused by this." He was not at all amused. "My feelings were constantly being hurt. It felt like 'death by a 1000 cuts,' that Chinese saying. I felt like I was bleeding from all these tiny little slices until finally I had no blood left in me whatsoever and I just gave up."

The actual words of reviews contributed to his dejection. Up through *The Magic Show,* he made the mistake of actually reading his reviews. Gradually, the responses crystallized into his self-image. It was no longer simply rejection—he came to believe what he heard. "It just felt clear to me that the New York theatre establishment saw me as an untalented upstart who had no business being part of their club. When *Working* took a nose dive, I started thinking, these are smart people, maybe they're right—maybe I'm no good. People thought I was a success, but I didn't feel like a success. I felt like I had tried really, really hard and I didn't achieve my goals. I wanted to be Richard Rodgers or Lerner and Loewe." He realized it was never to be and so would try to alter his goals.

As he shared his feelings with Carole, she tried to be supportive. She talked about the difference between how other people perceived him and how he perceived himself. His friends and family certainly believed in his talents, as Nina Faso's comments reflect. "Stephen Schwartz has the finest mind of anyone I've ever known. He's brilliant."

Equally, he was known for being tenderhearted. Says close friend Dean Pitchford, "Stephen is a very emotional man. He's a softy." It meant he could tap into deep emotions for songwriting,

In the books about musical theatre, I'm a footnote. I'm not a chapter.

STEPHEN SCHWARTZ

yet the same trait also made it harder to be Stephen Schwartz. He needed a thicker skin. Until he found that thicker skin, he would instead retreat from the world. Schwartz recalls, "I called my accountant and said, 'You have to structure things so that if I never make another penny I can still send my kids to college.'" Royalty and investment income made that possible.

For those years he was silent to the public, nothing could pull him into creating new musicals. Even with the Drama Desk Awards the following year, when he won for best director of the musical *Working*, his sour mood toward commercial Broadway theatre remained. When asked if attending the award ceremony lightened things he said, "No, nothing helped. I was really pleased to get it, but nothing helped."

Nor did the proliferation of regional productions of *Working* change his point of view. "That didn't change my antipathy for Broadway, for not wanting to write for theatre at all. I remember Joseph Papp, who ran the New York Shakespeare Festival, coming to my house because he was such a fan of the show. He and his wife came over to talk to me and maybe see if there was something I would do for them. I refused to discuss business at all. I just played with Scott. I absolutely deflected every attempt to discuss business. I didn't really do anything for three years. I took three years off. I didn't see a single Broadway play between 1978 and 1981. I refused to go to the theatre. So I never saw the original production of *Sweeney Todd*; that's the one thing I regret. I only saw it on television."

Parenting in Paradise

In terms of family life, *Working*'s failure was perfect timing. Jessica was two and Scott was four-and-a-half. Neither realized until much later that most dads don't spend so many hours playing with their children.

"I sometimes think that the happiest time of my life was the three years when I was depressed," Schwartz says. "My kids were little; I ended up spending much more time with them. It worked out in this strange way the way a lot of things in my life somehow work out in unforeseen, serendipitous ways."

Having been born with abundant energy, and continually maintaining his good health with fitness routines, he would never succumb to periods of staying in bed all day or shuffling listlessly around the house. "My way of being depressed wasn't to just sleep, it was to do a lot of projects. I practiced the piano—I was really playing well then—and I went back to all my student piano pieces. I taught myself to touch type. I played a lot of tennis and started playing local tournaments. I learned Spanish—why not? It was something to do—I think we were going to Mexico or something. But I basically hid out."

The Schwartz's backyard was especially ideal for the kinds of recreation Stephen loved. In addition to the tennis court and pool, there was the wide, sloping lawn with a rock formation and garden off to one side and a pond on the other. A small stream runs through the valley and a bridge crosses it to the forest beyond. This yard was ideal for various types of social gatherings.

Schwartz, ever the puzzle worker, concocted elaborate sets of clues and treasure maps for Scott, Jessica, and the children of friends like the Rushton family that included Jessica's friend, Sarah Rushton. (Jessica and Sarah developed a close friendship. Jessica's comments about it several decades later formed the basis of the song "For Good" from *Wicked*.)

The Schwartzes also held parties for adults. "It was all magical," Denise Boockvor recalls. "He would make a map where you go to one point, figure out the riddle and go to the next point. The property is huge so [the clues sent you] through all sorts of spaces. He made you think. He made you try to figure out to

I don't think Steve is an athlete's athlete, but he plays tennis well. He's got a lot of speed, he's quick, and he knows the game. He gets into it because there's a lot of art to it; there's a technique to it, and I think he accomplished the technique and is able to play at a really high level.

STEVEN BOOCKVOR

Steve [Schwartz] loves games. We used to play a lot of fun puzzle games over at the house, and treasure hunt games with clues. He just loved making these things up.

STEPHEN REINHARDT

solve the problems."

The congenial time with family no doubt contributed to the depth of feeling he cultivated as a parent. He had woken to the joy and responsibility of it when Scott was born. "All of a sudden there's someone who is more important to you than you are." As Scott and Jessica grew, his commitment to parenting grew with them.

Asked about the impact of being a father, he speaks with superlatives. "Unbelievable. I had no idea that I had the capacity for that depth of feeling. Before I was a parent I had no perspective on anything. All that was important to me was writing shows or whatever."

Getting Back to Work

The way Schwartz started back was with the invitation to direct *Working* as a television production for the PBS station KCET. He cast Carole in a role and they flew out to Los Angeles for the project.

While out there, a cast member named Bill Beyers helped nudge him from his resistance to seeing live theatre. "We were supposed to go have dinner and he drove. When he drove into the parking lot of the Shubert Theatre, I got all nervous. I was like, 'What are you doing?' He said 'Shut up, I've got two tickets to *Evita* and you're going.' I was really upset. I said 'I don't go to the theatre. I don't want to go.' He said, 'Well, it's too bad. I paid for the tickets, we're going.' And then I loved it. That sort of broke that cycle."

Directing the television production of *Working* (now available on DVD), he discovered that it could be fun to work again. Afterward, he started looking around for things to do.

Carole Schwartz appears in the DVD version of *Working*.

Stephen Schwartz drew elaborate treasure maps as a game for his kids. Note the ghost in the center playing a piano, while another holds a microphone.

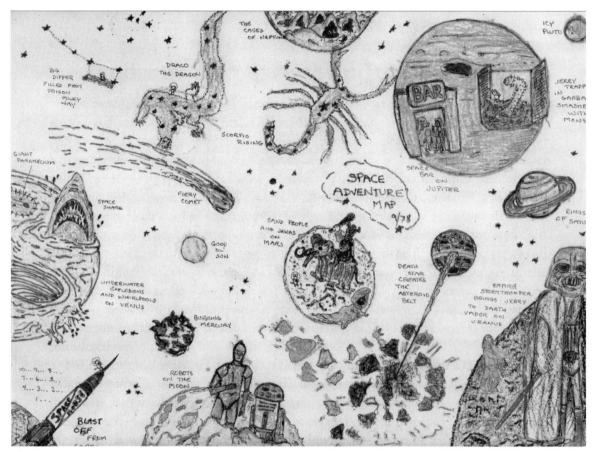

A space adventure map drawn by Stephen Schwartz for his children.

CREATIVITY NOTES

Dealing with Criticism

Once Schwartz accustomed himself to criticism, he found ways of dealing with it and advising others. To a disconcerted friend whose work had been negatively critiqued he sent the following email message:

"I thought I would remind you of a sign pinned to one of the walls in my house. It says:

THREE SIMPLE WAYS TO AVOID CRITICISM:
1. SAY NOTHING
2. DO NOTHING
3. BE NOTHING

"In the end, if you're going to attempt something, you're going to get criticized for it. And the higher you reach, the more intense will be the criticism. In the case of what you're attempting, right now whatever criticism you are receiving is clearly meant to be constructive. But if you let it inhibit you or deflect you from your own intentions, then it becomes destructive.

"So take it for what it's worth to you, and use it to the extent it resonates with you (and ignore those aspects of it that don't). It's no fun to be criticized—I certainly speak from experience on that account. But I would rather have the work that I've done and the criticism it has engendered than have neither."

Collaborators Joseph Stein, Charles Strouse, and Stephen Schwartz stop arguing about *Rags* long enough to pose for the camera. Stephen Schwartz later commented, "We are friends and all like each other, but something about that troika—it was a chariot with the horses running in different directions."

CHAPTER 12

R̃AGS AND THE 1980S

Sometimes we don't love things
Till we tell them good-bye

RAGS

In the 1980s, Stephen Schwartz emerged from his "retirement," tentatively ready to continue his career as long as he didn't have to submit himself to "the atmosphere of working on Broadway."

In Los Angeles in 1981, he directed a production of *Working* for television. He contributed to several off-Broadway efforts, including the score for a children's musical, *The Trip* (later re-worked and renamed *Captain Louie*), and music for a few songs for an off-Broadway show, *Personals*. He also explored the "adult contemporary" genre of songwriting, eventually recording an assortment of new songs on albums he titled *Reluctant Pilgrim* and *Uncharted Territory*.

He routinely said no to requests for songs for new Broadway musicals, and might never have contributed lyrics to *Rags* if he hadn't first been approached to direct the show. He explains, "I thought this is the way to have my vision: be the director and not a writer. From *Working*, I learned that I shouldn't be the writer *and* the director, so I thought now I'll just be the director." He later accepted the role of lyricist when it was decided that the collaboration between Charles Strouse and lyricist Hal David wasn't working appropriately for the show because they tended to write in too "pop" a style. "The producers thought the score required a more serious and historic overview," Strouse recalls. "Stephen and I knew each other—and I, of course, was aware of his collaboration with Bernstein, so I was greatly flattered when Stephen saw the potential of *Rags*."

I've always believed that Broadway is in Stephen's blood and that the wariness is a protective device.

CHARLES STROUSE

Before starting the whole effort, he talked to Carole about the prospects of working on another Broadway extravaganza. "Do you think that there's any chance that this experience won't be as horrible as I think it's gonna be?"

She looked at him and said, "Absolutely no chance."

But the material intrigued him, so he committed to help make the musical.

The development of *Rags* followed a similar pattern as that of *The Baker's Wife* and *Working*: hopeful beginnings, inspired moments yielding some memorable songs, and difficult endings. Yet the *Rags* journey was different because of the subject matter—the life of several Jewish American immigrants in 1910—and Schwartz's concentration on lyrics only. In the evolution of his career, writing lyrics for someone else's music proved helpful in many ways: the discipline of fitting words into Charles Strouse's song structures enhanced his craft, and it allowed him to be noticed as a lyricist.

While vacationing together in the Caribbean, Stephen Schwartz and Joe Stein spend part of their time finishing *Rags*.

Rags—A Brief History

Shortly after Stephen Schwartz launched into *Rags*, set on Manhattan's Lower East Side, he rode the subway down to the Tenement Museum at 97 Orchard Street. The field trip would help him picture what daily life was like for the many thousands of immigrants who had packed into apartments in the narrow, multi-story tenement buildings in the early decades of the 20th century.

As he toured the cramped quarters of the Tenement Museum, Schwartz noticed tall windows that allowed sunlight to flood in during the day—an observation that eventually filtered into song lyrics. With notebook in hand, he also took walking tours of the Lower East Side and learned about tragic industrial fires in the area, like the one at the Triangle Shirtwaist Factory in 1911.

He rode a ferry to Ellis Island before it had been opened as a tourist site, collecting thoughts and feelings about the first landing point for immigrants in America. He enjoyed "making notes, as always, of specific details that would help give verisimilitude and visual evocativeness to the lyrics."

I've always been concerned with themes of compromise and struggle in my life and in my work. I'm not interested in flag-waving. I'm fascinated by just how tough it was for immigrants in this country.

STEPHEN SCHWARTZ

Unlike the *Rags* bookwriter, Joseph Stein, Schwartz didn't have personal links to the Jewish immigrant experience—no memories of foreign-speaking grandparents around his childhood home sharing tales of "the old country" or of coming over to America. His father's German and Hungarian ancestors had arrived in the 1860s, and there were no special family stories passed along about them. On his mother's side, family connections to the Old World were similarly hidden in the distant past. One great-grandfather's origins could be traced to Vienna in the early 19th century, but others either had been born in America or their stories were unknown.

He connected to the topic by way of research. "I have so many books at home—*How the Other Half Lives, The Rise of David*

Levinsky, books about Yiddish theatre, the immigrant experience, and so on," he reports about the material he collected for the musical.

For Joseph Stein, the immigrant experience in the 20th century held personal significance. His father, Charles Stein, had left a small town outside of Warsaw (then part of Russia), traveling to America in the early 1900s. His mother crossed the ocean a few years later with his older brother and sister. Joe was born in New York City. Stein says about immigrants like his parents, "They were strangers in a strange land and it was a very tough life."

As librettist for *Fiddler on the Roof*, over the years he had often fielded "Son of Fiddler" jokes from colleagues as well as requests from producers for a *Fiddler*-like show. Although he didn't want to bring Tevye and Golde to America, he came up with an idea for a film about Jewish immigrants. After developing a treatment for a screenplay, he circulated it among friends. It fell into the hands of producer Lee Guber, who said, "I want to do it as a musical."

"Why not? Yeah, let's try it," Stein replied to Guber.

Who would try it with him? Composer Charles Strouse of *Bye Bye Birdie* and *Annie* fame agreed to write the score.

Strouse, a fifth-generation American, was immediately drawn to the *Rags* project. "My attraction to the story is directly due to the 'melting pot' of American music. The Black jazz, the Jewish klezmer, the tarantellas and the jigs." He would soon draw from a range of musical styles to create a varied score.

Music, Lyrics, and Story

In *Rags*, Rebecca Hershkowitz arrives in America several years after her husband. When she doesn't find him right away, her dream that she and her son, David, could escape misfortune in the New World suddenly evaporates. She finds a sewing job in a sweatshop. Saul, a labor advocate, tries to get her involved in a union and a strike. The two of them gradually fall in love.

Partway through the musical, Rebecca's husband, Nathan, shows up. She learns he has transformed himself into a posturing political climber without conscience. He has even removed the ethnic association of his name by changing it to Nat Harris. Rebecca struggles between wifely duty and her attraction to Saul, as well as to the new ideals Saul teaches her.

Schwartz and others especially liked the sideline story of the friendship between Rebecca and teenager Bella, whom she meets on the long ocean voyage to America. Bella, in a sense, rescues Rebecca and David when they arrive on Ellis Island with no contacts. Bella convinces her father, Avram, to allow Rebecca and son to stay with them at their relatives' tenement apartment. The story of their mutual support could have become the main story, but remained a subplot.

Early on, when Schwartz reviewed the developing musical story, he asked for another character, Ben. Ben was the type of immigrant "who got in there somehow, and made something of himself in spite of everything." He became Bella's boyfriend and provided, says Schwartz, "that kind of brash, young, energetic character" the story seemed to require.

He also wanted to toughen up the tale with tragedy. "The first thing I said when I came on was, 'Okay, somebody has to die.' It may be one thing too many, but it just sort of seemed as if we should do the Triangle Factory fire." And so they doomed Bella to perish in the fire, thus layering in more emotional as well as historical texture to the musical.

With a complex story in place, Charles Strouse and Stephen Schwartz planned and produced their complex score, often meeting at Strouse's Midtown Manhattan apartment. They wrote songs that reflected the multi-ethnic culture of Manhattan during

I have often cited my writing with Charles Strouse on Rags *as being the experience that taught me the most about the craft of lyric writing.*

STEPHEN SCHWARTZ

that period. "Brand New World," "Greenhorns," and "Blame It on a Summer Night" brought in ragtime and bluesy early jazz sounds. The song "Penny a Tune" provides the flavor of klezmer brought over from Eastern Europe, but with a twist. It begins with an Old World sound and by the end, the klezmer band is playing American jazz.

When the team decided that Bella's father and a neighbor widower needed a song, Schwartz remembered his trip to Orchard Street and wrote lyrics for "Three Sunny Rooms."

For Ben, Schwartz proposed a playful pastiche of a George M. Cohan song. He and Strouse developed "For My Mary" that Ben could sing to Bella, accompanied by a record playing on the gramophone.

The songwriters also wrote a standout number, "Rags," for Bella to sing as she shared her disappointment with America. The team decided to dub the entire musical *Rags* because of its multiple meanings, both musical and literal.

By the time they were finished with *Rags*, the writers had juggled a bountiful hodgepodge of survival issues, disappointment, angst, dangerous romance, longing, loss, freedom quests, compromise, idealism, and more. Schwartz believes he grew as a composer by listening to his colleague's varied work. "He leapt to ideas in ways that were different from how I work," Schwartz acknowledges. He feels *Rags* is Strouse's best score. "While other shows of Charles' were more Broadway-oriented, this is more classically and operatically oriented. *Rags* is Charles painting on a bigger musical canvas than he usually does."

Strouse returns the compliment, saying, "If this is true, it stems largely from Stephen's visions."

I still believe that Rags *contains the best lyrics that Stephen has ever written. Broadway is very unforgiving, but I recognize quality!*

CHARLES STROUSE
IN 2008

CREATIVITY NOTES

Tonal Disparity and Finding the Right Mix #2

For the genesis of the epic number, "Children of the Wind," Stephen Schwartz and Charles Strouse were agreeable to adjusting their drafts when their earlier versions of the piece weren't landing during backers' auditions. "Charles had written what I thought was a superb melody," Schwartz recalls. "I wrote two sets of lyrics but neither of them came off. People weren't responding to the music. Finally, Charles said, 'I'll just write a better tune.' I said, 'No, this is a great tune. It's not you, it's me. I believe in this tune. Let me take another shot at this.'

"The other two lyrics were too small for the music. The music has a kind of epic quality to it. When I first heard it I thought, 'This is a lovely little plaintive folk tune. I'll write a little personal song.' But it just didn't fit the music. I realized I had to be more poetic about it. I had to find an image and write more about the whole idea of the immigrant experience."

That version became "Children of the Wind," using Strouse's original tune. Schwartz reveals, "When the words had a larger thematic quality, they were riding correctly on the music, and suddenly everyone loved the tune. That was such a valuable lesson about lyrics and how they have to fit the tone of the music, and how the same tune can either work or not, depending upon what the words are."

In 1984, producers paid for a workshop for the Broadway-bound production co-directed by Stephen Schwartz and Nina Faso. (*Rags* was to be Faso's first co-director credit.) Actors and writers met in a rehearsal space at 890 Broadway in Manhattan.

During the workshop, the show's major problems came into focus. Production manager Bob Strauss remembers, "Everybody thought it was going to be a huge hit and loved the material, until we found out the book didn't work."

Afterward, Schwartz stepped down from the directing position because he and his colleagues, in his words, "were not solving the storytelling problems of the show; I came to feel that it needed an outside ingredient that another director would provide." He resigned on behalf of both himself and Faso—a decision that Faso long resented.

According to associate producer Madeline Gilford, after an exhaustive director search, the only two who agreed to direct the show were Martin Charnin and Joan Micklin Silver. Strouse wanted a director he hadn't worked with before, so Silver was it, even though her stage experience was limited. She had co-written and directed the 1975 movie *Hester Street*, another story of Jewish immigrant struggle set in Manhattan's Lower East Side, which meant she understood the milieu.

Schwartz was pleased with her ideas and vision for the musical. "She said it should be about the two women, with a focus on the relationship of Rebecca and Bella."

Production Details and Broadway Casting

Although an abundance of characters meant a larger cast and higher production costs, the writers made choices that they felt supported their story.

The sweep and size of the musical prompted the creators to think of hiring an opera singer for the important role of Rebecca. The creative team sought out Teresa Stratas, herself a child of Greek immigrants. They found in her a performer they believed could bring in the needed emotional layers.

Terrence Mann played Rebecca's love interest, "Saul," with Larry Kert as her compromising husband, "Nathan Hershkowitz." Judy Kuhn would wow crowds as Rebecca's friend, "Bella," who belted the show's angry title song, "Rags," and Lonny Price offered a bold "Ben." Dick Latessa (as Bella's father, Avram) and Marcia Lewis (as Rachel) added their charms playing the elders.

As more details of the complete production fell into place, the process became more challenging. The whole project was a struggle for everyone involved, from the creative team arguing about story issues, to the new director's inexperience with getting people on and off stage. Joan Micklin Silver departed partway through rehearsals for the pre-Broadway tryout in Boston in 1986. Schwartz and Strouse took over while they scrambled to find a new director.

The producers didn't rein in the production plan, even though covering costs for twenty-nine cast members and all their costumes, a large orchestra, and everything else would be tough. Everyone was feeling pressured with the responsibility for a show capitalized at five million. "It's difficult not to sit there and think about all that money," Schwartz told a reporter.

He was not the only one feeling burdened. Strouse said, "Because of the economics of Broadway right now, *Rags* is going to be either a landmark success or a landmark failure, and that's too bad, because it's stifling to have to work under that kind of pressure. You really hammer yourself into the ground doing a musical like this."

On the physical level, riches of setting seemed to hold them back. To convey the feeling of Manhattan's Lower East Side in the early 1900s, the set and staging for *Rags* overflowed with crowded tenements, cafes, and hawking peddlers. Scenic designer Beni Montresor didn't opt for simple backdrops or flats, but had full sets flown in from above the stage. And he arranged for the stage to be boxed in by mirrors that ran back to front and floor to ceiling, which could swing out to create city street scenes. A three-dimensional, stark white Statue of Liberty rolled on and off stage, and depending on where you were seated, would reflect off the mirrors. It was all pretty sensational.

By the close of Act II, the cast of characters has won the audience's empathy and sympathy. In Schwartz's words, "They have endured hardship, heartbreak, wrenching change, and the fairest of them has perished, but in the end Rebecca, David, Avram, and Ben have begun to make a new life in their new world…as another boatload of immigrants arrives."

Boston and New York

When the show opened in Boston, it was clear it had issues. Before it reached Broadway's Mark Hellinger Theatre, it underwent so many changes that each week audiences saw an entirely different show. Some fixes enhanced it. Publicist Josh Ellis recalls, as an example, that the song "Children of the Wind" was originally a trio sung by Avram, David, and Rebecca. In Boston, it became a solo for Teresa Stratas. "It worked really well as a trio, and it stopped the show as a solo."

While Ellis did notice Strouse and Schwartz head up to the swimming pool on the hotel rooftop every morning, he also remembers the tension of the times, especially with Ms. Stratas missing performances due to bronchitis. "Every single rehearsal day, and every single performance in preview, through the opening, through Teresa Stratas coming back into the show, was fraught with problems."

In *Rags* on Broadway, Russian immigrants arrive in America after a long ocean voyage. Left to right: David Hershkowitz (Josh Blake), Rebecca Hershkowitz (Teresa Stratas), Avram Cohen (Dick Latessa), and Bella Cohen (Judy Kuhn).

David and Rebecca adapt to the strange new world in *Rags*.

When Ben (Lonny Price, left) takes up gramophone sales, young David (Josh Blake, right) cleverly assists him while they sing "Sound of Love."

In Beni Montresor's set, a three-dimensional, stark white Statue of Liberty appears in various scenes. General manager Bob Strauss has remarked, "I think part of the problem with the show is that the set was so big that people on stage looked like little teeny midgets."

Tailoring 'Rags' for Broadway – Three showbiz veterans find that creating a successful musical hasn't gotten any easier.

NEWSDAY HEADLINE
FOR AUGUST 17, 1986

But that doesn't mean the show wasn't appreciated. At the curtain calls in Boston, appreciative audiences stood for enthusiastic ovations. "By the end of the run, the audience was absolutely captivated," confirms Ellis.

The producers tried to find a director who could pull together the disjointed elements of the show for New York and Gene Saks agreed to do whatever he could at the last minute. "I tried to clarify the story so people knew what was going on," Saks told a reporter, "but by clarifying it, I probably took away some of the camouflage that covered its deficiencies...as written, Rebecca was not a character but an all-purpose symbol, and that's always deadly."

With high expenses, weak reviews, and low advance ticket sales, the producers decided to close the show. Yet the cast and audience devotion to it was so intense that a march was held in an attempt to keep it running.

On August 23, 1986, the Saturday matinee crowd at Broadway's Mark Hellinger Theatre ended their ovations and waited, watching the stars and chorus members stand before them. Lonny Price stepped forward. "I don't know if you know this, but there is a good chance that *Rags* will close tonight," he explained to the audience. "However, after the performance the cast is having a celebratory march down Broadway from the theatre to Duffy Square. If you'd like to join us, we'll meet under the marquee in ten minutes." Price began to organize the unprecedented parade from the Mark Hellinger Theatre toward the TKTS booth to save a show that producers said had to close.

Journalist Masha Leon described the moment: "'Don't let the show close!' yelled an audience member, followed by cheers and applause on both sides of the footlights. 'Keep *Rags* open! Keep *Rags* open!' the audience chanted over and over. Then minutes later, over 1,000—yes, 1,000—audience members joined the cast, the musical's klezmer band, and cast member-stilt-walker Gabriel Barre on a thrilling march from West 51st Street to the TKTS tickets booth at 47th Street, to get people to buy tickets for that evening's performance of *Rags*. Within an hour, the TKTS booth had sold out all 784 tickets they had on sale. (The balance of the theatre's 1600 seats had been sold out in advance.)" Sadly, the colorful march could not save a show with poor reviews and insufficient advance ticket sales.

Critic Howard Kissel of *Women's Wear Daily* was among those with a mixed reaction. "Part of the problem is the show's ambitions. It tries to cover so many issues in the immigrant's experience, the plot has so many events, that few can be treated in any depth...[Yet] even if one's overall response is fragmented, 'Rags' taps into feelings so deep inside us we can't help but surrender."

With the sense of incompleteness of the show along with the over-budget production costs, the multi-million-dollar effort sank. Stephen Schwartz wrote out a vow, in front of Charles Strouse, never to work in a commercial Broadway venue again.

CREATIVITY NOTES

Production Values—Moving to Final Form

"The problem with musicals," Stephen Schwartz suggests, "is that you are only as strong as your weakest element. You can have a good show that gets sunk by one performance or an intrusive design element." Every artist faces form issues: a painter laments when a painting is poorly framed; an author worries that an unsuitable cover will misrepresent his or her book. For musicals, any number of things can obscure what the writers were trying to communicate: bad casting, distasteful costumes or sets, inappropriate orchestrations, or unappealing choreography.

Schwartz told one aspiring writer, "If you have a modicum of talent and craft almost anything will come off in a reading, because people in the audience are all seeing a different show in their heads." Options decrease as it becomes set in the "real world" of specific actors, fabrics, wigs, set pieces, spotlight cues, memorized dance steps, and orchestral arrangements. "You can't say, well, when they get the real person for the role that will be better. There it is. And many, many shows have foundered when they go to the final production."

For the original *Rags* set, Schwartz started working with designer David Mitchell. "We were going to do a set all out of cloth so the whole thing would look like clothes-lines with laundry hanging on them. In fact, at the first workshop, we had clothing racks with rags on them, and actors simply created different spaces by moving clothing racks. It was going to be much more low-tech—more of a *Nicholas Nickleby* feel."

Then Joan Micklin Silver hired Beni Montresor, whose set may have overshadowed the show and the budget. With production costs so high, *Rags* needed to be a sizable hit to succeed at all.

Losing Friends and the beginning of the AIDS Crisis

Meanwhile, in Schwartz's personal life, friends who had been close during *Godspell*'s heyday were moving away. Jeffrey Mylett and the Reinhardts had moved to Los Angeles. One day in the mid 1980s, the Reinhardts telephoned Schwartz to say that Jeffrey Mylett was quite ill. He had picked up an intestinal bug while spending time in India, or so he thought.

Schwartz remembers his phone call to Mylett in Los Angeles. "I phoned him from my house, and we talked for about ten minutes and then he said, 'I can't really talk anymore, I'm very tired.' I hung up, went to Carole and said, 'That was like talking to a ghost. It was like talking to a husk of corn with nothing inside it.'"

Two weeks later Mylett died of AIDS. "He was the first person I was really close to who died. And I just remember I said to Nina Faso, 'They're not kidding about this disease. This is going to be bad.'"

Schwartz continued his life in Connecticut, though with a different sense of its fragility. "I remember that for years after that, every day when I picked up the newspaper, the very first thing I did was read the obituaries. That's an unusual thing to do when you're in your thirties."

Stephen Schwartz in the woods at his Connecticut home. His daughter Jessica took this photograph for the cover of his *Reluctant Pilgrim* album.

Personal Songs

In 1987, Stephen Schwartz met John Bucchino, a fellow song-writer who would soon become his best friend. Schwartz later explained how he learned about Bucchino and his music: "I was doing a benefit, accompanying the wonderful singer Ronnie Gilbert, and among the songs she was performing was one called 'In a Restaurant by the Sea.' Blown away by the quality of the music and the evocative poetry of the words, I asked Ronnie who the writer was and if he had written anything else. She gave me a demo tape of several of John's songs, and driving home that night,

I popped the tape into my cassette player. A few minutes later, I had pulled over to the side of the road to listen. How could it be I'd never heard of this guy before? I became an instant fan."

The next time he was in Los Angeles, he phoned Bucchino and asked if he could meet him. They got together and played songs for each other. Bucchino, who didn't know his future friend's work, remembers being shocked that a songwriter would only write show tunes. "He started to play me songs, and he said, 'This is from this show, and this is from this show.' And I said, 'Isn't there something that is about you?' He was like, 'No, no, no, no, I don't do that!' I had *only* done that. It seemed bizarre to me that somebody wouldn't write just out of what they were feeling in their own life. So I think I inspired him to give it a try."

The two soon became close friends and Schwartz gave in to Bucchino's prodding, eventually writing enough personal songs to fill two albums: *Reluctant Pilgrim* and *Uncharted Territory*. As he wrote for the chorus of one of his new songs:

> *Time to sail, reluctant pilgrim*
> *My fear is all I've got to lose*
> *Life is nothing but a dreamscape*
> *And the dream is mine to choose.*

It wasn't a one-way influence. Bucchino had to stretch, under Schwartz's inspiration, to write for the musical stage or film. Among his achievements since the start of their friendship, Bucchino earned his first Broadway credit in the spring of 2008 with his score for *A Catered Affair*. He also wrote songs for the DreamWorks direct-to-video movie *Joseph: King of Dreams*.

Stephen Schwartz and John Bucchino (right) compare songwriting notes at a friend's house in Los Angeles in 1987.

Stephen and his teenage kids romp in their snowy backyard, winter 1989.

At home in Connecticut, the Schwartz family poses for their 1988 Christmas card photo.
Left to right: Stephen, Jessica, Carole, and Scott.

Charles Lisanby and his cat, Jefery, savor a quiet moment at home in Los Angeles. Lisanby, who conceived of a musical that began in Eden and ended after the Flood, grew up in an Eden-like environment on a Kentucky horse farm. Lisanby fondly remembered his pet ground-hog, as well as the horses, ponies, peacocks, dogs, and cats.

The London West End production of *Children of Eden*.

CHAPTER 13

CHILDREN OF EDEN – SECOND CHANCES

From this day forward nights won't seem so black
From this day forward we will never look back

CHILDREN OF EDEN

As with *Godspell*, the idea for *Children of Eden* was not something Stephen Schwartz sought out; rather it sought him. Very freely based on the first nine chapters of Genesis, it would be nearly as idiosyncratic as *Godspell*, although far more linear in structure. *Children of Eden* emerged after a decade of development as one of Stephen Schwartz's most popular shows for amateur production. When Charles Lisanby first shared his concept for the show, Schwartz realized it "had themes I've always liked: personal freedom versus authority, the quest for self-definition in a universe without definition, and parent-child relationships, in particular those between father and son."

Q: How do you approach God as a dramatic character in your work?

A: I approach all characters in shows of mine as people, rather than as types or historical figures. This goes for God as well as all other characters, be they Pocahontas or Charlemagne.

STEPHEN SCHWARTZ

In the Beginning

Schwartz first heard his next musical's concept in 1983, several years after Charles Lisanby had conceived of it. Lisanby was renowned as scenic designer for the Christmas Spectacular at Radio City Music Hall, as well as for his sizable list of credits for television and film, including the 1981 television production of *Working*. When he and Schwartz walked around the set before taping *Working*, the 6'1" tall designer easily towered over Schwartz. For their next collaboration, Lisanby would be looking up to the experienced musical maker.

After finishing *Working*, Lisanby envisioned a pageant called *The Glory of Creation* for entertaining throngs of summer season vacationers at the Crystal Cathedral near Disneyland in

California. He had already designed the scenery and special effects for the annual shows *The Glory of Christmas* and *The Glory of Easter.* In imagining the new show, he thought of Genesis.

"I was thinking about the cathedral and about all the special effects I could do with the creation of the world, with lasers and everything else, and it could be a sensational thing," Lisanby recalls. Years before *The Lion King* was staged on Broadway, Lisanby's imagination rolled through designs for giant giraffes and other animal costume magic. However, he soon realized the stage of the glass-walled cathedral wouldn't darken early enough on a summer evening for the light effects he wanted to use. Perhaps Radio City Music Hall would do it as a summer spectacular and add it to the annual Christmas and Easter shows Lisanby was already designing.

The concept evolved further after Lisanby watched interviews with Joseph Campbell, a comparative religions and mythology expert, that were playing on public television at that time. A comment triggered Lisanby's thinking about generational issues: In every culture, Campbell explained, a child is "…brought up in a world of discipline, of obedience, of his dependence on others." To become adults, young people have to learn to stand on their own. Dependence has to be "transcended" so that a maturing person moves into "self-responsible authority."

Lisanby then associated the relationship stories in Genesis with parent/child issues and the universal need to achieve independent personhood. "It started with God having a problem with Adam, or Adam having a problem with his Father."

His Act I could begin in the Garden of Eden, and continue after the expulsion when Adam and Eve had issues with their rebellious son, Cain. Act II could involve Noah and "Mama Noah" coping with their rebellious son, Japheth. In a larger spiritual context, the Flood in Act II might represent Father having trouble with his offspring, and then an acceptance or second chance after the Flood.

Lisanby penned a first draft of *Family Tree*, based on Genesis Chapters One through Nine, and then phoned Schwartz, who took to the concept immediately.

A representative from Youth Sing Praise, an annual youth musical event in Belleville, Illinois, had recently contacted Schwartz about a commission to write a choral piece for them. He wasn't given specific content—just something suited to their program that brings high school students to Our Lady of the Snows in the summer to produce a religious-oriented musical. *Family Tree* could fulfill the youth program requirements.

Another factor shaped the early development of this musical. Schwartz had attended a performance of *The Gospel at Colonus* at the Brooklyn Academy of Music. In this version of the Oedipus story set to Gospel music, lead vocalists narrated most of the story in song while performing in front of a sixty-person choir. The choral material was still essential to the storytelling, providing a Greek-chorus effect and commenting on the action. Schwartz wanted to try this structure in the new project.

A Carefully Planned Score

Preparing for Belleville, Schwartz not only worked at his piano, but also plunked around on a small collection of wooden xylophones he temporarily housed in his work room at home in Connecticut. He had brought them into the house after he and Carole attended a Christmas pageant at the private elementary school where their children were enrolled. The music instructor had taught students to play instruments developed by Carl Orff. These included xylophones with removable bars so that only the notes used in a particular piece can be played, thus reducing the potential for player error. For the Christmas show, the Schwartzes

Charles Lisanby thought of the idea of doing the Book of Genesis, *beginning with the creation and ending just after the flood. I was intrigued with doing a show about second chances and learning from past mistakes.*

STEPHEN SCHWARTZ

were transported by the tinkling sounds into a magical percussive world as youthful players plunked merrily away.

Stephen asked to borrow some instruments to develop sounds for a song called "The Naming"—a playful piece during which Eve and Adam name the animals. The song was part of an overarching plan in which musical coloring would support the story presentation.

"My thought was that when they were in Eden," Schwartz comments, "everything was going to be extremely simple…and with very pure chords. That's why 'The Naming' is basically A minor – no sharps or flats." The mallet instruments from Orff were primordially perfect for orchestration.

When the Snake makes its entrance in a scene with Eve, the music begins to get more harmonically complex with the introduction of 7th chords.

Then in the second half of Act I, when Adam and Eve leave the garden, guitars and other folk elements would suggest a homespun life.

Like the classic Greek chorus, the ensemble players tell the parts of the story that are not dramatized onstage, and react to the events that are shown. They are ever-present and an integral part of the play.

STEPHEN SCHWARTZ

Act II shifts again. "The second act, which takes place several thousand years later during the Noah story, is more pop and contemporary in style," says Schwartz. He also included world music and Gospel music, so that collectively the musical numbers of Act II would represent the growing diversity for the human population.

They workshopped the musical in Lisanby's living room, and by 1986 completed a two-act script with about eleven musical numbers, mostly choral pieces.

Stage Magic—A Ballooning-Off Point

On a sunny summer day in 1986, Schwartz sat in the audience in Belleville, Illinois to watch *Family Tree* for the first time. He had flown in from Boston where he'd been coping with technical rehearsals for the out-of-town trial of Broadway-bound *Rags*.

Lisanby had been in Belleville all week, working with the students and preparing a surprise for the attendees. He arranged for hundreds of multi-colored helium balloons to be tied on lines that looped just behind the bandshell arch at the back of the stage. They would be hidden for most of the show and be displayed as the post-Flood rainbow (referred to in Genesis) at the end.

From his chair in front of the outdoor stage, Schwartz watched young people performing in the costumes they had made that week. They had mastered rich harmonies and exciting rhythms for "Let There Be," "In Pursuit of Excellence," "Generations," "Ain't It Good," and others. He was already feeling satisfied, and there was still more to come during the finale, called "In the Beginning" — a lofty choral number celebrating a new beginning after the Flood. "Suddenly this rainbow floated up behind the stage while they were singing 'In the Beginning.' And then, at the very end, they let the ropes loose, so all the balloons floated up into the air. It was fantastic. And people went crazy."

It was clear from the applause and obvious enthusiasm that *Family Tree* could be a full musical. To complete the show, the writers would need more songs, an improved book, and a director, a producer, and a venue, among other things. Radio City Music Hall rejected their proposal.

Would London Be the Answer?

Schwartz was eager to try working in London. Having vowed never to work on Broadway again, he hoped, Pippin-like, to find his "corner of the sky" in the then-flourishing British musical theatre scene. He had heard how his favorite show, *The Life and Adventures of Nicholas Nickleby,* had been leisurely and lovingly developed by the Royal Shakespeare Company, and how the same process had then been applied to the recent musical

I don't think I would have gotten involved at all...if the first stop were Broadway.

STEPHEN SCHWARTZ

smash, *Les Misérables*. In keeping with the theme of his new project, Schwartz thought London could provide him with a second chance to experience the joyful collaborative creativity he had found with *Godspell*, and to work an ocean away from the pressures, egos, and critics of New York.

John Caird had co-directed both *Les Miz* and *Nicholas Nickleby*. Schwartz describes *Nickleby* as "the best thing I've ever seen in the theatre." So it was natural that when it came time to look for a director, he contacted Caird.

Caird was then directing the first national tour of *Les Misérables* in Boston. Schwartz invited him and his wife, the actress Frances Ruffelle, to come down to Connecticut. They arrived on their next free day and enjoyed the meal Carole prepared. After dinner, everyone moved into the living room under the cathedral ceiling. As the others settled around the grand piano, Stephen began playing through segments of the musical-in-progress. John was enthralled. The son of an eminent professor of theology at Oxford University, he notes, "I was very familiar with the material. I thought it was an amazing take Stephen had on this. He sang about seven or eight songs and I just sat there, mesmerized by how clever they were."

Conveniently, Caird was in a position to help bring a production to London. But the lovely music and story needed far more conflict for it to succeed as a stage musical. He spent part of that summer in California with Lisanby, attempting to make changes.

From the Londoner's perspective, "The characters were very stuck. I found myself doing the impossible job of instructing Charles how I thought it should be, and hoping that he would be able to rewrite it accordingly. He's a top designer and a wonderful imaginer of things, and I was enjoying working with him. But he didn't have the requisite skills to write the dialogue and take the story to the next level. The characters needed to be fully imagined just as the visual images had been imagined."

Weeks passed, and it appeared that Lisanby's slowly revised script wasn't going to be the supporting vehicle the full-fledged musical needed.

"So in the end, I said to Stephen and Charles, 'Why don't I just help you write this?' and Charles was happy with that until I proposed that I should be appropriately credited and remunerated for my work. That was when he objected to the idea of me being a co-author."

Caird approached Schwartz and said he wouldn't continue with the project. "I can't give away all my best writing ideas and have somebody else take the credit. If I'm a writer, I'm a writer. Let the credits tell the truth. That's what the word 'credit' is supposed to imply." He was the more experienced writer and man of the theatre, having served as a director and writer for plays, musical theatre, and opera for many years. At the time he was serving as Associate Director for the Royal Shakespeare Company.

Lisanby balked. "I had written the entire thing," Lisanby complained later, feeling it was his show. Caird saw the story as Genesis, which had been around for millennia, and couldn't come around to Lisanby's proprietary point of view. Schwartz didn't want to lose Caird, so they began making legal arrangements to enter into arbitration.

Lisanby was given the choice either to collaborate freely and share future credit and remuneration or drop out. "Stephen and I begged Charles to stay with the project," Caird recalls. "We said, 'Come on, share. Let's all do it together; it would be lovely.' He absolutely wouldn't do it."

Schwartz and Caird won an arbitration settlement and the show moved on. Only a tiny fraction of the original dialogue was kept. Lisanby would receive a percentage of royalties as part

Charles has brilliant ideas, and there were some beautiful turns of phrase…. What he's not great at is being a dramatist. He could not grasp the concept that it's conflict that makes drama and he could not succeed in injecting enough conflict into the play, and that's ultimately why John had to come in as the writer.

STEPHEN SCHWARTZ

of the settlement.

Moving Toward London's West End

About that time, Trevor Nunn approached Schwartz about reviving *The Baker's Wife* for the West End, which meant Schwartz could travel to London to address Nunn's concerns and move forward with Caird.

Everything for the new musical started to change, including the title. Inspired by the title of the French film *Les Enfants du Paradis (Children of Paradise)*, Caird thought *Children of Eden* would be a more suitable name for their show.

In London, he arranged for a no-cost workshop production. Soon the rehearsal room at Royal Shakespeare Company's Barbican Theatre was bubbling with youthful energy. Students of The Guildhall School of Music and Drama gladly offered their time as performers in trade for exposure to the expertise of John Caird and Stephen Schwartz.

Some young actors played assigned parts. All others could be "Angels" as the chorus was then called. The talented young players learned the material quickly and performed it well, so the writers could sit back and respond directly to their new material.

Characters, Themes, and Throughlines

Children of Eden's basic structure was in place. Act I included scenes in the Garden of Eden, the Snake, the expulsion from Eden, Cain and Abel's childhood, and Eve's last moments. Act II covered Noah's family preparing the Ark for the Flood, as well as scenes on the Ark and after the Flood subsides. Details and emphasis shifted at each step of the way, especially with regard to God as a character.

In *Family Tree*, God made His presence known by thunder—the sound by which Adam, Eve, and Noah inferred His approval or disapproval. In a later version, He was an off-stage voice. It now seemed clear that an onstage actor should appear in the role. Caird says, "In the medieval mystery plays, God was always a character who came on and related to the other characters—even chatting with the audience. He was always played by an ordinary working man. Our God derived from the same idea."

The writers labeled him "Father" to represent their human family themes. What they didn't yet know is that after London He would transform and in Act II become more forgiving (more the New Testament concept), just as does his earthly counterpart, Noah. For the time being, He was the stern creator depicted in the Old Testament.

Among the other characters, Schwartz found himself identifying with Cain. For him he wrote one of his most fervent rebel songs, "Lost In the Wilderness."

The story parallels between Act I and II deepened as the development progressed. Adam and Noah both struggled with their rebel sons. The boys' emotional journeys matched up as they expressed their need for self-determination.

Schwartz realized he could introduce the impulse for independent thinking earlier through Eve. Eve then passes it along, unconsciously, to Cain. With this concept in mind, he wrote Eve's solo, "The Spark of Creation." She passionately sings about the need to be curious, to discover, and to express. Her questioning nature later shows up in Cain.

The spark of creation
Is blazing in my blood
A bit of the fire
That lit up the stars
And breathed into the mud

Lyric for Eve

Another important discovery for the writers of *Children of Eden* at this time was the character Yonah. She existed in Lisanby's script as Anah, servant of the family and a lifelong friend of Japheth. Japheth chose her for a wife to bring along on the Ark, against his father's wishes. They originally sang, "Smile to Beat the Sun," a duet hinting at their warming love.

John Caird asked one of the Guildhall students for a list of Hebrew words related to their story. (In a "small world" coincidence, she happened to be the daughter of the original *The Baker's Wife* star, Topol). In her response, she included "Yonah" as a word meaning "dove."

When he switched the name Yonah for Anah, everything fell in place. Yonah would be a daughter of the race of Cain who was forbidden to go on the Ark. Schwartz wrote "Stranger to the Rain" as Yonah's lament when Noah's family members reject her from becoming Japheth's betrothed. Japheth decides to stow her away on the boat anyway, and before launching, the two sing a new love duet, "In Whatever Time We Have."

After forty days and nights, Yonah is discovered on the Ark. In a stressful moment in front of the whole family, Noah debates whether or not to cast them overboard. In a violent confrontation between father and son, Yonah serves as the peacemaker, the dove. She steps in and prevents a violent act, breaking a cycle of violence begun by Cain in Act I (when he struck down Abel). This added emphasis to the musical's message about second chances and the ability of new generations to make new choices.

Preparing *Children of Eden*

Our first production was trying to be the wrong thing. Children of Eden *works best on a smaller scale, on a human scale, in smaller theatres.*

JOHN CAIRD

When *Children of Eden* seemed moderately ready for a professional production in 1991, the Barbican Theatre, where Caird normally worked, had lost its state funding and cancelled its RSC London season. This meant that the not-for-profit route was no longer possible. The vast Prince Edward Theatre, with seating for over 1,600 people, was the only venue available. The producers decided to chance a run there, partly at the urging of scenic designer John Napier, who had designed *Les Miz* and *Nickleby*, as well as *Miss Saigon*. Schwartz was trepidatious—hadn't he learned from *Working* that one shouldn't plan a commercial production before the show was ready? But, he was reassured that there would be an unusually long rehearsal period. And besides, this was London; surely the West End was different than Broadway.

For scenic design, Napier developed a half-finished globe curving at the back of the stage, open so that audiences were looking from the inside at the various continents hanging on ribbing. Actors could climb ladders to several platforms above the stage, adding visual interest (as well as requiring actors to watch their step).

Matthew Bourne came in for choreography, making his pre-*Swan Lake* debut on the West End. Costume designer Richard Sharples created animal costumes so fascinating that they became museum pieces later on. (On the other hand, Father's oddball business suit with a cloak over it confused audiences.)

The team ended up with a cast of sixteen principals and twenty-six Angels, including actors talented enough to sing, dance, and play aboriginal instruments on stage during several numbers.

The search for a Father proved the most challenging. Schwartz and Caird auditioned British actors. The vocal necessities of that role were very similar to the quality and range of the cat, "Old Deuteronomy," in *Cats*, played by African-American actor Ken Page, whose vibrato-touched voice could hit notes ranging from high bass to low tenor. He was pleased to be cast and flew to London. As reported in *Time Magazine*, British Actors Equity union didn't believe that an American actor was necessary for playing the Almighty, and lodged an official protest—how could London audiences accept a Yank in such a role? Caird explained that auditions had not turned up another suitable actor. "British Equity backed off, but an official noted dryly that the union 'welcomes talented foreign artists working in our country even when they are required to play such an obviously British part as God.'"

MICHAEL LE POER TRENCH

Adam (Martin Smith) and
Eve (Shezwae Powell)
in the 1991 production of
Children of Eden.

*The London production
maybe reached too far in
terms of making a point.
People didn't really ap-
preciate the ideas, because
there were bloody costumes
and a lot of things being
layered into the show, and I
think people were not ready
to get there that fast.*

KEN PAGE

The company prepared for the show in rehearsal spaces in an old school building. Schwartz's mostly completed score was, if anything, overabundant. From that point on it would be difficult to make changes because Caird was overburdened as both book-writer and director.

Design and staging concepts probably contributed to the show's fragmented feeling. Caird's team reached for a kind of meta-theatre experience, a show commenting upon itself or at least consciously telling a story about creating. Sets, props, and some costumes appeared to be found material, suggesting that the *Children of Eden* company had made them or found them at a secondhand store—assorted street clothes dyed for Edenwear, a pterodactyl with wings made from a broken umbrella, unfinished plaster globs dangling on the half-made globe. "It was a very British concept," suggests Ken Page, "the way *Cats, Les Miz, Nicholas Nickleby* were created out of what was at hand. Sort of that raw bones theatre concept."

Whatever the visual appeal or lack thereof, the show wasn't ready and it wasn't working. "I knew we were in trouble in rehearsal," Schwartz recalls. "You can just feel it. I think to some extent John did too, because there were moments when he would just disappear."

The opening night, scheduled for January 8, 1991, should have been a cause for celebration, but instead was something to dread. The producers had arranged an apartment for Schwartz, and one day he slept in. Martin Erskine, who was on hand to create synthesizer programming, came over to the apartment because the composer was late for rehearsal. Schwartz heard him knocking on the door.

"You've got to get up and come to rehearsal," Martin called in to him.

Schwartz had such a bad feeling about it all that he told Martin he didn't want to get out of bed. "It was so horrible," he later revealed. "It was like being tied to the tracks and seeing a train coming at you. You know the opening is scheduled and there's nothing to be done."

London critics attended on the appointed January night and went home in the rain to write mostly unpleasant comments about the show. *The Times* called it "well-meaning, indecisive and gently soporific."

Many reviewers categorized it as very 1960s—not knowing what else to make of it. From the *Daily Express*: "In the beginning was a 2 million pound multi-racial musical based on the book of Genesis and financed by the Japanese. And the fashionable Spirit of the Sixties moved upon the face of the show, with archangels in blue jeans and hippie beads."

Kerry-Jane Beddows in one of the animal costumes from Act 1.

The *Punch* reviewer, who also labeled it as 1960s, wrote, "…this is yet another of those bloody quest musicals filled with soulful hymns to the mysterious, wonderful, Something Out There, the higher thought, the greater freedom, the incredibly awful banality."

Schwartz puts the blame on the level of preparedness of the piece: "It was like staging a first draft." There were elements they knew needed to be changed but it was too late. It closed after 100 performances, partly due to the escalation of the Gulf War in the Middle East. Since August of the previous year, trouble brewing in Kuwait with an Iraqi invasion was filling news headlines. In November, the U.N. declared January 15, 1991, as the deadline for withdrawal, so many Brits were staying home watching television to see if there would be a war.

"Nobody was going to the theatre for those three to four months," Caird recalls. "Everybody was glued to their televisions, watching the Middle East being blown up. They weren't going to any shows. Shows were closing all over the West End at that time."

John Caird (with daughter Eliza in his arms) and Stephen Schwartz take time out to enjoy some sunlight during their preparation of *Children of Eden*.

Stephen Schwartz stands by the poster for *Children of Eden*'s London production in 1991.

Frances Ruffelle, Stephen Schwartz, and John Caird, attend opening night for *Children of Eden* in London, 1991.

Caird says it wasn't an all-negative experience. "There were an awful lot of things about that production that I think many of us should still feel proud about. It was the first major piece of musical theatre work that Matthew Bourne did, for instance, and he is now one of the most sought-after choreographers in the world."

Children of Eden in America

"I thought this was going to be Stephen's biggest show since *Godspell*," Ernie Zulia recalls about the *Children of Eden* production about to raise its curtain in London.

Zulia, an American director with affection for all things Schwartz, had entered the songwriter's life by way of creating *Magic to Do*, a revue of Schwartz songs staged at the Cincinnati Playhouse in the mid 1980s.

When Zulia became associate artistic director at the Mill Mountain Theatre of Roanoke, Virginia, in 1991, he decided to pull *Magic to Do* out of the trunk. "I called Stephen and told him we were going do it in the summer of 1991, and he said that he had all kinds of new material that he was happy to send to me. He sent me all the *Children of Eden* songs and said, 'Use any of it that you want.' I just fell madly in love with the music."

"When *Children of Eden* didn't take the world by storm," Zulia continues, "I was shocked. Later on, when I had photographs and heard the recording, I could tell how large the production was, and that struck me as something that could have worked against it, but also it mainly sounded like they hadn't really ironed enough of the bugs out of it before going full blast with it. So after it closed in London, I called Stephen and said we would love to do a full-scale production of it in Virginia."

At almost 100,000 people, the population of Roanoke, Virginia, in the Blue Ridge Mountain range, was sizable enough to support a professional regional theatre. The not-for-profit Mill Mountain Theatre would host an official American premiere of *Children of Eden*, running from November 29 to December 22, 1991.

In addition to the paid stars, Zulia was able to add a standing choir of thirty and a children's choir of about twenty-five — to be called "storytellers" — in order to bring out the fullness of the choral numbers. For the first time, *Children of Eden* could be tested for its potential as a large school or community theatre production of the type that Music Theatre International likes to license.

Stephen Schwartz and his collaborator, John Caird, had to get busy tweaking the show. "We didn't really get the structure right until after London," Schwartz explains. Mill Mountain's effort provided the incentive for rapid change.

A New *Children of Eden*

Working mostly at Schwartz's home over the summer, the writers, with some input from Zulia, adjusted the show. He and Caird assessed the way the show had been received, both critically and by the London audiences, and sifted through the text looking for ways to communicate their story better.

Reviewers had been critical of Cain's accidental killing of Abel, so they changed it to a murder, bringing it closer to the Bible story. That meant changing Abel from a young boy, as was the case in London, to a teenager a few years younger than Cain. Schwartz wrote a new version of "Lost In the Wilderness" for Cain to sing.

The focus of change was making Father the protagonist of the show. "After London," says Schwartz, "John and I realized Father was the central character of the show." That meant the script had to be revised significantly.

Schwartz wrote a short piece called "Father's Day" that would emphasize Father's parental expectations in Act I. For resolving the emotional journey in Act II, it dawned on Schwartz that

Father could finish singing "Hardest Part of Love" with Noah, and that could be an epiphany moment.

With these changes and other adjustments, the show's structure felt more complete.

Casting for this production included top talent. The commanding presence and powerful voice of Broadway veteran Bill Nolte (*Cats, The Secret Garden*) suited his role as Father. Craig Wasson (*Godspell* tour) and Cass Morgan (*Hair, Pump Boys and Dinettes*) played dual roles: Adam and Eve in Act I, Noah and Mama Noah in Act II.

It turned out that Zulia's idea of casting the same actors to play the corresponding roles in both acts (Adam/Noah, Eve/Mama Noah, Cain/Japeth, and Abel/Ham) made a huge difference to the thematic continuity and audience involvement.

When opening night arrived on November 29th, critics found much to praise in this new version of *Children of Eden*. For his review in *Southern Stages Theatre Magazine*, Bruce L. Partin wrote, "It might be tempting to assume that this material has received ample attention in the past (*The Apple Tree* and *Two by Two* spring readily to mind), but the real strength of *Children of Eden* is that Schwartz and Caird have gone far beyond a simple retelling of Bible tales. This is a show that operates and succeeds on several levels, and it is one that should be providing satisfying production opportunities on both the professional and amateur levels for years to come."

"People came out at intermission just in a state of shock," Zulia recalls, "because the last fifteen minutes of that first act resonates so deeply. I think that Stephen taps into a part of the human condition as we try to handle death and grief. It was an amazing experience. By the time we got to the finale 'In the Beginning,' which is such a great song, you felt as though you had some kind of insight into our existence that you didn't have when you walked in that night."

Schwartz and Caird traveled around the country to work with other regional theatre directors who could take time to stage the ever-improving versions of the show. From Mill Mountain, to an evangelical music college in Quincy, Massachusetts, to a community theatre in Wichita, Kansas, about six or seven shows were mounted. The Las Vegas Academy developed a production in 1995.

In 1996, *Children of Eden,* directed by Stephen's son, Scott Schwartz, was featured at a theatre festival put on by The National Alliance for Musical Theatre (NAMT). This organization showcases new musicals to hundreds of producers around the country and the world. This led to the 1997 production at Paper Mill Playhouse in New Jersey, and ultimately to the 1998 RCA recording. Word of mouth spread and the show became a "hit" with regional theatres, despite never having played Broadway. It consistently ranks among Music Theatre International's top 20 most frequently licensed titles.

Schwartz has become a proud parent for this musical, and finds great satisfaction that "a very bumpy road led to a successful life, and in the perseverance involved in getting *Children of Eden* to the place where it's thriving." He once jested with an audience member for one of his question/answer sessions, "I promise you, it will be in a theatre near you within the next year or so because it's just everywhere."

CREATIVITY NOTES

Timing for Going Public

How do artists and producers of art know when a work is ready for the public? They often don't, and then commercial failure or criticism can inhibit further development.

Stephen Schwartz reports that for *Children of Eden* in London, he knew better than to go directly to the West End. "I had learned the lesson with *Working* not to be pressured into doing a large-scale production before the show was ready for it. I couldn't believe I let myself make the same mistake again. "

John Caird agrees. "I think most of our financial and commercial difficulties started from that decision that we would be brave and not cancel the show. We should actually, at that point, have said, 'Nope, we shouldn't do it. We'll postpone it. We'll wait until we get the right size of house.'"

For his next stage musical, *Wicked*, Schwartz insisted on a carefully paced development schedule, with enough time to retool the show after each reading and the out-of-town tryout.

The principle of containing one's unfinished work before sharing it is one that Julia Cameron often writes about in her books on the artistic life. Creativity, according to Cameron, is an artist's most valuable asset, to be invested soundly and protected conservatively. She warns writers not to show their work too soon or too indiscriminately: "Showing our writing to hostile or undiscerning readers is like lending money to people with terrible fiscal pasts. We will not be repaid as we wish."

"The Spark of Creation"

"Beyond"... "beyond"...
It sounds full of wind and mist, doesn't it?
It means other things exist, doesn't it?
"Beyond"... "beyond"...
It says, "Adam, leave your list," doesn't it?
Father, why does my head
Feel this joy and this dread
Since the moment I said, "Beyond?"

I've got an itching on the tips of my fingers
I've got a boiling in the back of my brain
I've got a hunger burning inside me
Cannot be denied
I've got a feeling that the Father who made us
When he was kindling the pulse in my veins
He left a tiny spark of that fire
Smoldering inside.

The spark of creation
Is flickering within me
The spark of creation
Is blazing in my blood
A bit of the fire
That lit up the stars
And breathed life into the mud
The first inspiration
The spark of creation.

I see a mountain and I want to climb it
I see a river and I want to leave shore
Where there was nothing, let there be something

Something made by me
There's things waiting for me to invent them
There's worlds waiting for me to explore
I am an echo of the eternal cry of:
"Let there be..."

The spark of creation
Burning bright within me
The spark of creation
Won't let me rest at all
Until I discover
Or build or uncover
A thing that I can call
My celebration
Of the spark of creation...

The spark of creation
May it burn forever
The spark of creation
I am a keeper of the flame
We think all we want is
A lifetime of leisure
Each perfect day the same
Endless vacation
Well, that's all right if you're a kind of crustacean
But when you're born with an imagination
Sooner or later, you're feeling the fire
Get hotter and higher
The spark of creation.

MICHAEL LE POER TRENCH

Shezwae Powell, Richard Lloyd-King, and the Company from the London cast perform "In Pursuit of Excellence."

GERRY GOODSTEIN

Eve (Stephanie Mills) sings "In Pursuit of Excellence" in *Children of Eden* at New Jersey's Paper Mill Playhouse in 1997.

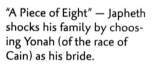

"A Piece of Eight" — Japheth shocks his family by choosing Yonah (of the race of Cain) as his bride.

The cast of the 1997 Paper Mill Playhouse production.

ACT III
1991–2003

~ Academy Awards 1996 ~

Alan Menken and Stephen Schwartz visit Paris during their October 1993 field trip for their second Disney movie collaboration, *The Hunchback of Notre Dame.*

CHAPTER 14

Pocahontas and *The Hunchback of Notre Dame*

What I love most about rivers is:
You can't step in the same river twice.
The water's always changing, always flowing

POCAHONTAS

Pocahontas

Chief Powhatan's daughter, Pocahontas, may not have rescued John Smith from death, as legend suggests. But she certainly could be given some credit for rescuing Stephen Schwartz's career. Historians agree that the Indian maiden played a vital role in the survival of the Jamestown colony after Smith and others arrived in America in 1607. Almost four hundred years later, her legacy would lead to a major turning point in Stephen Schwartz's professional life.

In 1991, before Disney called him, Schwartz had given up on show business completely for the second time in his life. Having failed in London with *Children of Eden,* as he had on Broadway with *Working* (1978) and *Rags* (1986), theatre once again seemed a dead end. That fall he commuted from Connecticut into Greenwich Village to attend graduate school classes in psychology at New York University with the intention of becoming a therapist.

"When *Rags* failed, I quit Broadway, but said, okay, I'll try London," Schwartz remarks. "When that didn't work, I gave up. I thought to myself, I'm one of those guys who had a little flash of success at the beginning, sort of like being slightly more than a one-hit wonder, but it's over for me, and nothing is ever going to work again."

We were taking the myth of Pocahontas and John Smith and the very real attitudes between Indians and the settlers, and then building our own mythology on top of that.

KEVIN BANNERMAN
DIRECTOR OF DEVELOPMENT
FOR *POCAHONTAS*

He considered alternatives. "I didn't really have my tail between my legs about life, though I did about show business. I thought, 'What else would I like to do with my life? I know—I've always been interested in being a therapist. What if I go back to school and become a therapist and that will be my new job?'" (He was himself in therapy once a week after *Children of Eden*'s failure.)

But the invitation from Disney to work on an animated feature for them brought him back into the world of musicals—and this time the experience would prove to be refreshingly new.

The connection to the movie came about a year after the gifted lyricist Howard Ashman lost his battle with AIDS. Disney executives had known in advance about Ashman's deteriorating condition. They would be hard-pressed to fill the shoes of Ashman, who had helped revive the status of Disney animated features with his Oscar-winning work for *The Little Mermaid* and *Beauty and the Beast*, credit shared with composer Alan Menken. The studio brought British lyricist Tim Rice on board to work with their New York-based songwriter, Menken, and together the two finished *Aladdin*.

At the same time, Disney also interviewed other songwriters, including Schwartz, to expand their talent pool.

Meanwhile, the director of development for *Pocahontas*, Kevin Bannerman, had to decide whom to bring on board as lyricist for this new Menken project. Like many of his colleagues, Bannerman loved musical theatre and was a fan of *Godspell*, *Pippin*, and other Stephen Schwartz shows. Tim Rice "…was always gallivanting around the world and it was difficult to get him and Alan together," Bannerman recalls. "And so here was Stephen, who had written scores that we all loved and we were all huge fans of, and he lived in the New York area!"

It would ultimately be up to Alan Menken to agree to a new writing partner. Menken, a year younger than Schwartz, had always admired him as a composer-lyricist. "He's a very talented man," Menken states. "I wouldn't have normally thought of Stephen, and then when his name came up for *Pocahontas* I checked out the work where he had just done lyrics on *Rags* and clearly as a lyricist he was very strong."

The two of them happened to be performing as part of a local benefit concert on March 1, 1991. They spoke backstage. Menken asked, "Would you be interested in working with me as a lyricist only?" He hadn't realized that, at the time, Schwartz had been planning to give up songwriting altogether.

A Disney team flew to New York, picked up Schwartz and drove to Menken's studio for a final interview/discussion on March 26th. During the brainstorming section of the meeting, they discussed the streams of the story.

The meeting had several important consequences. Bannerman sensitively notes, "Stephen needs to build trust in people when he first meets them. I think that's really critical for him. And then once he trusts you, it's full speed ahead. So it was important to him to get a sense of who everybody was and what the project was."

The interview went well and Schwartz signed a contract while story development for *Pocahontas* was underway. "I was definitely taking that job," he says, "although I actually thought I was pretty bad casting for it." He would soon find his way into the story and realize that he had something to contribute.

Breaking a Mold with *Pocahontas*

With *Pocahontas*, Disney Animation leaped out of the familiar fairytale-fantasy mode into the world of real historical figures—Pocahontas and John Smith. *Pocahontas'* co-director, Mike Gabriel, had first introduced the story concept during a "gong show" meeting some years earlier. In these regular gatherings (that were playfully labeled "gong show" after a television game show), employees at Disney Animation shared their ideas for movies with the executives. One day Gabriel pitched a story about a beautiful Indian princess who is torn between her father's wishes to destroy the settlers and her own love for one of them.

Peter Schneider, then President of Feature Animation, explains, "At Disney, we're always searching for projects with emotionally compelling characters set in big, mythic arenas. When Mike made his pitch, we had been thinking about an animated version of *Romeo and Juliet*, with its clash of two worlds and its especially timely theme of 'If we don't learn to live with our fellow man, we will all destroy ourselves.' *Pocahontas* has a very powerful message for all of us—that we must stop fighting, stop killing each other because of the color of your skin, who you are, or because you feel differently about religion."

It would be Schwartz's job as lyricist to step deeply into the Native American way of thinking, contrast it to the British mindset, and illuminate a common humanity.

Stephen was passionate, as I was, that our goal was not to do a docu-drama, but something that was inspired by the legend. We never wavered from the idea of how important it would be to make a story about the clash of two worlds.

PETER SCHNEIDER

A Pocahontas/John Smith story could provide the right context for the theme, although it deviated from the Disney formula. Adding to the challenge of borrowing from history was their quest to satisfy their usual audience while delivering a *Romeo and Juliet* or *West Side Story*-style plot that necessarily had a bittersweet or sad ending.

Kevin Bannerman describes Schwartz as someone who helped give the film its focus. "Stephen was critical in nailing the theme of the piece. We had Stephen and a screenwriter in a room together for a week, basically hammering out the structure of the story, song placements, and the thematic thrust, because not a single Disney project at that time moved forward without having a recognizable, strong central theme. And Stephen really did nail it. It had to do with, 'We're all one planet, all one people, and we need to learn to get along with one another to move forward.'"

The First Menken/Schwartz Collaboration: "Colors of the Wind"

For a Los Angeles meeting about *Pocahontas*, Stephen joined Alan Menken and the various directors in the company's studio. Around them on bulletin boards hung simple cards that served as the initial storyboards for the film. In this stage, before any images were drawn, the cards on the board included a few lines of text describing each prospective sequence and story beat (a beat is the smallest unit of a story). This represented a detailed outline of the work in progress, although the cards could be moved at any time. It was Schwartz and Menken's turn to transform the pattern before them. It was almost a game: Which card would change from a dialogue spot to a song?

Phillip LaZebnik, one of the screenwriters for *Pocahontas*, says, "I'm a big musical fan and working with Stephen was one of the more exciting things for me writing for *Pocahontas*. He certainly lived up to my expectations."

Thinking like stage musical writers, they considered an opening number, a finale of some kind, and a solo for their ingénue about what she wants. In this particular romantic tale, a song could introduce the divergent points of view for their heroine and John Smith. Drawing on Native American philosophy, Schwartz thought "Colors of the Wind" could be a good title for a song for Pocahontas.

It was time for creative magic. The new songwriting pair developed a general strategy of working together back home on the East Coast. By then, Menken had developed a substantial music studio as part of his large home in a pastoral setting of woods and fields in a corner of Westchester County, New York, where he lives with his wife and two daughters (Stephen lives in Connecticut, about a fifteen-minute drive from the Menken estate).

People often ask me if it's difficult for me as a composer to work with someone else's music. But by the time I've sat with Alan's music and played it over and over at my piano, it just becomes the music, *and I don't even think about who wrote it.*

STEPHEN SCHWARTZ

To begin the song, Schwartz sat near the piano in Menken's studio, and they discussed the feel of the song as well as the title Schwartz suggested. Schwartz had also brought an early draft of a few lines of lyric as a starting point. Then Menken heeded his own musical promptings. His hands moved over the black and white keys, and the melody emerged as Stephen made general suggestions, such as "Can it go up there?" "Could that note hold longer?"

In the early 1990s, Menken recorded songs on tape for his cohort to take home (and in later years on CDs and MP3 files). One advantage of Schwartz being a composer/pianist was that he could use a recording from Menken in his own workspace at home and pick up the tune relatively quickly, enabling him to test how a lyric would scan with the music. If the music was more or less fully developed, sometimes Stephen requested sheet music that Alan would print out from his computer (using Digital Performer software). Then a week or two later, when Schwartz brought the first draft of the lyric in, they would work on further refinements of the music/lyric coupling.

"The important thing," Schwartz explains, "is that the lyrics sit on the music. I think the music delivers the emotion…. The lyric has to sit on the music in such a way that it rises and falls and flows with it. If the music is going up into an emotional point, the content of the lyric and the words of the lyric need to make that same emotional journey so that it's one contour."

By the beginning of June, Menken had recorded Judy Kuhn singing "Colors of the Wind," and they shipped the demo recording to Disney headquarters in California. It was hard to predict what the response would be. "When I sent it in," Schwartz recalls, "I thought this was the end of my Disney career; they're never going to go for this. It just seemed so outside what they'd done before. Instead, they so loved the song that they built the whole animated idea around it. That's why there are leaves constantly blowing in everybody's hair through the whole film."

A Field Trip to Jamestown

To orient themselves further to the project, the production team took advantage of their story being based on real people. They traveled to Jamestown, Virginia, to capture images and impressions of the region where Pocahontas met John Smith. At the original site, 104 Englishmen had landed after four and a half uncomfortable months sailing the Atlantic Ocean in three wooden ships in 1607. In June of 1992, having comfortably jetted down to Virginia in a few hours, Stephen Schwartz joined Disney's filmmaking team for a research day at the historic location.

When the Disney team visited the Jamestown Festival Park in 1992, they toured the full-size replicas of The Virginia Company ships.

The visual artists took inspiration from the thick Virginia forests, the wide river, the restored Indian village, the fort, and the replicas of the three ships, while the writers and directors learned more about the history from their guides. Schwartz says, "Being on the spot was tremendously useful for atmosphere and specific details of the lyrics, and I bought some tapes while I was there."

These tapes proved central to the songwriting effort. One was called "Songs of the Virginia Company"—a collection of English sea chanties that he shared with Menken. They helped inspire "The Virginia Company," and "Mine, Mine, Mine." He also bought Algonkian music tapes, which inspired the songs "Savages" and "Steady As a Beating Drum."

As was his custom for a project of this nature, Schwartz steeped himself in the relevant culture. In New York City, he located a store that sold Native American poetry and related volumes. Settling into a comfortable chair at home, he read the poems as well as *Black Elk Speaks* and *The Last Algonquin*. "I have a joke about my process," Schwartz says: "In lieu of inspiration, do research."

Schwartz let the material inform and inspire him. "From a lot of research into writings by and about Native Americans, a whole pattern of thought began to emerge," he explains. "Their way of thinking about the natural world and man's relationship to it, their general philosophy as a whole, was inspiring."

"Just Around the Riverbend"

During the development phase of the film, Carole Schwartz watched her husband brood about how to solve a song concept. "We couldn't figure out how to start Pocahontas' story musically," Stephen remembers. "I kept saying, 'This character doesn't *want* anything until John Smith shows up. How do we launch her?' And, because dreams were so important to Native Americans, Carole came up with the idea that she has a dream that something's going to happen. Since *Pocahontas* was a Romeo-and-Juliet story, they thought about another Romeo-and-Juliet-based musical, *West Side Story*. There, Tony sings 'Something's Coming' as his first song. Our Pocahontas was the equivalent of the Romeo/Tony character. And so basically, 'Just Around the Riverbend' is the Native American version of 'Something's Coming.'"

Schwartz says that the song "didn't immediately land on the ear of the powers-that-be." He and Menken wrote another song for that spot, but asked the decision makers to listen to "Just Around the Riverbend" again after they made a few changes. They liked it the second time. (In musical writer parlance, "Just Around the Riverbend" served as the "I Want" number.)

Moving In and Writing More Songs

With the Disney project moving forward and his aspirations rising for future movie projects, Schwartz decided to find an apartment in Los Angeles. He'd been staying with Dean

One of the great things about Stephen was that he was more than willing to cut a song if everybody thought it wasn't working. That was one of the first things that impressed me; he'd do an enormous amount of work to write a song and then it would be gone if we thought something else would work better.

PHILIP LaZEBNIK

Pitchford on some of his trips there, but he now needed a place where he could move in a small piano and work in his own space, with Connecticut still his home base. This bi-coastal phase of his life would last through his busiest years in the movie business.

For the time being, Schwartz and Menken contin-ued working together on the East Coast, rolling out "Mine, Mine, Mine," "Savages," and various versions of songs that nev-er made it into the film, such as "In the Middle of the River."

Stephen Schwartz checks out the 100-foot-tall screens set up for the world premiere of *Pocahontas* on the Great Lawn of Central Park to take place June 15, 1995.

When all was sung and drawn, *Pocahontas* was ready to be re-leased on June 10, 1995. Disney decided to hold the film's world premiere in a natural setting—Central Park in New York City. More than 70,000 people attended the party that included bands, jugglers, a medley of songs from Disney films, and fireworks to cap the evening.

Reviewers and audience responses ranged from high praise for the artistry to anger about historical distortions.

Paul Hodgins, *The Orange County Register*, 6/23/95, offered a polite summary: "Composer Alan Menken delivers a tasteful if Disneyfied look at another culture…. By the musical standards of recent Disney fare…*Pocahontas* is about what you'd expect: a pleasing combination of heartfelt ballads, rousing choral scene-setters and hilarious comic-relief ditties, all wrapped in composer Alan Menken's slick, kid-friendly style."

Schwartz's lyrics were criticized for being didactic—a term that would be applied time and again to his work—with the suggestion that phrases like, "But I know every rock and tree and creature/Has a life, has a spirit, has a name," are too much of a direct lesson in Native American philosophy. Yet not long afterward, the Academy of Motion Picture Arts and Sciences voted "Colors of the Wind" the year's "Best Song."

CREATIVITY NOTES

Standing on the Shoulders of Giants:
Following Models

Stephen Schwartz often turned to models provided by other writers as an inspirational springboard for his original songwriting. In the case of *Pocahontas*, he specifically assigned himself the task of modeling lyrics after the style of two successful lyricists.

"Because I didn't think I was good casting as lyricist for the project, I consciously thought about who would have been better casting and then modeled my work on theirs," Schwartz explains. "I decided on Oscar Hammerstein II and Sheldon Harnick, because they wrote for ethnic people and folk people, and they dealt with issues of prejudice and cultural misunderstanding. And so as I wrote, I consciously tried to assimilate their styles. When I wrote 'Colors of the Wind,' I thought, 'What would Oscar do? What would Sheldon write?' I just recalled their sensibility. It was just a matter of adjusting my mindset to think how they would approach a song. I didn't steal anything specific from them. I just took in their sensibility and filtered it back out again."

For *Godspell* two decades earlier, he modeled some of the music after that of his favorite contemporary songwriters (*see the Creativity Note "Musical Diving Boards" on page 459 for more information*).

For *Wicked* a decade later, he would model the music for several songs on other writers' styles.

"Colors of the Wind"

You think I'm an ignorant savage
And you've been so many places
I guess it must be so
But still I cannot see
If the savage one is me
How can there be so much that you don't know?
You don't know…

You think you own whatever land you land on
The earth is just a dead thing you can claim
But I know every rock and tree and creature
Has a life, has a spirit, has a name

You think the only people who are people
Are the people who look and think like you
But if you walk the footsteps of a stranger
You'll learn things you never knew you never knew

Have you ever heard the wolf cry to the blue corn moon
Or asked the grinning bobcat why he grinned?
Can you sing with all the voices of the mountain?
Can you paint with all the colors of the wind?
Can you paint with all the colors of the wind?

Come run the hidden pine trails of the forest
Come taste the sunsweet berries of the earth
Come roll in all the riches all around you
And for once, never wonder what they're worth

The rainstorm and the river are my brothers
The heron and the otter are my friends
And we are all connected to each other
In a circle, in a hoop that never ends

How high does the sycamore grow?
If you cut it down, then you'll never know

And you'll never hear the wolf cry to the blue corn moon
For whether we are white or copper-skinned
We need to sing with all the voices of the mountains
We need to paint with all the colors of the wind

You can own the earth and still
All you'll own is earth until
You can paint with all the colors of the wind

Rhymes for "wind" that Stephen noted as part of his
initial brainstorming for the song.

All Thing have life
Rain and wind and river
Mountain and rock and *hemlock* ~~tree~~
Sturgeon and deer and turkey

We are just a strand in the web of life
we must live in harmony and balance
Forget ~~Pain~~ and sickness + misfortune comes
As surely as the rain in The Moon of Blue Corn

The same force That breathed into the first man
Flows through all Things
All Things are kindred

Grandmother Moon

How can you buy The sky?
How can you own The rain + The wind?
(How can you put a price on The earth?)

The sap in the trees
Is our life blood too

From Stephen Schwartz's *Pocahontas* notebook.

"Colors of the Wind"

To begin writing the lyrics for "Colors of the Wind," Stephen Schwartz drew from notes he made while reading Native American literature. "In the song, I wanted Pocahontas to address the Eurocentrism of John Smith; so in essence, it's a consciousness-raising song." He wanted to use a style and language with a Native American flavor, including locution and imagery he came across in his research.

Among the materials from which he drew was a letter to Congress written by Chief Seattle (or that was attributed to Chief Seattle in later years). The letter includes the lines: "The wind that gave our grandfather his first breath also received his last sigh. The wind also gives our children the spirit of life. So if we sell our land, you must keep it apart and sacred, as a place where man can go to taste the wind that is sweetened by the meadow flowers."

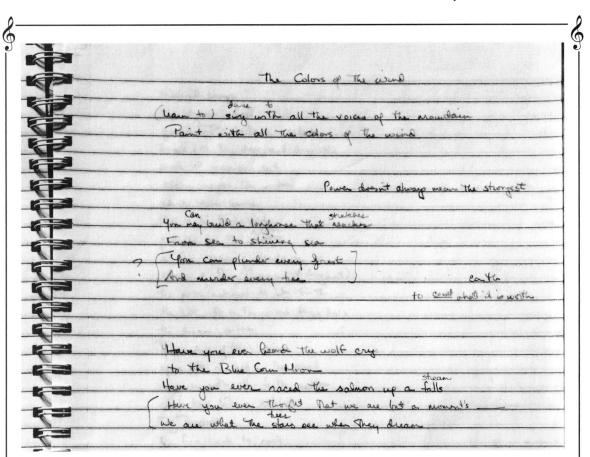

That helped inspire the title. Schwartz comments, "The title was something that popped into my head as I was exploring Native American poetry, and it had that metaphorical impossibility that can work as an image in a title. It's similar to a title like 'Corner of the Sky,' which is also a paradox. Paradoxes, I think, land in the ear and in the mind and make people think about what they're really saying."

He once explained to a fan where the "blue corn moon" line came from: "One of the phrases I came across, in a love poem, was: 'I will come to you in the moon of green corn.' (Some Native American tribes called their months 'moons' and named them according to something that happened seasonally, such as the arrival of green corn.) The phrase stuck in my head, but I didn't think the lyric 'have you ever heard the wolf cry to the green corn moon' really worked, because of the association of the moon and green cheese, plus the 'ee' sound in it, etc. So I changed it to blue corn moon, which I thought had a nice resonance, because of the phrase "blue moon" and the fact that there are things like blue corn tortillas, etc. Even though it's not authentic, and actually implies Southwestern tribes rather than the Northeastern Algonquians of *Pocahontas*, I used it in the lyric and it obviously served me very well."

The Hunchback of Notre Dame

About his interest in this project:
I write a lot about family relationships and twisted parental-child relationships, and the relationship between Frollo and Quasimodo, which was the thing that primarily interested me, contained those elements.

Stephen Schwartz

Whether or not adapting Victor Hugo's weighty French novel, *The Hunchback of Notre Dame,* was wise for Walt Disney Pictures, Schwartz and Menken were ready to step forward when the executives approached them for songwriting. This project would be much more of an artistic stretch than *Pocahontas* because they would need to combine adult-appropriate dark themes with child-oriented comic segments.

But it was not the songwriters' job to find an audience that suited the content. Rather, they needed to stir their creativity to write songs that would please the first audience, themselves, and then satisfy others working on the project. From the outset, Schwartz recognized that the film musical's core conflicts could trigger his artistry. In Victor Hugo's tale, villain Claude Frollo and the young man with a hunchback, Quasimodo, are thrown into a parent/child relationship fraught with issues—the kind of issues Schwartz enjoyed working with for *Children of Eden.* And he always liked dealing with fictional misfits. *The Hunchback* story, based in 15th-century Paris, had three: Quasimodo; Esmeralda—a gypsy girl; and Phoebus—a military man with principles who could not be jostled about by authority.

The story also gave his imagination a chance to dive into the delusions of villain Claude Frollo, his favorite part of the assignment puzzle. Could he articulate feelings that could both pass G-rating standards and reveal twisted innuendos? An adventure in lyric writing awaited him.

As this 34th Disney animated feature film took shape under Jeffrey Katzenberg, the songwriting duo thrust their full creative energies into the work. Over the next four years, as many as 600 artists, singers, actors, and others contributed to the making of this one film.

From A Dense Novel to 90-Minute Screenplay

By 1993, Disney writer Tad Murphy had outlined the film and developed a script draft that the songwriters received when they were invited into the project. Many of the storytelling decisions had been made.

Victor Hugo's novel, published in 1831, had been set in the late 1400s so that readers would remember a time when the cathedral was at the heart of society in medieval Paris. Hugo's aim was to inspire preservation efforts for the cathedral, hence the original title of the book, *Notre Dame de Paris.* He invented the central character of a deformed baby who was abandoned on the steps of the cathedral. Priest Claude Frollo raised the child who became the bell ringer.

Disney storytellers would, of course, simplify and condense the long novel. Troubled by the implications of a priest character as villain, their Frollo became The Minister of Justice. "There was a lot of discussion about whether Frollo was going to be the Minister of Justice or whether he was going to be the Archdeacon," Stephen Schwartz recalled about the development of the *Hunchback* film and subsequent versions. "It's frankly much better if he's the Archdeacon. If he's not the Archdeacon, what the hell's he doing in Notre Dame with this kid? You have to create a whole backstory to justify the relationship."

That backstory had to be covered near the film's opening. In the Disney version, Frollo is encouraged by the Archdeacon of Notre Dame to raise Quasimodo as his own, to atone for killing the baby's gypsy mother. For that, Schwartz and Menken would write "The Bells of Notre Dame."

Other story elements were altered from the original as well. Most significantly, Esmeralda lives at the end of the movie, whereas in Hugo's novel, she dies.

Schwartz and Menken made note of the likely song moments. One might be Quasimodo looking out from his belltower where

I read chapters and passages of Notre Dame de Paris *several times while working on the film. The song "Hellfire" is derived largely from a three- or four-page Frollo interior monologue, and much of "Out There," "Topsy Turvy," and "The Court of Miracles" came from repeated readings of the source material.*

STEPHEN SCHWARTZ

he was required to stay, longing to attend the Festival of Fools. The holiday celebration was another essential song spot. Somewhere in there, too, would be a song for a baritone or bass—a villain's ballad. And a song for the Court of Miracles scene seemed appropriate.

"Out There" on a Field Trip

As they began pondering the songs, Schwartz remembers his writing partner "fooling around" with a tune he thought might work for *Hunchback*. He drove over to the Menkens' and listened while Alan played a complete melody. "Alan had written a tune that he liked, which seemed appropriate for this project. The way the harmonies shift underneath it is very Saint-Saens, very French in feel. He played it for me and I loved it."

They already knew they would need to have Quasimodo sing in his tower while looking out over Paris. In the lyricist's mind, two words were a perfect fit for both the song's meaning and the rhythm provided by the first two notes of the chorus: "The chorus went plunk, plunk, da da da da da, and I said, 'Well, it's 'out there...' obviously, because this is a story about a guy who wants to go out there.'"

October of 1993 brought Schwartz into one of his favorite parts of the musical writing journey: the field trip. This time he flew to Paris with other members of the production team.

By special arrangement, he was able to enter the great cathedral of Notre Dame in the early hours before tourists arrived. For several days in a row, he arrived near dawn at the gothic stone structure beside the river Seine. Entering through the giant doorway, he headed for the bell tower and climbed up the seemingly endless winding staircase, then perched in the tower where he could look out over the city as Quasimodo might have done. In his chameleon-like fashion, he mentally slipped into the character. "By that point I had done a lot of research into what Paris would have looked like in 1482 and I would sit there and look out and imagine what Quasimodo might have seen, and how he might have felt about it, and I scribbled down ideas and phrases. While some people start writing lines of lyrics, I'm much more free-associative; I just write anything that comes into my head."

"Hellfire" and "Heaven's Light"

For *Hunchback* Schwartz directly applied his high school Latin studies. He brought in a Latin liturgy to be musicalized and sung by a chorus of villagers during the explosive finale and integrated several lines for Frollo to sing in "Hellfire." Schwartz comments, "It just seemed appropriate to use sections of the Latin liturgy to accompany this material. Frollo's slightly stilted and pretentious locution was just an extension for me of his character, and it was also influenced by the way the character spoke in the original novel (albeit I read it in translation)."

Another inspiration for "Hellfire" came from Italian opera composer Puccini. Conceptually (but not musically), Schwartz and Menken based the song on the end of the first act of *Tosca* in which the villain sings about his nefarious plans while a chorus of worshippers sings in church at the same time. "Hellfire" is set up in a similar way.

Schwartz was surprised that Disney did not object to the song's lyrics or ask for rewrites (although they reanimated Frollo's fantasy of Esmeralda in the sequence to make it a little tamer sexually). He comments, "I was (and remain) grateful to the Disney organization for allowing me so much creative freedom."

"Heaven's Light" emerged afterward. "We thought Quasimodo needed a moment to express his delusion or hope that Esmeralda might actually think of him in a romantic way." They planned to put it just before "Hellfire" and decided it should have "Heaven" in the title as a contrast.

My favorite character I have ever written is Frollo, who is probably the most despicable human being in anything I've done; I love him as a character. He was so totally self-justifying and in such denial of his own true motives. It was really fun to go to dark places in myself I would never let myself do in real life. It made me understand why actors love to play villains.

STEPHEN SCHWARTZ

"God Help The Outcasts" & "Someday"

Menken and Schwartz wrote Esmeralda's song "God Help the Outcasts" for her first entrance into Notre Dame when she is awed by the serenity and splendor of the place. Jeffrey Katzenberg suggested the songwriters try a more liftable song of inspiration, so they wrote "Someday" for the same spot in the movie. In Schwartz's words, Esmeralda "brings with her a bitter and acute awareness of the injustice of her situation and that of her people and the less fortunate of society. So the song is meant to be a sort of prayer for justice and fairness, for society to change its ways." Ultimately it was decided that "Someday" would be run over the end credits instead and "God Help the Outcasts" was returned.

Finding an Audience

The Hunchback of Notre Dame opened in America on June 21, 1996, and fared slightly less well at the box office than *Pocahontas*. Critics tended to welcome it. *Entertainment Weekly* writer Owen Glieberman wrote, "…the Alan Menken-Stephen Schwartz score, for all its showpiece numbers (where would a Hunchback musical be without singing gargoyles?), has been woven into the action as seamless recitative. *The Hunchback of Notre Dame* is a true folk-pop operetta."

Parents and kids were not all thrilled to have such adult themes covered in a "cartoon." One reviewer in Austin, Texas, wrote, "Some children are certain to be frightened by the dark machinations of the storyline (as some howling at the screening I attended seemed to bear out). The musical score by composer Alan Menken and lyricist Stephen Schwartz leaves little impression on the memory and is not likely to have the kids replaying the songs ad nauseum."

Schwartz later expressed, "Despite some tonal inconsistencies, it's my favorite of the three animated features I worked on. And I think it's Alan's finest score (so naturally it's the one he didn't win an Oscar for)."

But for adults who would accept animated drawings as an adult film medium, it was exciting. Fortunately in 1999, the team was able to pull a stage version together for Germany, which resulted in an additional recording of some of the songs on the soundtrack as well as new ones.

(As of this writing, plans for an American stage version are in the works.)

CREATIVITY NOTES

Finding the Song Moments in a Story

Question: What is it that makes some moments demand a song?

Stephen Schwartz: This is always a decision based on the instincts and experience of the songwriter(s). The classic response is the dictum ascribed to Oscar Hammerstein (I have no idea if he actually said it or not) that a character should sing when the emotion has become too high for ordinary speech. That's certainly one criterion, but I can think of several successful musical theatre songs to which it doesn't apply. Another consideration is that a song extends a given moment or beat and focuses on it more. Therefore, the choice of what is musicalized is an indication of what characters and ideas the writers think are important.

It's been said that a character in a musical doesn't really "land" until he or she sings, and I think that's true. And if there are important themes or ideas, they need to be sung about too. Lastly, there is the sense of the rhythm of the storytelling that leads one to feel, "We need some energy here," or, "We need to laugh here," or, "This is the point where we should find out what the show is really saying."

All these factors go into making the decision, which, as I say, is usually instinctive. When I worked on animated features for Disney and DreamWorks, I (or I and Alan Menken) would look at a board with the story outlined on individual notecards very early on in the process. And we would say something like, "I think this card should be turned into a song," or, "I think there should be a song between these two cards," or, "These two or three cards can be combined into a song." In other words, it has to do with a sense of the architecture of the whole show.

Stephen Schwartz enjoys the attractions of Egypt as part of his field trip with the DreamWorks team.

CHAPTER 15

MULAN AND THE PRINCE OF EGYPT

No life can escape being blown about
By the winds of change and chance,
And though you never know all the steps
You must learn to join the dance

THE PRINCE OF EGYPT

In June of 1994, travel-loving Stephen Schwartz arrived in Beijing on his first trip to China. As *Mulan*'s songwriter, it seemed as if Disney had offered him a fortune cookie with multiple fortunes: "You will cross the great waters," and "You will find happiness through your work." He'd been pleased to work at Disney under Jeffrey Katzenberg, and now, while finishing *The Hunchback of Notre Dame,* the company had expanded his role, assigning him both music and lyrics for *Mulan.*

His goal for the China tour was to notice everything that might make the folktale-based story seem grounded in authenticity. Traveling with a team of about a dozen moviemakers, Schwartz made notes that might serve his future lyrics while visual artists sketched images from the sights around them at the Forbidden City and other attractions.

He particularly enjoyed the last leg of the tour—a side trip to the Guilin region, a land studded with peaked green mountains often seen in Chinese landscape paintings. He would later tell friends, "It's *unbelievably* beautiful; maybe the most beautiful place on earth."

Before visiting Guilin, the group traveled to the Great Wall of China—a spot that would be featured in the film, and also toured several Chinese homes as well as temples with curving red roofs. In village shops, Schwartz collected tape recordings of traditional

Jeffrey Katzenberg is really, really smart about story. He is very gifted in that way.

STEPHEN SCHWARTZ

Chinese music—anything that might suggest a feeling or tune or rhythm. Standing in a market, he held up some little metal Chinese bells, ringing them to test their appeal. Convinced they could be used in a recording session, he purchased them.

During this trip, Schwartz became fascinated with the pentatonic (five-tone) musical scale used in the folk music of China. He planned to ignore the traditional eight-toned scale familiar to Western musicians and use the pentatonic scale for all his songs for *Mulan*.

Schwartz wrote two complete songs for *Mulan* before his fortune cookie crumbled.

Disney To DreamWorks

At Disney headquarters, nothing was running like a fairy tale. On April 3, 1994, company president Frank Wells had died in a helicopter crash while on a skiing holiday. In subsequent months, Katzenberg made an unsuccessful bid for the vacant post. Then, after a well-publicized feud with Michael Eisner, Katzenberg left the company. He had managed to convince Stephen Spielberg and music mogul David Geffen to form a new studio with him, DreamWorks SKG, a competitor for Disney.

Shortly thereafter, Schwartz received a call from Katzenberg inviting him to a meeting in Los Angeles about the first animated feature for DreamWorks. Schwartz signed on the dotted line for *The Prince of Egypt,* knowing that, from his side, there would be time to complete the limited number of songs needed for both this project and *Mulan*.

Soon enough the powers-that-be at Disney found out about Schwartz's second job. They objected to having their songwriter work for a competitor, especially when a bitter former Disney executive ran the rival company. Schwartz felt as if he had walked onto a minefield. "A battle was raging that I got caught in without wanting in any way to be involved." Disney gave him an ultimatum: Be exclusive or leave. No matter which way he looked at his own destiny, he realized an exclusive contract would not make his own dreams work. "When Disney said, 'You have to make a choice,' I said, 'This is nonsense. People work for different companies all the time.'"

Peter Schneider, then President of Feature Animation, came to a recording studio where Schwartz was working to have a talk with the independent-spirited writer. "He was very upset with me," Schwartz recalled later. Schneider suggested that if Schwartz wrote for DreamWorks, his name would be removed from the publicity for the two Disney movies he had already worked on. "I just said, 'Peter, I don't want to be exclusive to anyone. I have the contractual right to do this, and it doesn't threaten you. And besides, Jeffrey has told me that they are willing to wait to release *The Prince of Egypt* till a year after *Mulan* comes out, so they are not in competition with one another. I just don't see how this hurts Disney at all.'"

Since Schwartz wouldn't budge, he received a call from company CEO Michael Eisner. Eisner explained Disney's tradition of using artists who worked exclusively for the company. Schwartz pointed out that the very first sentence of his contract, which Eisner had countersigned, said he would work on a non-exclusive basis. Schwartz remembers the following exchange:

"Michael, why would I have had that sentence in there…if I didn't intend to act on it at some point if the opportunity presented itself?"

"I didn't really think you meant it," Eisner replied.

"Think about the opposite, Michael," Schwartz responded. "Think about me coming to you and saying, 'I'm not doing *Mulan* because I've taken this other project instead.' That would be reprehensible, and I won't do it to either project."

"Then we'll have to replace you on *Mulan*," Eisner decided.

"Well, I'll be very disappointed, but that's *your* decision, not *my* decision. *My* decision would be to do both of them." David Zippel and Matthew Wilder took over as songwriters for *Mulan* and Schwartz's work went unused.

"I don't regret my decision," Schwartz says in retrospect. "And after all, *The Prince of Egypt* was a very successful film and exciting to work on."

The Prince of Egypt

Recalling his entry into a DreamWorks project by way of a phone call from Jeffrey Katzenberg in November 1994, Schwartz says, "I was predisposed to take whatever assignment Jeffrey, Steven Spielberg, and David Geffen offered." Having a chance to work with Steven Spielberg appealed to him, as did working again with Katzenberg. Schwartz excitedly attended a meeting with the "triumvirate" at Spielberg's Amblin headquarters. But when they said, "We want you to do the songs for our first animated feature, *The Ten Commandments*," his heart sank. "I thought, 'I can't turn this opportunity down, but I really don't want to do *The Ten Commandments*.'"

He felt he'd done enough Bible-related musicals and didn't want to get tagged forever as just being a specialist in that genre. Disappointment must have shown on his face because Spielberg quickly said, "But we're not calling it *The Ten Commandments*, we're calling it *The Prince of Egypt*." They then discussed the project.

Schwartz soon realized the film would actually be a dramatic tale about a man who finds out his entire life was a lie and who has to reinvent himself. *That* angle appealed to him. "What was interesting to me was finding the personal, human story that we all can in some way relate to. It can be a metaphor, in some way, for all of our lives." So he signed on to write original songs.

Hans Zimmer would write the film score, often borrowing from Schwartz's themes to create a more integrated sound.

The Making of "Deliver Us"

Before any artwork existed or the storytelling team had looked at any details of the tale, Stephen Schwartz prepared the opening number, "Deliver Us."

"Almost as soon as I heard that we were doing *The Prince of Egypt*, I knew how to do the opening," Schwartz recalls. "It seemed to me so obvious that if this whole show was going to be about somebody changing his entire life in order to deliver these people from bondage, we had to feel what the bondage was like. It wasn't enough to say, 'Oh, well, they're in bondage.' We really had to experience it emotionally."

His memories from *The Ten Commandments* would now help him make creative decisions. In 1956, eight-year-old Steve Schwartz begged his parents to drive him to see the movie when it played on suburban Long Island. As he watched the film, one scene especially struck him and he remembered it many decades later.

In the scene, Hebrew slaves are engaged in building a city when a woman—Moses' mother, as it turns out—gets her garment caught between some stone blocks that are being moved. Egyptian guards stand by, heedless of her desperation. Just as she is in the greatest danger, Moses saves her. "It was the image of that single woman caught there and about to be crushed by these stones," Schwartz says, "and the fact that the Egyptians didn't care at all because 'it's just another Hebrew slave.'"

For the choral number "Deliver Us," Schwartz says he was trying to do something as compelling as that scene in *The Ten Commandments*.

The tone changes to a tender mood for the "River Lullaby" section of the number, in which Moses' mother, Yocheved, takes the baby to the river's edge and floats him in a basket. Schwartz tried to imagine what it would be like for a mother to send her helpless son into the unknown, hoping to save the infant's life.

Writing this part of the song with words in English didn't seem to create the right effect. "It started to feel like a musical as opposed to an emotional experience," Schwartz recalls. He needed another strategy and was instinctively drawn to the idea of having Yocheved sing in Hebrew instead. "I thought, 'Well, maybe it would be better not to quite understand what she's saying, but just to feel the emotion of it, sort of like seeing an opera in a foreign language.'"

So he called an Israeli friend, Sariel Beckenstein, who spoke Hebrew, and asked if he would write some lines in Hebrew for the mother to speak to baby Moses. Schwartz then musicalized them.

Recorded by popular Israeli singer Ofra Haza, the natural accent and perfect Hebrew create a genuine, heartfelt sound:

YAL-DI-HA-TOV, VEH HA-RACH (*My good and tender son*)
AL TI-RA VEH, AL TIF-CHAD (*Don't be frightened and don't be scared.*)

In the animated scene, we see inside the home where the mother is cradling her child and looking warily out the window at the Egyptian guards.

My son, I have nothing I can give
But this chance that you may live.
I pray we'll meet again
If He will deliver us.

Schwartz appended the main melodic theme of "River Lullaby" to the beginning of "Deliver Us," which became the opening for the film. "It was really important to come up with a melody that expressed the place and the time and emotion of the situation," he explains. "It's the very first melody you hear. I knew that I wanted to open the movie with this simple solo melody, probably solo trumpet because I love the sound of solo trumpet—it's very mournful."

When the film's newly hired directors heard the demo tape Schwartz made with his New York City singer friends, plans for the whole project were still in the formative stages. Co-director Steve Hickner remembers how the song was a "gift," providing a template for the whole film. "'Deliver Us' was the first song that Stephen played for us when we began *The Prince of Egypt,* and it really did set the tone for the movie. At the time we were uncertain as to how to best realize on screen the difficult themes of infanticide and slavery in animation. When we heard those haunting first notes of the Moses lullaby, we knew that the movie had moved from a cartoon into the truly epic world of a David Lean film [Lean directed sweeping movies like *Dr. Zhivago, Lawrence of Arabia,* and *Passage to India*]. Somehow that simple melody felt as memorable and timeless as 'Lara's Theme' [*Dr. Zhivago*] from the instant we heard it.

"His Hebrew slave chorus of 'Mud, sand, water,' etc., also helped to set the gritty, realistic tone of the movie, and it was beautifully tempered by the haunting melody of the lullaby. All in all, Stephen wrote a piece of music that proved that we could indeed create a movie from this material. Then, when Hans Zimmer arranged the song, the music was elevated even further and we knew we were off the blocks and onto a truly exciting project."

I like working with Stephen because he's just as crazy about his commas and his full stops as I am about mine, and his ideas are good; he always has a point of view.

HANS ZIMMER

A Field Trip to Egypt

On November 26, 1995, Schwartz, Katzenberg, Hickner, and about a dozen others headed for Egypt. In addition to the tourist attractions—remnants of the ancient civilization—they viewed (in Schwartz's words) "crummy little towns with the kind of ancient tenements where the Hebrews would have lived."

They spent two days exploring the ancient palaces and temples of Luxor and Karnak, the colossal figures in the Valley of the Kings and Queens, and even some newly opened tombs where the tawny reds, azures, and browns of wall paintings were still vibrant.

From Luxor they boarded a tourist sunboat for a trip up the Nile River. By nightfall, the boat docked near the temple of Kom Ombo, north of the Aswan Dam. Temple guardians granted them special permission to visit the temple at night when there were no tourists around.

At the time, Schwartz was contemplating a crucial musical number where Moses would wrestle with his awakening to his heritage.

Kom Ombo had no street lamps; the only illumination that night was moonlight and beams from flashlights carried by the art directors. "I could see the lights swirling around the columns," Schwartz recalls. "I pictured Moses holding a torch and going around and looking at all these things, having just learned that he wasn't actually a prince of Egypt." Floating in from his recent memory came images of disheveled dwellings, and in the juxtaposition, inspiration flashed. "I saw the contrast between that and this beautiful, cool, elegant, clean stone. And then the lights going around it, the lights of the art directors."

"I could hear the motion of the water, and this sort of Phillip Glass-like theme started in my head. I didn't have anything I could write it down on, so I went around singing this musical phrase to myself. I pretty well got a whole first verse there."

The moonlight, the temple, and the Nile had cast their magic to inspire "All I Ever Wanted."

> *Gleaming in the moonlight*
> *Cool and clean and all I've ever known*
> *All I ever wanted.*
> *Sweet perfumes of incense*
> *Graceful rooms of alabaster stone*
> *All I ever wanted...*

After traveling inland up the Nile to the Aswan Dam and Abu-Simbel, Schwartz and the others crossed into the Sinai Desert. There he collected images and ideas that later proved essential for future songs "Through Heaven's Eyes" and "When You Believe."

The trip ended with a few days back in Cairo. With their exotic wares, the open-air shops of the amber-toned marketplace lured the movie team to browse. As he had done in China for *Mulan*, Schwartz scouted for recordings of music that might inform his writing. Expecting to need historical folk music, he was surprised to find contemporary Arab pop music more useful. "Although they were meant to be pop, they used Arabic scales and chord patterns as well as vocal ululations all set to a techno-beat." This inspired him to "work within a specific scale that could summon up that sound."

"Playing with the Big Boys"

While *The Prince of Egypt* staff contacted hundreds of religious experts and scholars as part of their research for the film, Schwartz and Hans Zimmer huddled over the score and storyboards. At one point they took a break and flew to Las Vegas to see the famous act by illusionists Sigfried and Roy. As they watched pyrotechnic displays and wild tigers and all the glitz of a big magic spectacle, they wondered whether they could

We started doing very much the Disney model. Lots of jokes, you know, and some of our characters were awfully cute. We shed all of those things and went, 'We're just going to make a good movie...'

HANS ZIMMER

Hans Zimmer and
Stephen Schwartz

adapt the entertainers' style for a sequence in the middle of their film—a meeting between Moses and the Egyptian priests.

Back home, Schwartz wrote what he describes as "a broadly comic number, a sort of send-up of Las Vegas-style magicians, complete with a chorus of female acolytes. I know a lot about magic illusions from doing *The Magic Show*. I know that with those big illusions, essentially all the magician is doing is making gestures in front of them. And it's the way the box or whatever is constructed that creates the magic, so it's a lot about showmanship. And we decided that was what we were going to do with the Egyptian priests."

His aim was to "show how showmanship, pomp and pretension are often used as a distraction from lack of real content in a lot of areas, from religion to politics."

"Through Heaven's Eyes"

A section of the movie known as "the Midian sequence" became a matter of debate in story meetings between Stephen Schwartz and the directors, sometimes joined by Jeffrey Katzenberg and Stephen Spielberg. It needed a song or image montage that could compress about twenty years into four or five minutes, including almost the entire time Moses lived in the Midian desert in the Sinai after leaving behind his life as a prince. Co-director Brenda Chapman wanted to be sure to avoid duplicating what they had done in *The Lion King* during the song "Hakuna Matata," when Simba grows up: "In *The Lion King*, Simba literally grows from cub to full-grown lion in one swift dissolve. I didn't want just another cross-dissolve, age-quickly progression accompanied by a happy-go-lucky tune. It worked great for that movie, but we needed to say more about our Moses."

What would that "more" be? That was the songwriter's challenge. Schwartz made the first of four passes at the song with a number called "All in Your Attitude."' He comments: "It was basically about how to deal with being poor and that it's all in your attitude. It was a funny song (basically Jewish humor) but it was too lightweight for that sequence. We didn't really want it to be that funny."

One thing that did come from this draft was the line, "When all you've got is nothing, there's a lot to go around." Schwartz says, "Steven Spielberg loved that line and said, 'Whatever you do, make sure you can still have that in the final song!'" Naturally, that line appeared in all subsequent songs for that spot in the movie.

Then the thought was, since Moses had left what turned out to be a false home, the song could be about him finding his true home and fitting in with a new group of people. Schwartz went back and forth from piano to group meeting with two more drafts of the song along those lines. "I wrote a song called 'Don't Be a Stranger.' People didn't really like that too much—a little too cute, a little too complicated, and again it didn't really seem to be delivering the emotion that was needed for the sequence. Then I did a song called 'One of Us,' which had a really strong, hooky tune. We thought we had finally solved it. But Jeffrey felt that even though it seemed to be a successful song, we were on the wrong track. It needed to be about something larger."

It was Katzenberg's suggestion that the song be more about the philosophy of Jethro, the spiritual leader of the tribe. It should also reflect the change in Moses' way of thinking.

Schwartz says, "I realized then that I had actually been going in the wrong direction. In the rest of the film we were trying to take big events, famous iconic events, and bring them down to human scale—to say, 'If this really happened to somebody, how would he or she feel?' The opposite was true in this Midian sequence. We needed to take a human passage of time and give it a huge philosophical context. A man spends twenty years becoming part of a tribe, falling in love, taking a wife, et cetera. But these very human events needed a broader context. This was great to think about from a theoretical point of view, but of course I had no clue what to do. And you can imagine, having written three songs for this spot already, I was a little bit played out. I just said, 'I don't know what to do here.'"

Co-director Steve Hickner remembered an anonymous poem that might serve as a touchstone. It was called "Measure of a Man." Hickner says that when he handed Schwartz the poem, he could see the light click on. "What I did," Schwartz recalls, "was take the poem and translate the idea into 'Midianese.' I basically took the idea that the measure of a man is not what he owns or how much he's worth monetarily, but in how much he gives to other people. Then I translated it with images that were appropriate to that tribe—stones on top of a mountain, or water in the desert, or tending a sheep. All the imagery of the song is appropriate to the life of that tribe. So all the metaphors that they use are things that they know in life."

Humbly, Schwartz likes to give credit to Hickner for finding that poem and to Katzenberg for knowing what the feeling and philosophical size of the sequence had to be. "All I did with the song is take the idea contained in the poem and make it feel appropriate to the movie."

But Hickner gives Schwartz full credit for taking fairly simple ideas and connecting them to a larger vision that was more angled toward God. "Stephen's song reflects what would be authentic sentiments for the singer, Jethro, the high priest of Midian. 'Through Heaven's Eyes' is truly a Stephen Schwartz original."

"The Plagues"

By 1997, *The Prince of Egypt* filmmakers had reached the eleventh-hour moment both in the storyline of the film and in its production. Katzenberg was getting edgy about the budget and he wanted the project to wrap up quickly. Philip LaZebnik, who had been brought over from Disney after he finished *Mulan*'s screenplay, next completed the screenplay for *The Prince of Egypt*.

"Stephen had a lot of trouble with 'The Plagues,'" LaZebnik recalls. In the story, Moses is involved in cataclysmic events—the infamous ten plagues—that seem to be a last-ditch effort on the part of the cosmos to persuade Rameses to release the slaves. The moment called for a song but it wasn't working.

Says LaZebnik, "The song got pretty tedious and repetitive by the third or fourth plague. Then he came in one day all excited. He said he had it figured out, and the key was not to do the plagues chronologically, but to have the song be about the conflict between the two brothers. That was a real breakthrough. Suddenly everyone saw the light and said, 'Yes, this will work,' and things fell into place."

Hans Zimmer suggested using "All I Ever Wanted," which already had emotional resonance for one of the characters. Schwartz wrote a *Carmina Burana*-type chorus as a musical backdrop, and let the brothers sing a version of "All I Ever Wanted" over it in countermelody.

Jeffrey Katzenberg remained nervous. Schwartz jokes, "Jeffrey's contribution to this song was to say, 'We don't have a lot of time, and we're almost out of money, and we can't do a four-minute animation sequence. Whatever you do, you've got to do the plagues in two minutes and thirty seconds.' And I said, 'Okay, that's part of the assignment then—two minutes and thirty seconds.' We all laughed. But the final song is two minutes and thirty-seven seconds."

"When You Believe"

The original inspiration for "When You Believe" dawned in the Sinai desert, when the directors suggested a song celebrating the

I like thinking about the larger issues that are contained in shows like Children of Eden *and* The Prince of Egypt— *about the ethical and philosophical issues that concern me and others. I'm interested in the themes in those pieces.*

STEPHEN SCHWARTZ

Hebrew tribes' joy at their liberation. Hickner describes the moment: "'When You Believe' was hatched during that ride out to Mt. Moses [at St. Catherine's Monastery]. What we discussed was to try to create a signature song that would be both the anthem for the Hebrews as well as for the entire movie. We also discussed that it would be great if it could accomplish all that and end up being an anthem of sorts for DreamWorks as well, the way 'When You Wish Upon A Star' is for Disney."

Hickner acknowledges the success of Stephen's efforts. "It was an amazingly tall order and, incredibly, Stephen accomplished it! I think the song works so well and is so beloved because it not only stands out in the movie, it is a great song in itself."

Stephen describes the process: "In 'When You Believe,' one of the things I was looking for was how to make a transition from the mournful quality of the first half of the song into the triumphant feeling at the end. At a certain moment in the writing, I'd kind of run out of things to say in English that wouldn't feel hackneyed or sentimental. I'd said what I had to say, but I knew there needed to be this transition moment.

"So I began to think about the possibility of using Hebrew lyrics. I called one of the religious advisers on the project, Rabbi Robbins in Los Angeles, and asked him if he knew of any Hebrew poetry that might be appropriate. He suggested the 'Song of the Sea,' which the Hebrew tribes were supposed to have sung after they crossed over the Sea of Reeds. He thought it would be all right if I used some of the words for the beginning of the Exodus, and I selected the ones I thought were most appropriate for the situation, and then set them to music, trying to use a simple folklike melody. It was Hans' idea to begin the section with children's voices—yet another of his excellent contributions."

But the song needed to acknowledge the ambivalent and compassionate feelings that the Hebrews may have had at that moment. When Rameses tells Moses that his people have permission to leave, the Pharaoh's son, the boy Moses had considered a nephew, has just died and suffering has filled the land Moses once called home. Schwartz remembers saying to his colleagues, "You must show that this guy feels horrible about what happened. You can't just have him going out into the streets, whooping it up and celebrating." And so the animation scene shows Moses collapsing and weeping outside the palace. The same applied to the song, which couldn't begin with the Hebrews dancing for joy if the audience was to retain sympathy for them. "'When You Believe' is written to have a very slow build from a mournful quality to joy and triumph," Schwartz says.

Worldwide Release of *The Prince of Egypt*

In December 1998, four years after its inception, DreamWorks' audacious undertaking was simultaneously released to 6,000 screens around the world. The tremendous gamble paid off and the film drew in over $300 million worldwide. Many religious leaders applauded DreamWorks' effort, making statements like, "Hollywood got this one right." The DreamWorks founders had successfully launched their dream. The participants were rewarded for the gamble they had made. Brenda Chapman says, "Although I don't think the public was quite ready for dramatic animation, everyone who worked on *The Prince of Egypt* gained the respect of their peers for taking the risk and doing an excellent job in the process."

Schwartz was fifty years old when *The Prince of Egypt* was released. Reconciled at last to a life in show business, for better or worse, he planned to spend several more decades exploring new creative ventures. He was, in fact, readying for the next major plunge, which he'd actually dreamed up two years before on a boat ride in Hawaii.

Stephen Schwartz visits the Great Sphinx of Giza near modern-day Cairo.

CREATIVITY NOTES

Adventure and Risk

When *The Prince of Egypt* came out on DVD, it included a special feature in which Jeffrey Katzenberg praised the talented artists who joined his team for taking a risk. Schwartz later turned the credit back over to Katzenberg: "I think the risk was felt most keenly by Jeffrey, since he was literally putting his money where his mouth was in committing his new company to this huge undertaking. I didn't feel any more risk than I have with most of the other projects I have done, most of which have seemed a little loony to undertake."

Do creative people need to be risk takers? Schwartz doesn't think of himself that way. As his son, Scott, explains, "I think a risk taker is somebody who takes risks for the thrill of it, because they need the high. I wouldn't say my dad is a risk taker, although, God knows, artistically he has taken many risks over the years and continues to. I think of him more as bold and strong and confident about what he wants. A small example: On family vacations he'd always be very clear about what he wanted to do, and very organized. I do think he's adventurous. I don't know if that's a risk taker so much as someone who is always excited to try and learn new things."

Stephen also labels himself as adventurous rather than a risk taker. "I don't like staying in the same place. My joke about myself is that I have an extremely short attention span." If his attention span is a liability, his exploratory nature is a constant plus for his creative career. He loves to expand his horizons by traveling to out-of-the-way places he's never seen, from the Galapagos to Greece. And this fills his creative reservoir and helps keep his imagination from getting stuck within boundaries.

He remembers his friend Alan Menken advising him to stick with Disney. "He said, 'You found this niche and you should just stay in it,' and I was like, 'Well, I've done that already.' There's something to be said for Alan's situation: when you've found your niche, stay there and explore it and deepen it. But that's not inherent to my personality. I tend to ask, 'Okay, I did that, now what's new to do?'"

At sunrise, Stephen Schwartz and colleagues climbed up Jebel Musa, the peak traditionally known as Mount Sinai in the Sinai Peninsula.

Measure of a Man—An anonymous poem

Not—how did he die?
But—how did he live?
Not—what did he gain?
But—what did he give?

These are the merits
To measure the worth
Of a man as a man
Regardless of birth.

Not—what was his station?
But—had he a heart?
And how did he play
His God-given part?

Was he ever ready
With a word of good cheer,
To bring a smile,
To banish a tear?

Not—what was his church?
Nor—what was his creed?
But had he befriended
Those really in need?

Not—what did the sketch
In the newspaper say?
But—how many were sorry
When he passed away?

"Through Heaven's Eyes"

A single thread in a tapestry
Though its color brightly shine
Can never see its purpose
In the pattern of the grand design

And the stone that sits on the very top
Of the mountain's mighty face
Does it think it's more important
Than the stones that form the base?

So how can you see what your life is worth
Or where your value lies?
You can never see through the eyes of man
You must look at your life,
Look at your life through heaven's eyes

A lake of gold in the desert sand
Is less than a cool fresh spring-
And to one lost sheep, a shepherd boy
Is greater than the richest king.
If a man lose ev'rything he owns,
Has he truly lost his worth?
Or is it the beginning
Of a new and brighter birth?

So how do you measure the worth of a man
In wealth or strength or size?
In how much he gained or how much he gave?
The answer will come,
The answer will come to him who tries
To look at his life through heaven's eyes

And that's why we share all we have with you,
Though there's little to be found
When all you've got is nothing,
There's a lot to go around

No life can escape being blown about
By the winds of change and chance,
And though you never know all the steps,
You must learn to join the dance
You must learn to join the dance

So how do you judge what a man is worth?
By what he builds or buys?
You can never see with your eyes on earth
Look through heaven's eyes
Look at your life,
Look at your life,
Look at your life through heaven's eyes!

WICKED

Spoiler Alert.
This *Wicked* section of the book contains details about the plot of the musical that give away some of the surprises. It's best to see the musical first, and then read this afterward. The author assumes many readers will have already seen the show.
For more information, see www.defyinggravitythebook.com

Glinda (Kristin Chenoweth) rides her bubble in *Wicked*.

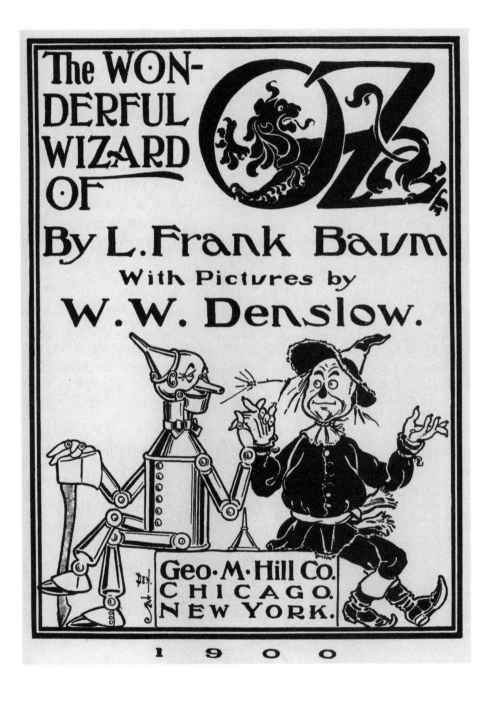

CHAPTER 16

LANDING IN OZ

Elphaba
It's time to trust my instincts
Close my eyes and leap!

At the start of 1996, Stephen Schwartz never imagined he would end the year envisioning his next Broadway musical, *Wicked*. Movie songwriting seemed to be his ideal calling, especially after one eventful evening in March. He donned his black tuxedo and white dress shirt, strode across the red carpet, and met up with his *Pocahontas* writing partner Alan Menken at Los Angeles' Dorothy Chandler Pavilion. For forty-eight-year-old Schwartz, being nominated for an Academy Award was a welcome twist on his childhood dream of writing musicals for the stage. With his kids at home watching the ceremony on television, and his parents and wife in the audience, he waited for the announcement.

"And the Oscar for Best Original Musical or Comedy Score goes to…" An expectant silence settled in the hall while presenter Quincy Jones opened the envelope.

"Alan Menken and Stephen Schwartz." Applause burst from every direction while the pair made their way to the stage. As Menken spoke about their *Pocahontas* songwriting, Schwartz clutched his golden statuette and grinned, soaking in the acknowledgment from Hollywood. That evening he and Menken also stepped up to accept the award for Best Original Song, "Colors of the Wind."

Back home in Connecticut, he placed his golden statuettes beside his Grammy gramophones in a trophy case converted

Backstage at the Academy Awards ceremony, Menken and Schwartz pose for photos.

from an aquarium that his kids no longer used. That summer, far from the pressures of show business, he swam in his pool, read, played with his little wirehaired terrier, Archie, dined and socialized with Carole, and basically enjoyed his life.

As his financial security had long since been assured, only his creative urges could compel him to agree to a new project. Perhaps a movie song request would come his way if his next project, *The Prince of Egypt*, did well. Why would he want to endure the Broadway scene again? Painful memories lingered from his difficult collaborative journey with *Pippin*, as well as the disappointment of commercially unsuccessful shows.

"I don't like conflict at all," says Schwartz, whose idealism had clashed with Broadway realities. "Shows are struggles. Every one of them is a struggle to get it right, but the sort of 'us against them' or the armed camp way of doing a show is not my game at all. I really don't enjoy it."

But he did love to travel. An upcoming excursion would change everything.

His new journey began that December. He was in Los Angeles finishing some work on *The Prince of Egypt* when his long-time buddy, songwriter John Bucchino, called him from the island of Maui in Hawaii. Folksinger Holly Near had hired Bucchino as a piano accompanist for her performances at a conference at the tropical getaway. Once on Maui, Bucchino decided it was too good not to share. His room included an extra bed, and he had a car and free food. "If you can cash in some frequent flyer miles and come for the weekend, you'll have a free vacation in Hawaii," Bucchino offered.

"I am *so* there," came Schwartz's answer from L.A., and by December 16th, he was.

When Bucchino and Near had a block of time away from the stage, they organized a snorkeling adventure with Schwartz and

Near's friend, Pat Hunt. A small boat sped them over to Molikini, a mostly submerged volcanic crater popular for its rainbow spread of sea creatures that delight snorkelers.

On the trip back, Holly casually mentioned to Stephen, "I'm reading this really interesting book called *Wicked,* by Gregory Maguire."

The novel's title sounded intriguing. "I think I've heard of it. What's it about?" he inquired.

"It's the Oz story from the Wicked Witch of the West's point of view." In an instant, Schwartz's imagination flashed through the implications of a backstory for *The Wizard of Oz* told from the perspective of the unpopular witch. It was the best concept for a musical he'd ever heard.

As soon as he returned to his L.A. apartment, he called his attorney in New York, inquiring about Maguire's 1995 novel *Wicked: The Life and Times of the Wicked Witch of the West.* "Okay, this book has been out for a while, so somebody has the rights. I need you to find out who has them. Meanwhile, I'm going to get the book and read it, because I think I want to do this."

From that first "Aha!" moment, visions for a stage musical adaptation of Maguire's *Wicked* swept into Schwartz's mind as readily as a dream. He loved the vision of a green witch-to-be becoming a social outcast when she is labeled as "wicked" in spite of her good intentions. He pictured a theatrical first act climax in which the green witch would fly. He heard ambitious choral numbers and the instrumental sounds of a sizable orchestra.

There was no way around it. This was a Broadway concept, not one for a film or a small-budget nonprofit theatre company. Although he had firmly decided, indeed pledged, never to work on Broadway again, his instincts didn't leave him a choice. He believed it was *his* story to tell.

There were things that I knew right away. I knew how it was going to begin, I knew how it was going to end, I knew who Elphaba was, and I knew why—on some strange level—this was autobiographical even though it was about a green girl in Oz.

STEPHEN SCHWARTZ

But with such a popular novel, surely someone in Hollywood was converting it to the silver screen. Schwartz would have to stop them, and somehow inspire the rights holders to consider instead the risky and time-consuming venture of producing a musical in New York City.

While his attorney, Nancy Rose, followed clues on the rights trail, *Wicked*'s prospective composer-lyricist read the novel and confirmed that his hunch had been right: musicalizing the Wicked Witch's story seemed "quintessentially an idea for me," meaningful enough to be worth the effort and potential struggle.

For one thing, he loved looking at traditional stories from a new angle. *Godspell* approached the New Testament in a fresh way, *Children of Eden* reworked Genesis for a new take on family life, and *The Prince of Egypt* explored the Exodus story from the standpoint of the brother relationship between Moses and Rameses. Now he was responding to Gregory Maguire's twist on *The Wizard of Oz.* "I recognized immediately that this was a genius idea and that it was an idea for me: the way it took a familiar subject and spun it," Schwartz recalls.

Wicked also held the attraction of its focus on "Elphaba," the quirky and misunderstood green girl who becomes the Wicked Witch of the West. Maguire named her after the author L. Frank Baum, who penned *The Wonderful Wizard of Oz*, when he pondered the sound of the initials "eL" "Fa" "Ba." Schwartz recognized in her an emotive power suited to filling a stage with song. "Elphaba is a very musical character with big emotions. She is fantastical. The world is fantastical. Glinda is very musical." He felt confident about musicalizing parts of the story.

Most importantly, Elphaba's story felt close to his own experience. He knew what it's like to be "green," and what inner resources are needed to carry on with life. "The idea of the story created a sympathetic resonance in me," Schwartz affirms, "and I know that I'm not alone. Anyone who is an artist in our society is going to identify with Elphaba. Anyone who is of an ethnic minority, who is black or Jewish or gay, or a woman feeling she grew up in a man's world, or anyone who grew up feeling a dissonance between who they are inside and the world around them, will identify with Elphaba. Since that's so many of us, I think there will be a lot of people who will."

Schwartz bought a spiral notebook in which he would catch all his story and lyric ideas—snatches of inspiration, research notes, lists of rhyming words, first drafts of lyric lines, and later drafts. On the black cover, the manufacturer's slogan, "Five Star–In a Class By Itself," hinted at what would become of the musical that began as penciled-in writing on the lined pages.

Schwartz knew that converting a 405-page novel into an enchanting evening at the theatre would take months, if not years, of planning. Maguire had created, as the author himself described it, "a dense, almost 19th century type novel that takes place over thirty-eight years and has thirty-eight speaking parts." Could any group of musical collaborators successfully distill and remix ingredients while still preserving the original flavor?

About adapting the novel *Wicked* to a musical:
It has so much plot; it's all over the place. It wasn't simply a matter of cutting. It was a matter of taking the basic idea and re-examining it—of letting go of some of the pieces and yet staying true to the essence.

STEPHEN SCHWARTZ

Alan Menken and
Stephen Schwartz accept
their Academy Awards for
the score of *Pocahontas*.

Stan and Sheila Schwartz hold their son's
Pocahontas Oscars.

The Fateful Moment: Stephen Schwartz and Holly Near discuss Gregory Maguire's novel *Wicked* on a boat ride in Hawaii.

Friends John Bucchino and Stephen Schwartz relax on a snorkeling trip off the coast of Maui.

No One Mourns the Wicked

No one mourns the wicked
No one weeps when they are gone
No one builds them statues in their name
The good man scorns the wicked

Goodness knows we know goodness
when we see it, don't we?

There are commandments we've been given

She broke ev'ry one // before she was done

How much more

Just how wicked could she can you get?

(Goodness knows we know what
goodness is)

When a good person dies, a survivors cries
with grief

Relief

No rose or laurel on their head

No
But instead

What adorns?

Only thorns

And when they're dead

No one mourns

The wick-ed

No one mourns the wicked.

right & wrong are simple, right?
we know it when we see it
Goodness knows we know what goodness is

Pages from Stephen Schwartz's *Wicked* notebook.

CHAPTER 17

STRUCTURING TWISTS AND TURNS

Tourists in the Emerald City
...Ev'ry way
That you look in this city
There's something exquisite
You'll want to visit
Before the day's through!

In the spring of 1997, emerald-skinned Elphaba held Stephen Schwartz's imagination, while around his backyard at home, nature's verdigris filled his visual field. Near his tennis court and in the woods at the edge of the grassy lawn, new leaves on oak, maple, hickory, and beech trees spread a jade awning. Ferns uncurled their fiddle-like heads, and moss around the base of the trees emerged from under the snow.

For the new musical, Schwartz needed fresh ideas for Elphaba's fictional life story. Maguire had intentionally left trails open, allowing readers to imagine possibilities. Schwartz, as dramatist and creative puzzle-solver, wanted to complete them. "Part of the fun of the show for me was explaining how everything we knew from *The Wizard of Oz* happened. There are hints of that in Gregory. But that certainly was not his focus." For example, Maguire established Elphaba's romantic relationship with Prince Fiyero, and then later played with the possibility that Fiyero could have become the Scarecrow. For the stage, Schwartz seized such suggestions and built them into the character arcs in his carefully structured plan.

Unable to take a field trip to Oz for his usual research phase of writing, Schwartz instead drove a few miles to his small-town

Like a froggy, ferny cabbage,
The baby is unnaturally
Green!

MIDWIFE AND FATHER
IN *WICKED*

library, where he pored through L. Frank Baum's series of *The Wizard of Oz* books. Making notes about the Wicked Witch's reputation, he recorded a question from Baum's text: "Which road leads to the Wicked Witch of the West?" and the answer: "There is no road, for no one ever wishes to go that way." No one, he thought, is saddened when the Wicked Witch melts. Soon a song title, "No One Mourns the Wicked," slipped into his mind.

Among his favorite brainteaser problems for the story was how to reverse-engineer the green witch's end-of-story situation in order to make the musical synchronize with *The Wizard of Oz* movie and novel. He believed *Wicked* could be in the family of shows like *Annie* and *Gypsy*. In both cases, the musicals begin earlier in the life of their title character (comic strip subject Little Orphan Annie for one, burlesque performer Gypsy Rose Lee for the other). Even though audiences know who Annie and Louise will become by the end of the show, they get involved in the way their story unfolds. Schwartz was fond of "the pleasurable jolt one gets when one finally sees Annie come down the stairs in her signature red dress and curly orange hair, or when you hear the announcer say, 'Wichita's one and only burlesque theatre presents Miss Gypsy Rose Lee'...I thought there could be a moment like that in *Wicked*."

The show could also be structured with additional theatrical jolts, "not just the creation of the Wicked Witch persona, but the Scarecrow, Tin Man, ruby slippers, flying monkeys—all the Oz icons. I felt the show had to deliver on *all* of that, and it would make it really fun."

This was part of his plan to heighten what he called the *Rosencrantz and Gildenstern Are Dead* quality of the show, referring to Tom Stoppard's play in which two very minor characters in Shakespeare's *Hamlet* are made the central characters, with the action of *Hamlet* playing just off-stage. In other words, at least for the latter part of *Wicked*, it might seem like the events of the movie *The Wizard of Oz* were all transpiring in the nearby environment off-stage.

Gathering his *Wicked* notes in September of 1998, Schwartz typed an outline describing details of scenes but without any dialogue or lyrics. This outline, Roman numerals and all, would be a starting point for discussion in meetings with unknown future collaborators. It didn't matter that the structure might change completely with their input; it had to make logical and artistic sense to him.

Choosing from the 38 speaking characters in Maguire's *Wicked*, Schwartz focused the musical by dropping, among others, Nanny, Ama Clutch, and Turtle Heart. He downsized the number of characters at Shiz University, the school where the future "good" and "wicked" witches would first meet, believing that this reduction would concentrate and thereby enhance the power of the plot. (He favored keeping the "Boq" character, partly because he liked the name.)

He included talking Animals, as featured throughout the novel (the talking kind are always labeled with a capital letter), represented especially by Dr. Dillamond, a talking Goat and biology professor at Shiz. The conflict between the Wizard's regime and Oz's talking Animals, Schwartz realized, served as a metaphor for earthly politics.

He also preserved the novel's clever concept of the blonde girl's name alteration, but made it more prominent. As an aside in Maguire's text, readers learn that Miss "Galinda" has changed her name to "Glinda" as a belated apology for her initial rudeness to her professor, Dr. Dillamond, who had pronounced it "Glinda." Schwartz imagined a flamboyant moment for the stage production, where she ceremoniously shortened her moniker in public. The scene would highlight her nature as an attention-loving socialite.

Inspired by his memory of the 1980 film *Resurrection*, Schwartz envisioned a different ending from the Witch's melting. Watching *Resurrection*, he had felt drawn to this story of a woman, played by Ellen Burstyn, who nearly dies in an auto accident and then comes back to life, heals herself, and begins to heal others. Burstyn's character dislikes notoriety and finds a way to "die" again, at which point the movie skips ahead, showing her continuing as a healer in a desert region in contented anonymity. At the end of *Wicked*, Elphaba could somehow fake her melting death and then hide away in a virtually uninhabited region where she would heal Animals.

Outlining took months. Future audiences of the show needed a compact and focused version of the story, and Schwartz treasures story clarity.

The 1998 Outline—First Scenes

In Schwartz's conception of *Wicked* on stage, the audience is immediately reminded of the Wicked Witch of the West's demise by melting. "Today is a joyous day for all Oz," a narrator declares, "because they are celebrating the death of the Witch."

Then the witch's story flashes back to her birth, with material condensed from the novel—about 100 pages equaling a few minutes on stage. It begins with her unhappily married mother, Melena, bidding farewell to her husband, Frex (whom Schwartz changed from a religious minister to the Governor of Munchkinland), as he departs on a trip. Melena allows a traveling salesman to seduce her with the aid of an elixir in a green bottle. Moments of stage time later, she becomes visibly pregnant and gives birth to a queer green baby girl while Frex, horrified, looks on.

I knew that it should start with everybody celebrating the death of the witch. And that everybody would be really happy because this villainess, this wicked person, the enemy, was finally dead.

Stephen Schwartz

Time shifts forward about eighteen years, when Elphaba leaves her homeland on a train to go to college. Next, the Shiz University section introduces some of the students, including Elphaba's handicapped younger sister, Nessarose (who is the future Wicked Witch of the East), Boq the Munchkin, and Winkie Prince Fiyero, as well as the Professor, Dr. Dillamond.

A scene involving a witch hat serves as a pivotal scene for Act I. Maguire had already concocted a special moment for the possible hat discovery. When their dorm room window blows open, Glinda ("Galinda" at this point) asks Elphaba to secure it with a luggage strap in her closet. Maguire wrote, "Elphaba found the strap, but in doing so the hat boxes tumbled down, and three colorful hats rolled out onto the cold floor. While Galinda scrambled up on a chair to organize the window shut again, Elphaba returned the hats to their boxes. 'Oh, try it on, try that one on,' said Galinda." Schwartz asked himself why couldn't that be *the* hat, the classic black witch hat?

For the musical, he has Glinda tricking her roomie into wearing the ugly pointy hat to an orientation dance at the beginning of the school year at Shiz. When Elphaba shows up, students laugh and make fun of her. Glinda's sense of guilt drives her to dance with Elphaba and they begin to accept each other, transforming their former enmity into friendship.

Act I continues, partially adopting the storyline from the first half of the novel. At the Act I climax, Elphaba realizes that the Wizard of Oz is worse than a fake—he has oppressed the Animals—and she turns against him. The Wizard calls in Madame Morrible, the former headmistress of Shiz, who has become his assistant. She tries to cast a spell on the rebelling young woman, but Elphaba grabs the book of spells (*The Grimmerie*) and flies off. (In Maguire's and Schwartz's versions of the story, Madame Morrible has sinister powers—a story element that would shift

Lyrics for Galinda, referring to a pointy black hat she offers to Elphaba:

*It's really, uh, sharp,
don't you think?
You know black
is this year's pink.*

as the show evolved.)

For the fifteen scenes of the musical outline for Act II, Schwartz greatly condensed the second half of the novel. Elphaba has gone underground. She and Fiyero get together, but the Wizard's men capture Fiyero and she escapes. The green heroine travels to the Governor's palace in Munchkinland, the Wizard's palace, Fiyero's castle at Kiamo Ko, and other locales, trying to right the wrongs of Oz, all the while being labeled as "wicked."

She also attempts a spell in an effort to save Fiyero. She later finds out that she did save him, but the spell turned him into the Scarecrow.

In the end, Dorothy throws a bucket of water on the Witch, appearing to melt her. She brings Elphaba's green bottle keepsake to the Wizard. The bottle falls from his hands as he realizes he has killed his own daughter, who was conceived when he first arrived in Oz.

The audience soon finds out that Elphaba has faked her death so that she can escape the Wizard's regime and live out her days in obscurity with the Animals. Scarecrow (Fiyero) finds his way to the Badlands, where he and Elphaba reunite and sing a reprise of a song that might be called, "As Long As You're Mine."

[See also: "Extras: Wicked *Outline by Stephen Schwartz," page 503, for the complete original version.]*

With Schwartz's plan, a musical of workable length was at least conceivable. What would ultimately work on stage was anyone's guess. He was quite prepared to discuss options with his future colleagues.

CREATIVITY NOTES

A Structuring and Compartmentalizing Mind

While Gregory Maguire's mind could allow stories and characters to slip in and out according to his instincts for long narrative, Schwartz sought to impose suitable divisions on the material—breaking the story into two acts, each with a limited number of stageable scenes. His skill in doing so related to his experience in segmenting time.

In his work and personal life, he can stay focused on one task with one group of people, and then completely drop it and move into the next activity. "I think of it as like an egg carton, as being able to keep the eggs separate in each compartment and not have them mush and run together. Sometimes I do that to a fault. I think I do that in my personal life too; everything is quite compartmentalized, but it works for me."

This way of thinking allowed him to pocket pieces of the prospective musical into their scenic compartments and move them to the most helpful spots along the story timeline.

As musical development evolves from ideas to carefully planned outlines, the egg carton metaphor shifts to architectural blueprints. Schwartz once explained to writers in a workshop: "Musicals, like films, are essentially about structure, and if you get the structure right, then a multitude of sins can be forgiven. But if it's wrong, the individual brilliance of the writing is hard-pressed to deliver anything. It's kind of like building a house. Once that basic frame is there, if it's solid and it's going to stand up, then you can add a window or take out a wall or whatever; but if you're decorating a room and meanwhile the house is falling down, then you're in trouble. So it's best to take a lot of time to test the structure."

Not only does he believe in structuring, but also his songwriting mind works in organized patterns—so many carefully matched musical measures, so many rhymes that fit together. His creative process includes inspiration and flow—but it's just as much about ordering pieces of the artistic puzzle.

Marc Platt

Stephen Schwartz and author Gregory Maguire consider the appropriateness of staging a musical based on Maguire's novel.

CHAPTER 18
ON THE RIGHT TRACK

Elphaba
Some things I cannot change
But till I try, I'll never know

In their phone call from opposite coasts, Nancy Rose exchanged greetings with Marc Platt, who was then president of production for Universal Pictures. His and Demi Moore's company were to partner in developing a movie of *Wicked*. "This is where luck took over," Schwartz later recounted. "It turned out that, unlike most motion picture producers, Marc had a love for the theatre, liked musicals, and had been in a production of *Godspell* in college."

It was also lucky that the early versions of the screenplay fell short of Platt's expectations. When Nancy Rose explained what her client wanted, both the timing and the idea were perfect. "The moment she said it," Platt reveals, "I thought, 'That's what's missing from the development process—music!' It's Oz and it's a fantasy world. It felt like it lends itself to music, and so once Nancy said it, it clicked in my mind immediately that it was a wonderful idea."

That didn't mean that he was ready to reverse several years of work and commit to Stephen Schwartz's association with a new stage musical. They had to be able to work together to transform a relatively dark and complicated novel into the kind of elevating evening at the theatre that audiences expected when buying tickets for a pricey Broadway musical.

Schwartz flew to L.A. for a meeting on November 13, 1998.

"Look, here's why I don't think it will work as a movie," he told Platt in his office at Universal Studios. The forty-year-old movie

You're letting yourself in for an enormous amount of grief if you don't get rights in advance. Horror tales abound.

STEPHEN SCHWARTZ
OFFERING ADVICE TO
AN ASPIRING WRITER

executive had trained as a lawyer. Along the way, he'd acquired the critical judgment necessary to keep hundreds of movies-in-progress on track when he served as president of production at Orion, TriStar and finally Universal Studios, guiding such films as *Dances With Wolves*, *Philadelphia*, and *Sleepless in Seattle*. Perhaps his limited experience producing an off-Broadway musical many years earlier would make a Broadway venture seem more comfortable. In his calm manner, he welcomed the famed composer-lyricist who was nine years his senior, and listened to his persuasive perspective on Maguire's *Wicked*.

"First of all, it's an internal story," Schwartz continued. "There's too much about Elphaba's motives that are internal, so how are you going to express those? You either do a soliloquy or have a voice-over. You can't rely on close-ups to get the subtleties across, and that's exactly what songs do. Number two: audiences won't accept characters in a movie that don't look like the characters in *The Wizard of Oz*, but the abstractness of theatre mitigates that!"

Platt appreciated the composer's reasoning and his passion for the *Wicked* story. "I was thrilled to work with Stephen and trusted him from the first instant that we met," the producer asserted later. "As a teenager, his music influenced me a great deal."

The movie producer agreed to pursue an option for a stage musical project with Stephen Schwartz's name attached, even before a single song had been written. "I was all for it, right from the get-go," Platt affirms, "and it really was just a question of convincing Gregory Maguire and negotiating with him to change directions."

From the outset, both Platt and Schwartz identified themselves as project leaders. Fathers in real life, they each expected to father the musical, metaphorically speaking, taking significant responsibility in the growth of their child. Platt, as lead producer, would be in charge of securing financial backing and the success of the venture as a whole. Schwartz, as the only core team member with extensive experience on a big Broadway musical, would assert his seasoned perspectives, instinctively protecting his new offspring when it strayed too far off the path he believed was right for it. Their mutual interest in the welfare of their new creation was a setup for progress as well as potential conflict down the road.

In any case, the book's author had to agree to let his novel be musicalized. Schwartz remembers his concern about countering a typical author's dream come true. "He had already sold his book to the movies and was waiting to have a great big motion picture made from it." Would he be flexible enough to approve a live Broadway musical instead?

Gregory Maguire

It was a gentle and friendly voice Stephen Schwartz heard at the other end of the phone line. Maguire was staying in Connecticut on a farm belonging to the family of his partner, Andy Newman. He agreed that if Schwartz drove out to the farm, they could confer about *Wicked* as a possible stage musical.

After the call, Maguire described the arrangement to Newman, saying, "We're going to go for a walk and then we'll come back and pick you up to join us for lunch. On the basis of which of the two restaurants I propose—the pizza parlor or the more upscale establishment—you can tell if I think the meeting went well and I am feeling positive about the prospects."

When Schwartz arrived a few days before Thanksgiving, the two creative artists went for a walk in a wooded area around a reservoir. "I don't know how much you know about the Broadway theatre," Schwartz began. Maguire feigned ignorance.

"I know you have a following as a writer," Schwartz continued, "and *Wicked* has its own following. I would like to talk about why

The wonderful thing about music is that it has no filter for people. Music seeps into you somehow. And Stephen's music, however you want to label it, is music that people love. It is emotional music and it wears its emotion on its sleeve.

MARC PLATT

I think it should be a musical rather than a film." He made his pitch about why Elphaba's story should be sung.

The author didn't reveal how much of a fan he was of Schwartz's work. In fact, he had taught himself to play the piano from the scores for *Pippin* and *Godspell*.

Even so, he knew a lighthearted show wouldn't do justice to his novel, so he raised his concern for preserving some of the tone and larger perspectives of the text. As they walked, he listened to the songwriter's approach. "Stephen saw the comic and the melodramatic possibilities in my sprawling slice-of-Oz-history novel," Maguire acknowledged later, "and he promised that however the plot evolved to suit the stage, the grim themes of the novel would inform the show."

When they returned to the house, Maguire selected the better restaurant for their lunch. "I was not hard persuaded," says Maguire. "I was pretty convinced even before he showed up that I knew his line of argument and I was going to buy it."

Before the *Wicked* project got very far, Schwartz heard that Platt had left his post at Universal Pictures. His heart sank. Would his lawyer have to negotiate for the rights all over again? Soon, though, he learned that in forming Marc Platt Productions as an independent company, Platt took the project with him, wishing to continue as producer of the live stage show.

Schwartz's own transition into songwriting for *Wicked* would have to wait. "I never write songs for a show before there is at least a very detailed outline," he reveals. And that would depend on finishing rights arrangements, finding a book-writing collaborator to work with, and writing up a version of an outline to present to him or her as a jumping-off point.

In this case, a "her" seemed ideal. "I felt because the main characters are women, and so much of it has to do with their coming of age as women, that it would probably be good if I could find a woman writer."

A Female Writing Partner

Stephen Schwartz agreed to join *Pocahontas'* producer Jim Pentecost in Disney's dining room for lunch one day to discuss an idea that Pentecost had for a new feature film. The producer also wanted Schwartz to meet a popular TV writer named Winnie Holzman to encourage the two of them to work together on his project.

When he arrived, Schwartz greeted the dark-haired woman whose ready smile would soon become familiar to him. He had admired her *Birds of Paradise*, a musical for which she wrote lyrics and co-wrote the book as part of her training at New York University's prestigious Tisch Musical Theatre Writing program. And he was a fan of *My So-Called Life*, an Emmy-nominated television series about a young girl coming of age, which Holzman created.

As they conversed over the meal, both writers realized Pentecost's proposed venture was not their cup of tea, but they discovered their common fascination with *Wicked*. When the novel came out, Holzman had looked into optioning it for a screenplay, but gave up when she learned the rights were already taken.

As with many of his decisions, Schwartz allowed luck and serendipity to play their roles—between his affection for Holzman's work and her appearance in his life at that moment, she seemed a perfect fit. They exchanged contact information and left the meeting not knowing what might transpire.

One factor could have blocked any future agreement: Schwartz planned to write both music and lyrics, while Holzman was accustomed to writing song lyrics in addition to the libretto for her

I was so intrigued by the basic premise of the novel — taking this extreme figure of iconic wickedness and making her the heroine.

Winnie Holzman

V.PAUL.SMITH.JR

Paul Dooley and Winnie
Holzman. Schwartz chose
Winnie Holzman as book-
writer for *Wicked* and says,
"Winnie is particularly good
at writing female characters
who are funny, real and believable, and that seemed to
me to be particularly apt for
a show like *Wicked*."

stage scripts. But he'd cross that bridge if he came to it.

Another issue could be any complications from working with a writing partner who lived 3,000 miles away; Winnie had settled in Los Angeles when she married actor Paul Dooley and established a television career. Yet by 1999, when they would begin, collaborators could close distances by email as well as phone communication. Besides which, Stephen enjoyed coming to L.A. (especially during winter), and Winnie could stay in one of his guest rooms if she came out to Connecticut for a week of writing.

⌘

A few months later Schwartz telephoned Holzman with news.

"Guess what? I think I have the rights to do *Wicked*! So let's talk and see if we agree on things."

She recalls, "I was very surprised because neither of us thought it was possible to get these rights. It had been kind of a dream that couldn't be realized."

Right away Schwartz said, "I hope it's okay, but I have to tell you I want to write both music and lyrics. I don't know how you feel about just writing the book." Still stunned, she replied, "I'm honored."

Glinda (Kristin Chenoweth), Elphaba (Idina Menzel), and the citizens of Oz in the Emerald City.

JOAN MARCUS

Shiz University Headmistress, Madame Morrible, insists that Glinda and Elphaba be roommates. The photo is from the 2005 tour, with Carol Kane as Madame Morrible, Stephanie J. Block as Elphaba and Kendra Kassebaum as Glinda. *Wicked*'s creative team spent a year working out the storyline for the way these reluctant roommates become friends.

CHAPTER 19

STORY BY COMMITTEE

Elphaba
Dreams the way we planned 'em

Glinda
If we work in tandem…

Schwartz's new writing partner, Winnie Holzman, had reason to admire his gift for story structure. She didn't bring in a territorial "I'm the bookwriter" edge to their first discussion over Schwartz's outline. "Stephen had been thinking about the book for a long time," Holzman explains. "He had read it and read it, and he was coming in with a very strong vision of how to do the show. And then I kind of caught up to that."

By the time Schwartz, Holzman, and Platt were ready to meet regularly in the summer of 1999, Platt's operations had moved to a small office in a one-story brown bungalow on the back lot of Universal. As the planners sat in a quiet corner of the movie world, with celebrity photos from Platt's projects overlooking them, they edged their future show *Wicked* from initial treatment to a story breakdown for the libretto-to-be.

While the banter was cheery enough, the foundation-laying task proved intellectually difficult. Schwartz likens their structuring process to that of J.K. Rowling, who worked out the world for the *Harry Potter* novels for a year before she began writing.

One thing Schwartz had felt sure of was the starring role for the musical. "I saw it as Elphaba's story," he reveals. "It was going to be a show like *Funny Girl*: one central character and you follow his or her journey." For the time being, flighty blonde Glinda the Good remained in the secondary role as Maguire had conceived her.

Yet when Winnie Holzman pictured Glinda, Elphaba, and Fiyero moving through Oz, she realized that a love triangle involving the three of them would add drama. It was one of "the first big contributions that Winnie made," Schwartz remembers.

It wasn't a simple addition, but part of Holzman's process of working over the novel's complex collection of characters and subplots. Maguire's Fiyero was married to Sarima but had an affair with Elphaba. For the stage adaptation, the extramarital affair story gave way to a stronger alternative. Schwartz recalls, "Winnie felt it was very important that Elphaba do something wicked, so she really wanted Elphaba to commit adultery or the equivalent thereof. But we realized very early on that it would be…much stronger if Elphaba's betrayal was of somebody she actually knew and cared about, so Fiyero's wife went and Glinda came in instead as his pre-Elphaba love interest."

Another love triangle might serve as subplot: Nessarose would grasp for the affections of Boq, the Munchkin, who, in turn, would yearn for the dismissive Glinda. Schwartz and Platt applauded these contributions from their TV-writer colleague, who was now feeling her way into her first major stage musical outline.

Because all three teammates had worked in Hollywood, they naturally turned to the familiar storyboarding process to support their structuring efforts. Platt made notes on index cards when they first began, writing out each story "beat"—each tiny shift in plot or the emotional story—as a brief phrase. "We worked for a long time on, sort of, 'beating it out,'" Platt remembers.

Essentially, the story that I was interested in telling was the two girls; the relationship between the Wicked Witch of the West and the Good Witch.

MARC PLATT

At one point the writers attached white and blue 3"×5" cards to a simple white foam-core board about four feet wide by three feet tall. Using their homemade storyboard, they could rework their configurations as needed. White cards were for story moments, blue for songs, with a sentence or song title on each. One white card said, "Meet Morrible," referring to the manipulative headmistress of Shiz University, where the witches-in-training first meet. It is Madame Morrible who assigns the girls to be roommates, which led to the next song card. The blue card said, "Elphaba and Glinda don't like each other," holding a place for a song that had yet to be written. The card text described the action. "By doing musical numbers in a different color," Schwartz explains, "you see if there are too many white cards in a row. It really works." In later years, when the story structure became confused, they would return to the storyboard.

Stephen Schwartz works in the Manhattan apartment that serves as his studio and office.

The three planners had other projects that needed attention, so their *Wicked* sessions spread out over time; it took a full year to complete a detailed scene-by-scene outline with which they felt confident enough to begin actually writing the show. They usually met in Platt's office, although they also sometimes gathered in the backyard of Holzman's suburban Los Angeles home, or on the black sofa and chairs in Schwartz's studio/office space in an apartment he'd recently acquired in Midtown Manhattan.

In conversations by phone or in person, *Wicked*'s team spoke of the invisible inner storylines as much as their characters' visible actions. They viewed Elphaba's inner journey as involving a subconscious search for an accepting father figure, as well as acceptance by society—longings she relinquishes for the sake of a greater good. The future "Glinda the Good" craves the affection of her peers, Fiyero, and the Oz citizenry, and later realizes how much more she values true goodness over popularity. The musical writers hadn't yet conceived of how Fiyero would mature through time, but that would come up before their final draft.

They needed to carefully align story elements in Act I with events in Act II. "The way the show works is that the whole first act is a setup," Schwartz explains. He likens it to the effect created when you stand dominoes on edge in rows and then tip over the

Elphaba is a girl whose green skin has shaped her character, made her feel an outcast, made her long for acceptance. But her inborn integrity and empathy prevent her from betraying her conscience in order to achieve the acceptance she craves.

Stephen Schwartz

first one so it hits the next and they all tumble down sequentially. "The whole second act is about watching the dominoes fall." It was all part of reverse-engineering the details of the familiar Oz story. Not only did they have to set up the variable friendship between Elphaba and Glinda, but also future developments for Fiyero/Scarecrow, the Wicked Witch of the East, and so on.

The storyline for Elphaba's sister, Nessarose, added a special complication. In the novel, she is born without arms. For the stage version, the creative team decided to give her arms but confine her to a wheelchair. That allowed them to write a scene with the famous sparkling shoes—the ones that, in *The Wizard of Oz,* the Wicked Witch wants but Dorothy gets. In their stage adaptation of Maguire's book, Elphaba would cast a spell on the shoes to help her sister walk.

But nothing was simple. Some story dominoes would wind up in every incarnation of the show, while others fell out of the game. At least for now, major and minor storylines were carefully intertwined and ready to be tried in dialogue and song.

CREATIVITY NOTES

Paths of Least Resistance

Writers like Winnie Holzman and Stephen Schwartz agree that it's not always best to "begin at the beginning." Many experienced writers zoom into the center of a project based on whatever naturally draws their attention.

Winnie Holzman says, "I tried to just respond to what in the novel was leaping out at me. For me it was the two girls and just the fact that in amongst all the brilliant things Gregory Maguire did in the novel, he had made them roommates in college, which I think is really a stroke of genius." Holzman and Schwartz talked for hours about how much this meant to them and what the implications were. "So we felt that we really had to start from there, because that was what gripped us both emotionally, humorously, in every way, that was so right," Holzman remembers.

As for getting started on a score, Schwartz says: "I tend to follow the 'path of least resistance,' rather than try to write sequentially, like the advice to Alice in *Alice's Adventures in Wonderland*: 'Begin at the beginning and go on till you come to the end; then stop.' When starting the score for a show, I tend to start with the song that seems easiest to me, the one that comes most naturally. Often, it's trying to get at the emotional or philosophical center of the story—'Colors of the Wind' from *Pocahontas*, 'Out There' from *The Hunchback of Notre Dame*—but not always. It's most important just to open the door and step into the show somewhere." For individual songs, Schwartz almost always decides the title before anything else, because the title crystallizes what journey the piece is meant to take.

One of novelist Gregory Maguire's techniques for warming up his thoughts about writing in a fictional world is to use images of famous actors for his characters. His mental cast for *Wicked* included Melanie Griffith as Glinda, Angela Lansbury as Madame Morrible, singer k.d. lang as Elphaba, and Antonio Banderas as Fiyero.

Schwartz avoids this specific casting approach but uses a related strategy: "I picture what I think the characters look like."

These prolific, creative people have accustomed themselves to making their mental images more vivid in their mind's eye, and to heeding their emotional response to their material.

Norbert Leo Butz and Idina Menzel sing "As Long as You're Mine" in the Broadway production of *Wicked*.

CHAPTER 20

Somewhere Over the Keyboard

Wizomania Chorus
Who's the mage
Whose major itinerary
Is making all Oz merrier?

While sitting at the grand piano in his living room, or pacing the floor pondering lyrics, Stephen Schwartz turned his attention to song moments represented by blue cards on the storyboard. Following his habit of beginning with titles, his structural mind came up with a scheme: every song title would include the words "good," "bad," or something synonymous. He wrote down possibilities: "No One Mourns the Wicked," "Making Good," "Bad Situation," "For Goodness Sake," and others. He soon gave up the needlessly constricting plan, but the titles offered mental nooks in which song ideas could coalesce.

He soon abandoned another constricting goal—finding an other-worldly or Ozian musical palette. "The biggest musical challenge," Schwartz acknowledges, "was trying to come up with a coherent sound for the show that didn't sound as if it came from our world, but could believably be 'Ozian' (except for the Wizard's number, which I thought should sound very old-time American). I experimented with trying to invent a different scale or system of harmonization, but that just became wearisome to the ear very quickly and was pretty inaccessible. So then I just tried to write in my own style, but to avoid any of the pastiche-type numbers that I often use in my other scores."

He eventually drew from his broad repertoire of styles and musical inspirations, including Beethoven, Bernstein, Hindemith,

For both me and Winnie, the first draft is just murder. Once you get something down, it's easier. You can say, 'Okay, we can fix this, and this isn't working, and that song doesn't work.' Then you get more ideas.

Stephen Schwartz

Rachmaninoff, vaudeville soft-shoe, Asian folk music, The Weavers folk music, Sting, "bubblegum" pop, and musical theatre.

To unify the score, he would develop recurring musical motifs that elicit emotional responses, on the model of composer Jule Styne. "I remember being a kid," Schwartz comments, "and hearing the 'I Had a Dream' theme in *Gypsy*, which gets repeated over and over again, or 'Nicky Arnstein' in *Funny Girl*." He believes a composer can add "another layer of understanding of the emotion or complexity of the action" by repeating a motif in different songs, using it to mean something new emotionally. He'd been successful with this strategy for *Children of Eden*, and planned to approach *Wicked* in this way as well.

More specifically, he'd look for "leitmotifs"—themes associated with important characters and ideas, as utilized in Wagner's operas and in film scores. Just as the *Star Wars* score included special music for Luke, Leia, and Darth Vader, perhaps *Wicked*'s score could suggest aspects of Elphaba, Glinda, and others by way of leitmotifs.

Sometimes a character's words are belied by what motif is being used, or there's an illumination of the content of the scene because of the motific reference.

STEPHEN SCHWARTZ

Schwartz would associate several themes with Elphaba. One possible leitmotif had already turned up out of his "trunk" of unused music. After reading *Wicked* the novel, he sat at his piano penciling out song fragments, and remembered a 1971 pop melody that he had composed for a song about romantic partners stuck in a complicated, unsatisfying relationship. But while he never did anything with the song, he says, "I always liked this tune a lot." Then when thinking about a duet for Elphaba and Fiyero's romantic scene in Act II, he wrote new lyrics for this melody, changed the bridge, and thereby created "As Long As You're Mine," a love song set in a troubling time. "It starts out with them in danger and they know that they have very little time to share together." Played gently, the introductory chords that are repeated twice (C minor, A-flat, C minor 7th without the fifth, and B-flat—over C pedal tone throughout), establish the necessary mood.

When he set out to write a song for *Wicked*'s first scene, he discovered he had already written the opening chords: "When trying to find the theme for Elphaba, I played the 'As Long As You're Mine' opening in sort of Rachmaninoff style. I thought if I did it that way, it would sound like the Wicked Witch, like a giant shadow terrorizing you."

This was all part of his richly conceived approach: "It was clear that since *Wicked* was going to be about seeing the Wicked Witch of the West and the other characters with more complexity and less as black and white, we needed to start with an extremely black and white point of view—she's bad, she's dead—and then by the time we get to the celebration the second time, we have an entirely different perspective on what is happening and how we feel about her."

From a musical standpoint, he wanted the opening music to be oddly celebratory and dark at the same time. It would begin by introducing danger. "I thought the very first thing you heard needs to be 'Uh-oh, the villain is coming,'" Schwartz explains. "It's supposed to sound like horror movie music." Any closing reprise material would be similar, only possibly more plaintive, suggesting a changed reaction to the destruction of the witch.

In the mini-overture for the musical, he used the chords from "As Long As You're Mine" almost like a sudden thunderclap—evoking Rachmaninoff's "Prelude in C Sharp Minor." These came to represent the darker of two themes for the Wicked Witch of the West.

For the opening of the "Good News" section in "No One Mourns the Wicked," Schwartz wrote what he later described as Bernstein-like polychords (different tonalities in the treble and bass) to add a harsh, disturbing subtext to the celebration.

Then for the main melody (for "No one mourns the wicked/ no one weeps when they are gone..."), he turned from Western music to Eastern for a sound that would feel unfamiliar to the theatregoer's ear. Recalling his trip to China that preceded his initial work as the first songwriter for Disney's *Mulan*, what spontaneously came to mind was the pentatonic scale he'd chosen for his unused work for that project. In fact, when writing a song called "Written in Stone," he'd discovered a tune and chord change that he loved. "I was trying to summon up a different world of ancient China, adhering to the Chinese scale," he once said about it.

"Making Good" and the "Unlimited Theme"

As he continued to write, *Wicked*'s composer would discover additional elements of cohesion that would provide more of a continuous texture to the score (more "through-composed," in his terminology). One of these elements was Elphaba's second leitmotif—her "Unlimited Theme"—which he delighted in discovering while writing her first solo.

Ever since deciding that *Wicked* should be a stage musical, he'd imagined the future Wicked Witch of the West singing her heart out to reveal her motives and feelings. She'd express her wants in her musical number that would set up the audience's expectations for the show (forming the so-called "I Want" song). That's what Schwartz intended "Making Good" to accomplish.

He first wrote the "Unlimited Theme" for a musical bridge for this "I Want" song called "Making Good," and although he eventually replaced the song with "The Wizard and I," he always kept the segment in which Elphaba sings, "...Unlimited/ My future is unlimited...."

This theme would also filter into both the Act I and Act II end-ings. It occurred to him that he could borrow the first seven notes from "Over the Rainbow" to pay homage to *The Wizard of Oz* film songwriter Harold Arlen (using a different rhythm), so those be-came the theme's first notes.

"What I thought was amusing—and I wondered if people would get it, and of course people did—is that it's the first seven notes of 'Over the Rainbow.'" That means: "Un-li-mi-ted, my fu-ture…" corresponds to "Some-where o-ver the rain-bow." "The reason that that's a joke," he continues, "is because according to copyright law, when you get to the eighth note, people can say, 'Oh you stole our tune.' And of course obviously it's also dis-guised in that it's completely different rhythmically. And it's also harmonized completely differently over a different chord and so on, but still it's the first seven notes of 'Over the Rainbow'."

Besides the fun of the Arlen association, "Unlimited" served as a unifying theme. "I always knew that 'Unlimited' was going to be our 'I Had a Dream.' I wanted to have Elphaba say, at the very beginning, 'Unlimited. My future is unlimited," and at the end of the show say, 'I'm limited.'" Later, when he wrote "Defying Gravity," he used this theme as well.

On his next trip to L.A., Schwartz played these songs for Marc Platt. When he finished, he knew something about them was bothering his producer. Platt remembers wanting "additional colors," ideally something more production-oriented. Schwartz's recollection is that Platt edged gently through some "um, ah, I just wonder…" types of expressions and said, "I have a question for you."

"You want to know if anything in the show is ever going to be fun, right Marc?"

"Well, yeah."

"All right, I *promise* you that the next thing I write will be a fun song." It was that exchange that inspired the sparkly "One Short Day" production number about Elphaba and Glinda's few hours as tourists in the Emerald City.

As Schwartz later explained, he and Holzman developed the idea that when Elphaba and Glinda go to the Emerald City, it could be like two girl tourists going on a spree in Paris for the first time. As part of their whirlwind visit, they would attend a show, *Wizomania*, showing, Schwartz says, that Oz was "like Mussolini's Italy, where everything is in service of 'our great leader.' It also allowed me to poke fun musically at some old-fashioned Jule Styne musicals that I love by making the rhythm of 'Wizomania' recall 'Don't Rain on My Parade.'"

To complete the piece, he drew on his counterpoint skills to create a delightful collage such as he'd previously employed for *Godspell*'s "All For the Best." More than any other song in the score, "One Short Day" reflected the buoyant spirit of Arlen's *The Wizard of Oz* music, as well as the composer's own love for travel adventures. (It also contains a little musical joke in the orchestration: a reference to Arlen's "Optimistic Voices" ("You're out of the woods...").

CHAPTER 21
FIRST DRAFTS AND "ADJUSTIFICATIONS"

Glinda
And when someone needs a makeover,
I simply have to take over:
I know I know exactly what they need

On the West Coast, Winnie Holzman's imagination entered Oz. She worked on *Wicked* in the little office in her backyard and in the local Starbucks during spare moments while maintaining her role as a producer and writer for the television show *Once and Again*.

Holzman was accustomed to formatting character dialogue using screenwriting software, in this case Final Draft, but while her TV-scripts for *Once and Again* included names like "LILY" and "RICK" centered above dialogue (formatted in all capital letters), in her quirky new assignment she typed in the odd inventions of Gregory Maguire: "ELPHABA," "FIYERO," and "MADAME MORRIBLE."

She and Schwartz kept in touch by phone and email, working on countless adjustments to story and song. Easing the normal collaboration tensions, the two understood each other's turfs. "Winnie is a very good lyricist in her own right," Schwartz insists. "So she understands, for example, when a song is going to take over and often she will write things knowing that they are going to become musicalized."

As a working pair, she and Schwartz matched up well. "From the beginning there was just a 'click,'" she reveals. "It became clear that we had a natural affinity to collaborate." Like Schwartz, Holzman had grown up on Long Island at the same time, and they had a similar enough sensibility for artistic matters.

The first major contribution that Winnie made was the writing of the character of Glinda. She got her from the get-go, and it just leapt off the page.

STEPHEN SCHWARTZ

Winnie and I laugh every day. We find each other's sense of humor very funny. So the way we talk is to make each other laugh with the absurdity of putting on a show. There's a lot to laugh about.

STEPHEN SCHWARTZ

Humor helped them face the endless reworking required for this vast project. For an early draft, Holzman created a kind of "Oz Speak," mostly used by Glinda, in order to further separate the setting from our world. When Glinda describes something as confusing, she instead calls it "confusifying." When she needs to say, "He means no disrespect," it becomes "disrespectation," giving an additional bit of whimsy to her character. Soon Holzman was hearing Oz speak spoken back at her. When revisions had to be made, Schwartz would say with a wry smile, "Well, we'll have to make an 'adjustification.'"

Over time, Holzman came up with such words as "braverism," "discoverates," "disturberance," "festivating," "gratitution," "hideodious," "linguification," "moodified," and "rejoicify." Once Schwartz got the hang of what his colleague was doing, he added such Ozisms as "definish," "de-greenify," and "surreptitially" to the lyrics.

He was pleased that she also took familiar cliché phrases and altered them slightly, as when "thrilled to pieces" becomes "thrilled to shreds." "This is just one of the many ways in which Winnie is a brilliant writer," the songwriter says of his ideal teammate.

She reports a lot of joking around in story meetings. "Stephen definitely has a very funny sense of humor. There's plenty of playing. I think being creative together is a great feeling."

Getting Glinda: A "Popular" Collaboration

Holzman loved writing Glinda. She took clues for Glinda's youthful vanity from Maguire's novel. He wrote about her as a seventeen-year-old aboard the train to Shiz: "Galinda didn't see the verdant world through the glass of the carriage; she saw her own reflection instead. She had the nearsightedness of youth. She reasoned that because she was beautiful, she was significant, though what she signified, and to whom, was not clear to her yet."

Holzman breathed her in and rewrote her in quick strokes for the stage. Glinda (Galinda) expects Madame Morrible's attention as dorm rooms are assigned, so she introduces herself: "I am Galinda Upland. Of the *upper* Uplands." When she writes a letter home and reads it aloud, it begins: "Dearest darlingest Momsie and Popsical." When she corrects Dr. Dillamond over her name, she says in a testy way, "It's Ga-linda. With a 'Ga.'"

As the young blonde would-be witch began charming her self-deluded way off the page, Holzman suggested psychological issues just below the surface. As a writer, she liked to work on characters "who have problems, who behave badly, who have much to learn, who lie, who do things without knowing why." Her Glinda became such a character.

Schwartz knew the importance of showing off Glinda's superficial personality in song as an essential setup for all the transformations to follow. "I could not blow this," Schwartz remembers assessing. But he didn't yet have enough particulars for how Glinda might behave. He only knew that Elphaba wanted to be like her.

Schwartz's floor-pacing at home continued, as he struggled with a song concept for Glinda. One day Marc Platt and Winnie Holzman remembered a modern takeoff on Jane Austin's *Emma*, the 1995 teen flick *Clueless*. In it, a popular high school girl in Beverly Hills takes a "clueless" transfer student under her wing to help her win a boyfriend. During the movie, she gives her friend a new style with new makeup, hairdo, and clothes. Holzman had the idea that when Elphaba and Glinda become friends, Glinda would give her dowdy green roommate a makeover.

Schwartz seized the makeover session for a song moment. He loved the absurdity of having Glinda attempt to transform the future Wicked Witch of the West into somebody like her. He pulled out his notebook and started penciling in a list of what it takes

I wrote "Popular" for all of us who weren't the most popular in school. It's sort of my revenge!

Stephen Schwartz

to be popular, as per someone like Glinda. He based some of his ideas on a pretty girl he knew in high school who, of course, won a place on the cheerleading squad. "She was the most popular girl at school, and she went out with the captain of the football team. She was the homecoming queen, blond with a little perky nose—the whole thing."

Drawing from this list, he headed for the piano and created the sprightly number "Popular." It flowed pretty quickly. He sang the melody while playing "bubblegum" pop-music chords and rhythms (such as had been in vogue in songs in the late 1960s and again in the mid 1990s). From then on, the collaborators playfully labeled that scene the *Clueless* section of the script. For the rest of the scene, Holzman wrote dialogue that sounded right for teenage-girl dorm-room patter. (Like other writers, Holzman is a coffee-shop eavesdropper. There she collects real conversations that inspire her drama and television writing. She says, "I love to sit in public places and listen to people. And sometimes I do it too much and people look at you like there's something wrong with you.")

After they become friends, Elphaba (Idina Menzel) gets a makeover from her roommate Glinda (Kristin Chenoweth). This photo was taken in San Francisco in 2003 during *Wicked*'s pre-Broadway tryout.

JOAN MARCUS

CREATIVITY NOTES

The Delicate Question of Who's Right

Stephen Schwartz had a gut sense of rightness about "Popular" as a song for Glinda, especially when it sprang out so naturally. He rarely sends lyric drafts off to a producer without a demo, but this time he made an exception: "I was so pleased with this when I got it that I sent the lyric to Marc Platt. He hadn't heard the music. He called me and said, 'I'm not sure about that song 'Popular.'" Marc couldn't yet see how it would be appropriate.

Somewhat deflated, Schwartz thought for a moment. "Here's this very smart producer for whom I have an enormous amount of respect, and he reads this lyric and says, 'I don't think this is it.'" Checking his own conviction level about it, Schwartz decided to ask Platt to wait and see.

"You know what, Marc? You need to trust me on this. I think it's going to work." At the next workshop it became clear "Popular" was a winner.

Schwartz later reflected, "If someone says to you that a song isn't working, you think, well, maybe they're right. So when do you stand up and believe in yourself? When do you say, 'I don't care what you're saying, I know this is right'—when is it stubbornness or arrogance, and when is it [appropriate] conviction? It's a tricky thing."

In this case, Schwartz asked his song's evaluator to postpone a final judgment until the piece could be considered in context. The strategy worked well.

The songwriter's friend, John Bucchino, recalls other situations over the years where Stephen preferred to start again, based on a colleague's suggestion for a new approach. Says Bucchino, "That's the difference between someone who is just a bully and someone who is passionate and opinionated, but also willing to say, 'Oh, you know what, that's the better idea; I can let mine go.'"

As the only green girl at Shiz University, Elphaba Thropp (Stephanie J. Block) finds college life uncomfortable.

Block was the first actor to play Elphaba during *Wicked's* development, and later stepped into the role on tour and on Broadway. The photograph was taken during the tour.

CHAPTER 22
WE'RE OFF TO SEE A READING

Elphaba
So I'll be back for good someday

Elphaba and Glinda
To make my life and make my way,
But for today, we'll wander and enjoy

A big Broadway show calls for plenty of testing along the way. If budgets allow, a series of readings or workshops can provide essential feedback, as well as deadlines that both motivate and challenge the writing team. Schwartz says, there's no better way to "find out what's working and what isn't in the dramatic structure and storytelling." As *Wicked* morphed its way to final rehearsal, seven such readings were needed.

In the spring of 2000, the writers prepared a modest presentation for Universal's Stacey Snider and a few others. To play Fiyero, they recruited actor Raúl Esparza, and for Elphaba they brought in Stephanie J. Block (who would later tour in the role and play it on Broadway). A small room with a piano on the Universal Studios lot became the stage for the private performance.

Winnie Holzman was thrilled to be narrating the fledgling creation. Schwartz sang "No One Mourns the Wicked," Block performed "Making Good" and joined Esparza in singing "As Long As You're Mine." Together the "cast" debuted "One Short Day." Esparza remembers, "It was really wonderful to be part of that day and to get everybody excited about it. It's not so easy to know in Los Angeles when people are excited, but they seemed genuinely excited. And Marc Platt was very happy. I thought it was thrilling that Stephen Schwartz was coming back to Broadway with a big musical."

As we went through the story, we created one version of it, and then you get some distance and new ideas appear to you and solutions to problems that you didn't see before, and so the material morphs and evolves into what it ultimately becomes.

MARC PLATT

After this audition, *Wicked*'s writers received their first of many green lights. Schwartz flew back to the East Coast feeling confident about his pending return to the Great White Way. Winnie Holzman's partial draft was working well enough, and over the subsequent weeks she scurried through the rest of Act I so that Schwartz would have a context from which to create more songs.

Next up was a reading in Los Angeles of *Wicked*'s Act I, and that meant a serious deadline. "...I've just *got* to write; I'm in a lot of trouble here," Schwartz told his assistant in July as he made plans to take August as a "writer's hibernation"—a self-imposed sequestering when he would not answer email or socialize, but only work on the show. "We're supposed to do a reading of the first act of *Wicked* right after Labor Day," he explained. "That means I purportedly will have all the songs, which I don't now. The deadline is somewhat self-imposed, but the options clock is ticking."

Of course, perfection wasn't expected. During the upcoming and future table readings, a "pick-up cast" of local actors hired just for that reading would sit around a couple of large tables with the *Wicked* script in front of them and read it aloud. Even this minimal performance would let the producer and writers know if they actually had a viable musical in the making.

Before the appointed day for the makeshift reading, Schwartz and Holzman called around the Los Angeles area, recruiting talent. Winnie's husband Paul Dooley agreed to drive over to voice Dr. Dillamond. Stephanie J. Block was pleased to come back for Elphaba. With Marietta DiPrima as Glinda, David Burnham as Fiyero, Lenny Wolpe as the Wizard, Marian Mercer as Madame Morrible, and a few others, the parts were covered.

For the key role of *Wicked*'s first music director, accompanist, and vocal arranger, Schwartz invited Stephen Oremus. The composer had spotted the wavy-haired pianist when he music-directed Andrew Lippa's *The Wild Party*. Oremus was born the year *Godspell* opened (1971) and grew up playing *Godspell* and *Pippin* songs on the piano. He graduated from the film-scoring program at Berklee College of Music and had arranging skills that would prove useful later on. When the September reading cast assembled, Oremus, as *Wicked*'s newly hired music director, flew out to teach songs and then prepared to accompany singers on what he remembers as a "crappy little spinet piano."

When it was at last time for this first reading of Act I, the actors, writers, and about a dozen audience members headed down the steps to the basement level of the Coronet Theatre in West Hollywood, entering a tiny black box theatre. The writers had generated so much material that it took well over two hours to read and sing through the songs for what was supposed to be the first half of the show. As over-abundant as the material was, the room shimmered with their delight. Marc Platt remembers, "I myself was surprised at the power of it. From then on it became an expectation."

Wizardy Zeitgeist

One of the writers' goals for the reading was to assess the fore-knowledge an audience would bring to the show, and how that would affect their perception. What could they presume everyone would know in advance? Although their reading audience was not a cross-section of Broadway-goers, the writers were pleased to get a good hint for the future from this carefully selected group of theatre-going friends whose opinions they trusted.

Only a small percentage of viewers had read Maguire's book or any of Baum's original Oz series. Not surprisingly, audiences brought in memories of the ever-popular *The Wizard of Oz* movie with Judy Garland, and the "general zeitgeist knowledge"

(Schwartz's term) of Oz that is part of the cultural consciousness.

So Schwartz and Holzman had a new platform. "We decided that the movie was a 'documentary' of what really happened," Schwartz recalls, "and that everything that we did had to be explainable within that context." That meant that certain essentials became "facts" in Oz and nothing in the show could contradict them. In Ozian reality, for example, Glinda the Good comes and goes by bubble, Glinda and the Wicked Witch argue at the site of the fallen house, the Wicked Witch of the West covets ruby slippers, and when Dorothy throws water on her, she appears to melt.

(This decision would open them up to a range of complaints down the road. Critics who admired Maguire's dark novel faulted the musical for sidling up too closely to the upbeat movie. Others complained that the movie connection was not drawn carefully enough.)

Changes—A Friendship Story

Feedback from this first reading also helped the show evolve toward a more personal story of the friendship between the two witches of Oz—an updated, fantastical version of the venerable "buddy story." An acquaintance who attended said to the writers afterward, "When the two girls are on the stage together, it's golden. It's in the other places that you have problems." They agreed, as did their story-wise producer.

Platt's next motion picture, *Legally Blonde,* featured its own Glinda-like character and was set for release the following summer. In the *Wicked* story, he had latched onto a more-or-less balanced focus on Elphaba and Glinda. What interested Platt was "the idea that the one I thought was 'wicked' is really good, and the one that I thought was 'good' is kind of manipulative and not that good, and how they change each other."

In synch with his colleagues, Schwartz was ready to let the musical's emotional core evolve toward the intertwining journeys of the two witches-to-be, backing away even further from his original notion that the show was basically Elphaba's story.

To make the musical drama complete, the future Glinda the Good would need to become a better person through her friendship with the future Wicked Witch of the West. "Glinda's story is a character who's redeemed through experience," Schwartz realized.

Schwartz compares Glinda with superficial characters in movies who deepen over time, "…like the Harrison Ford role in *Star Wars*—the character who starts out as this kind of selfish jerk and winds up being the hero—or Humphrey Bogart in virtually every movie he ever made, from *Casablanca* to *Key Largo*. There's Bill Murray's character in *Groundhog Day*. These are obviously all quite different, but they are all stories of people being redeemed through experience."

He also believed that the Animal and the Nessarose/Boq subplots were necessary, even though they used too much stage time.

There was so much structuring left to do. Even so, it was time to consider who would descend in Glinda's bubble.

Kristin as Glinda

Schwartz easily imagined Kristin Chenoweth in the role of Glinda the Good. He'd seen her in various performances around New York, including her Tony Award®-winning turn as Sally in *You're A Good Man Charlie Brown*. He also knew Chenoweth was around Los Angeles at that time, taping a television series pilot, *Kristin*. So he phoned her about the reading for the show coming up the following winter.

I felt like I knew how to write Elphaba and Winnie knew how to write Glinda, so between the two of us, we kind of got there.

STEPHEN SCHWARTZ

"I've got this show, and there's a part that I kind of wrote with you in mind, and I can't imagine anyone else doing it," he said.

She said she was too tired to do it.

Schwartz said, "I'm going to send it to you anyway and you can read it."

When the script arrived, Chenoweth read it and loved it. Of course she could play Glinda, at least for a reading. She decided to take cues from the Glinda portrayal in the 1939 *The Wizard of Oz* film by actor Billie Burke, including the slightly over-the-top voice with its edge of pretentiousness. As she told a Playbill reporter, "I had to harken back to the voice a little—it's so right for the character. And it makes people laugh, because they immediately think of the character they've known and loved all these years."

By then the writers had mapped Glinda's character development. Chenoweth knew that beneath a cheery veneer is a more complex layer of personality. "She has issues," Chenoweth would frequently say in interviews, and that heightened the demands on the actress. She looked forward to the challenge.

Over time, as *Wicked*'s cast concocted their interpretations of their characters without any models, the writers began adjusting their material with the performers in mind. In a pre-Chenoweth period, Schwartz wrote Glinda's pieces for a Broadway belter or alto voice. When Kristin came into the show, she would sometimes come up to him in the workshops for readings and hint things like, "You know, I can sing high."

The songwriter remembers feeling in a quandary about it. "I didn't know what to do because I didn't know how you can come out and belt sometimes and then all of a sudden sing 'Glitter and be Gay.' And then one day I had a concept. I said to her, 'I think I have an idea of how to do this. I think when you are the Glinda that we all know, you are a soprano, but when you are just yourself, then you'll sing in spoken range.' I would never have conceived of doing soprano material for this character if it hadn't been for the fact that Kristin Chenoweth was cast. It really helps to know who you're writing for."

JOAN MARCUS

Kristin Chenoweth and the *Wicked* ensemble sing "Thank Goodness." The Congratulotions sign features one of Winnie Holzman's "Ozisms." The homage to *Evita* in Chenoweth's pose at the microphone was her idea.

CHAPTER 23

TURNING POINTS IN OZ

Fiyero
You've got me seeing through different eyes

Referring to their outline, *Wicked*'s bi-coastal writers settled into their separate workspaces to write Act II. Their goal, in terms of plot development, was to artfully topple the numerous dominoes they had set up in Act I. For example, love triangles introduced in Act I would test the evolving friendship between Elphaba and Glinda as well as Nessarose's moral behavior. Also, the Animal story that serves as a focal point of the conflict between Elphaba and the Wizard needed to pay off in terms of consequences for their relationship. Finally, the carefully devised setups for such Ozian icons as the Scarecrow, Tin Man, Cowardly Lion, and the ruby slippers would have to play out as satisfying surprises.

They didn't necessarily write the songs and scenes in the order in which they appear in the show, but over time, the whole tale came together.

"Thank Goodness"

In the fall of 2000, Universal Pictures had allowed the *Wicked* project to become public. Around that time, a website for Schwartz musical fans began sending out an email newsletter called *The Schwartz Scene*. Stephen Schwartz agreed to contribute an update for each issue, and these *Scenes* ended up becoming an archive of his activities for *Wicked*, as well as for other shows.

In his first update, he mentioned Gregory Maguire's "extremely clever idea of telling the story of the Wicked Witch of the West — how a little green Oz girl named Elphaba grew up to be the greatest villain in the land." Then he expressed what had captivated him: "This is a story about how appearances can be deceiving and how life is more nuanced and complex than we like to think it is."

Adaptation complexities remained challenging, even after several years of work. "There's a whole subplot in the book about talking Animals," Schwartz mentioned in a November interview. "Frankly, we tried to get rid of it because it's confusing, but so much of the story hinges on it there is nothing that can be done. That is the biggest thing for us to solve—figuring out how to do that subplot without bogging the whole show down."

Work on "Thank Goodness" for the Act II opening occupied the end of the year. Finally, late in December, Schwartz curled up at home to reflect on the challenges of the previous months. For *The Schwartz Scene* Issue 2, he showed readers the subtle play of puzzle-working required for an original musical.

"I am sitting here watching what looks as if it is going to be a record amount of snowfall white-out the sky and make a bleak but beautiful monochromatic wilderness of my yard. Since my house is warm enough and I have a fire going and enough food for a couple of days, this gives me a feeling of coziness. I have no choice but to do the work I have assigned myself on *Wicked*."

He explained how much he wanted each song in the intricate and complex musical to tell the exact right story. But that hadn't been easy to work out.

"...Act One ends with the transformation of the leading character into the Wicked Witch of the West we have come to know (and love), and Act Two opens some months later. We want to find out how her fame, or rather infamy, has spread throughout Oz.

"I spent several weeks compiling material for a chorus number in which various rumors and exaggerations about her would be exchanged. I had pages and pages of lyric ideas and musical sketches. Yet every time I tried to write the actual number, something stopped me. The tone felt wrong. It kept feeling as if I had suddenly slipped into the world of children's theatre, and it lacked the subtextual richness and satiric bite that we think we have found for the first act. Finally, after a long discussion with Winnie Holzman, we discovered that it was the wrong event for the number. There was no story context, and thus the number was telling us something we more or less already knew.

"We decided to have the people of Emerald City gathering, not simply to gossip about the Wicked Witch, but for a specific purpose—to watch celebrities arrive for the fabulous engagement party of Glinda, who has recently been named Good Witch of the North. Since we also know the character she is becoming engaged to and have feelings about him [i.e., Fiyero], it gives a strong forward push to the story. Within this context, the people can still worry about the Wicked Witch arriving to spoil the celebration, and they can gossip and exchange misinformation about her, but there is immediately a more sardonically comic tone to the scene. Once this discovery was made, I was able to write the number relatively quickly…." In this way, the second act opening number, "Thank Goodness," was born.

Also high on Schwartz's "To Do" list was Elphaba's turning-point song, during which she'd finally acknowledge her assigned "wicked" appellation.

Schwartz reasoned that when the famous tornado in *The Wizard of Oz* shows up, "Elphaba sees it as a metaphor for what she has brought down upon them all." His notion was that, "When everything was falling apart in her life, Elphaba would sing a song called 'Reap the Whirlwind.'"

The title "Reap the Whirlwind" came from his memory of a passage in the Torah, when people's sins were drawing natural disasters upon them. Says the verse: *They sow the wind and* reap the whirlwind." But when that title proved a dead end, he filled this spot in the show with "No Good Deed." In this song, Elphaba vents her building frustration and fury and latches onto the saying, "No good deed goes unpunished," one of Schwartz's favorite aphorisms. How often had he felt punished rather than rewarded for his efforts to create something good? And now Elphaba could express that for him.

As if writing an opera aria, in one measure his vocal line included a loud and long-held note diminuendoing into a note that's almost whispered. It was an effect he'd been fond of in

BELOW: A section of the incantation that opens "No Good Deed," Elphaba's second act "aria." Schwartz says the words of the spell "just sounded like a magical chant to me, and could also move quickly enough to convey urgency and desperation."

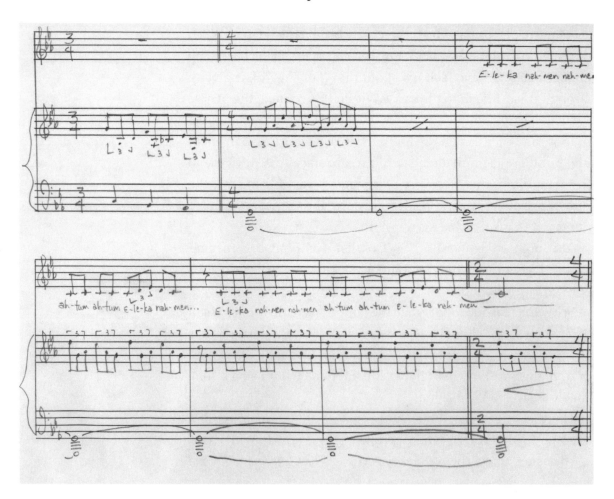

many operas he'd heard.

To find a musical texture for the accompaniment that was anxious and intense, Schwartz turned once again to the rhythmic drive in the work of composer and concert pianist Sergei Rachmaninoff, who often wrote fast-paced and complex concerto passages. A concert pianist Schwartz would never be, but he had developed enough skill to compose and play a piece like "No Good Deed," with its multiple sixteenth-note arpeggios. Then he cleverly spun out "March of the Witch Hunters" as a march variation on "No Good Deed."

CREATIVITY NOTES

Dramatic Anger and Creativity

Although few people are proud of their angry outbursts in real life, dramatists love characters that spout off. "I think anger is very theatrical," Schwartz suggests. *Wicked*'s "Defying Gravity," "No Good Deed," and "March of the Witch Hunters" join his list of powerful, angry songs like "Alas for You" from *Godspell*, "West End Avenue" from *The Magic Show*, "Rags" from the musical *Rags*, and "Lost in the Wilderness" from *Children of Eden*.

Schwartz says, "I think different writers write well out of different emotions. I find it difficult to write love songs. And I find it very difficult to write happy songs. Angry songs are very easy for me, and I think many of my best songs are essentially written out of the character's anger."

In such moments, when the emotion is so clear and direct, a character gets set up for a turn in the story, and audiences are prepared for something new to happen. For "No Good Deed," they would also witness a sensational stage event, with illuminated smoke swirling up around Elphaba as she waves her arms around to finesse the spell.

"I loved that song from day one," recalls original Elphaba, Idina Menzel. "It was such a motherf—ker for me to learn. It changes time signatures a lot, but I love it. That song to me, every emotion I feel fits exactly with what the notes and the words are saying. It all becomes one."

Finding "For Good"

Apprehensive about the first Los Angeles reading of the entire show coming up in 2001, Schwartz knew he could no longer put off writing a major song. He decided his work in 2000 had to yield a perfect duet for Glinda and Elphaba to sing at the end of the show. "It was daunting because that is *the* song," he shared in an interview. "That is the key to the show. And I knew before writing it that if that song was right, we had the show."

To research the song, he decided to talk with his daughter, Jessica. He was aware that Jessica and her best childhood friend Sarah Rushton had stayed in contact even though Sarah had moved to San Francisco. So daughter and dad got together in the living room in Connecticut. Stephen sat at one end of the couch with a notebook and pencil on his lap, ready to capture ideas. "What if you knew that you were never going to see Sarah again and you had one opportunity to tell her what she's meant to you?" Stephen inquired. "What would you say?"

As Jessica spoke about her friendship, Stephen scribbled, "People come into your life for a reason. They teach you things you need to learn. There are things you have to teach each other and maybe the purpose has been served…"

It wasn't long before she had given him most of what he would use for the first verse of the song—all based on a real-life experience of a deep friendship. Jessica imagined speaking to Sarah: "No matter what person I become, there will always be in me the girl you knew, and no matter who I become, I would never have been that without knowing you."

Her comments were not all sweetness and light. But with the idea she might *never* see Sarah again, she continued, "There are things I could apologize for, and there are ways to clear the air. But I'll just let them go. They don't seem to be important now. Thanks, but it really doesn't matter anymore."

I love phrases that mean more than one thing. Obviously, the phrase "for good" is a double entendre: It means both 'forever' and 'for good as opposed to bad.'

STEPHEN SCHWARTZ

Before Stephen could shape these heartfelt comments into a full song, adding metaphor, rhyme and Glinda/Elphaba interaction, he needed a title. He telephoned Winnie Holzman in LA, and they brainstormed about possibilities. Stephen was penciling notes while Winnie free-associated. Reflecting on the meaning of the moment, Winnie said, "You know, they've been in each other's lives, and they've basically changed each other for good."

The light went on in Stephen's awareness as he instantly recognized the perfection of that title—the power of the double meaning of that seemingly ordinary phrase. Trying to be polite, he said, "Okay, stop," and told her he was going to hang up. "I don't think she consciously understood the reverberations of that phrase, but as soon as you hear it, it's a gift from heaven," Schwartz later recalled. After a few days at the piano he called her back with the completed "For Good"— almost. Another family member had an essential contribution to make.

Back when he was working on *Pocahontas*, producer Mike Gabriel had suggested that footprints were a visual image symbolic of making impressions. Without too much thought, Stephen had written "like a footprint on my heart," in a line for Elphaba. Carole Schwartz, for whom Stephen first played the song, wasn't going to let that one pass.

"That's such an icky image," Carole frankly commented.

"Well, you know, like footprints on the sands of time," Stephen said to defend it.

"But footprint on my heart? It's just icky, it's like someone stepping on my heart," she insisted.

"All right, uh, handprint." And that was it.

The song would go on to become one of Stephen Schwartz's most frequently performed pieces. As one fan writes about the song: "It sums up everything that I feel for all of my family and friends."

With "For Good" I was looking to find the heart of the show, to really sum up in some way the emotional experience of these two women.

STEPHEN SCHWARTZ

"For Good"

GLINDA:
I've heard it said
That people come into our lives for a reason,
Bringing something we must learn
And we are led
To those who help us most to grow
If we let them
And we help them in return
Well, I don't know if I believe that's true
But I know I'm who I am today
Because I knew you...

Like a comet pulled from orbit
As it passes a sun
Like a stream that meets a boulder
Halfway through the wood
Who can say if I've been changed for the better?
But because I knew you
I have been changed for good.

ELPHABA:
It well may be
That we will never meet again in this lifetime
So let me say before we part
So much of me
Is made of what I learned from you
You'll be with me
Like a handprint on my heart
And now whatever way our stories end
I know you have re-written mine
By being my friend...

Like a ship blown from its mooring
By a wind off the sea
Like a seed dropped by a skybird
In a distant wood
Who can say if I've been changed for the better?
But because I knew you...

GLINDA:
Because I knew you...

BOTH:
I have been changed for good...

Megan Hilty and Caissie Levy

LYRICS BY STEPHEN SCHWARTZ. USED WITH PERMISSION

ELPHABA:
And just to clear the air
I ask forgiveness
For the things I've done you blame me for

GLINDA:
But then, I guess we know
There's blame to share

BOTH:
And none of it seems to matter anymore

GLINDA:
Like a comet pulled from orbit
As it passes a sun
Like a stream that meets a boulder
Half-way through the wood

ELPHABA:
Like a ship blown from its mooring
By a wind off the sea
Like a seed dropped by a bird
In the wood

BOTH:
Who can say if I've been changed for the better?
I do believe I have been changed for the better

GLINDA:
And because I knew you...

ELPHABA:
Because I knew you...

BOTH
Because I knew you...
I have been changed for good.

Sarah Rushton and Jessica Schwartz, whose friendship helped inspire "For Good."

Turning Points Somewhere in Time

Throughout the long evolution of *Wicked*, Schwartz and Holzman sought ways to bolster themselves and each other. Often puzzle pieces didn't fit right or the opening didn't completely gel with the closing or their storytelling for either Glinda or Elphaba outpaced or overshadowed the other.

To help keep on target, they made a little sign patterned after James Carville's concept during the 1992 presidential campaign; Carville, Clinton's campaign strategist, hung a sign in Bill Clinton's Little Rock campaign office that reputedly said, "It's the economy, stupid." His intent was to keep everybody focused on an important issue of the day that his political opponent had not adequately addressed. Schwartz reports: "Our sign, which we would show to each other when we felt the story was veering off course, simply read: 'It's the girls, stupid.'"

But what about the girls? When they made one stronger, it was hard not to make the other one weaker. Winnie wanted input from "…someone who hadn't been discussing every beat of it, who just came to it fresh, and had his own point of view."

So Winnie called her former mentor, playwright Arthur Laurents of *Gypsy* and *West Side Story* fame. By phone, Laurents told *Wicked*'s writers that their script lacked a clear direction. "Arthur felt that we had focus problems. He didn't know *who* the show was about," Schwartz recalls, "and he didn't know *what* the show was about. Winnie and I were incredibly depressed." They decided to meet with the seasoned pro to discuss script issues in person.

After riding the subway downtown to Christopher Street one night, Schwartz and Holzman walked along the narrow streets of Greenwich Village to his townhouse. Over dinner at a nearby restaurant, Laurents listened to Holzman reminisce about the mid 1980s. She and her classmates at New York University's musical theatre writing program had often gathered in Laurents' living room in the Village.

Holzman told him that she and Schwartz playfully labeled their *Wicked* project *The Way We Woz*, a spin on the title of Laurents' 1973 movie *The Way We Were*, because it had some similar elements. He got a kick out of that.

Winnie joked about a witch brawl in Act II in which Glinda and Elphaba lunge at each other after exchanging taunts over Fiyero.

"You know I stole that from you from *The Turning Point*," Holzman said, grinning at her former teacher. Laurents just laughed. She was glad to receive his implicit blessing for borrowing from the ballerina catfight in Laurents' 1977 Shirley MacLaine/Anne Bancroft film about competitive friendship.

As they ate, their conversation covered a variety of storytelling concerns. "It was about us getting ideas in his presence," says Holzman, "because the conversation that ensued from talking to him was very exciting, and it helped open our minds." Laurents wasn't really playing fix-it doctor, but rather sharing his perspective from a one-time reading of the script. "He had lots and lots of reservations," Schwartz later recalled, "and that was really helpful to us because it pinpointed stuff we had to do, and I think we addressed a lot of those issues."

Among Laurents' comments that Holzman and Schwartz took seriously was one regarding Fiyero's attitude toward Glinda in the opening scene of the second act. Even though he hasn't asked her to marry him, Glinda surprises Fiyero with an engagement party. Laurents suggested that instead of Fiyero appearing annoyed and angry, he is cavalier about the pending marriage, as if it didn't mean anything to him.

After that, Holzman added Fiyero's line, "And look, if it'll make you happy—of course I'll marry you." Glinda responds, "But—it'll make you happy too. Right?" Fiyero replies before he runs off, "Well, you know me—I'm always happy."

Audiences would empathize with how pained Glinda felt at that moment. There couldn't be anything more disorienting for her as she began collecting public adoration as "Glinda the Good."

Glinda the Good (Kristin Chenoweth) and Elphaba, who is now the Wicked Witch of the West (Idina Menzel), quarrel in Act II of *Wicked*. The photo was taken in San Francisco, and shows the original designs for Glinda's "bubble dress" and Elphaba's black dress. Designer Susan Hilferty says that she thought of the two female lead characters as iconic representations of the heavens and the earth. Glinda the Good's costumes reflected imagery of air and lightness, such as bubbles and stars (her tiara is made of glass stars). Elphaba's represented deep earth as in the color of coal and rock.

CHAPTER 24
IF WE ONLY HAD A TEAM

Wizard
Since once I had my own day in the sky
I say ev'ry one deserves a chance to fly...

In February of 2001, the first full draft of *Wicked* would receive a workshop and a reading at Universal Studios in Los Angeles. That month Schwartz's personal assistant, Michael Cole, flew to L.A. to help close down his boss' apartment there, now that the songwriter was shifting away from film work and back to Broadway. There was no time for regrets about leaving a somewhat glamorous recent past. On February 23rd, Cole watched his boss reworking lyrics for "As Long As You're Mine" up to the minute they had to leave to drive to Universal Studios for the reading. When they arrived, Schwartz took aside Stephanie J. Block, who was playing Elphaba, to teach her the new lyrics, partly to surprise Winnie Holzman.

The gathered crowd of about a hundred and fifty people sat in the audience while Kristin Chenoweth, Stephanie J. Block, and the other cast members sat at a long table on a raised platform at one end of the room. Scripts, scores, and bottles of water were the only props. Stephen Oremus provided accompaniment that day as he conducted from a baby grand piano in one corner of the studio space.

"The overture started and we were off to an Oz we've never seen before," Cole remembers. "There was a feeling in the air that we were witnessing musical theatre history. The amazing thing was that this was only the second time this script had been read publicly, and I was transported to Oz without one single costume, set piece, or magical illusion. At one point, I saw Winnie rush over to Stephen, full of surprise and delight at the new lyrics."

Schwartz was relieved to hear bursts of laughter and exuberant applause. "I was especially pleased to see how funny the show played, and yet how the audience could go from laughing one moment to becoming teary-eyed the next without the show feeling inconsistent in tone."

But he wasn't ready to sit back and soak in praise. Schwartz had invited some of his 'brain trust' friends—people in the business who could give feedback based on years of experience with dramatic storytelling. "What's really more helpful is knowing what you didn't like," he told record producer Bruce Kimmel, who tried praising him for the material presented in the reading. "What's different about Stephen than most of the creators of new works that I run into," Kimmel later commented, "is his absolute willingness and need for input. Not that he uses it all, but he thinks about it. And maybe even if he disagrees with the particulars it might lead him to a different solution."

Marc Platt and others also offered advice and the writers made additional improvements in time for a second reading on March 2nd before Universal executives. Schwartz recalls, "Most of the [musical] numbers seemed to work well, and I was able to do some reshaping and rewriting in the week between the two readings that helped the ones that needed it."

As a result of the March reading, Universal Studios head Stacey Snider and her cohorts agreed to fund the remaining series of readings to test the material.

Although it wasn't made public for another year, Chenoweth had clinched a new role for Broadway. When her TV show fell through, there was no question that she would be *Wicked*'s first Glinda. She later told a reporter, "I wish that I had more to sing, but I took it more for the journey that this character takes." Schwartz believed it was good for her career to play Glinda, even

About Kristin:
She's a comic genius, and she just makes me laugh.... A friend of mine called her "heaven in a ponytail."

NORBERT LEO BUTZ

though, at the time, *Wicked* was still more about the Wicked Witch, and hence Chenoweth would not be the primary star. "What's great" Schwartz observes, "is that Glinda evolves from the cliché of who you think this person is and also in a way from the cliché of the characters that Kristin has played in the past. Through the whole first act she is pretty much what you expect—a self-centered young woman who flaunts her attractiveness. And then suddenly in the second act she starts to grow as a person. And, I think to the audience's delight and surprise, she turns out to be, in some ways, the hero of the show."

The Glinda role would call upon Chenoweth's considerable dramatic skills, and ultimately her vocal prowess. It would turn out that Chenoweth was at least as good for the writers as the role would be for her, and her imprint on it would prove to be considerable.

David Stone

A fortunate bit of behind-the-scenes casting for *Wicked* involved a Broadway-savvy man in his mid thirties. David Stone had assisted Broadway producers Barry and Fran Weissler before starting to produce shows on his own, both on and off-Broadway. Like Marc Platt, he'd been a fan of *Pippin*. He played the role of Theo in summer camp as an adolescent, and in 1988 became friends with Stephen Schwartz after meeting him when a mutual friend directed music for an off-Broadway revival of *Godspell*.

Stone later met Marc Platt when Stone was producing a Broadway run of *The Diary of Anne Frank*. In the early days of *Wicked*'s development, Platt invited Stone to be his producing partner for the show as soon as they were ready to do a full reading.

Stone flew out from New York for the 2001 L.A. reading. "I went to the reading expecting to be charmed," he shared later.

David Stone

"What really stunned me was my emotional involvement in the show. By the time they sang 'For Good' at the end I was sobbing. I went back to Marc's office, where Marc, Winnie, and Stephen looked at me and said, 'Okay, now what?' I started talking about directors, designers, choreographers, and schedule." Stone created a budget, hired personnel, and set the production in motion.

Over the next several years, *Wicked* team members gained entry into the unique world of Broadway pre-production by pressing a little silver button outside the locked entrance to Stone Productions on 44th Street in Manhattan's theatre district. When the buzzer sounded, an employee on the 5th floor could unlock the glass door at street level, just west of where *The Producers* was playing, that opened onto a narrow hallway with an ancient elevator. Stone subsequently moved to more spacious quarters, but at the time his office was crowded with rows of desks for half a dozen employees.

A small conference room became the setting for many future agreements and arguments. Shelves stuffed with spiral binders filled one wall, organized by the names of musicals or plays indicated on the binder spines. A small window delivered a few rays of light for a lone plant.

A blond wood table took up most of the workroom space. As Stone and others hashed out details of the show's expensive requirements, the table would periodically fill with the elements for audience enchantment: scenic design sketches and models, drawings for dozens of handcrafted costumes, lighting notes, versions of scripts.

Finding a Director

Before any other decisions were made, *Wicked* needed a director whom everyone on the creative team could agree to hire. Platt's goal was to have *Wicked* open on Broadway in the spring of 2003, and that necessitated the immediate hiring of a director who could guide upcoming readings.

As the spring wore on, Schwartz became, in his words, "increasingly frustrated by how long it's taking to find a director." The Broadway veteran believed it was vital to find a seasoned pro for the job—"someone who has had experience doing a big musical like this, under the kinds of pressures that Broadway can generate."

Stone had a different idea. Since he had produced several shows directed by Joe Mantello (including *The Vagina Monologues*), he put forward the thirty-eight-year-old's name for helming *Wicked*. Although Mantello hadn't directed a musical piece other than the opera *Dead Man Walking*, he seemed suited. "Every now and then you see plays, and you think that the director could do musicals," Schwartz notes, referring to Mantello's impressively staged *Corpus Christi*. So the songwriter consented to having Mantello direct *Wicked*, and shortly thereafter Gregory Maguire did, too (as his contract gave him veto power over the decision).

The oldest son of Italian-American parents, the short, thin man with black hair had replanted himself years earlier from his hometown of Rockford, Illinois, to North Carolina School of the Arts, and then, in 1984, to New York City. He found work as an actor but realized he wanted to direct shows himself. "I like being the person who says, 'We're going north,' if I believe that north is the best way to go," he explains. Usually, he was not aggressive about his guidance. Naturally both ambitious and shy, he is often seen in photos with his hands in his pockets—a guy on the sidelines who is there to witness and evaluate before he speaks.

As *Wicked* meetings continued, Mantello's teammates expected him to be both more of a sergeant at some points and less dictatorial at others. "I hang back at first," Mantello reflects about his

Joe Mantello

practiced, gentle side. "I know it was unnerving at first for Marc and probably Stephen. I listen to what people are saying and I try to get the feel of what's going on. And I'm also trying to learn in life to be patient—a kind of patience that doesn't come naturally to me."

Schwartz was pleased when the newly hired director formed his vision and began to assert himself in his role. Then the inevitable tug of war started as he began reining in the writers' fanciful extremes with regard to production pragmatics and vision.

Schwartz and Holzman wanted a scene in the musical to parallel the crystal ball scene in the movie, but instead of Dorothy seeing Kansas, they imagined the ball revealing animals of our world via black and white film clips. Mantello intervened. If a real audience were shown clips in the crystal ball (which they actually tried during a rehearsal), only the first two rows of people would see them. Or if large clips were projected, then the whole feel would change. "Then all of a sudden you're getting into showing a movie," Joe complained. As he described later, "Then we're asking, 'are we showing real cows, or real goats? Because our goat [character] doesn't look like a real goat.' It begged so many questions; it was one step too many. And that was an example of a moment I thought, 'That's not our show.' We don't have that kind of visual vocabulary."

The writers understood, and found it easy enough to give up this time. Later, they disagreed as much as they would agree on story issues, and quibbled about casting. Authors of a show always get a vote on which actors will originate the roles, as do the director and the producers.

When Mantello came in, he really wanted to cast Elphaba right away, and the others went along with the idea. Stephanie J. Block had certainly been wonderful in the readings, but Mantello maintained that because of his own inexperience for doing a big Broadway musical, he needed an experienced leading lady, and Block had yet to debut on the Great White Way.

He pitched the idea of Tony Award®-winner Audra McDonald. She was well known but was either busy or unwilling to audition.

"You know what?" Schwartz said to Mantello. "I've never seen Audra do anything like this. I think she's a great talent, but I don't know if she can do this kind of role and I simply will not cast someone if she won't come in, if she doesn't care enough about this role." Holzman agreed.

After some time off in the summer, Schwartz invited his Los Angeles-based colleague to stay with him in Connecticut while they worked on script revisions. Auditions for the Elphaba role were scheduled to begin September 12th, which meant he and Holzman would drive or take the train into the city. On the morning of September 11, 2001, Stephen turned on the television and was "shocked beyond belief" by the tragedy of the World Trade Center destruction less than 50 miles away.

Holzman recalls, "I was up in his house writing and I think, in a weird way, we felt lucky; lucky that we had something we could turn to." The auditions that were to be held the next day were cancelled. A few days later, they received a call from the casting director who said he thought they should go ahead because people needed something to do.

Idina Menzel had been performing as Amneris in Elton John and Tim Rice's *Aida* at night when her agent found out about selective auditions for the Elphaba role. "All I knew was that it was a new musical," says Menzel about the audition appointment. "The story sounded intriguing, but most of all, it was going to be directed by Joe Mantello and have music by Stephen Schwartz, and I didn't care if it was the phone book, those were the kinds of people I wanted to be working with."

On September 20th, the decision-makers prepared to watch and listen to nine or ten nervous singers scheduled to perform for them. Holzman recalls, "The first person that walked in that day was Idina Menzel." Holzman's instincts took over. She told the others she had a feeling about that girl, that she was the one.

Idina Menzel had trained classically as a child, but when she began singing pop songs at weddings and bar mitzvahs near her Long Island home, she needed to sound *less* trained. She began working with vocal coach Tanya Travers, who trained her in a technique based on natural speaking style. So she had cultivated the pop-music voice that would work with contemporary theatre songs.

It didn't hurt that the prospective *Wicked* star was already popular as a result of her earlier work. In the original production of *Rent* (as well as later in the movie version), she played performance artist Maureen. When the show transferred to Broadway, Menzel was nominated for a Tony Award® as Best Supporting Actress. She later performed in Andrew Lippa's *The Wild Party* at the Manhattan Theatre Club.

I put on green lipstick and smoky black eye shadow and went to audition for the green girl.

IDINA MENZEL

For audition callbacks, the casting director arranged for Idina to have the music for "Defying Gravity," which she carefully prepared to sing. She remembers being asked to stay. "You always know it's going pretty well if they keep you for a little while and they work on other things with you. So they were like, would you mind going over to the piano and trying this song? I'd never heard 'I'm Not That Girl,' so I'm like 'Oh God, I'm going to be winging this song I don't even know.' And so that was the song that we did at the piano. And I had to sight-read it in front of all of them. Sort of, uh, terrifying."

Schwartz liked Menzel but was enthusiastic about Ana Gasteyer in the role as well. In the end, Menzel's contrast to Kristin made her best-suited as the original green girl. (Ana Gasteyer eventually played the role in the Chicago production of *Wicked*.) Schwartz explains, "Kristin is so precise and controlled and she has such amazing technique, and Idina seems much more raw."

Menzel assumed the role of Elphaba in time to prepare for the first New York City reading in December 2001. After she was hired, she practiced songs with Stephen Oremus.

Then Schwartz invited her to his Manhattan studio where computer printouts of sheet music rested atop the ebony Yamaha grand piano. This working session would be among her favorite memories of the whole *Wicked* experience. "I was standing at the piano and he starts to play me the songs and to teach me stuff, and get my voice, and figure out keys. There's something that's so pure about always wanting to be a singer, and then standing at a famous composer's piano, and just singing with them. Forget about a huge orchestra and agents and managers; just standing in a room singing at a piano is where you start as a child."

Sometime later, in a practice session, the originator of the Elphaba role started influencing the way "Defying Gravity" would be sung from then on. Schwartz had kept Elphaba's song in the alto vocal range. Menzel began picturing the actual scene as it would unfold on stage, with a chorus of singers below her. Reflecting on her abilities, she thought, "I couldn't project over all the ensemble members in such a low voice." As she pictured herself rising in the air, she also had the idea that the music could mirror what was going on. "I'm going up into the air, and then I wanted to sing up there." At the same time, she wanted to show Schwartz "the different places of my voice so that in the future he could play with that."

She was considering how she'd sing the last stanzas beginning with, "So if you care to find me/Look to the western sky."

As she recalls, "I said, 'How would you feel if I sing this up an octave?' And he was cool with it. I'm really glad that he liked the idea. You know, you're flying physically; you're flying vocally. Elphaba's becoming the Wicked Witch of the West and there's something about being more in that tonality that felt more synonymous with the sort of stereotype of Margaret Hamilton, so I was just trying to merge all these worlds together and come up with my own character."

Inside the First New York City Reading

I stayed as far away from [the stage adaptation process] as I could, and let them work their magic and let them be theatre people. I'm the humble writer in the background, having provided some canvas upon which everybody else could dance and sing and make merry.

GREGORY MAGUIRE

It was finally time for Gregory Maguire to check in on *Wicked*. He agreed to come down from his home in the Boston area for a reading to be held December 14th at the end of a two-week workshop in New York City. Schwartz and Holzman were apprehensive as Maguire's scheduled arrival approached. "Once we finished reading the novel, we put it away," Holzman emphasized in an interview around that time. "Because, as brilliant and powerful a book as it is, it wasn't what we needed to make this musical. It was the jumping-off point. But we needed to use our own inner life to make this musical."

Even though Schwartz felt justified in their approach to adaptation, there was a certain "moment of truth" feeling about having the author show up. "We've taken his child, pulled its limbs off and put them back in different ways, and dressed it up in a whole other outfit," he commented in an interview. "I'd feel terrible if Gregory thought we'd destroyed his work or didn't realize what he was hoping for."

Partly because their adaptation was so different, the writers needed feedback that the workshop could provide. For a cast, Schwartz brought in friends with Broadway or cabaret voices, including his assistant, Michael Cole, and then let Joe Mantello start to direct them. Stephen's pal, Jayd McCarty, came in as a narrator to read stage directions and help weave the story together. Other actors included Elizabeth Franz (Madame Morrible), Amy Spanger (Nessarose), Deven May (Fiyero), Gavin Creel (Boq), Steven Skybell (Dr. Dillamond), and Lee Wilkof (Wizard).

Idina Menzel was still starring in *Aida* on Broadway when the workshop was being planned, but she arranged time out and then ended her run in *Aida* shortly thereafter. Kristin Chenoweth carried on as Glinda.

Even with the actors' high level of experience, it took about a week for them to master the demanding music. Schwartz and Holzman provided printed scripts in loose-leaf binders, but then kept adding colored sheets for script revisions inspired by the workshop. So over time, the binders became a rainbow collection of papers.

Joe was the best editor Kristin could have because she is so inventive, and Joe was able to say, no that's too much.

DAVID STONE

Kristin Chenoweth knew her breadth as an actress and stepped into the role of Glinda with such flair that directing her would be about focusing her creativity. Her work immediately enchanted her peers. McCarty commented later, "I walked into that first rehearsal for the first reading and watched what Kristin did and went, 'Whoa, she's f—king phenomenal.' She knew what was going on, what she was doing. She knew who this person was. She figured it out." Because of her skills and instant assimilation of the character, the writers wanted to give her more to do; they could see how she sold the show.

"For a while," Menzel says, "I felt dwarfed by Kristin's perfection." Her own process was intentionally more exploratory.

For Mantello, directing Menzel would be a building process. "She can't do it until she has all the information," he reveals. "So rehearsal for her is a completely different thing. It's a gathering of information." The rehearsal setup became a parallel to the fictional setup for awkward Elphaba and glitzy Glinda. Mantello recalls about Menzel, "She felt awkward about her role. She would watch Kristin and say, 'Kristin, you're perfect. And I just feel like…' And I would say, 'That's the story of the play! You *do* feel like that. You're looking at the most perfect creature God ever created and you don't know where you are. And you're always in the wrong place, and you're stumbling over things, and that's what Elphaba is! So instead of trying to look for it outside, that's what you use. You start from that, and then build on it."

It was partly Menzel's sense of inadequacy that had helped the creative team cast her as Elphaba in the first place. "She brings with her a sort of wounded quality," Schwartz comments. "She may just have been the happiest girl in the world for all of time, but the quality she brings is of someone who has sort of a hole in her, a wound, and that's very right for Elphaba."

On December 14th the actors readied themselves to present the latest rainbow-sheet printout of the script to Gregory Maguire and about 75 guests who could fit onto the black plastic chairs in the rented studio space at the New 42nd Street Studios. Fluorescent bulbs lit the open space where the rows of chairs began filling with guests, including Stephen's friends Andrew Lippa and John Bucchino, the cast's family members, and industry people. To the left of the chairs, Stephen Oremus stood near an old upright piano, on which he would accompany the reading.

For Schwartz, this was a work session. Not one for such formalities as a jacket and dress pants, he appeared in black jeans and a short-sleeve gray T-shirt under a black vest that December day. His self-assigned task was to sit on a tall stool at the back of the room next to Holzman, observing audience responses.

When the security guard notified him that the novelist had arrived, Schwartz met Maguire downstairs and, as they rode up the elevator, nervously warned him not to expect the musical to be like the book.

The cast assembled in front of a black velvet curtain backdrop and filled in the chairs on two rows of risers. Over the next few hours they would pull up the metal music stands holding their scripts each time they stood to perform. Taking their places in the center: blond Kristin in a pastel outfit and dark-haired Idina in a long, black dress.

Schwartz crossed his arms over his chest in a wait-and-see pose.

"We're especially happy to have Gregory Maguire, the author of the novel, here today," Marc Platt told the group in his introduction. Maguire nodded to the applause and the reading began.

At various points during the reading, Schwartz slid off the stool and stalked around in back of the audience to check on Maguire. "I was waiting for him to make an angry face," he explained later.

But the forty-seven-year-old, lightly bearded novelist sat peacefully enthralled, often laughing with the rest of the audience and applauding the musical numbers, now and then wiping back tears.

Even though I had several reservations, my overall appreciation for the work was profound and genuine.

GREGORY MAGUIRE

From Elphaba's birth to Shiz to the Emerald City and beyond, the words and music transported the audience through Oz. Bursts of laughter and applause filled the moments. When the finale finished and the cast took their bows, Maguire was the first audience member to rise, offering a standing ovation for the presentation.

Through the cheers, someone called out Stephen Schwartz's name and he raised his hand, gently taking in the implied praise. He slipped off the stool to receive hugs and handshakes from friends and colleagues. Moments later, he and Winnie Holzman accepted Gregory's congratulations with relief. They were delighted that their inner life had led them somewhere that could satisfy his intent.

2002: More Writing and Rewriting

Schwartz surprised himself with how confident he felt about *Wicked*, as he made plane reservations to fly to Los Angeles for a private reading in front of the upper echelon of Universal Pictures. He knew Universal Chairperson Stacey Snider and others would understand how much work was left to do on the show, but he believed they'd be captivated by the poignancy of their tale and would agree to final funding.

Before leaving for the West Coast, he and Winnie crammed in a few weeks' work on the script and songs. "We learned a great deal about the material," Schwartz reported in *The Schwartz Scene* newsletter about the reading the previous month, "and what rewrites and revisions we want to make. Bookwriter Winnie Holzman and I are busily at work on them now, and we will be trying a lot of new things in Los Angeles. This is a part of the process I really enjoy, so even though it's been a great deal of work, I've been having fun."

Fortunately, the presentation in L.A. went well. Universal Pictures agreed to put forward a large portion of the $14,000,000 needed for *Wicked* to run on Broadway. Stone and Platt raised the rest. They earmarked nearly $4,000,000 just for sets and costumes, ensuring this would be a sensational production if nothing else.

By early spring, challenges kicked up a notch for the *Wicked* team. For Schwartz, as a lover of structure, when everything is in doubt, it's hard. He described recent efforts in *The Schwartz Scene* spring issue: "We had reached the stage where it was time to pull the show apart and put it back together, using the insights gained from the series of readings we had done over the last year or so. We decided to concentrate on the first act, since that was where we felt we had our main storytelling and structural problems to solve. Although it was, as always, unsettling to question every moment of the show and consider changing anything and everything, ultimately I feel it has yielded excellent results."

In strained times likes these, Schwartz found comfort in camaraderie. He played a lot of tennis in Connecticut and socialized in Manhattan cabarets and restaurants with songwriter friends. He and Bucchino had established what they call "Whine and Dine," when they can get together over wine and dinner to vent their frustrations over life. "Nobody is just strong and sure all the time," says Bucchino. "I've seen him have bursts of incredible self-doubt. We all do. And one of the other things I love about our friendship is that we talk about everything, and when he's going through a difficult period or I'm going through a difficult period, we can share it and help each other through. He's a good person to 'Whine and Dine' with."

Friends Stephen Schwartz
and John Bucchino.

Fiyero (Adam Garcia) lazes in his car as he arrives at Shiz University. Elphaba (Idina Menzel) stares at the new arrival. Photo from the London production of *Wicked* (2006).

In 2001, Adam Garcia flew to New York for a workshop and reading of *Wicked*. He would read the part of Fiyero. He recalls that the writers focused the role shortly after he arrived, making Fiyero very shallow. But the character would have an emotional arc.

Adam Garcia: "I like Fiyero, as on the surface he seems incredibly shallow.... But there is quite a depth to him. And despite his richness and his Princeliness, I don't think he really thinks he is worth that much and so he doesn't mind being sacrificial. He is quite generous in that respect."

CHAPTER 25

CHARACTER DEVELOPMENT

Fiyero
They want you to become less callow,
Less shallow

As the script evolved, so did Fiyero, as well as *Wicked*'s secondary characters of Nessarose, Boq, Dr. Dillamond, Madame Morrible, and the Wizard. "One of the things we tried to do in the show," says Schwartz, "is give many of the characters, and certainly the three leading characters, a big journey to take. They don't go from A to B, but they really are transformed as people by their relationships with one another."

For a long time, Fiyero was rather undefined—a rich prince, an eye-candy type who was there to attract both Glinda and Elphaba. By way of introducing Fiyero's character, Schwartz originally wrote a solo, "Who Could Say No to You?" which he later revised as "Easy As Winkie Wine." Neither song seemed ideal.

In another version, Fiyero and Glinda sang a few lines as they went off together to the "frolic," a school dance. In typical Glinda fashion, she sang:

Anybody who's as handsome as you
Deserves the prettiest girl on his arm.

Fiyero replied,

And anybody looks the way you do
Deserves a beau of overwhelming charm.
…We deserve each other.

The thing about Fiyero is that when we first meet him he's extremely un-self-aware.

STEPHEN SCHWARTZ

He's sort of a party boy. He's attracted to Glinda, who's beautiful and fashionable. But then he falls madly in love with Elphaba, this mysterious and passionate girl with green skin. And that experience transforms him.

NORBERT LEO BUTZ

The writers realized the audience didn't really know who he was or why the girls would like him.

Australia-born actor Adam Garcia was invited to play Fiyero in a reading in the spring. Garcia recalls that after a few days of the workshop, the writers started distinguishing Fiyero's inner qualities from his surface charm. Schwartz explains, "We knew that Fiyero had to come on and be incredibly attractive and seem kind of shallow and dumb at the beginning." It could later be revealed that he wasn't shallow, but actually compassionate and courageous. He'd evolve personally through time and that would make him more interesting. Schwartz and Holzman decided, "He's hiding from things. He doesn't want to be hurt; he doesn't want to be challenged. It's out of fear. But because of his relationship with Elphaba he turns into a braver person."

Schwartz took time off from his work to see a revival of Rodgers and Hammerstein's *Oklahoma!* that had just opened on March 21, 2002, at the Gershwin Theatre. "I was sitting and watching it and they say, 'Oh, Will Parker's coming to town,' and they all go to meet him at the train. This guy gets off the train and sings 'Everything's Up to Date in Kansas City' and does a big dance number. The audience didn't know anything about him. He just walked in and kind of took over the stage and did this number. And I thought, 'That's what I should do with Fiyero. I should just have him enter and do a big number right away.'"

Back in meetings, Schwartz and colleagues agreed that Fiyero could be a party boy who could organize all of the students into party mode. At home at the piano, and with actor Adam Garcia in mind for the role, Schwartz composed "Which Way's the Party?" as Fiyero's song, as well as a big dance number for the students at Shiz. (Segments of the song were later recorded by PBS and included on *Broadway: The American Musical DVD*, with Fiyero played by Norbert Leo Butz.)

Boq and Nessarose

The writers continued to be challenged by Nessarose and Boq as characters and in terms of their relationship. Schwartz recalls, "One of the most difficult things to work out was Nessarose and Boq, and how to weave them in so they are part of the plot without having them grind everything to a halt. It was very difficult. You can't know how many times we wanted to cut Nessarose out of the show. She's very inconvenient from a storytelling point of view. This is a story about the relationship between two women, but there's this third woman hanging around and it's a pain in the neck. We would say, 'If only we could cut that role, it would be so much easier.' But we all know that the house falls on Elphaba's sister, so we couldn't cut her."

They wrote into the script that her father would gift her with the famous jeweled shoes. Then, in a dramatic moment, Elphaba casts a spell on them and Nessa starts to walk for the first time. Schwartz attempted several songs for this moment, including one that focused on winning the affections of Boq, now that she could walk. No one understood why the songs, good ones out of context, didn't seem to land well when they were included in Act II. "You know, maybe she shouldn't have a song," Mantello said in one meeting.

"No, no, no, no, it's a huge event—it has to be musicalized," Schwartz insisted. "It can't just be a scene!"

The night before a mid-workshop presentation for the December 2001 reading, with Amy Spanger as Nessarose, Schwartz came up with a song for Spanger that would fulfill the needs of that scene. Then, during the morning run-through of all the new material, he and Winnie decided to give up the piece. He had an epiphany about it: "Maybe the problem is that it shouldn't be a new song; it should be reprise material in some way."

He decided to let Nessarose's music be drawn from some "We Deserve Each Other" material he'd written for Glinda and Fiyero.

With her father, Frex, looking on, Nessarose inspects the jeweled shoes he has just given her. Frex is played by Sean McCourt, and Nessarose by Michelle Federer, in the Broadway production of *Wicked*.

OPPOSITE PAGE: Stephen's handwritten lead sheet for a section of the musical sequence called "The Wicked Witch of the East." In this duet, Nessarose pleads with Elphaba to save Boq, whose heart she has shrunk with a botched spell. Then Elphaba chants a spell, turning Boq into the Tin Man so he can survive without a heart. To write the language of the spell, Schwartz modified Greek, Latin, and Italian words for "heart," "life," etc.

JOAN MARCUS

The Animals

Of all the challenges in *Wicked*'s story development, the Animal story proved the most elusive. "At one point we were even thinking, well, maybe we can't make this work," Holzman recalls, "and we'll just think of another plot because it was so upsettingly difficult."

In the first draft of Act I, Schwartz and Holzman invented what they called a "Rain in Spain" moment that took place in a laboratory at Shiz University. In the scene, Elphaba, Fiyero, and Dr. Dillamond sang and danced over a breakthrough in Dillamond's research findings, echoing the "Rain in Spain" scene from *My Fair Lady* in which three principal characters sing and dance over Eliza's improving diction. Schwartz wrote a song called "As If By Magic." In the course of the celebration, Elphaba and Fiyero realize they are attracted to one another.

"It read okay on the page, but when we heard it in an early reading, it felt kind of like a 'B' sci-fi movie. It was wrong tonally. We needed to take it more seriously because our leading character takes it seriously and important choices she makes hinge on it. So that was a discovery, that it couldn't be sort of funny or campy or kind of a sci-fi send up." The writers abandoned this approach and left the Goat songless for a long time.

Holzman tells of one scary meeting in the spring of 2002. She and Schwartz, Platt, and Mantello met in the living room of Schwartz's Manhattan condo for hours, trying to figure out the Animal subplot while poring over the storyboard. "At times we wanted to kill each other," she says. "It felt like you were stuck in an est group and you weren't allowed to go to the bathroom, that's the only way I can describe it."

An offhand remark uncovered a solution. Holzman continues, "Marc Platt said something about how in Oz, Animals can speak and that's what's so magical. Somehow we came upon this whole realization that the tragedy would be if they lost their powers

Neither Stephen nor I think of it as animal rights. It really has nothing to do with actual animals. It's much more to do with injustice — people being scapegoated, people being singled out as not good enough.

WINNIE HOLZMAN

of speech, if that was re-moved from them. And Joe somehow understood how to tell that story in a way that Stephen and I really struggled with."

One of Mantello's vital suggestions pertained to Dr. Dillamond's speech. Originally, Dillamond bleated like a goat every now and then, as a kind of joke. He'd pronounce "Miss Elphabaaaaa" and it added charm and brought

Stephanie J. Block as Elphaba and Timothy Britten Parker as Dr. Dillamond in *Wicked* on tour.

laughter in early readings. But the director told the writers, "I need to see him as the great teacher he is, so that his disintegration is more compelling." That meant that the professor would need to speak very perfectly at first; and later, audiences would witness his deterioration (when he unwittingly bleats about something "baaaad" instead of speaking "bad").

Once the team found the speech concept, they clung to it, knowing they had a powerful yet simple story element. The journey proved worth taking. Schwartz could finally write the right song for the Goat at that moment. "We thought his situation really needed to land, so I wrote 'Something Bad.'" Dr. Dillamond frets about the rumors that Animals are losing their powers of speech, and during the song he seems to be starting to lose his.

One of the things we came to feel was that the Animal story worked best when it was a metaphor. And when it was somewhat poetic, which is the idea of them losing the power to speak, which is a sort of poetic idea.

STEPHEN SCHWARTZ

In the Throes of Change

As the pace of *Wicked*'s development hastened, Schwartz found himself constantly in New York City rehearsal spaces witnessing auditions, or sitting in David Stone's meeting room in "the throes of negotiations with actors, a potential choreographer, etc." It would be a time for racing through emotional hills and valleys toward the deadline, with the April 5th reading as a definite peak. "The reading went spectacularly well," Schwartz expressed in an email. "We're all extremely excited about the progress we have made. Carole [Schwartz] came and thought the improvement in the show since she last saw a reading was 'unbelievable.' So I'm very exhilarated."

Joe Mantello was finding his stride and ready to assert what he felt would be workable on stage, including the ending. Schwartz wrote for *The Schwartz Scene* update, "I would like to say for the record that our director, Joe Mantello, was extremely helpful to Winnie and me in helping us reshape and sharpen scenes and incidents, and I am enjoying our collaboration immensely."

In the subsequent newsletter, Schwartz wrote that Winnie Holzman had arrived in New York, "...and she and I are feverishly working toward another reading at the end of the month. We are then planning to do some sort of staging/choreography lab in October, and then (eek) we go into rehearsal in February for our first production, which will be at the Curran Theatre in San Francisco beginning the week of April 14, 2003. I know that may sound far off to some of you, but believe me, when you're working on a new musical, it's not!"

It's interesting about Stephen, he's so ultra respectful of the bookwriter; he even values and used Winnie's words and sometimes was loath to cut them at the expense of having a song. I think he loved Winnie's dialogue so much that he kept breaking up his songs with it. There were just a couple of places that I felt that we have to deliver an uninterrupted song!

JOE MANTELLO

Revised Ending

In an early version of the script, Holzman wrote a final scene with Elphaba and Dr. Dillamond to be acted out downstage (while upstage, at the Wizard's palace, the celebration of the death of the Witch continued). It was to take place on a scruffy farm in an isolated area of Oz called the Badlands.

Doctor Dillamond! Oh Doctor Dillamond! Do you remember me? It's Elphaba. Oh Doctor— I wish there were more I could do for you—

She's given up the *Grimmerie,* a book of magic spells, and doesn't know what she can offer. And then Schwartz had her sing the reverse of her unlimited song.

> *I'm limited—*
> *I'm sorry, but I'm limited…*
> *I don't have the powers I once had when this began*
> *So all that I can do for you*
> *Is do the best I can…*

He liked the down-to-earth feel of having her use natural healing abilities rather than magic. Dr. Dillamond then bleated with difficulty: *El-pha-baaaa.* She became a healer for these Animals who were destroyed by the Wizard's policies.

"On some emotional and philosophical level, it was why I wanted to tell the story," Schwartz later revealed about the last scene where Elphaba heals Animals. "It's the fact that it's completely anonymous and she'll never get any credit for it and she'll never get any public affection for it, but she does it anyway. That was the end of the Elphaba story to me." The concept of a return to life after death made sense for Schwartz in his own life—wanting to work without the ballyhoo that accompanies fame.

But as the work on endings evolved, it became clear that they had too much to tie up to dwell on the Badlands moment. There was Glinda and Elphaba's goodbyes, the Wizard's dismissal, the reprise of "No One Mourns the Wicked" by the citizens of Oz, and the departure of Elphaba with the Scarecrow. So many endings, so little time.

Schwartz did his best to argue for keeping the Badlands scene. If it had to go, he had to be sure everybody knew what they were cutting. "This is very important to me," he told Joe Mantello,

There were things that added nuance and dimensionality to the ending of a show that's about nuance and dimensionality, which unfortunately simply had to go from a theatrical pacing point of view.

STEPHEN SCHWARTZ

Eden Espinosa sings
"Defying Gravity."

CHAPTER 26

The Countdown Begins

Glinda
   ...Though it is I admit
   the tiniest bit
   unlike I anticipated

To Marc Platt's disappointment, the script's lagging development and Mantello's previous commitment to direct *A Man of No Importance* at Lincoln Center meant he couldn't bring *Wicked* into New York by spring 2003.

"When's Halloween?" someone asked in a meeting with the creative team around David Stone's conference room table. "Is it on a Thursday?" Thursday had become the traditional day for opening a big new Broadway musical because it allowed for reviews to be published in Friday theatre sections. They decided to open on Thursday, October 30th, Halloween eve, as would suit a Witches of Oz musical.

The team gave up the idea of trying out *Wicked* in a scaled-down regional theatre production in Seattle in the fall of 2002, and would instead aim for a traditional out-of-town tryout in late April 2003 at San Francisco's Curran Theatre, followed by the Halloween Broadway bow. Many hundreds of decisions remained to be made.

Even with San Francisco in the plans, Schwartz argued for a wait-and-see approach before the decision-making team gathered in Stone's office. He wanted a substantial gap between the trial production and the opening, ideally without committed dates for New York. "I've had enough experience to know that you can't make major revisions while the show is running." He was ready to make any change necessary to tighten the story (even though a few previous collaborators had faulted his zeal

We raised the bar very high for ourselves. We made unusual choices.

MARC PLATT

in this regard). But he wanted to be able to stop the express train to do it.

Although the producers weren't willing to leave the show in pending mode, they did agree to an unusual three-month delay between the out-of-town production and Broadway—a decision they would not regret.

They chose the Gershwin Theatre for mounting the show in New York.

Designing *Wicked*'s Oz

When it came time to hire the professionals who would envision *Wicked*'s appearance—its color, texture, light, and motion— the creative team made final decisions together.

For scenic design, originally, the director sought out Academy Award-winning Japanese designer Eiko Ishoka. "Eiko is a visionary," Mantello tried to explain to the others. He brought her down from Montreal, where she was designing for *Cirque du Soleil*, to attend a meeting with the creative team. However, her style of conceiving a show wasn't a match. "She would bring in these beautiful drawings," Mantello remembers, "but there wasn't a big idea. It was just scene-to-scene. And I'm such a novice at it myself. And I would say, 'Well, how do we get from here to here?'" When it didn't seem that Eiko would work out for the production, he came up with a plan for design auditions. "We thought the best way to not go down another dead end," Mantello explains, "was to just get inside the head of a few people."

For their auditions in Stone's office, some designers brought in computer-assisted design drawings, and others just talked. When Rhode Island-based Eugene Lee arrived for his appointment in June 2002, he filled a table with a large white model.

Schwartz responded as a boy with an intriguing new toy. "He came in with this model, and we were like, okay!!! It looked as if the Wizard character from *The Wizard of Oz*—this sort of Kansas, turn-of-the-century medicine man with his little cart—had designed the set. There were little Victorianesque kinds of gadgety things with some wheel that turns that doesn't really do anything."

When Schwartz conceived the show, he pictured sets in his head that were high-tech and sleek, but he quickly adapted to Lee's angle. "It's all aggressively low-tech, sort of like *Nicholas Nickleby*. You see everything that gets brought in." Mantello was especially pleased about the concept of an actor-driven curtain opening, and he made it something for the monkeys to do.

Lee and his associates, who included Edward Pierce as associate designer, Nick Francone as assistant designer, and others, began their work by reading Gregory Maguire's novel, which triggered a basic concept. When they were given a script that listed more than twenty scene changes, they realized that this show called for an "environment" as opposed to isolated set pieces. As Pierce explains, the design couldn't be literal but rather "conceptual" and "textural." It was important that "within that environment, with very little effort, we could transform ourselves from one place to another place. So when you bring out two beds, and you manipulate the unit set a little bit, you're in a dorm room. You fly in a couple of portraits, you change the upstage picture and light it in a different way, and you're in the parlor at Shiz University." It was the only way to create a seamless show.

Clocks

"The clock in my head has started ticking louder and faster," Schwartz wrote in his summer *The Schwartz Scene* update, referring to deadline pressure. Meshing their story with the clock in Eugene Lee's design theme became one of his and Winnie Holzman's challenges. Lee had absorbed Maguire's novel before

In creating an environment you're not only creating a physical structure, but you're creating an emotion and you're creating a world in which a story can unfold. Then you only introduce specific elements for those moments where you need to know that you're in a very specific human place.

EDWARD PIERCE

he read the *Wicked* script and loved his notion of the Clock of the Time Dragon—a complex clockwork structure topped with a Dragonhead and pulled around on a wagon. Elphaba was born inside of it. Maguire says he made it up to suggest, on the one hand, something artificial from the Wizard's reign, and on the other, the possibility that the green girl born inside of it might in some way "be exempt from being seduced by the glamour of the mechanics of power and spectacle."

For Lee and his team, if the whole show took place as if inside the clock, the Wizard's power would make more sense and provide high contrast for Elphaba's struggles against it. They would use clock gears for visual unity and affix a dragon's head to the front of the proscenium, breathing smoke as the show began.

But from the writers' standpoint, it had little to do with the show. "The first thing you see is this great big dragon hanging over the set, and what the hell is it?" Schwartz questioned. "We had to make something up. So we decided, since in Gregory's book he refers to the Time Dragon, we'll just refer to the Time Dragon Clock and then people will be like 'Oh, that's what the dragon is,' and then everybody can forget about it." He added, "Now that we've explained the dragon, I kind of like it."

For costumes, it was Marc Platt who was really keen on Susan Hilferty's drawings. "Susan was just so bold with them and specific with her approach and it felt like, 'You know what? That's the way to go!'" With a nod to Dr. Seuss, Hilferty created an Ozian visual vocabulary. About her concept, Platt says, "It has its own unique language. It doesn't look like anything you've seen before and yet it looks like, in bits and pieces, things you've seen before. Like Oz, it was supposed to remind us of our own world and yet be very different from our world. And so that was genius, I think."

The design team of Eugene Lee, Susan Hilferty, and lighting designer Kenneth Posner began meeting to coordinate their approach. The William Denslow illustrations from the 1900 *The Wizard of Oz* novel inspired much of the vocabulary and tone of the art design for *Wicked*, but of course the designers were also influenced by what Schwartz and Holzman had written. "We were trying to create a [visual] language based on the musical itself," Hilferty recalls.

For dance and musical staging, the songwriter agreed to Wayne Cilento, based on his work on *Tommy*. "What he did for *Tommy* was he created a style of movement for these people that had its own look. It was sort of like the monster bar in *Star Wars*. It had references to other things but it just looked like completely its own world."

It was time to begin collaborative planning for the peak moment of the show: Elphaba's ride to the highest part of the stage as she reveals her deeper nature.

Ozians in *Wicked*.

FOLLOWING PAGE: Idina Menzel and the Broadway company of *Wicked*.

SPECIAL SECTION

Collaborators Create A Peak Moment
—Defying Gravity—

JOAN MARCUS

Just before *Wicked*'s intermission, Elphaba, in her heavy black dress, and Glinda, in a cheery yellow travel dress, arrive at the doorstep of their dream as they are presented to the Wizard in his palace. As in any good quest story, they are tested. The "Defying Gravity" song and scene displays the moment the show's heroine takes an ethical stand.

Early on, Stephen Schwartz wrote the scene's centerpiece, the song "Defying Gravity." To begin, he read Holzman a list of possible titles he'd made up. "Fortunately, her favorite was 'Defying Gravity,' which was my favorite too," he reports. He liked the nuanced meaning of "defying" that conveyed defiance of authority as well as of the earth's gravitational field. Once he got the title, the song "wrote itself" quickly, originally as a solo for Elphaba, and later with duet sections added in.

Holzman's ideas helped structure what Glinda's role in the scene could be. The blond sorceress wannabe sought acceptance by authorities Madame Morrible and the Wizard, regardless of their vile deeds. When Elphaba follows her convictions and breaks from them, Glinda cannot summon the courage to be unpopular. From this turning point on, the two young women go down different paths: Glinda will be "Glinda the Good," and Elphaba will be the "Wicked Witch of the West."

Schwartz structured the piece with a mid-song turning point, when things could have been different. At first, Elphaba and Glinda snap at each other, singing: "I hope you're happy," sarcastically, because they believe the other person screwed up. Glinda decides not to join Elphaba's flight. They part as friends, singing, "I hope you're happy" as a sincere wish.

"I wanted the music to be powerful and empowering and thrilling," Schwartz adds. "I wanted a series of simple notes that sounded like strength, coming into your own, feeling the power come up from below, from your feet and spreading up through your body."

By the time Joe Mantello and the designers heard the song in context during readings, Idina Menzel knew how to belt it into the stratosphere. They watched her sing from behind a music stand, without any set or light, and draw thunderous applause. They now had the opportunity to create an event so stunning that it would linger in the theatre-goers' minds as a reason for attending a live Broadway-level performance.

To stage it, Mantello instinctively knew not to use the traditional Peter Pan type of flying back and forth. He believed people would start looking for wires and stop listening to the deeply emotional song. "It's a transforming moment for the character. She has this epiphany, and the whole plot hinges on it. And so I wanted to keep the audience in that mind-set and yet deliver 'She's flying.'" He wasn't sure how that could be accomplished. He believes in encouraging an audience to bring their creative mental pictures to the scene. "Their imaginations can do so much more than anything we are capable of doing in the theatre. So my job, I felt, was to engage their imaginations so that they said, she's flying—I didn't *tell* them she was flying, but in their imaginations they saw her flying."

One winter night in early 2002, he and Platt held a meeting over dinner at the Odeon, a popular dining spot in downtown Manhattan. Odeon covers their tablecloths with paper and provides crayons, enabling kids of all ages to entertain themselves as they wait for food. Mantello grabbed a crayon and went to work drawing lines for

Elphaba's upward motion. He explained to Platt about having Elphaba rise from the stage floor with black cloth flowing behind her. "There's a cape that goes the full size of the stage, and that's what makes the expansive gesture." Platt caught the excitement of the possibilities and they started to make a plan for the spectacular scene.

Once the steady upward movement was in the plan, Hilferty designed a huge cape for the witch to wear. "It's like a mountain," she says about the shape. "It's really about being in an incredibly powerful position. Elphaba comes forward right at the audience, and as she's moving forward, she grows and grows and grows. It's a kind of spectacular visual that also really goes with the music. It doesn't do something different than the music is doing. It just lets her build and build and build. It's such a triumphant moment."

When it came time to rehearse the whole scene, Wayne Cilento worked with Mantello to be sure the actors' movements around the set pieces would visually support the effects they wanted to achieve. Lighting designer Kenneth Posner planned for eerie blue-green beams to layer in atmospheric mystery and pizzazz, and special effects designer Chic Silber arranged for stage smoke to rise up into the light.

Orchestrator William Brohn worked with Stephen Schwartz on instrumentation and wrote out the score for the orchestra pit musicians who practiced the challenging piece. "The song 'Defying Gravity' is loaded with drama," says Brohn. "It has a very active string figure that Stephen requested directly. That figure gives that swirling effect of levitation."

Finally, the actors would bring the force of their emotions and talent to interpret the scene and song, and sound designer Tony Meola's team would make sure they were heard.

In this way, the Act I climax, "Defying Gravity," became their collaborative spectacle that allows audiences' emotions to soar along with Elphaba.

OPPOSITE: Notes that Stephen Schwartz wrote while brainstorming ideas for "Defying Gravity." FOLLOWING PAGE: Completed lyrics for "Defying Gravity."

I feel a kind of wild freedom I've never felt before —
I feel like I've cut ties I didn't even know were binding me
Years of trying to please my father, my sister, the
people around me, even you —
Years of thinking I could change them — "if I did this,
if I did that, they would love me
All at once I don't care —
All at once I'm following my own star — and it's like a star
just learning how to shine

Too late to worry if my actions are wise
Too late to fear I'm out on a limb
I only know there's no looking back
Trust my instincts
Close my eyes + jump into my future

No one to trust but me

Something has changed within me
Something is not the same
(I won't just pause to play by the rules)
Of someone Else's game
                    or
(Something that will never again be tame)

"Defying Gravity"

ELPHABA
Something has changed within me
Something is not the same
I'm through with playing by
The rules of someone else's game
Too late for second-guessing
Too late to go back to sleep
It's time to trust my instincts
Close my eyes
And leap...

It's time to try defying gravity
I think I'll try defying gravity
And you can't pull me down.

...I'm through accepting limits
'Cuz someone says they're so
Some things I cannot change
But till I try I'll never know
Too long I've been afraid of
Losing love I guess I've lost
Well if that's love
It comes at much too high a cost
I'd sooner buy defying gravity
Kiss me goodbye, I'm defying gravity
And you can't pull me down!

Unlimited
Together we're unlimited
Together we'll be the greatest team
There's ever been - Glinda!
Dreams the way we planned 'em

GLINDA
If we work in tandem

BOTH
There's no fight we cannot win
Just you and I defying gravity
With you and I defying gravity

ELPHABA
They'll never bring us down!

(GLINDA decides to stay behind.)

GLINDA
I hope you're happy
Now that you're choosing this

ELPHABA
You too--
I hope it brings you bliss

BOTH
I really hope you get it
And you don't live to regret it
I hope you're happy in the end
I hope you're happy, my friend

ELPHABA
So if you care to find me
Look to the Western sky!
As someone told me lately
Everyone deserves the chance to fly
And if I'm flying solo
At least I'm flying free
To those who'd ground me
Take a message back from me:

Tell them how I am defying gravity
I'm flying high, defying gravity
And soon I'll match them in renown
And nobody in all of Oz
No Wizard that there is or was
Is ever gonna bring me down!...

LYRICS BY STEPHEN SCHWARTZ. USED WITH PERMISSION

More Casting

Bernie Telsey Casting, Inc. ran open auditions and assembled stars for this Equity production. Sometimes decisions were a breeze. Dana Ivey declined the Madame Morrible role offered to her due to an allergy to stage smoke, and that's when Carole Shelley showed up to audition for the role of the bullying college dean. British-born Shelley interpreted the role with an almost Dickensian grotesqueness. Her layered portrayal of the superficially encouraging yet villainous sorceress would help define the character. "Carole came in and she was wonderful," Schwartz recalls. "That was easy. She got cast almost immediately." Other parts were harder. Adam Garcia's agent had made arrangements that precluded his continuing on as Fiyero after he performed the role in one of the readings. However, Norbert Leo Butz came in, bringing his considerable strengths as an actor and singer to the role.

Schwartz had carefully chosen some of his favorite performers for the earlier readings, expecting that they'd please his colleagues and make the final cut. He was overruled, which meant calling his friends, like Scott Coulter, on the phone to say how disappointed he was that they didn't get cast. Mantello brought in a few actors he'd already worked with, and persisted in getting them cast, including the relatively inexperienced Michelle Federer for Nessarose.

Although Schwartz ended up being a fan of Federer in the role, at the time he dug in his heels, insisting on a seasoned Broadway dancer. He had envisioned an important dramatic scene with the famous ruby slippers from *The Wizard of Oz* film. Nessarose would be sitting in her chair as her sister enchants her shoes, and then she would take her first steps. "I thought we should cast a dancer, but Joe didn't see it that way," Schwartz recalls. "I thought there could be a really great moment when

There's so much talent around. There's nobody there in Wicked *who just sings and then has to crawl off stage when the dancing happens; and there are no dancers in it who are just moving their mouths.*

STEPHEN SCHWARTZ

she stands up and walks. There could be some weird thing of clumsily and yet spectacularly doing something physical. I still think that's a missed opportunity. If Joe had been Bob Fosse or Gower Champion or Michael Bennett there would have been a dance at that section. It's screaming for it in devising a musical and Joe just could not see it."

For the ensemble, Schwartz needed singers, Wayne Cilento needed dancers, and Joe Mantello wanted people he could work with comfortably. "I don't have any control over the outcome or how a show's received," Mantello explains about his perspective. "What I do have control over is: who's going to come to the party. Are we going to have a good time along the way? This is why I put all my energy into casting, though I despise the process, probably because I have sympathetic nausea for every person who walks into the room."

"In the casting process, Stephen drew a lot of lines in the sand," David Stone later explained regarding the songwriter's arguments. "Finally Joe just said, 'I'm the director, either I have who I want, and you have to trust that I can get the performance out of them, or you have to have another director.' And Joe was right. Ultimately Stephen backed down because he knew Joe was right about that."

From Joe's side, he was feeling his way into his job, and that meant standing his ground on some issues. "I think Stephen has had particular experience in theatre that makes him, maybe, nervous or protective or gun shy. And I have to say, for the most part, it's so hard for me to work this way, because I've never been second-guessed to this extent." He understood that Stephen was skittish but wanted more trust, and wanted to say, "It's not that what I'm asking for is carte blanche. But I'm the director; you've got to trust me at a certain point."

Joe was really strong [in his opinions], and I wanted someone strong. There were directors I turned down because I said they're not going to be able to stand up to me. But then, in the moment, you get annoyed if everybody is not doing everything your way.

STEPHEN SCHWARTZ

In October, Schwartz wrote his update for *The Schwartz Scene* while working in his Manhattan apartment. "I'm sitting here in my studio as my engineer, John Angier, hooks up the cables from the Yamaha Disklavier to the computer so we can prepare the music for one of the new songs for *Wicked*. It has been a busy few months of preparation—rewrites, readings, meetings, and more rewrites—as we get ready for *Wicked* to kick into another gear. Winnie and I have completed what we hope is our rehearsal draft, and I have one more major new song to write, and then it's time to put this puppy on its feet and see what we have wrought. I am both terrified and exhilarated."

2003

In January, at the top of the year of *Wicked*'s public debut, the show was a collection of patched-together pieces. Wayne Cilento planned Ozian dances for ensemble members and principals. Costume shop employees busily sewed hundreds of individual beads on gowns for Glinda and Madame Morrible. Susan Hilferty accompanied every cast member to the shops of the Broadway costume makers. There actors would be fitted for costumes three times: with a muslin pattern, then in a version with the specific fabric for the costume, and finally in the completed piece.

The set department and contractors finished constructing pieces like the clockworks, the Wizard's puppet head, wheelchairs, and the dragon. Everything had to be designed for shipping to San Francisco and then to Broadway.

Earlier, Schwartz had met with Kristin Chenoweth and Idina Menzel to sculpt their songs. Now the leading ladies were practicing with their vocal coaches with a specific deadline by which their singing muscles would have to be ready for eight performances a week.

I do a lot of preparation before I get in front of people, even in rehearsal. I take songs to my voice teacher and work on everything ad nauseum.

Idina Menzel

Footloose and *Fame* songwriter Dean Pitchford (left)
joins Stephen Schwartz
on a walk on the Schwartz
property.

It was the job of Joe Mantello and Marc Platt to picture the whole, and Schwartz felt challenged knowing almost every aspect of the show's success was now out of his hands. "This is the time that's really tough for me," he revealed whenever asked. To his friend, Dean Pitchford, he grumbled that the fun is over once the show is written. Pitchford replied, "Well, this is why you get paid." Schwartz laughed, at the time, but that was the truth of it—if the show was a hit, he would make money; if it flopped, he wouldn't be paid anything but a minimal advance.

One thing Schwartz wanted was a hand in his show's public image. Instead, the concept for *Wicked*'s logo and poster would be determined by Stone and Platt in meetings with ad agency Serino Coyne, Inc. Soon the witches of Oz in a yin/yang-like curve of black and white with a green-sky background emerged from an artist's drawing based on the group concept. It gave a sleek, contemporary profile to the show that visually presented an archetypal motif of opposites coming together.

Schwartz had wanted something that more clearly evoked the actual story of the show but admits the ad agency was smart about it. "Nancy Coyne [from the agency] said to me, 'Look, I'm not trying to appeal to *you* with this poster. I'm trying to appeal to women who buy tickets, to tourists, and to mothers and their daughters. If the show's a flop, it doesn't matter what your poster is. If the show is a hit and we can reach that market, this is the difference between running five years and ten years.'"

Mr. Songwriter stayed busy with the music.

William (Bill) Brohn had come on board as orchestrator. He would set up the final flourish for the score by translating Schwartz's piano-vocal music sheets into larger works for a twenty-three-piece orchestra. Brohn was accustomed to working on big shows and had a long list of impressive credits. *Ragtime*, for which Brohn received a Tony Award® for Best Orchestrations, was one of Schwartz's favorite musicals. "I was very flattered when he called," Brohn says.

Pre-production craziness whirled around Michael Cole from his post in the Schwartz office. "Yesterday, Stephen spent the entire day in a meeting with Alex Lacamoire [assistant music director], Stephen Oremus, and Bill Brohn, going over every second of the show musically," Cole reported in an email at the time. "It was a great meeting (where they all seemed to be 'on the same page' in terms of how the show will sound), but Stephen was exhausted after it was over. He also had a long meeting with Winnie to go over a couple of scenes that are being tweaked. He has been a busy boy."

Michael Cole, Stephen Schwartz's assistant, prepares for the busy days ahead when *Wicked* opens.

Even when the score was nearly ready for rehearsals, Schwartz still had doubts about "What Is This Feeling?" He said in January, "I've written four versions of this song. I know this version is the best I've done so far, but I'm not sure it's going to work." It didn't, and he'd need to rewrite it again during rehearsal.

He wrote in *The Schwartz Scene*, "As I begin this first quarterly newsletter update of 2003, it is with the discomforting realization that when the time for the next one rolls around, *Wicked* will already be in rehearsal. After all this time doing rewrites, readings, and more rewrites, it seems to be coming up alarmingly quickly. But I feel we have assembled a very strong team to try to bring it to life on the stage of San Francisco's Curran Theatre this coming May. This is a strange time for the writer of a show. My work is more or less done for the time being, until we see the show in front of an audience or at least get into rehearsal. So I basically have to sit around anxiously, hoping that other people are doing their jobs!"

What Is This Rehearsal Feeling?

New York's winter of 2003 begrudgingly gave way to a cool March as *Wicked*'s cast headed into rehearsals for an out-of-town tryout. In a practice room at 890 Broadway, actors peeled off their heavy wraps, filling metal coat racks at one edge of the room, and then stepped out onto the wood floor beneath the flourescent lights in the concrete beams overhead. A row of portable mirrors lined one wall, offering visual feedback for performers.

A Chorus Line's Michael Bennett had purchased this old eight-story factory in 1977 and converted it into dance and theatre spaces. The rented rehearsal room for *Wicked*, a few blocks uptown from Manhattan's East Village, became a temporary Oz as rehearsals ran from 10 a.m. to 6 p.m.

For the first session, the new company gathered in full force, including assistants. As Michael Cole remembers, one table was piled high with bagels, croissants, fruit, juice, coffee, and tea. While the actors were having their Equity meeting (when an official from the union covers legal details and the actors select one of their members to represent them to the union), others ate and greeted each other. "It felt like a small army—lawyers and press agents and advertising and hair and lighting and sound and choreography and assistants and programmers and drummers and the stage manager and assistant stage manager and on and on. It was remarkable."

After Marc Platt welcomed everyone, he praised Stephen and Winnie for their beautiful work, and Joe Mantello for his passion for the piece. "He spoke of what the show was about—love and friendship, etc.," says Cole, "but then he told us what *Wicked* meant to him personally, and underscored the theme of being different and finding friendships in spite of appearances.

The thing that amazed me about it: Usually these meet 'n' greet producer speeches are so cold and stuffy and boring and who the hell cares? Every word that Marc spoke was true and honest and heartfelt and not the slightest bit corny. Then everyone introduced themselves. When Stephen said his name, the crowd *burst* into applause. Same for Winnie…then the cast did a read-through of the script. Everyone was just terrific, and there were lots of laughs, lots of tears."

From the first day, Joe Mantello asked Stephen and Winnie to be present at all rehearsals in case script adjustments were needed. Winnie brought her notebook computer, and Schwartz showed up, but he would often drop in at the piano where Stephen Oremus and Alex Lacamoire were finalizing vocal arrangements.

Part of my job as director is that I'm the stand-in for the audience until the audience gets there. So I try to listen to it with no agenda, as if I'm coming to it for the first time.

JOE MANTELLO

As actors moved into Oz, their personalities and talents filtered into staging efforts. One of the harder parts to work through was the "catfight" between Glinda and Elphaba in Act II. "I'm not a big fan of stage fights," Mantello says, "because I always think they look cheesy. So I was just trying to make it humorous." Fortunately, Kristin Chenoweth already knew how to twirl a baton, and had the notion of twirling her wand in Elphaba's face—a moment future audiences would love.

It was during these rehearsals that Schwartz finished work on an earlier moment in the show, when Glinda and Elphaba face off. The song began its journey as the "Elphaba and Glinda don't like each other" card on the storyboard. Opposites thrown together—there was inherent drama. Over time, Schwartz wrote two different songs with "Bad Situation" in the title and then tried another one he called "Far Be It For Me." He says, "They were all about the two girls being roommates and not getting along. I just never came up with anything that was good enough."

From Stephen Schwartz's
penciled notes about
possible songs for
Elphaba and Glinda:

> *Nothing in Common*
> *Just My Luck*
> *And Yet…*
> *Oil and Water*
> *Insufferable*

At one point, he questioned the director about it. "Is this an obligatory song?" But there was no way out of it. That moment provides a foundation for the central transformation in the show—the "bad" and "good" characters shifting from loathing to deep caring.

Finally, Winnie Holzman suggested the roommates could sing a song about hate-at-first-sight. It would be like a spoof on falling-in-love songs. That inspired Schwartz to write, "What Is This Feeling?" Version One while finishing the score for rehearsals. Originally he set the lyrics of loathing to a lovely waltz tune so that it became a playful satire. Sung in a practice session, it got a lot of laughs and pleased both writers, but not Mantello.

Schwartz couldn't understand the director's resistance and wasn't sure what to do about it. "When I first played the song for Joe, he didn't really like it. Winnie and I asked ourselves, 'Why doesn't he get it?' He couldn't put his finger on it, and finally one day he went to see *Hairspray*. He came in the next day and said, 'The first act of *Hairspray* is so high energy. I think what's bothering me about that song is that it's so early in the act, I want more energy.'"

Schwartz waited to test it in rehearsals when the cast read and sang through the show in sequence. "As soon as I heard the song I thought the whole act has just gone into the toilet," Schwartz recalls. Mantello was right. The show needed energy at this point. He talked to Joe afterward. "You said this to me a month ago and it's been in the back of my head since you said it, so I think I can do this for you very fast because I think it's there and I've just been waiting to summon up my own energy to do the work."

That night Schwartz wrote another version of a song for Elphaba and Glinda in the form of new music for "What Is This Feeling?" He adjusted the lyrics slightly and brought it in. "People were very impressed that I wrote it in a day, but the fact is that I didn't. I actually wrote it over the course of about two-and-a-half years; it's just that there were several first drafts of it. But I did five separate numbers for this spot and I think this is it." It was.

Every big musical needs dance numbers to contribute to the energy. *Wicked*'s choreographer Wayne Cilento amplified the zestful energy of "What Is This Feeling?" by sending a wedge of college coeds to dance zippily behind Glinda, visually implying their support for her.

Finally, *Wicked* was ready for the next big step.

San Francisco Tech and Dress Rehearsals

The *Wicked* principals and creative team gathered at the Clift Hotel by the Curran Theatre in San Francisco, where they would form a family bond over about eight weeks. The cast arrived in time for three weeks of technical rehearsals before May previews. For such things as the loading in of the set and the setting up of the lights, producer David Stone stood by Joe Mantello, making sure that everything

Music Director Stephen Oremus, director Joe Mantello, and choreographer Wayne Cilento plan song staging for *Wicked*.

The setting is a leased space at the 890 Broadway building (a rehearsal center in Manhattan established by *A Chorus Line* creator Michael Bennett). Here the company of *Wicked* prepared for the San Francisco tryout.

Idina Menzel and Stephen Schwartz pause for a break during a *Wicked* rehearsal at 890 Broadway.

QUESTION: *Could you talk about Elphaba as someone who is different? Stephen thinks of himself as an Elphaba, partly because, as an artist, he always felt kind of different. So did you see him as an Elphaba at all?*

IDINA MENZEL: No, I see him as this legendary guy and I'm just trying to do a good job and not get fired! I don't see him like that. But I can appreciate that everybody obviously goes through that in their life in some way or another, when they feel completely alienated and like an outcast, whether it's for a short time or for their whole lives. And yeah, of course, when you're an artist, usually you have to take risks and usually you have to put yourself on the line and go against the grain in order to be great and unique. And then you sort of stand up for what you believe, and have to be able to resist the negative things people will say to you.

Kristin Chenoweth and Idina Menzel rehearse a scene for *Wicked* at 890 Broadway.

worked.

It was a time to walk through the entrances and exits for this complicated, multi-scene drama. Michelle Federer as Nessarose performed from two different wheelchairs. The first time she tried one in San Francisco, it careened down the stage, almost landing in the orchestra pit. After that, the crew made sure she was proficient with the brake.

Wayne Cilento, whose credit on the playbill would be musical staging, not just choreography, served as an extra guide for Mantello, who was not as used to moving such a large cast around a stage. The director would say things like, "Wayne, how would you want to get them on or off?" And then Mantello would judge what he liked or didn't like. Sometimes Mantello would jump up and try something; other times Cilento would. "It was great to have sort of a tag team on those sort of things," recalls Stone.

Legally *Wicked*

At a distance from the puzzle-working of tech rehearsal, *Wicked*'s writers stepped through a labyrinth of entertainment-industry politics and legalities. Holzman was called into a meeting with Universal in Los Angeles roughly a week before previews were to begin. Although L. Frank Baum's books are in the public domain, Universal owned the rights to Maguire's novel but not *The Wizard of Oz* film, which had come to be controlled by Warner Bros. Out of fear Warners could sue them for infringement, the lawyers told Holzman to make certain cuts and rewrite certain lines or the show would be closed before it opened.

Designers had already accommodated to the rights restrictions handed down to them. "There was a lot of pressure from the producers, who were getting pressure from the lawyers," Hilferty recalls, "but, in fact, I was never interested in the film costumes because the film was reflecting 1938 [the year the movie was made] American culture."

To avoid Glinda's pink bubble image, Eugene Lee had already designed a gray, clock gear-like contraption that encircles the actress, which could be lowered and raised, or "flown in" by winches as needed. On this mechanical "bubble" his staff installed several automated bubble-generating machines with an electric motor that made the machines spin and blow soap bubbles out into the space around Glinda. The device, invented for fairs, had never been used in a major stage production but created better magic than a puffy pink bubble would have anyway.

While the designers were not restricted further, Schwartz was incensed that the script was suddenly being censored, and angry on behalf of his audience, whom he feared would get an inferior show. For all his years of meetings with Marc Platt and Holzman, the whole notion was to make *Wicked* a prequel to *The Wizard of Oz* people know best—the film. And in three years of periodic performances at readings, the audiences had roared their approval through laughter, so they were sure they were on the right track. This sudden restriction, even though the brunt of the problem fell on Holzman, seemed unconscionable. It was "playing by the rules of someone else's game," to the hilt—exactly contrary to the musical's message.

Schwartz recalls, "Glinda used to say 'Goodbye Dorothy.' Huge laugh. Gone. And a line about the green witch: 'Did you just disappear in a puff of nasty-smelling smoke?' Cut. And a line, 'Making poppy fields for people to fall asleep in; what was that all about?' Huge laugh. Cut." He found the cuts idiotic.

The tense moment was at least as hard on Kristin Chenoweth as it was on the writers. "Here was the co-star of the show," Schwartz rants, "and she didn't have the big songs in the same way that Idina did, but what she had were some great scenes and some really funny lines. And suddenly her two funniest scenes were going. We had to cut all those lines. We had a list of lines that the lawyers for Universal made us cut or they were going to close the show. She had somewhere between six and ten giant laughs that had to go."

In order to break the news about the enforced edits, Holzman and Schwartz held a private meeting in the Clift Hotel with the star, who had accepted the part three years earlier. They spent time with her over several days as the script was reworked. "I have to tell you that this was a place she really impressed me," Schwartz shares. "Kristin stayed composed. She cried one day but she didn't have a fit. She didn't call her agent and say get me out of this show. She didn't do things that a lot of other people I know would have done. That was a place where the chips were really down and she could have behaved in a lot of ways that were not as constructive. Many people with their names above the title would have behaved in those far less constructive ways and she did not. And I will always admire her and always be grateful to her for that. But we said to her that she had every right to be very upset. We were incredibly upset, and very angry. But we promised her that we would come up with other lines for her." Winnie Holzman took her shopping in San Francisco as comfort.

Schwartz had good reason to acknowledge his colleague's endurance and ability to rewrite. "That's what Winnie is brilliant at. I was never more impressed with her than when those lines had to go, because as a writer I would have killed myself. It would have been as though they came to me a week before opening in San Francisco and I was told, 'I'm sorry but we're cutting 'Defying Gravity' and 'I'm Not That Girl,' and then I would have had to write different songs. And yet Winnie stayed calm and she just went to work and she came up with new solutions."

Settling in at the Clift Hotel next to the Curran, Holzman got to work on changes while Stephen paced the floor behind her, pondering new humorous lines for Kristin. The next tangle would be over the lighting on the ruby shoes.

Schwartz's passion remained unwavering with regard to the iconic images embedded in our culture's collective psyche by the popular film. For him, the Wicked Witch of the East's distinctive shoes that her sister coveted were the epitome of the message. Although in Baum's Oz they were silver, they were made ruby for the film, apparently to add to the Technicolor dazzle.

"You can't imagine the fight we had about the fact that Winnie and I were saying they *have* to be red," Schwartz reports. Jeweled shoes were about as close as they could get. But Schwartz-the-dramatist wanted red spotlights cast upon them to make them glisten the proper hue. "You have to put a red spot on her shoes," he tried to insist. When Platt passed along the "No," Schwartz retorted, "Then don't do the show."

Finally the shoes were lit to turn red.

Although Schwartz and Holzman lost many of the battles, they were finally able to keep a line that was unique to their work:

Nessarose: *What's in the punch?*

Boq: *Lemons, and melons, and pears!*

Nessarose: *Oh my!*

From producer Marc Platt's perspective, the changes were all about artistic inventiveness and their intention. "There was a line to walk, simply because many people's memory of *The Wizard of Oz* is from the MGM film and so we just wanted to be careful that we didn't take any protectable expressions of ideas that were in the film that were unique to the film. We don't own those and had no intention ever of using them. We wanted to be original."

Kristin Chenoweth, as Glinda, descends in her mechanical bubble.

CHAPTER 27

SHOCK AT FIRST SIGHT

Midwife and Witch's Father
…It's a healthy perfect lovely little…
Ohhhhh! Sweet Oz…

When Schwartz and Holzman first saw Mantello's vision of their story on stage during technical rehearsals, they were temporarily too stunned to be contributive. "Winnie and I spent a couple of days sort of glowering in the back of the theatre and never saying anything to Joe, which drove him a little crazy," Schwartz recalls.

After seeing *Wicked* in his head for six-and-a-half years, it was hard for Schwartz to adjust to this quite different actualization of the show. He especially worried over the dark appearance of the opening scene in terms of the bulk of the set and somberness of the overcoat costumes for the citizens of Oz. In early rehearsals, his imagination could still supply things, but he says, "When you actually see it concrete on the stage, it's a very shocking moment." Adding to the *Twilight Zone* nature of Schwartz's experience was the extensive amount of time the group spent working through this opening scene. Stuck and uncomfortable, he remained silent and waited.

As the company struggled to get ready, dress rehearsals for each act took up the two evenings prior to the first preview, so *Wicked* had never been performed in its entirety before it went public. Then on Wednesday night, May 28th, the Curran Theatre filled with 1600 people. The first audience would either cheer their approval or leave the theatre jabbering their disappointment. No one knew.

I was just in such shock that I couldn't speak to Joe for a while. But then with the first preview the audience responded extremely well from the beginning. So I think Winnie and I relaxed and thought our show is still coming across the metaphorical footlights.

STEPHEN SCHWARTZ

As it turned out, the audience eased readily into *Wicked*'s version of Oz from the moment actors in monkey costumes pulled open the curtain and Glinda appeared high above the stage in her mechanical bubble. They laughed, they applauded, and they stayed through the performance. At the bows, the crowd cheered wildly and rushed into a standing ovation as the cast members, with Kristin and Idina in the center, held hands and acknowledged the success. When the curtain finally closed, many cast members hugged each other excitedly. As Idina later reported, Kristin turned to her and said, "Oh my God, I've never been in a show where they stood like that!"

It had taken countless script drafts to reach that point and the affirmation helped ease some of Stephen's doubts. "It was going to make it easier for us to do our work. Is it good enough to succeed? That's another question. But it was clear that we were not just going to fall into the ditch, so that was very encouraging. I was pretty relieved."

Over breakfast in the Clift Hotel lobby the next morning, *Wicked*'s mastermind team of Marc Platt, David Stone, Stephen Schwartz, Joe Mantello, and Winnie Holzman faced each other for their first out-of-town notes meeting. With approximately twenty pages of notes on his lap, Schwartz asserted points about what he wanted to see happen.

There was never a lot of actual yelling. But it was very tense. It was people carefully navigating their way around one another.

DAVID STONE

David Stone remembers that being the worst meeting. "It was terrible, mostly because Stephen just came on too strong. It's natural for a writer to feel a little disoriented, but Stephen's instinct, because of his previous experiences, was to push very hard back. It was just like a bulldozer and the tone was really wrong. It wasn't a conversation like, 'Joe, I don't think that's quite working,' or 'These things are good but I want to talk about some other things.' Nothing complimentary. So that was a very bad day."

Schwartz comments in his defense, "Winnie and I felt we had never been given an opportunity to voice our opinions during the entire rehearsal process, always being told to wait until the show was up and running. Now that it was, we were determined to be heard." Everyone left the meeting with much still to be settled.

Mantello was already feeling bad about not being trusted to do his job. He expected to deliver the show in the script. "Not necessarily the show that they saw in their heads, but the show that they wrote." He didn't intend to cave in to every one of the writers' requests but would consider their comments.

On Saturday the five show leaders reconvened in Holzman's hotel room. Tension lingered over the revision process because, according to Stone, they had seen that *Wicked* worked, which meant they were "ten times more stressed" about fixing the problems. "We knew we were close to having something big— and we didn't want to screw it up. "

Having seen several previews, Schwartz was clear which scenes "stank" and which "worked," and offered his suggestions for cuts, since they needed to trim the show from its three-hour-and-twenty-minute running time. The group agonized over how much they could implement during the next week's rehearsals: what changes could the cast memorize, what cuts could the orchestra make? According to Schwartz, this was the most contentious meeting of the entire process. "Joe reduced Winnie to tears, and I really laid into him."

But things were about to look up. After an intense few hours, Schwartz left to give notes to the music director. "I stalked out of the hotel and I'm walking toward the theatre and there's this big mob in front and I thought, 'Oh no, somebody has had a terrible accident.' I was worried that maybe someone in our cast got hurt. Then I realized it's too early for anyone to be at the theatre. When I got to the crowd, it was a line at the box office that was

The pressure all of us had put on ourselves was especially intense. Everyone involved in the show had a great deal riding on it— more than usual, in fact.

DAVID STONE

stretching out into the street." He stood, stunned for a moment, realizing that positive word of mouth about *Wicked* must have spread. For the first time since long ticket lines formed for *The Magic Show* twenty-nine-years earlier, a Broadway-related musical of his had a momentum of its own. Maybe the hairsplitting details of the previous hours were less consequential than they had seemed.

While David Stone strove to create company unity by housing a core group at the Clift Hotel, Schwartz moved out as soon as the company manager could arrange it. Not one for bonding with the group at a time he needed to think clearly, he chose a newer hotel around the corner that he could walk over to when he needed perspective. Schwartz, who is always inclined to establish structures and boundaries, believes in the principle of keeping business relationships separate. It was a strategy he observed used by director Trevor Nunn, who, during his production of *The Baker's Wife* in London, separated himself from everybody else involved, including Schwartz. "I thought that was really smart," Schwartz affirms. "I did that on *Wicked* and it turned out to be an extremely good choice. If you mix business and your personal life, it makes things messy and unnecessarily fraught and complicated. I also don't need for the people that I work with to be my friends and my family. I have a family. I have friends. These co-workers are people I like and I'm happy to be in touch with over the years. But until the musical has opened, I really keep it quite separate."

The new room in the elegant Nikko Hotel served as a spacious, quiet getaway. In the dining/living room of his suite, he had room for a synthesizer keyboard to use for reworking songs. Many East Coast friends and relatives were flying out to see the show, and he could invite them up.

His parents, Stan and Sheila, and sister Marge came to enjoy *Wicked* in early June. As well as offering her suggestions, Marge also praised her brother, saying she wasn't surprised that the show was really good. Sheila suggested a scene be cut, and that went into the grab bag of impressions her son was collecting.

In his alone time, Stephen began rewriting and cutting song verses that were "overstaying their welcome, that seemed superfluous or redundant." Rewrite, test, rewrite, and test again. There was always a danger something could be tweaked to death, but he reasoned that an out-of-town tryout was about fixing things; when family and friends gave feedback, he pondered it, and then shared it.

Mantello wasn't pleased. "We can't start rethinking everything because a friend of yours didn't like it," he insisted. "I believe in keeping my own counsel. I feel like I'm good at my job most of the time and I feel like if the other people are doing their job, which in this case they were, WE can figure it out."

Two days before *Wicked* opened, Mantello won a Tony Award® for directing the Broadway play *Take Me Out*. It was his turn to be the experienced Broadway veteran when advising the relative newbie, Marc Platt, who seemed upset that some people walked out during previews. "I'm going to save you a lot of trouble," Mantello told Platt. "There's going to be a lot of people who don't like this show. And this is San Francisco; get ready for New York! You can't be devastated because a couple of people walk out. Maybe they didn't pay the babysitter past ten. Maybe they didn't like the show. Maybe they have a problem with witches. You don't know. There are people who don't like *Gypsy* and *Gypsy* is a masterpiece."

Mantello speaks of Schwartz and Holzman as an entity, and himself as another:
I remember feeling at that point that we were on two totally different tracks with one another. We were missing each other as people. It was very hard for either group to hear the other.

JOE MANTELLO

Stephen Schwartz and Kristin Chenoweth on opening night in San Francisco.

Opening Night

Wicked had enough going for it in its current incarnation to enchant the thousands who flocked to see it, who then spread the word before any reviews were printed. Still, it was judgment day. Critics who attended would cast their verdict over the likelihood of the show's future success.

Naturally, Schwartz wanted friends on hand for the special occasion. Holly Near, John Bucchino, and Pat Hunt, the original group from the 1996 Hawaiian boat ride, were only too glad to be there. More than anyone else, they would be awed that his imagined musical had become a gigantic two-hour and forty-five minute show, featuring eighteen songs plus reprises.

One of the Curran Theatre's prop staff had fallen in love with the dragon perched above the proscenium (whom the cast had named "Ozwald") and had been spending many hours refining his rigging so the operation went smoothly. Chic Silber, the special effects designer, had arranged for it to breathe smoke. Irrelevant as it might be to the whole show, it helped charm audiences into the unusual Oz opening up before them.

After a one-minute overture, actors in monkey costumes drew up the muslin curtain painted with an antiqued map of Oz. Kristin Chenoweth glistened in her bubble and Idina Menzel received enormous applause for "The Wizard and I." What the San Francisco audience would see that the New York audience wouldn't was a funeral scene for Dr. Dillamond midway through Act I. During it, Glinda claimed the spotlight with her eulogy and her change of name from Galinda to Glinda in his honor (while really hoping to please Fiyero by her act).

For "Defying Gravity," when the green girl rose to the top of the stage, all the effects worked smoothly. As the second act ended, the audience offered a standing ovation while the cast beamed. *Wicked* was off to a good start.

Wicked novelist Gregory Maguire attends opening night in San Francisco.

Reviews were mixed but generally hopeful. Although *Variety*'s reviewer complained about the "gluey banal sentiment" of the latest Schwartz musical and rated the score as Andrew Lloyd Webber crowd-pleasing schlock, several of the reviews were quite upbeat. *San Francisco Chronicle* critic Robert Hurwitt used the headline: "Every witch way: Spellbinding 'Wicked' a charming vision of Oz, but is a few bricks shy of a road." He insisted *Wicked* could use a few new songs and scenes but praised the approach. "Their primary choice is a good one…winnowing down Maguire's tale to focus on the relationship between Elphaba and Glinda—from being thrown together as college roommates ('I will be loathing, loathing you my whole life long') to becoming best friends and worst enemies…. The story of the two witches-in-training is well developed and expertly performed."

"*Wicked* is a smart, sassy and wildly different musical look at the Land of Oz," wrote Pat Craig in a review for *The Contra Costa Times*. "And, with a dollop of Munchkin wax and a bit of dramatic liposuction, *Wicked* could fly like a farmhouse in a hurricane and land on Broadway with all the explosive clatter of a spontaneous standing ovation."

There were now only 119 days until the show was to open on the vast stage of the Gershwin Theatre. As word-of-mouth spread and reviews reached the public, the new musical quickly sold out for its West Coast run. Oz-giddy audiences clearly delighted in the show, which they greeted with rapturous applause and standing ovations.

Judging from both critical and audience response in San Francisco, Glinda's part provided the best stage magic, especially with lines and songs written specifically for Kristin Chenoweth, who glistened in the role like a comic enchantress.

The story of Elphaba, according to Schwartz, "wasn't tracking." Fiyero, the girls' shared love interest, stuck out like a character dropping in from the show next door, and other parts of the puzzle dangled in draft mode.

Tone—It's Not *Les Miz*

About a week after opening night, Schwartz sat in his hotel room with a stack of newspaper reviews, email printouts, and notes from friends—in all, about thirty sources. Without heeding the nature of the source, he read everything, assuming the attitude of a statistician. In the responses for *Wicked* he looked for trends like the high points on the bell curve.

It wasn't because he aimed to please the next batch of critics. "What I would never do," Schwartz insisted in a San Francisco interview, "is change our show to be a different show than we want it to be just because we think someone will say nicer things about it in the press. What we *will* do is to try to understand where the show *we* are trying to do is not succeeding and try to correct it so that it's communicating more what we want to communicate."

He was completely surprised that both reviewers and friends commented that the opening number reminded them of *Les Misérables*. "How can they possibly think this has anything to do with *Les Miz*? I realized from the reviews that the costumes for the opening number were wrong and I wanted them to change them. They look like a mob. It *looks* like *Les Miz*." Mantello apparently supported Susan Hilferty, who had not had *Les Miz* in mind at all. She had designed the costumes for the "March of the Witch Hunters" scene for the Oz citizenry, and then it seemed that the same group of Ozians should appear in those costumes at the beginning. Says Hilferty, "The mob for me was basically the mob from any 1930s movie that goes to hang somebody in prison and they're heading toward the square with torches. So I literally was imaging the overcoat and fedora, with a twist." Schwartz was overruled and the "mob" costumes remained.

The songwriter *was* able to influence Fiyero's costume, noting that he didn't stand out enough. Hilferty designed a red vest to cover his shirt for his sporty polo duds. Then he'd slip into a princely new tux with tails for the ballroom scene.

In the songwriter's own turf, Fiyero's number, "Which Way's the Party?" seemed most problematic. "Butz works overtime trying to pump some life into the tired 'Which Way's the Party?' number," the *Mercury News* printed. "The ensemble gets down and gets funky Oz-style, and it looks like they're all doing a dance called the Spastic Scarecrow," wrote the *Oakland Tribune* reviewer. As well, the feedback Schwartz collected from colleagues suggested problems with this number. The piece would have to be scrapped completely.

I've wanted to work with Norbert since I saw him in Thou Shalt Not *and particularly in* The Last Five Years. *He's a lyricist's dream. In* Wicked, *I wrote 'Dancing Through Life' especially for him to take advantage of both his voice and charisma.*

STEPHEN SCHWARTZ

"I think what happened with 'Which Way's the Party?'" he said afterward, "was that it didn't translate for people into illuminating the character, into understanding that that's how this guy looks at life. It just seemed as if we were trying to do a production number for its own sake."

The third weekend in June, Schwartz was scheduled to give a workshop in Colorado. Just before getting on the plane he was discussing the issues about this song with Michael Cole. Several hours later, Cole received a phone call. His boss just wanted to share that he'd written an entire lyric on the plane for a new version of the song, and called it "Dancing Through Life."

For Schwartz's summer plans, composing music for "Dancing Through Life" would be high on the priority list.

More San Francisco Fixes

Another song that needed attention was "I'm Not That Girl." When Schwartz originally wrote it, he'd remembered a folk ballad called, "I Know Where I'm Going," sung by Ronnie Gilbert of The Weavers. That song ends in an unusual way, on what musicians call a $\underline{V}$ chord, rather than on the root chord. "I'm Not That Girl" ends on an E-major chord, rather than its root chord of A-major. This makes the ending feel unresolved. Schwartz used the music to represent Elphaba's emotional state when she sings this piece about unrequited love. But the ending made it harder for audiences to know when to applaud.

When watching Menzel sing it in San Francisco, the composer asked himself, "Should I end on the one chord? Should I put a button on it?" Those were all the things he didn't want to do. "Joe helped me out there," he later affirmed. "He fixed the lighting. And Stephen Oremus helped me to make sure that the audience knew the song was over." When those adjustments were made, the audience more readily understood the closure on the piece and then acknowledged it with their applause.

Behind the scenes, the company carried on with the nitty-gritty details of getting the job done. The cast adjusted to the constant changes given them by the writers. Schwartz praised their adaptability, particularly mentioning Idina Menzel, whose lines for Elphaba were a work in progress. "We'll be in rehearsal and changing many, many things. There will be eight scenes with changes in them. We'll get to performance that night and she's just letter perfect, as if she's been performing it that way for weeks! She's one of the hardest-working performers I've ever dealt with."

The orchestra, too, coped with the flux. "It was a very intense time," recalls Stephen Oremus. "They would make changes on stage during rehearsals and they'd be like, 'Oh, that's one tiny little change' and I'd be freaking out because I had to communicate that to twenty-three people in the orchestra. So I'd write a long list and everybody would get there early knowing we were changing things. We'd have pages and pages of notes for the orchestra on the stands."

In San Francisco the writers would say, 'Do you think you could put this in tonight?' So I'd have stuff written on my hand, and I'd have my dresser writing little Post-it notes with a one-line change in the scene, and I'd go, all right, what's the new line for the scene? Then I'd go out and do it.

IDINA MENZEL

Cast and crew members accrued experience so as to reduce mishaps on Broadway. One night the wardrobe door wouldn't stay shut and had to be fixed. Another night the audience heard a loud crash as a set piece fell over backstage. Norbert Leo Butz, in the role of Fiyero, recounts: "I have this Errol Flynn moment where I swing in on this rope. One night in San Francisco, I let go of the rope and the rest of the actors started cracking up. I turned around and the rope had literally tied around Kristin's head and got caught on her crown and was pulling her off stage. It was like watching Barbie get hung." Another night, a portable stand with spotlights mounted on it fell over on Chenoweth, a heads up for everybody to watch those backstage traffic routes. It knocked her out for a moment but she got up and finished the show.

Chenoweth had invented a hair-toss move as part of her characterization of a coquettish college girl. She overdid it one night and gave herself whiplash, aggravating an old injury. For several weeks, she had to wear a bejeweled version of a neck brace.

Despite temporary problems, the show had much going for it. To a friend, Schwartz commented, "The thing we're so lucky about is no matter how we change the show around and what we cut and what we add and make the right change or the wrong change, every time you re-deal that hand you're starting with two aces. You've got these two amazing women, so that's a big step ahead of the game."

A factor that helped Schwartz face the challenges of finishing a Broadway musical was the one he counted on at the beginning when he invited Winnie Holzman to share the project. Over the past few years they had spent hundreds of hours on the phone, or working together in one or the other's home, or in her hotel room or his, or going out for meals, or watching the show together from the back of the theatre and talking afterward. Their mutual support made the demanding process more manageable.

CREATIVITY NOTES

Collaborative Support

For Stephen Schwartz, the labels "bookwriter" and "songwriter" are not what they seem. While reworking *Wicked* in San Francisco with Winnie Holzman, he shared this story: "I was at lunch today with a television writer who was asking, 'Supposing you disagree on something, do you approach Winnie and say: You have to change this book scene? Or would she dare to say: I don't like that song?' But it doesn't work like that at all! There's no differentiation. We go back and forth. Even though she is ultimately responsible for the dialogue, there are lines that I wrote, and even though I'm ultimately responsible for the music and lyrics, there are lyrics that she wrote. It's a much less proprietary way of thinking."

He adds that teaming up is essential. "One of the things I have learned about doing a Broadway musical is that the writers must hang together as a team. Winnie and I often consciously said to each other, 'Don't argue in front of the kids.' We never disagreed in front of anybody. And if we had something where one of us felt one thing and the other of us felt another thing, whether it was about specifics in the book and score, or whether it was about how to handle a given situation in casting, or what we felt about staging, or anything like that, if we disagreed about anything, we always worked it out between the two of us so that we always spoke with a united voice, and that was vital."

Holzman was also confident in their team of two. "The relationship with the two of us is that we always ended up being able to come to the answer," she says. "It would sometimes take a long time, but we would get there. And I guess that's probably the definition of a good collaboration. We would end up getting there. It wouldn't always be easy or fun but we would get there and we would look at each other and go, 'Oh, I love that! I love that answer!'"

Carole Shelley as
Madame Morrible and Joel
Grey as the Wizard of Oz.

CHAPTER 28

PRE-BROADWAY SUMMER

Elphaba:
> *Too late for second guessing*
> *Too late to go back to sleep*

Packing and moving a farmhouse and other pieces of *Wicked*'s multimillion-dollar set by truck across the country to Broadway wasn't easy. But it was a cinch compared with getting the creative team to agree on a final version of the musical. And because rewrites for other out-of-town tryouts have been known to necessitate major rebuilding of sets, nothing could be installed in the Gershwin until the script was ready. The pressure was on to finish the final version of the script as soon as possible.

Could the composer and director work peaceably in the same room? "Joe and I are both a little bit 'My way or the highway' guys," Schwartz acknowledges. "It's odd because he's Italian and I'm not but I behave more stereotypically Italian and Joe behaves much more Jewish. I tend to do it very kind of openly and emotionally. Joe just kind of says, 'I'll just sit in the dark,' and goes away by himself and broods. It's odd because we behave exactly opposite from our ethnic stereotype."

Schwartz slipped into his "my way or the highway" ultimatum mode several times during the ensuing weeks, especially while speaking to Marc Platt. As an observer recalls, the second to the last night for the San Francisco production, "Stephen was screaming at Marc about something in front of the theatre after the show."

On the surface Schwartz was saying, in so many words, I'm the author of this show; if it's got my name on it, I have rights about what goes in—otherwise take my name off it and I'll go home. Platt had the power of purse strings, and seemed equally identified as Schwartz was with responsibility for his baby—it was *his* show, *his* company. If the two glared at each other in a cartoon image, the shared thought bubble above their heads could read, "I'm the father and I know what's best for *my* child."

Schwartz reports, "I was saying to Marc, look you have three choices. You can close down the show and walk away. Or you can do in New York exactly the show that we ended with in San Francisco. You have the legal right to do that, in which case you'll never see me again, but you can do that and take your chances. I don't think it will work but good luck to you. Or Winnie and I are going to make the changes we want to make and we're the authors and that's how it goes. And I really had to stand my ground on some things. I had to hang very tough. And Winnie had to hang tough, which is new and difficult for her."

As thermometers tracked summer heat waves, *Wicked*'s collaboration temperature remained feverish from late June through mid August.

To begin with, Stephen Schwartz and Winnie Holzman wanted to regroup on their own after San Francisco. They sent a polite email to Joe Mantello saying they needed time to rewrite. It was Mantello's turn to be shocked over expectations not meeting the reality confronting him. "They don't want to hear from me," was the message he took in, and the blockade seemed a violation of the rules for collaboration.

"It really, really, really, really pissed me off," Joe said later. "Because I felt like, yes, we have three months, but that three months is going to go by like that. And I thought that they had made such drastic changes that (A) I wanted to know why, and (B) I wanted to register my opinion of them. I thought I had earned that. And to be told, 'We're not ready to hear that right now,' was upsetting to me. I was feeling that I was being excluded at a time when we needed to roll up our sleeves. We knew after opening night that there were certain things we had to address. The writing of Elphaba needed to be stronger. And what I felt at the time was that they were putting Band-Aids® on things, but the real problem they weren't addressing was the character of Elphaba."

The writers wanted to address Elphaba, they just wanted to do it alone for a while, and they believed that relatively small adjustments could make a huge difference. Schwartz later explained they had several goals in mind after San Francisco. "The main one had to do with making the character of Elphaba more active and making the stages of her journey clearer so that each scene was a distinct and clear step in her journey."

Another goal was to retouch the political story by working on the Wizard's role, which necessitated recasting it. And they wanted to integrate Fiyero more successfully into the show with a new song and new lines.

After a one-week vacation in early July, *Wicked*'s Marc, Joe, Winnie, and Stephen gathered in Schwartz's living room in his Manhattan condo, meeting over the script from 8:30 a.m. until after midnight. "Oh my God, what a night," Schwartz remembers. "And then we continued the next day, working our way through the script line by line." Then it was "no rest for the wicked," as they geared up for the final push to get the job done.

As a group, the creative team decided to replace Robert Morse (Wizard) with Joel Grey, Kirk McDonald (Boq) with Christopher Fitzgerald, and John Horton (Dr. Dillamond) with William Youmans—changes they believed would support their new plans for the script.

They had asked Grey two years before but he was busy and didn't take it seriously. But then he was told about the father aspect of the role—

I am a sentimental man/ Who always longed to be a father. / That's why I do the best I can/ To treat each citizen of Oz /As son or daughter.

"That sounded interesting to me," reports Grey about the Wizard of Oz character. "That he never had that [experience of fatherhood] in his life and here he is in a very alien land."

Over dinner with Joel Grey one summer night, Schwartz and Holzman discussed his ideas for the role. "He asked a lot of questions," Schwartz explains, "And it made us think we could write him more Kansan," and they subsequently sprinkled some American sayings into his part of the script. Grey also suggested he should dance with Elphaba as part of the staging of "Wonderful."

The Wizard was becoming more likable, which suited the writers' perspective (overriding Maguire's view of him as being like Hitler). He was somebody who got caught up in the lavish attention poured on him in Oz, and who'd been corrupted by fame. Schwartz had written "Wonderful," in which The Wizard could make his case, and Grey's performance could come close to convincing the audience that he was an okay guy, all the while hinting at another layer to his personality.

Keep Dancing Through

If "Defying Gravity" was the *Wicked* team's collaborative tri-umph, the Fiyero introduction and student dance scenes were their biggest trouble spots. As Mantello would later reflect, "That section, in terms of costumes and the tone, was our hardest. It re-ally took the longest time." They already knew "Which Way's the Party?" wasn't working. But that was only one of the prob-lems. When the outfits for the dance arrived in San Francisco, the gowns were in jewel tones with saturated color, and were too busy from Mantello's point of view. One actress wore a black-and-white outfit, which he loved. He asked Hilferty to redo the others and "keep the palette of the ensemble very tight—black-

and-white formal wear—so that our principals would stand out among them."

At home at the piano, Schwartz slipped into musical brain-storming mode in order to replace "Which Way's the Party?" with his new song. He'd already tried one style of music, but Joe Mantello's lukewarm response to a private demo meant the journey wasn't over. The composer said in an early-July interview, "I'm going to write four different approaches to the music and play them for my collaborators and say 'pick one,' and then I'll do it that way because I can't make up my mind, so I'll let them make up my mind for me." It was an approach he'd used once before to satisfy movie executives. For *Wicked*, lyrics were ready and he had no problem writing a verse of music in a variety of styles for a potential "Dancing Through Life."

He tried a crooner tune as something Frank Sinatra might sing. He wrote some measures for a zippier dance piece that Fred Astaire might dance and sing to, similar to "They Can't Take That Away From Me." Moving up in musical time periods, he came up with something very piano-based, "Billy Joel-esque," as he describes it. He even attempted something more atonal, but decided it was too reminiscent of Stephen Sondheim to pursue. Finally, he brought to mind a long-time favorite composer, Sting, and wrote a tune with a danceable beat and strong baseline.

At the piano in his Manhattan apartment during the next meeting of the minds for *Wicked*, the songsmith set out a musical buffet before the gathered guests. He reports, "It was Wayne Cilento, our choreographer, who was most (pardon the pun) instrumental in the decision to use the Sting-like version of the music."

Schwartz finished this version of "Dancing Through Life" and supplied music for dance arranger Jim Abbott, who quickly prepared the number for fast-approaching dance rehearsals. Unfortunately, Mantello never liked the number. Schwartz recalls,

"He said to me in a difficult conversation we were having, 'Look, I just don't think it's a very good song.'"

As for the efforts for Elphaba, the writers reworked virtually her entire role. "I don't think she has one scene that hasn't changed," Schwartz explained in an interview around that time. "We tried to look at where she was in each scene, what had happened that made her different than where she started the scene before. We had done that before, but we felt after San Francisco that we hadn't done that job sufficiently well."

They also had story surgery on their minds: cutting an eight-minute funeral scene at Shiz for when Dr. Dillamond supposedly dies. From the songwriter's side, the idea first formed when his parents flew from Long Island to San Francisco to see their son's new musical in previews. It was Sheila Schwartz who said, "What do you need that funeral for? He isn't really dead anyway." That started her son thinking about cutting it. Independently, Winnie Holzman suspected that the scene was misleading and led to an awkward story twist for getting Elphaba to an appointment with the Wizard. But cutting the scene might mean a battle with her colleagues other than Stephen. She decided to face it.

The hardest thing on any musical, especially when there are so many people involved, is making sure that we're all making the same show. The good thing here is that the show on stage has the style and tone that we all wanted. For Wicked, we agreed about the big stuff.

DAVID STONE

Show Surgery

Even though the show had succeeded financially and in terms of popular appeal in San Francisco, the team knew it had to be perfected

Schwartz spent most of July and early August on his backyard patio in a bathing suit and a baseball cap, rewriting while getting a tan and dipping occasionally into his swimming pool. Hanging out in the sun, he often paced around while arguing with people on the phone. About the summer showdown he says, "I can tell you exactly what things we were fighting about: the structure of 'Dancing Through Life,' the elimination of the funeral scene, and the first three scenes of Act II. Those were the *huuuge* fights of the summer."

He had never been particularly skilled at negotiating with tact for what he wanted, and so he just tried to be as insistent as he could. His work philosophy could be expressed as: It's not about being nice; it's about getting the job done. He was task-oriented, and his intensity was hard to counter. "Maybe part of the reason I haven't experienced a musical being easy to create is that I'm part of what makes it difficult, because I have such strong goals for what I want the show to be. And if I feel that it's going away from those goals, I fight tooth and nail to return it to that track, and that can produce conflict when my collaborators are not necessarily agreeing with me. Joe weighed in and Marc weighed in with their opinions about the writing, but when it got contentious, I really dug in my heels and Winnie fortunately hung tough with me." He added later, "There were things that I absolutely believed. I held 'these truths to be self-evident.'"

A partial solution to the summer's issues would come from a more neutral party—David Stone. Stone was focused on the show's business aspects. He'd been occasionally pulled in for story decisions, and now he joined the fray as a kind of mediator and perspective-giver. "I was a little fresher to the creative process at that point," says Stone, "because I had been outside of it for a while. Marc had really carried this show on his back for five-and-a-half years. But because I had ten years of friendship with Stephen and with Joe, it was my turn to do some heavy lifting in the creative process. It was really only hand-holding, making sure that everyone kept talking even when they didn't want to."

He reports about the last week in July and beginning of August: "I went away for vacation, stupidly, in the middle of the summer. My cell phone bill was forty-nine hours in one week! A little tiny bit was from Joel Grey when we were talking to him. But the rest of it was from Marc and Stephen and Joe. My role was to navigate the emotional mine fields between Stephen and Joe, and Marc and Winnie. So I got to get yelled at the most because they would all vent at me instead of at each other."

Discussing the elimination of the funeral scene, Schwartz said calmly about a month afterward, "That was the biggest fight we had on the show. Susan Hilferty was upset and Joe was incensed and I realized later that some of it had to do with the fact that in his mind, that's where Elphaba first wears black, and he couldn't justify why [Elphaba] was suddenly in black. And I was like, 'Who cares, she wears a black dress one day, and that's what she happens to be wearing when she goes to the Emerald City, or she's got this hat and now she's got a dress to match the hat. I don't care why she's in black, I'm not going to give you an eight-minute funeral scene just so she can show up in a black dress.' But they were very upset, and from their point of view, I understand why, because they had their own visual through-line, and eliminating the scene pulled one of the tent pegs out from that."

Schwartz adds that Marc Platt was very concerned about the funeral scene. "He talked to Stacey Snider about it. I think if Stacey had said, 'They're crazy, we can't cut that scene, it's so important,' it would have gotten very tough. Fortunately, Stacey agreed with us. And that was the beginning of the turnaround for Marc."

In other areas of conflict, there were dance department/music department quarrels, especially over "Dancing Through Life." Cilento's way of staging it was different musically from what the songwriter wanted. "There were places that they really took it out of my hands in a way that's kind of unconscionable, because I should have had more authority over certain musical decisions that were made," Schwartz claims. "Because I had gone to the mat on other things, I felt, you know what, I'm going to give them this." He later admitted, "I have to say on this one, although Joe never liked the number, it's really Joe's structure that wound up in the show, and I think it's a good one."

By late summer, the image of the green girl in *Wicked* had become a personal symbol for Schwartz. For one thing, continuous disappointment had set in, and Elphaba's lyric, "Wishing only wounds the heart" (from "I'm Not That Girl") applied to his expectations and hopes and dreams for *Wicked*. It was hard not to be cranky when so much seemed to turn against him. For another, he had to struggle constantly to maintain congruence between his convictions and what others expected of his creations. He was isolated and ready to stay that way. "At this point I'm feeling something has changed within me, and I'm not going to play this game anymore—exactly the sort of turn that Elphaba takes at the end of the first act. There are certain things [over which] it's going to be this way, or I'm out of the show."

Walking to meetings in Manhattan, Schwartz sometimes ran into friends around the theatre district. "People say, 'Aren't you excited?' And I think, 'You're insane.' I'm not excited at all. No, all I feel is dread, because there is only one thing that could go right and there are so many things that could go wrong! It's like what a football coach once said: there are only three things that can happen when you throw a pass and two of them are bad.'"

Not surprisingly, that August he was burned out. One day he argued over the phone with Mantello while sitting in Stone's conference room. Schwartz scribbled out a note on a blank piece of paper and left it on Stone's desk: "David, I don't want to do this show. I quit. You can use my score but take my name off it, please. Do not call me. Speak from now on to Nancy Rose only. Goodbye—Stephen Schwartz." He walked out of the office, but came back to retract his comment. Stone was sympathetic.

Ultimatums are not the best way to handle things and it's a little embarrassing that I do have a tendency when I get tired or I run out of patience or tact to say, you know what, forget it. Let's just not do it.

Stephen Schwartz

Schwartz wasn't the only one feeling the strain of the collaboration. Marc Platt later revealed that everyone felt it, but at least the efforts to resolve conflict were based on the work details rather than egoism. "All the individuals involved in the show have had what I'll call their 'dramatic moments' at one time or another," says Platt, "where statements were made that were dramatic and, sort of, ultimatums. But those were few and always passing, fleeting moments, because it was always based on the merits of something. What emerged is a show that I think each of us is very proud of and very happy with."

CREATIVITY NOTES

Holding Steady and Being Flexible

In the summer of 2003, Stephen Schwartz and Winnie Holzman struggled to find the right course of action. They wanted to make changes to the script, but their colleagues asked them not to alter it too much. "People are afraid of change sometimes," Schwartz comments. "Writers are less afraid of change because that's what we're used to doing: thinking of something and saying, 'Oh, that didn't work,' and then just thinking of something else." Oddly enough for them, *Wicked*'s writers were accused of rigidity and of not accommodating the wishes of the group.

At the same time, they were listening to opinions and trying to sort out their choices in relationship to an inner vision of how their story should unfold. "It's hard to do at this time because you're hearing everything that everybody says, and everybody has an opinion and it's very hard to just shut all that out," Schwartz told another writer. "Ultimately, I think you have to take everything in and understand what in your show is communicating and what's not…and then write what you think *you* would like to see, informed, of course, by what you have learned. My experience has taught me that when I write what truly moves, amuses, or interests *me*, it usually communicates with others."

It was never easy, because he still believed in the principles of collaboration and working things out. Who is to say what was "right" when no one sees eye-to-eye? Time will tell. Time will heal.

"Ozwald" the Dragon over a map of Oz on the curtain for *Wicked*.

CHAPTER 29

WICKED ON **BROADWAY**

Glinda
> *Don't worry—I'm determined to succeed*
> *Follow my lead*
> *And yes, indeed*
> *You will be….*
> *Popular!*

As technical rehearsals finished, the company readied itself for previews and the October 30th Broadway opening. On the main two floors above the stage, *Wicked*'s stars selected dressing rooms and personalized their cinderblock hide-a-ways with fabric, furniture, and photographs. Ensemble members chose spaces in front of mirrors in shared rooms below the stage. Their Oz-twist costumes filled half a dozen clothing racks. In an out-of-the-way corner of the wardrobe area, black costumes for the abandoned funeral scene hung on a long rack.

The wardrobe and wig staffs also set up work areas on the lower level. Over seventy wigs needed to be maintained. In the hours before shows, Glinda's blond locks, Elphaba's black ones, and all the others would be brushed and readied.

Susan Hilferty oversaw the creation of duplicate Elphaba and Glinda costumes for the understudies and adjusted styles for a few others. In San Francisco, Michelle Federer as Nessarose wore a luxurious pink robe in Act II. "In New York," says Hilferty, "she was doing something different. Instead of it being about this wealthy, spoiled, overwrought invalid who had given in to incredible robes and jewelry, Michelle's Nessarose became more controlled and introverted—more like Emily Dickenson." To match the change, Hilferty asked Federer to switch to the black dress with a high black-lace collar that Kristin Chenoweth had worn during the now-deleted funeral scene. Federer would wear it without adornment and with her hair pulled back in a tight bun.

At stage level and in the hall, the set team unpacked and adapted their multi-million-dollar scenery system. Audiences would see as deeply as 40 feet to the back wall of the stage, depending on whether any of the clockwork gears or other set pieces were moved in or out. The design called for irising down the almost fifty-foot-wide stage in order to cozy up the view. To transform the cement-barn appearance of the austere Gershwin, the staff "grew" vines along the walls near the stage where they would hang hidden lights and speakers. They also augmented the Ozdust Ballroom, adding an arch of small lights, and carefully checked how the new script changes would affect the moving scenery.

Originally, Elphaba was much more of an observer. She was on stage a lot, but she didn't have an opinion about things—we couldn't see her point of view. The revised version after San Francisco gave her more intelligence and more of a sense of humor.

IDINA MENZEL

Idina Menzel came in before previews to practice walking backward into the "levitator arm" that provided a small platform for her to stand on for "Defying Gravity." (Safety arms snapped around her waist and locked around her.) In these days before the show opened, she also sped up her facial greenification, and got her routine "down to about forty minutes doing everything—with my wig and everything on. It's fun. It's like I'm a kid and I get to paint my body."

September and October — The Journey's End

Michael Cole was surprised at how little control his boss had, at this stage, over the musical he had conceived. Cole observed Stephen adapting to the situation by working on radio spots with his engineer and finalizing the score.

The music work seemed to provide a kind of solace. Schwartz said at the time, "I'm concentrating on the music because that's what I *can* do something about. I'm trying to make the music sound as good as I can make it sound. And I just have to let everybody else do his or her job as far as everything else is concerned, and hope that they do it well enough."

Now that "Dancing Through Life" was complete, he could make subtle refinements on the score as a whole. He commented in a message to fans: "At this point, there is only one brand new song, 'Dancing Through Life,' a replacement for Fiyero's first number, 'Which Way's the Party?' I have done much trimming and reshaping on other existing songs, and there are several new intro verses to songs which involve reprise material—this is one of my favorite techniques and makes the score feel more through-composed, and it was something I couldn't do too much of until I knew what the final songs were going to be."

When *Wicked* opened in previews in New York on October 7th, audiences embraced the show as they had in San Francisco. Worries began to lighten up, although Schwartz remained edgy. He and his teammates sat in the back of the house watching the show, and then met about changes they needed to make. Together they faced necessary cuts. Although a longer version had more depth, it had to be cut back. "The show was more moving when it was three hours and ten minutes," Schwartz said about the San Francisco version that told a more complete story. "That's the tough part about cutting. Everything we had in that show was there for a reason, so every time you take a little something out, the question is how much of a loss is this?"

Around Broadway, buzz for *Wicked* rose quickly. John Moses, who plays clarinet and other instruments in the *Wicked* orchestra, reported by email before opening night, "The talk on the street is very positive, and the best it's been in years for a new show. I think the merchandise kiosks have been doing great business with their stuff; we seem to be very well received every night by each theatergoer. I've been involved in over 25 new productions on Broadway,

Enough of the show was working that we could not be panicked; yet there was a level of panic that's just built in. With a new musical, I've never heard anybody say, "We had so much fun, and it was exactly what we wanted."

JOE MANTELLO

and I believe we have a hit here with *Wicked*. I'm guessing 5+ years; we will see. Mixed reviews won't matter, people want to see and be involved with this show. It's a feel-good show."

Still worried about the outcome and regretting his lack of control, Schwartz still sometimes went into panic mode. By then, David Stone had learned to smile and let his friend out of his numerous ultimatums about quitting if things didn't change. In mid October, Schwartz ranted over some minor detail, saying, "If this is the case, I'm never going to see the show after the opening night." Stone burst into laughter. "It was so funny. And then we went out for drinks afterward and he said, 'Forget that I said that.'"

Wicked would "freeze" about a week before the official opening to give the cast time to work into a final version before critics arrived. That meant that even up through the third week of previews the team of creators met to hash out final fixes.

Marc Platt helped add a last piece. It had to do with the monkey, Chistery, who had served Elphaba in her castle. When Elphaba fakes her death, Chistery remains and gives the *Grimmerie* to Glinda, at first in silence. "We had him speak when he was giving the book to Glinda. It wasn't at the right moment, and it wasn't landing," Platt reports. He realized that if Chistery found the green bottle that links Elphaba and the Wizard, it would be more touching, especially if he, an Animal, were to practice speaking to Glinda. "It became a poignant moment for the monkey character, and it also underscored the fact that the green bottle is a clue of some sort."

I never felt like I knew what I was doing the whole time, until maybe a few weeks ago and a few times in San Francisco, but I had Stephen Schwartz and I believed that he knew what he was doing.

WINNIE HOLZMAN
OCTOBER 2003

And so the bittersweet ending found its best staging. Holzman closed the book on the book. The last notes on the score, the last costume and set fixes, the final dance moves—all were tweaked and put in place for the cast to memorize.

By this time the creative team members were mostly pleased with their work. And they believed it was an important musical.

Schwartz later summarized the show's essence: "Its themes deal with ethical and philosophical questions: What is 'wicked' and what is 'good,' and what is the difference between how we see (and label) people in those terms and who they really are? Why are we so easily fooled by people who pretend to be good but whose actions are reprehensible? (There are certainly plenty of current examples in American life.) Don't all people have both wicked-ness and goodness within them, and isn't it how they come to rise to the best of themselves or succumb to the worst that ultimately decides what kind of person they are? Aren't things always more complicated and nuanced than they seem on the surface, and cer-tainly more complex than we tend to define them publicly? In a society such as ours in which public discourse has become in-creasingly simplistic and simple-minded, it seems to me these are highly relevant issues."

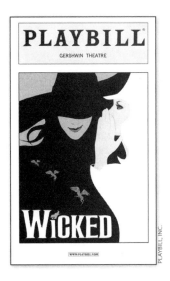

Finales

ASCAP hosted a party in honor of *Wicked*'s premiere, with Stephen Schwartz as a special guest. On Monday, October 27, 2003, the artistic glitterati of the musical theatre world showed up at this reception at Manhattan's Thalia restaurant after the show's evening performance. Musical theatre creators like Marc Shaiman, Charles Strouse, Lynn Ahrens, Stephen Flaherty, Lucy Simon, and others came out to toast Schwartz. The private gathering would be his only opening festivity, as he has a personal policy of never attend-ing his own openings. ("I hate opening nights for my own shows; they're horrible," he insists. "There are all these people who had absolutely nothing to do with the show...." He doesn't like the so-cial hubbub with a bunch of strangers blocking the food table from all the people who worked really hard to get the show mounted.)

His close friends were on hand for the ASCAP gathering, includ-ing Craig Carnelia, Dean Pitchford, who flew in from Los Angeles,

David Stone and Idina Menzel on Tony Award® night.

and John Bucchino, who had been witness to the show's development from its inception.

"It just feels so well balanced now," Bucchino told Winnie Holzman at the party. "Elphaba truly is the lead character and the strongest character; the most present sort of character."

But his most Elphaba-like friend would not be present at the October 30th glamour night when the green carpet spread in front of the Gershwin Theatre entrance and camera flashes lit up the night as celebrities and guests of the production filed into the hall.

Stephen and his wife Carole packed their Jeep and drove to a remote hideaway in the mountains of Vermont for a long and finally restful weekend.

Idina Menzel and Kristin Chenoweth mimic the *Wicked* poster as they pose for a photo at the opening night party at Tavern on the Green.

A Few Critics' Negative Comments
About the *Wicked* Score

"…Mr. Schwartz's generically impassioned songs…have that to-the-barricades sound of the ominously underscored anthems of 'Les Misérables.'"—Ben Brantley, The *New York Times*

"There are Sondheimesque numbers that have more than a passing suggestion of "Into the Woods," and these don't coexist well with the bushel of creamy generic scream-it-to-the-second-balcony pop ballads."—Linda Winer, *Newsday*

"…nothing really jells. The original material does not have much emotional sub-text, but a more insightful director might have forced Schwartz to create some." —Howard Kissel, *New York Daily News*

"The merits of Stephen Schwartz's score are meager…"— Michael Feingold, *The Village Voice*

"Schwartz… has produced the kind of bland, generic Broadway music where you tend to hear the orchestration…before you notice the tune. If you notice it."—Clive Barnes, *New York Post*

"The show's twenty-two songs were written by Stephen Schwartz, and not one of them is memorable."—John Lahr, *New Yorker*

A Few Fans' Comments on the Show's Score and *Wicked* Cast Recording

I loved, loved, loved the score and during "Defying Gravity" all the hair on my body stood up on end. —Stephanie

I can't even tell you how obsessed I am with *Wicked*. I know every word to all of the songs. —Alyssa

I was washing dishes when I played the CD and stopped dead in my tracks when I heard Idina sing "Wizard and I." After that, I was hooked. —Brian

I love every song from the show. —Samantha

From the first time that I heard that amazing music I fell in love! I play it non-stop. —Steven

My favorite pieces, such as "Defying Gravity," "What is This Feeling?" and "For Good" still give me the chills every time I listen to them. —Shawn

If I could pick where I had to die, it would be at a performance of *Wicked*. If I could pick the last words that I heard, it would be the last note of the song "Defying Gravity." This show is utterly amazing! — Jen

Wicked **as an International Phenomenon**

In May of 2008, as *Wicked* celebrated the fifth anniversary of its first performance in San Francisco, David Stone commented, "Nothing prepared any of us for the unbelievable success that *Wicked* has enjoyed. Every one of us worked on the show because we loved it, and we thought that other people would too. But the level of its popularity is far beyond anything that one can even dream about. Peter Marks of *The Washington Post* said that '*Wicked* is a breathtaking success story,' and the enormity of the success really does take your breath away. We recently hit a cumulative worldwide gross of $1 billion dollars (faster than any show in history) and there is no end in sight. There are productions now in New York, Chicago, Los Angeles, First North American Tour, London, Tokyo, Stuttgart and Melbourne. Upcoming productions are scheduled for San Francisco, Second North American Tour, and Amsterdam. What is truly amazing is not just that the productions are running, but that they are still selling out everywhere.

"Marc refers to *Wicked* as an "8 to 80," as they say in the film business. Our audience is incredibly diverse because there are very few people of any age, especially in America, that don't have a deep relationship to *The Wizard of Oz*. What has been especially interesting is how well the show has been received in England, Australia, Germany, and Japan, where *The Wizard of Oz* is not a part of the culture in the way that it is here. In Japan, in fact, hardly anyone knows that source material, yet they are coming because they are attracted to the story of a strong relationship between these two amazing women. And I think that this points to why it is a success for so many different groups of people. Children, young adults, older audiences, all find something in the show that appeals to them: from the putting together of *The Wizard of Oz* story, to the exploration of what it means to be an

Marc Platt, Stephen Schwartz, and David Stone celebrate the 1,000th performance of *Wicked* on Broadway.

When the tour hits a city, tickets are gone within hours of going on sale.

DAVID STONE

outsider, to the examination of the idea that societies judge value based on appearance, to many other deep and personal meanings. A large family can all appreciate the show on completely different levels—and then walk out and talk about what it meant to each of them. And, most importantly, *Wicked* appeals to anyone who believes that a friendship can change your life in profound and unexpected ways. And that is an experience that knows no cultural boundaries and an idea that remains timeless."

Stephanie J. Block and the ensemble perform "Defying Gravity" in the 2005 *Wicked* Tour. The sets, props, and costumes for the tour fill fourteen 52-foot semitrailers when being transported from city to city.

Megan Hilty, Caissie Levy, and the ensemble perform "One Short Day" in the Los Angeles production of *Wicked*.

JOAN MARCUS

John Rubinstein, the original Pippin, plays the Wizard in the Los Angeles production of *Wicked*.

"Both John Rubinstein and Ben Vereen, original stars of *Pippin*, have performed the Wizard. It's interesting that these two extraordinary performers, who provided such a contrast to one another in *Pippin*, should wind up playing the same role in *Wicked* thirty-plus years later."

—STEPHEN SCHWARTZ

"After over thirty years, what a joy and a wonderful twist of professional fate it is to find myself once more enjoying a long run in a Stephen Schwartz musical. *Wicked* touches so many people on so many levels; it is a great story, beautifully told, with great roles for actors and singers. I am loving every single minute of being the Wizard of Oz!"

—JOHN RUBINSTEIN

Stephen Schwartz at the
Gershwin Theatre.

AFTER THE TONYS

...So keep dancing through...
WICKED

An Interview with Stephen Schwartz at the Gershwin Theatre

In September of 2004, I drove into New York City to meet Stephen Schwartz for an interview before he headed off to a Dramatists Guild meeting that afternoon. We met at the theatre where *Wicked* had been playing to sold-out houses for a year.

Going into the Tony Awards® season the previous spring, he had hopes of winning the recognition he'd aspired to, but *Avenue Q* collected Best Score, Best Book, and Best Musical awards.

I had scheduled the interview with Stephen at the Gershwin because I had more to learn about his self-perception regarding fame, fitting in, and his outlook about the future. The following are highlights from our conversation, with minor edits for clarification.

I guess somewhere in the back of my mind, I always thought I'd have a Tony someday. It seems ironic to me that the kid who dreamed about writing for the musical theatre wound up with Oscars and Grammys but no Tonys. Of course I'm the one who always says awards don't matter.

STEPHEN SCHWARTZ

"I've always liked this theatre," Stephen remarked as he opened the Gershwin stage door on 51st Street. "I saw the very first show that was here—*Via Galactica*."

A vigilant backstage door manager, who was sorting mail for the cast, looked us over.

"Can I help you?" he inquired.

"He's the composer," I said with a grin, feeling like I owned the place just by standing next to him.

"Oh, sorry, I didn't recognize you," the guard replied, and shrank back to his desk.

Stephen punched the Up button on the old freight elevator and we climbed aboard. We passed through the backstage hallways to the upper lobby of the theatre.

"This is the Broadway Hall of Fame," he showed me. Along the white walls, columns of names formed of gold-painted letters rose high above our heads. A section of lettering that described the display caught his attention: "It says here, 'The Theatre Hall of Fame honors those who made outstanding contributions to the New York Theatre. Eligibility requires a career spanning 25 years on Broadway and at least five major credits. Selections are made annually by the nation's drama critics and editors.' The name of every major American theatre composer is on that wall," Schwartz pointed out, noting that his is not included.

"Here's Tom Jones and Harvey Schmidt," I said as I read the names. "Betty Comden, Jerome Kern, Irving Berlin, Stephen Sondheim…"

I'd seen the golden list before, but it was just a bunch of names, and in another part of the hall, black-and-white photos of the people listed. I had figured these displays were a theatre owner's way of attracting attention, but apparently a Broadway organization maintains it.

We sat on the black-cushioned benches beneath the golden letters.

"When I was a kid," Stephen began in a quiet voice, "of course neither the Gershwin Theatre nor this wall of names existed, but this was going to be my 'corner of the sky.' I wanted to make a contribution to musical theatre; maybe help to advance it in some way or expand its boundaries like people whose names are on this wall, like Richard Rodgers, and Stephen Sondheim, and Bock and Harnick, and Kander and Ebb and all these other people. That was my dream.

"And I think concomitant with that dream was an acceptance by the Broadway establishment, which I think is what this wall symbolizes. And that's what, for whatever reasons, didn't happen

We don't get everything we want in this life. That's kind of what I write about. If we are persistent and tough and determined, we can get some of what we want, but no one gets it all.

STEPHEN SCHWARTZ

for me. I won't even say it's a disappointment anymore, because at this point I've accepted it. It's simply a fact of life. I've had to accept the fact that it's a dream that didn't come true. And that's okay, because so many other things have come true and have exceeded my expectations.

"I couldn't ask for more from the score for *Wicked* in terms of response that I've gotten, in terms of what's happened with the album and the sheet music and the unbelievable way they have sold, the fact that I hear constantly from people about how the CD is never out of their car, and their family has four copies of it, and their children have the music and they know all the songs, and so on and so forth. This may be a stronger response to a score of mine than I had for *Godspell,* which was a pretty amazing response. That's all gratifying to me. But there was an aspect of my dream of being among these people." He gestured mildly to the names on the wall.

In planning this interview, I'd recalled a line from the musical *Pippin,* which I wrote out and brought with me. After traveling to battle with his father Charlemagne, Pippin is ready to give that up completely, and speaks the line I now gave Stephen to consider.

"'I thought there'd be more plumes,'" he read aloud. "Roger Hirson's line, not mine. But that's my favorite line in the show. I guess that's how I feel about Broadway. I thought there'd be more plumes."

I suggested, "In a certain way the plumes are about the reward for a contribution. They are the fruits that you hope for, but we don't undertake any action for the sake of the fruits, necessarily."

"No, that's true," he agreed. "When I started I didn't do it for the money, I didn't do it for the fame. It wasn't that I wanted to *be* something, it's that I wanted to *do* something. I thought I had been given certain gifts and talents, and I could use them within the form of musical theatre, if not to advance the form necessarily, at least to add to the literature."

Sitting below the names, we spoke about who made it into the musical theatre "canon" and who didn't. We shared our mutual bewilderment over the way some critics and theatre pundits treated Broadway efforts—as if they would be happy if the majority of shows failed.

Heading out of the hall, we walked past the part of the theatre with a photo gallery. "Here's Jerome Robbins," I pointed out. "Did you like him?"

"There were three people who were around in my lifetime that I wish I had worked with," Stephen replied. "The major one was Jerry Robbins. The couple of encounters I had with him were very positive experiences." [The other two on his wish list, he later explained, were Hal Prince and Michael Bennett.]

"But you know what, Carol? After all this time, I walk through the Gershwin, and I see that line at the box office, and there's a sign that says 'This Performance Sold Out'—how can you feel bad? I'm stunned by what's happened with the show. I'm overwhelmed by the success. Plus I actually like the show. That's the other thing: it's not only a success but it's a show I actually even like."

As we left the building, even though it was pouring rain, I decided to walk with him toward his Dramatists Guild meeting several blocks away. I held my tape recorder toward him as he sheltered me from the torrent under his black umbrella. Remembering something I had meant to bring up about the ending of *Pippin*, I started singing a stanza from the finale to the show: "*I wanted magic shows and miracles/Mirages to touch.*"

He joined in to sing, "*I wanted such a little thing from life/I wanted so much.*"

"What about it?" he asked.

"Doesn't that tie in?"

He paused for a few seconds. "Actually, you're making me feel good about the ending of my Broadway story. Because you're right, if I were writing it, if I were writing me as a fictional character, I would never have written an ending like *The Bad News Bears* or one of those movies where they win everything in the end. If I had written my life as a story, this is the ending I would have written: mitigated—not unmitigated—success. Not a perfectly happy ending; not someone getting everything he wanted; something that was basically positive but with that dash of bitters thrown in. So maybe it worked out the way it was supposed to after all."

Winnie Holzman and Stephen Schwartz on the Hollywood Walk of Fame. Four and a half years after *Wicked* opened on Broadway, Schwartz was honored in Los Angeles for his contribution to theatre. He attended the unveiling ceremony at the Pantages Theatre where *Wicked* enjoyed a record-breaking run.

Extras

Stephen Schwartz attends the opening of *Golda's Balcony*, a Broadway show that his son directed.

Author Carol de Giere

Jessica, Scott, Stephen, and their beloved (and according to Carole Schwartz, deliberately spoiled) Archie.

ABOUT AN AUTHOR AND A SONGWRITER

Like a comet pulled from orbit
As it passes a sun

WICKED

When Stephen Schwartz and I first "met" by way of his website, we lived 1,000 miles apart and he was lifetimes ahead of me in terms of success and its rewards. He was born in 1948, chose a career direction at age nine after seeing his first Broadway show, and wrote the score for *Godspell* at twenty-three. By the time we met in person in the summer of 2000, he had already been working at the top of his field for three decades. His activities involved multi-million-dollar projects for which he wrote songs at home on his 15-acre country estate in Connecticut or held meetings in his 7th floor condo near Manhattan's theatre district. As eminent as he was, he often spent time answering questions from people who wanted to learn from him.

I was born in 1952 in Madison, Wisconsin, and watched my first Broadway show at age forty-nine. I lived with my husband, Terry, in an 800-square-foot bungalow in the small Iowa town of Fairfield, about five hours southeast of *The Music Man* writer Meredith Willson's hometown, Mason City. Like Marion in Willson's musical, I worked for several years as Madame Librarian; however, I longed to express myself creatively by writing articles, books, and songs. After studying professional writing in graduate school, I started a new career writing feature stories for local and regional publications.

My songwriting efforts reached their peak when a local elementary school group performed a few of my songs in their pageant, but small-time creativity seemed to be the limit. My inspiration lived by its own whimsy; my writer's voice flickered like candlelight in a prairie breeze. As a fan of creativity how-to books, I believed that artistic energies could be heightened with training and practice.

One day, for a freelance job as part of a team creating a large website, I was assigned to write several pages of text about musicians whose last names begin with the letter "S." On the Internet I researched guitarist John Schneider and jazz singer Diane Schur.

The next name, "Stephen Schwartz," looked somewhat familiar. Although I had been a casual fan of musicals, I wasn't yet theatre geek enough to know his work by his name. I logged on to www.Stephenschwartz.com, and after noting his impressive bio (that included one of my favorite musicals, *Godspell*), I read Mr. Schwartz's articulate and charming answers to fans' questions about his work. I'd struck gold: not only had I discovered someone whose creativity was reliable, but I'd "met" an accessible artist who was self-aware enough to describe his process in a way that would help me and others absorb it.

It made sense to enter his world by way of writing about it. I emailed him, requesting permission to cover his story in a book. A few days later he replied, "No one to date has asked," and he agreed to cooperate with my efforts as long as I focused on his artistic output and not his personal life.

By summer I was in New York for our first interview, lifting one of his golden Oscar statuettes out of the glass cabinet in his Manhattan condo.

"Whoooa!" I yelped. The unexpected weight of the Oscar he'd earned for writing song lyrics for Disney's *Pocahontas* nearly tipped me off balance.

"I told you; that's what everyone says— 'They're so heavy,'" he commented about the eight-and-a-half pound trophy. "This one is actually peeling." He showed me how the gold covering had flaked off on one of the feet, exposing a gray metal. He never wanted to have it fixed because he likes how it comments on the thin veneer of show business glamour.

I looked forward to peering beneath the surface of the entertainment world. Standing for the first time in the hallway of Stephen's Manhattan condo, I noticed a visual clue for the prevailing metaphor of his profession and my book project—puzzle-solving. Hanging in a small black frame was a page from a magazine that included *Key of C*, a British-style crossword puzzle he co-authored. Over time, I learned that brainteasers and bridge, Scrabble® and Boggle® crosswords and Sudoku are mental exercise gyms for a songwriter whose profession involves solving storytelling riddles, addressing intricate rhyme schemes, and carefully connecting songs to shows.

In my case, the puzzle work involved fitting interview material into a whole pattern for the jigsaw puzzle that was Schwartz's multi-decade journey. The special challenge for my book jigsaw was that the goal kept changing.

Stephen originally pointed me toward some of his favorite books that might serve as models for my work. One recommendation was Craig Zadan's *Sondheim*

& Company, which reveals how Stephen Sondheim and colleagues worked through show development problems. Another was William Goldman's *The Season: A Candid Look at Broadway*, in which Goldman covers a particular Broadway season, exposing behind-the-scenes creative issues and commercial concerns.

These books got me started and helped me to realize that from such a great physical distance, I couldn't really describe what it was like to be around musical makers.

In 2002, as Stephen and his colleagues compacted *Wicked's* storylines into a musical, my husband and I wrestled with packing issues of our own. We had decided to relocate to the New York City metropolitan area so I could work on the book and Terry could find a new job.

"I can't believe this is going to fit," I remember muttering as I studied the empty U-Haul truck backed up to the porch and then eyed a snarl of boxes and furniture in the house. But Terry found a way to wedge everything in, and we left our familiar life behind. (The difficult-to-fit theme traveled with me, transferring to my piles of manuscript drafts and research materials.)

Our relocation proved essential for my book and confirmed how giving in to promptings from a muse can change your life! Living within commuting distance of Manhattan meant I could catch a busy songwriter for interviews at Starbucks coffee shops, on subway rides, over tea after his workshops, and while walking with him to his next meeting.

During our first interview session, held around the glass dining table in Stephen's city apartment, I began reading on his soon-to-be familiar face a reflection of his complex character that matched his far-ranging output. His serious nature appeared in the long cheeks, prominent nose, and sometimes furrowed brow beneath a crop of brown hair. This matched my sense of him as an earnest composer of musicals with significant themes. Yet when his face curled into a smile, I glimpsed a boyish elfishness glistening in his blue-green eyes. It started to make sense that the same man who wrote the majestic "When You Believe" from *The Prince of Egypt* also wrote the goofy "All For the Best" for *Godspell*.

That first day I also noticed his hands as they wrapped around a large tea mug. His fingers are not the long, slender kind I previously associated with artistic people, but are sturdy and wide, more like those you'd expect on a carpenter. Over time I realized he is a builder of sorts. He usually helps to construct the framework of a musical-in-progress and then helps determine the placement of songs within that story structure.

The positive results of his storytelling successes are on display in his private corner of Manhattan. In an office converted from a bedroom, posters for *Godspell, Pippin, The Magic Show,* and other productions fill a wall with neatly framed splashes of red, off-pink, lavender, and blue. In the living/dining room area, Pocahontas waves from a framed animation cel on the wall, her hair flowing in the "colored" wind. Posters for *The Prince of Egypt* and *The Hunchback of Notre Dame* hang in a hallway, and later a Wicked Witch of the West teapot took over some counter space in the kitchen.

Of course, there is no framed portrait of Bob Fosse, a director with whom Schwartz tangled; no replica of the closing notices for *The Baker's Wife, Working,* or *Rags.*

For the first few years I attempted to describe how these musicals evolved, but as I studied the stumbling blocks of Stephen's journey, and looked past the Oscars, Grammys, and royalty checks, a new kind of story emerged. I finally understood the degree of disappointment he experienced along his path, and the amount of healing he needed to do in order to carry on.

David Friedman, a fellow songwriter, summarized Stephen's journey for me during an interview. When I mentioned that Stephen seemed to have some contradictory qualities, Friedman said, "If I think of a dichotomy for Stephen it's that he is sensitive and yet he has the fortitude and strength to survive and be successful. Stephen is often viewed as difficult. He has been thrown out of rehearsals because he is very opinionated, and yet that comes from sensitivity—a sense that he's going to be walked over, a sense that he's going to be hurt. Stephen, also much more than I, has had the ability to navigate that sensitivity. He shows up and gets out there and goes in and tries and works and presents and fails and gets fired and comes back. He just keeps going."

With this in mind, the goal of my puzzle settled into the more manageable and interesting task of telling Stephen's "creative career" story instead of reporting more generally on the making of each musical.

In my new attempts to fit Stephen's career into one volume, I recognized an organizing pattern I could use after listening to a talk by another biographer who had noticed that her subject's career fell naturally into "three acts." For *Defying Gravity,* I divided Schwartz's career in a similar way, and as I collected material, I subsumed it within this framework.

❧

For me, a great benefit in writing an authorized career biography was the interaction with the principle subject. For one thing, it was often fun to confer about the book. There were rare but delightful warm-weather moments spent on the back deck at my rented house in Connecticut. Stephen and I discussed my chapters while downing tea, grapes, crackers, and cheese. As well, over the eight years of the project, he helped by breaking myths about creativity that were holding me back.

I had assumed pros like him always hit the mark first time around, and that I was probably inferior because it took me countless drafts to get something workable. But I learned that having songs or stories pop out fully formed is a relatively rare phenomenon. Writing usually takes time and a lot of effort.

Stephen quips, "I envy people who say 'I just channel and things flow.' God bless them—I don't know how they do that. I sit there with these notepads and pencils, and a little phrase will come to me that I'll scribble down, and then a totally unrelated phrase comes that doesn't rhyme and has nothing to do with it, and I scribble that down. The notes all look like pages and pages of patchwork stuff. Eventually something will emerge and I'll go back and start to think, 'I could take this and put that with that.' It's more like assembling pieces that arrive. It's very, very rare that something just flows on out. It's exhilarating and a huge relief when that happens, but it doesn't very often."

Another myth he broke for me was that writers aim at pleasing an audience. Although this is true to a limited extent, from Stephen I learned that pleasing the masses is not necessarily the aim and it comes late in the game. That's why a conversation we had in San Francisco during *Wicked*'s out-of-town tryout in 2003 was so significant to me. I'd held some over-the-rainbow notion that everyone would delight in his new musical, and was disappointed to learn that some didn't. He shook his head and said, "There's just nothing that everybody likes. You can't please everybody."

His freedom in this regard shook me in its boldness and helped me move forward with my own choices. I had been worrying about pleasing my audience, and that held me back. And, of course, I worried about satisfying his taste.

"It's your book," he emphasized when our talk turned to my project. "You need to write it the way you want to write it. It's not what interests me, it's what interests you. If and when I write a book, I'll write my book."

I hope he does, as I will always have things to learn.

CREATIVITY NOTES

Writing to Please an Audience of One

Writers are often advised to write with their audience in mind. Stephen Schwartz follows the advice in an unexpected way. "The audience I always write for is myself. I hope and assume that if I would like something, find it interesting and moving, and consider the work of high quality, others will too. I find that makes me tougher on my own work and avoids pandering and second-guessing. I'm writing what I want to hear; I'm writing what speaks to me. And somehow it speaks to enough other people. It may not ever speak to anyone who reviews for the *New York Times*, but it's speaking to enough people."

At another time, when he explained his thoughts about an audience, he said, "I think the trap that writers fall into is in trying to second-guess the audience, or the critics, and thus not really writing what they believe, or feel, or care about. The audience can smell your passion, your commitment, and audiences are really smart as a collective entity. They really can spot phoniness a mile off, and so you can trust that if as a writer you can get to the truth (and that doesn't all have to be heavy duty— it can be comic, it can be satirical, it can be political or whatever), it will speak to people."

Stephen Schwartz at work out of town.

From Idea to Audience:
The Odyssey of a Song

There's things waiting for me to invent them
There's worlds waiting for me to explore
I am an echo of the eternal cry of:
"Let there be…"

CHILDREN OF EDEN

What happens to a show tune before it reaches you or me by way of a performance or cast album? After meeting Stephen Schwartz, I decided to trace the journey of a song as it manifests. With his help, I eventually learned how music moves from the most silent, inner ruminations and creative leaps of a songwriter through layers of storytelling decisions, physical scoring, and on to stage productions and cast albums.

First Impulses: The Inside Story

Back in November of 2000, when I was still living in the Midwest, I boarded an Amtrak train for the ride from rural Iowa to Chicago. Stephen had agreed to grant me most of his free time for two days before evening concert appearances there.

Heedless of the long, quiet prairies the train pulled past, I studied my questions about the creative terrain of his working process. My most anticipated duty that weekend was to uncover colorful little stories for my readers based on Stephen's real life encounters—the ones that inspired specific passages in his musicals. Or so I thought.

I had secured a suite in a downtown hotel where Stephen and other performers were staying, to provide us with interview space. When I opened my door early in the morning for our scheduled meeting, he bounded in, his energy lifting as if into a tennis match. Dressed in pre-concert casuals, his blue jeans contrasted with the velvety olive upholstered chair he settled into. The world traveler made a few comments about the unsuitable smallness of his room on the floor below, and then we began. I served up questions about *The Prince of Egypt* and his field trip to Egypt, as well as his other film projects and shows.

"When you went to the Sinai, did you see Bedouins with handmade rugs?" I inquired, with a National Geographic-type scene as my reference point. I had in mind "Through

Heaven's Eyes," a song with the lines:

"A single thread in tapestry/Though its color brightly shine/Can never see its purpose/In the pattern of the grand design."

He must have browsed a street bazaar in Egypt and picked out a special tapestry to bring home. Or perhaps he'd visited some hut where some Egyptian craftspeople were sitting on the floor weaving rugs.

"I didn't see rugs in the desert," he answered, returning my gaze with mild surprise. "All of the imagery in 'Through Heaven's Eyes' is clearly related to research I had done. After a while it's hard to know whether something came from a picture I saw or a book or something I saw on the streets of Egypt or whatever. You know, it all blends into closing my eyes and putting myself in the Sinai."

It was actually the most helpful answer for how he works. But I completely missed the point. "He just doesn't get what I'm trying to ask," I thought to myself.

When we got to stories about the short-lived Broadway musical *Rags*, an immigrant tale set in New York City around 1910 with lyrics by Schwartz, I asked about the sultry "Blame It on a Summer Night," a song from the show that later became popular among cabaret singers. Surely singers would want an anecdote about this piece.

I asked, "Can you remember a certain summer night that inspired that song?" He'd

no doubt reveal a story about tooling around with friends in New York City late some night as the basis for lyrics like:

> The street is full of lunatics
> Sharing some pagan rite
> If we're here till dawn
> Can we blame it on
> The summer night?

"That was not something that came out of my life, particularly," he replied nonchalantly. "It was really what the music sounded like to me."

Darn.

Throughout the day I gathered material for other aspects of my research. We ate lunch and continued until late afternoon, when the songwriter headed for the door to prepare for an evening performance. I squeezed in a question about the sparrow metaphor—a powerful image for the need to let go of someone as they grow (as parents do their offspring). It's from a *Children of Eden* song, "Hardest Part of Love."

> As a child, I found a sparrow
> That had fallen from its nest
> And I nursed it back to health
> Till it was stronger than the rest
> But when I tried to hold it then
> It pecked and scratched my chest
> Till I let it go…

I had so clearly visualized a boy holding a fluttering brown creature that I was *certain* Stephen would share memories of an injured sparrow he'd looked after while growing up on Long Island.

Instead he just laughed and said, "Carol, you keep wanting to find a source, but I didn't have a pet sparrow. I just made it up."

Several years and a move to New York later, I met Stephen for an interview in his Midtown Manhattan condo/office one evening. I made another attempt to spark his memory of song origins, this time for *Pippin*. I knew that, like me, he is a morning person who writes early in the day. I asked what I had always imagined would be true: "Did you wake up one morning to see a beautiful sunrise and then write 'Morning Glow'?"

"No, Carol, you're still not getting how I work," he said in a slightly exasperated but gentle tone. "You keep asking about these external influences. It's not like that; it's internal. Let me explain to you how I work."

As he spoke, I could imagine him at home in rural Connecticut where he handwrites lyrics. ("Computers stifle my creativity.") And he "noodles" on the piano until a song emerges.

"It may be other people's processes," he allowed. "It may be that Paul Williams wakes up one Monday and looks outside and it's raining and he's grumpy so he writes a song

called 'Rainy Days and Mondays.' I don't do that. I usually have an assignment that I give myself, which is that I'm working on this moment in the show right now. And I go into a room that has a piano in it, and places where I can pace, and yellow pads, and I close the door…"

At this point he closed his eyes and gestured with his right hand as if slipping it into a puppet.

"…and I try to become the character at that moment and feel what he or she is feeling, see what he or she is seeing, and most importantly, want what he or she is wanting."

He opened his eyes.

"Then I write down phrases that come to mind. And if it comes out, 'this is going to be a new morning for me and glowing like a new morning,' then I get an idea to write a song called 'Morning Glow.' It comes from inside. It's not from, 'Oh look, it's a sunrise. I know! I'll write a song called 'Morning Glow' and stick it on this character, Pippin.' It's completely the opposite. It's all internal with me! It's really not affected at all by external events, by external sensory realities."

He next used a metaphor that dated us both as Baby Boomers. In the pre-video games era of the Hula Hoop® and coonskin caps there was a mass-produced toy divination product known as the Magic Eight Ball®. The ball had a window with a floating black plastic octagon inside that had different sayings written on each side, any one of which could happen to come up when you shook it or turned it over while asking questions about your life's direction.

Stephen continued: "You know that Magic Eight Ball? Where you shake it and you look at it and something floats to the surface and it says, 'Signs point to yes,' or 'Ask again later'? A lot of the experience of writing is like that for me. I sit there and sort of shake my internal Magic Eight Ball and something floats to the surface. And I write down whatever floats to the surface. Do you know what I mean? And it may be something from a long time ago or something that I just imagined or a phrase I heard that I've always liked and suddenly seems appropriate. Deciding to write is a conscious and deliberate choice, like deciding to meditate. But what happens once you put yourself in that place is not so conscious and deliberate. It's unconscious and instinctive. And, as I say, it has very little to do with what's around me at the time. I'm almost completely unaware of my surroundings."

At that point we had to become aware of our surroundings because he had to leave for a film screening. I finally realized that at its core, Stephen's artistry is an inside story: although he consciously and subconsciously collects impressions before he begins, a song ultimately emerges from what he hears and feels inside himself.

Rewrites, Testing, and "The Wizard and I"

Before studying how musicals developed, I somehow expected that they unfolded in a linear fashion. Growing up watching the standard licensed shows that played in Madison, Wisconsin, the musical theatre genre appeared pat and patterned, and easy enough to spin out.

It wasn't until I met folks in the business that I grasped how flexible and creative they really needed to be in order to meet the unexpected demands of an evolving work of art. At one point Winnie Holzman tried to help me relate to the making of *Wicked* by comparing it with reading a novel. "You know when you read something, if it works it just looks inevitable. But to arrive at it—" Holzman sighed and continued, "—all I can explain is that it was extremely difficult."

Years earlier, Stephen Schwartz accustomed himself to the constancy of change. Over tea at his dining room table in his condo one day, he and I discussed what it was like to write so many versions of songs for his musicals. While talking about *The Baker's Wife* I noted, "You wrote a ton of songs for the show."

"Oh, millions of songs!" he quipped. I couldn't help but wonder how someone at his level deals with so many cuts and changes. I said, "It amazes me, your objectivity in terms of your babies. You don't seem to have this thing of 'these are my babies' that everybody does with their creations."

"It's not about that," Stephen insisted. "I'm very fond of quoting Tom Jones [the lyricist/librettist of *The Fantasticks* and author of *Making Musicals*] who said that in a musical, 'Everything is more important than anything.' That simply means that it's about the totality, and you have to be willing to change or sacrifice any given thing in order to make the entire thing work. So individual songs or moments or lines—if they're not serving the piece as a whole, they have to go. And I have absolutely no sentimental attachment to them whatsoever."

What he proved to himself through his many efforts was that there is always some other solution, and that you find out what works through testing.

"Songs in shows have a different purpose than individual songs," he re-explained to me as I tried to crystallize my understanding in a later interview. "Individual songs just have to work within themselves and they are their own context. A song in a show has responsibilities. It has to be moving the plot along or illuminating the character

or having some purpose in the storytelling or in the audience's understanding of the overall show. It's a tile in a mosaic. It doesn't matter how beautiful that individual tile is if it doesn't fit in the overall picture. Whereas an individual song, you just go and look at the tile by itself."

"Making Good" was a tile that fell out of the mosaic of *Wicked*, to be replaced by "The Wizard and I." After *Wicked* opened in 2003, Schwartz developed a presentation about the evolution of "The Wizard and I" to use while satisfying the frequent requests he received for speaking engagements. I brought my tape recorder along to a talk he gave at a local senior center in Connecticut. I include the following transcript because it so well exemplifies how songwriting works. (The transcript includes very minor edits.)

Stephen Schwartz: "I had this notion to write a song called 'Making Good,' and I was very happy with this title because of the double meaning, the phrase meaning 'being successful' as well as doing something 'good' as opposed to 'bad.' I thought there was something delicious about having the character that the audience knows is going to be the Wicked Witch of the West come out and sing a song about what she most wants: to be making good.

"The song 'Making Good' was her first in the show, at the train station where she is leaving home to go to school. After four readings I began to get the feeling that the song didn't really put the character over the top and launch her the way we wanted it to do. Then Idina Menzel came into the picture. I thought about the things she did, the high-energy roles, and thought I would write something different, high energy and tougher, that seemed more like Idina. So I wrote a version of the song that sounded like moving fast music, train music. It was a different take on the same song.

"This worked a little better. But, there was still something that felt disappointing about it. I just felt it was not effective enough. My colleagues were getting nervous about my futzing around with this song. I just wanted it to score a little better. And then Scott, my very smart director son, came to a reading. He said that the whole situation with the train station was cliché. He commented, 'Maybe you could have done that thirty years ago, but you can't do that anymore because everybody knows about the "I want" song now.' He recommended that we cut that entire sequence and start with Elphaba in school, and have her do something that earns her the right to sing.

"So there is this scene at school where something disturbs her, and she inadvertently does something that's magical. This act gets the attention of the head of the school, who happens to be a sorceress. She says, 'I'm going to help you get to meet the Wizard of Oz.'

"Winnie Holzman, our very intelligent bookwriter, was also thinking about this issue, and she said, 'You know, when you think about *The Wizard of Oz*, what does everybody want? They want to meet the Wizard and have him fix whatever is wrong with them—give them a heart, give them a brain, give them courage, take them home to Kansas, whatever they want—they go to the Wizard. Surely that should be involved with what Elphaba wants as well.'

"All these ideas came together, and we decided to try doing a song about her meeting the Wizard of Oz and completely scrap the idea of her getting on the train and going off to school.

"Now, as I began to work on this new song, I remembered something from when I first saw *A Chorus Line*. They have a famous curtain call where they all suddenly come out in gold lamé costumes with gold top hats. I remembered when I saw this show, thinking that of course they're going to do a kick line and the audience will go 'ahhh…' and I was very resistant to being manipulated. Sure enough, they all danced around in their gold costumes and they came downstage and got in a big line… but they did not kick; they danced around some more, and I found myself thinking, 'Well, they're going to do a kick line, right?' And they all came downstage again after dancing around for a while, and got in a big line, but again, they didn't kick, and they danced around some more. By this time I was thinking, 'Where's the kick line?' Sure enough, at the very, very end of the show, they all came downstage and did the kick line, and I was the first one standing up and cheering.

"Afterward I realized that Michael Bennett, who had created *A Chorus Line,* had done something very smart. He'd taken the obligatory moment that he had to deliver, and he made everybody wait for it, until they were grateful when it finally arrived. This is easy to say, but you have to be smart to do this.

"So I started thinking about this new song, and the fact that we now had Idina Menzel in the cast as Elphaba. People who knew her would be expecting her to come out and do this great big belt. I thought that as long as I was writing this song again, what if I saved the big belt until the very end of the song? So I really tailored the song to Idina in that way. Notice that the big belt section comes way late, at the very end of 'The Wizard and I.'"

And with that, he sat at the piano, accompanying himself as he sang the final version of Elphaba's song with its delayed belt that so effectively energizes that moment in the show.

High-Tech Composer Prints Out a Score

For this next segment of the odyssey I include a revised version of a journal entry from the summer of 2002.

It's about a twenty-minute walk from the inner sanctum of Stephen Schwartz's studio/condo to the Lincoln Center plaza where I sit on a marble bench on a hot summer afternoon. Through the windows of the Metropolitan Opera House building on my left, I can see a Marc Chagall mural. On the vast painting, childlike primary color images float against a yellow background, and in the center, a woman plays a harp. The whole image suggests muses and musical inspiration in an ethereal world, all of which my mind wants to link to my experience from earlier this afternoon.

A few hours ago, while running errands in the city, I stopped by Stephen's place to loan him a book that he had expressed interest in reading on an upcoming trip. He surprised me by inviting me to a work session as part of his scoring of *Wicked.* He thus allowed me to witness the way melodies move from a composer's musing into visible music that can be printed and distributed to cast members, and performed for audiences.

I recall that at the apartment door I tugged off my sneakers and slipped stocking-footed onto the carpeted floor. The hushed air-conditioned safety of Stephen's condo felt like a summer cave shaded by window blinds that averted sunrays from the southern exposure.

I grabbed my notebook and followed him into the back room. The composer/tennis player was padding around in sweat socks, beige polo shirt, and shorts, as if ready to play his favorite sport. He was in the midst of his music game, which draws upon another set of practiced talents, but one he can approach with equal ease, aided by electronic wizardry.

In the studio area, deflected light from the north window gently lit the room. Under the window was his Roland synthesizer keyboard. There was a computer keyboard to the right of it, and next to that a monitor flickered. Somewhere behind the furniture, a computer fan purred.

I shook hands with Stephen's "music guy," John Angier, who manned the mouse and watched the screen. Stephen had often spoken about the thirty-something musician who had been on retainer as his arranger and engineer for half a dozen years. He seemed a gentle man, barefoot that day. I learned that John uses a software program called Logic instead of the commonly used notation software program, Finale, because Logic doubles as a tool for recording and sequencing.

Stephen slid into a cushy office chair facing the synthesizer and I took a place behind the duo on a soft, red silk oriental rug that covers most of the parquet floor.

They were reworking the notation of the accompaniment for "Making Good" from *Wicked,* and although the song was later abandoned and rewritten, the process I was about to witness would remain the same.

"Did you work this out before and just memorize it?" I asked. He nodded yes.

"I used to keep everything in my head until I was ready to write down the whole show," he said, referring to his risk-taking younger days. He showed me a score sheet he created by hand at home, the way music had been written, revised, and laboriously copied for centuries. But with the computer, Stephen explained, once something is done, "if a singer requires a different key…"

He finished his sentence by gesturing with one finger hitting a key to represent the instantaneous change that can be made with the latest technology.

Stephen then turned his attention to his song and began warming up. "Let me just remember this a second," he said, and twittered through a few bars. When they were ready to start the notation process, the songwriter pressed the keys of the Roland to play the song. I could just imagine how the impulses in his brain that made up the music he heard in his head traveled through synapses and neurons that ultimately moved his fingers over the appropriate keys on whatever keyboard he was using.

His touch started red and yellow lights pulsing on the computer screen. When he finished several measures, John clicked the mouse. In a flash, a page of music notation morphed into view on the monitor. Stephen immediately began proofing it. He read the music off the monitor that the software had generated, playing on the Roland what he saw on the screen. In this way the composer was able to verify that this represented the music he wished to share with the world.

He and John worked back and forth with adjustments. Stephen would say things like, "Here go to B-flat Major," "Get rid of that C," "Do the enharmonic here," "Let's put a G on top of that," "Let's take the bottom note and put it on top." He experimented until he was happy.

That was just the accompaniment. Next, Stephen played the melody and they layered it in through the same process.

John explained to me that he would integrate the changes into the score and print out the new version. At the end of this process, the musical information would be sent to the orchestrator, and eventually to the conductor and orchestra members.

The pace of the afternoon was summer-ease appropriate. It doesn't sound like much, but in that relaxed atmosphere of Stephen's condo, a sense of everything working out had enveloped me.

As I emerge from my reflections, the doors on one of the theatres of the Lincoln Center complex have just opened and matinee audiences now stream into the plaza.

For a moment, in an abstract kind of way, my mind seems to hold the beginning, middle, and end of music as a whole phenomenon—from the most inward stirrings within a composer, to the recording and transfer of notes that performers learn, to audiences savoring them. It's very satisfying to connect this all together as I glance again at the Chagall and enjoy a visual artist's commentary on the art of music.

Wicked Cast Album Recording Session

Along with live performances, recording sessions mark the culmination of the long process of moving an abstract idea into a completed score. Two weeks after *Wicked* opened, Decca Broadway arranged for three days of recording sessions at Right Track Recording's facilities in a warehouse building about a dozen blocks south of the Gershwin Theatre. On the second afternoon,

November 11, 2003, I was granted permission to witness one of the sessions, also to be attended by filmmaker Dori Berinstein's team for her documentary, *ShowBusiness*. (The DVD includes several minutes of footage at Right Track.)

The tightly planned, high-budget venture would need to clip along quickly under Stephen Schwartz's control as album producer. Under Equity rules, cast members were being paid a week's salary for a 12-hour session, and no one wanted to consider overtime. As always, Stephen organized separate recording sessions for various tracks and groups of performers. The orchestra came in first, although they would also return each day to accompany singers. Then cast members came in for multiple sessions over several days, carefully staggered so no one worked more than one twelve-hour session.

In the afternoon, I beamed myself up, notebook in hand, to the bridge of a starship, entering a world light years from my normal experience. In the control room, all chairs and equipment were aligned for a view through a large window overlooking the orchestra space. I could see a galaxy of musicians beyond the glass. A few bright stars twinkled off in a corner quadrant: Kristin Chenoweth and Idina Menzel behind more glass in smaller isolation booths.

Captain Schwartz, as record producer, commanded from his perch behind recording engineer Frank Filipetti, who managed four dial-filled consoles that stretched along the front of the room.

Orchestrator Bill Brohn and his assistant sat quietly at a table overlooking the consoles and studio space. With white score sheets spread on the tables before them, the orchestration team would scrutinize the central stellar map throughout the day, making sure the ship stayed on course. Record company executives from Decca Broadway and Universal Music sat beside them. Schwartz's assistant, Michael Cole, sat near the captain, keeping his eyes on the libretto—the flight plan for reaching the next destination.

The rest of the environment switched from starship to family living room. In the back of the control room space were comfortable chairs and couches where onlookers stayed out of the way while watching in wonder. Someone had filled a coffee table with Poland Spring water bottles and bunches of grapes that trailed over platters.

Seated on a comfortable couch, *Wicked*'s bookwriter Winnie Holzman seemed the mellow mom, warming the surroundings with her nourishing smile and the autumn russet and orange designs of her floral shirt.

As she listened, she knitted a scarf for her daughter, using heather green yarn tinged with gold that she kept in a plastic bag marked *Wicked.*

During a break, Kristin Chenoweth in a Page Six tee snuggled up to Winnie and repeated some lines from the script, like: "I know, that's what makes me so nice." Winnie giggled even though she must have heard the lines a thousand times. Later, when Norbert Leo Butz sang "Dancing Through Life" and spoke the lines from the show, "What's the most swankified place in town?" Holzman mouthed the reply in a stage whisper, "That would be the Ozdust Ballroom."

The session was technology-driven and time-conscious, but exciting. I saw plenty of smiles exchanged, stories quietly twittered between friendly colleagues, and backs patted. Enhancing this atmosphere were the melodic textures of *Wicked*'s score piping through the speakers into our area as it was recorded. I watched it stir the room like a musical breeze: heads bobbed, shoulders swayed, and feet tapped the beat.

The main studio measured 85′×55′ — large enough to hold symphony orchestras and suited to a Broadway cast recording where as many as sixty singers and instrumentalists might be in a room at one time.

Stephen Schwartz, Joel Grey, and Winnie Holzman talk in the control room at the *Wicked* cast album recording session.

Stephen shouldered the responsibility for the enterprise like it was second nature, having produced most of his previous cast albums. He listened and directed proceedings based on his carefully prepared schedule and the results he was getting. Dressed for the day in colors of absorption — black jeans and dark green long-sleeve shirt — he remained totally focused on his task. As he worked, he paced the green-carpeted floor, checking his watch about every twenty minutes, scratching out notes on a yellow legal pad, and sometimes tapping his pencil to the rhythms of his own music. When he needed to communicate outside the window, he pressed a talk-back button on a microphone box in his hand as if clicking a TV remote.

Through the glass and on a monitor we could see the mussed crop of dark hair on the head of the conductor who Stephen Schwartz tended to call "Stephen Oremus," his full name, in order to keep the multiple Stephens straight in everyone's mind. Oremus stood on a riser farthest from the control room. He was visible from about the waist up, and everyone could watch his arms and hand movements while he conducted in his T-shirt and jeans.

Between the conductor's stand and the control room, acoustic partitions separated string players from brass, and from Gary Seligson on drums. Fortunately for the observers, percussionist Andrew Jones had ensconced himself near the control room window, so we could watch him pinging on the more exotic percussive instruments: gong, bongos, djembe, wind chimes, and more.

Collectively the orchestra musicians brought hundreds of years of performing experience into that session, as well as at least two months' work with this particular score. The vocalists brought their own carefully trained instruments, their Broadway-groomed voices. Although we couldn't see everyone, we could hear them by virtue of a network of microphones and speakers. In final mixing sessions many hours later, all the audio-isolated pieces would be blended as needed.

❧

The "Thank Goodness" session began a little before 2 p.m. Everyone adjusted microphones and headphones as they eased into the precisely planned recording procedure.

Stephen Schwartz: "Uh, hello, can you hear yourself?"

Kristin Chenoweth: "I can hear me just barely."

Adjustments are made.

Stephen Schwartz: "So, sweetheart…I'm going to do three takes just for choices."

Stephen closes his eyes and enters his inner listening space. The orchestra starts up and Chenoweth begins singing. She is "Glinda" now as she croons the bittersweet moment at the opening of Act II, when "Glinda the Good" feels surprised that getting what she wanted hasn't brought the anticipated satisfaction.

> *There's a kind of a sort of…cost*
> *There's a couple of things get…lost*
> *There are bridges you cross*
> *You didn't know you crossed*
> *Until you've crossed…*

Schwartz raises his arms as if conducting—or is he soaring on her long-held note for 'crossed…'?

They finish the take and are pleased. Kristin says there were some good moments even though it was "sometimes a little pitchy."

Schwartz: "This is what I'm going to do, honey. I have three or four tracks and I go in and find the best of each one."

Chenoweth: "Thanks, Stephen."

They start other takes.

Schwartz: "That's fabulous. Kristin, you don't have to enunciate so much. You can be a little more relaxed." Several times through the afternoon they discuss the difference between stage precision and recording studio work. A slightly more conversational delivery is what he wants, though later he said, in terms of infusing personality of the characters, it needs to "feel like the show and yet musically sound as solid as a record."

Chenoweth playfully exaggerates her enunciation, quoting Eliza Doolittle in *My Fair Lady*: "How *kind* of you to let me come."

Take Three is done. They break and prepare for "Popular."

Stephen turns to Platt. "We had a really good morning. Joel was fantastic!" He raves about Grey's performance and says he was also pleased with Carole Shelley, who had come in the morning as well while other orchestra tracks were being laid down.

Now in the afternoon, the focus is on Chenoweth, Menzel, and later Butz. By necessity, the day proceeds in carefully pre-planned segments as dictated by the sequential parts of the score. Everything else is ignored while each part is brought to perfection.

Stephen Oremus to the orchestra: "Cell phones off. Are we ready?"

Chenoweth is in high spirits and sings her response on a soprano note: "Yes!"

They pause to check their headphones. Gary needs some adjustments to his.

Stephen Oremus: "Gary needs a little less of Kristin."

Kristin Chenoweth: "That's what all the men say."

Still, she begins to sing as the self-assured Glinda, advising her roommate Elphaba on how to become popular.

After the introductory section, Oremus raises his baton to begin Take One of the main section. At the precise moment he brings it down, we hear the orchestra musicians start their harmonies while Chenoweth launches into "Popular, you're gonna be pop-u-lar." I'm dazzled: How can these dozens of separate individuals begin so exactly in unison with just this little gesture?

Over the speaker system we hear more of "Popular." Stephen sits sideways for a moment on the swivel chair at the desk behind him, pencilling on a yellow legal pad, swaying back and forth in the chair to the rhythm of the music. His face is a study in delighted innocence.

When the take ends, Stephen tells Stephen Oremus he wants to hear the strings for a particular marked segment of the score. "I'm hearing one wrong note there." They check through the possibilities. A player says, "I have a 'G'," while someone else says, "I have an 'A.'"

Oremus and Schwartz: "Aha!"

Schwartz: "Everyone should be playing a D minor chord." The player made the correction and they continued.

It's not the only time during the session that Schwartz revealed his musical sensitivity. Through the interweaving strains coming from a dozen or more instruments at once, I'm astounded he can hear one wrong note.

After three takes on "Popular" they move on. Without green makeup, Idina Menzel flops into the control room, exhausted from the weeks of performances at night and publicity appearances by day. Although "Defying Gravity" is next, she tells Schwartz he won't get anything good from her until later. They decide to put the two stars in separate sound booths so they can redo tracks individually. Menzel would add her trademark flourishes the next day,

but tired or not, she sang perfectly, if a little more quietly than usual.

Over the break, Chenoweth comes into our room and chums around with Winnie. I hear her fancying herself as "One-Take Tina—that's what I like to be—get in, get out." When it's time to begin again, the tiny woman strides toward the studio's heavy metal gray door and struggles with it. Schwartz is standing near. "I'll get it; I'll get it."

Stephen gives instructions to Idina, calling her "Dee." He hurries everyone to get ready. "We need to move along or we won't get one of the songs on the album."

This is where I move up and sit on the edge of the platform beside the table with the orchestrator. I want to observe the percussionist throughout "Defying Gravity," and the strings on his left, watching as their bows quiver for the tremolo effect at the beginning that musically evokes Elphaba's own trembling as she moves into her new powers.

I can see Andy Jones through the graded-length chimes that create the back side of his exotic haven. He moves swiftly between the two copper timpani that, with the gong, form the left side of his percussion fortress; the chimes are in back, something that looks like a xylophone in front, the two sets of wind chimes hanging from a pole on the right that he tinkles at precisely the right moment, and some hollow vessels—perhaps a series of bells—hanging over his head.

Idina:
> Unlimited
> Together we're unlimited
> Together we'll be the greatest team
> There's ever been

I settle back for a moment as the timbre of the instruments and of the singer's voice washes over the room. I stop attending to individual notes and instead listen to the totality, enjoying the way the various musicians unite to create an artistic whole that is so much more than a collection of parts.

Stephen wrote in his quarterly report for *The Schwartz Scene*: "I always enjoy being in the recording studio; it probably appeals to the control freak in me. In this instance, too, I was blessed with a superb recording engineer, Frank Filipetti, who is one of the best I have ever worked with. In addition, each of the principal cast members really stepped up with their solos, so that I feel we were able to capture each performance at its best. The only slight drawback was the necessity to have the CD ready for release in time for Christmas, which led to a few very late

nights mixing. In fact, the last night I left the studio at 4 a.m., thinking I would walk back to my apartment through the empty streets of New York, only to find the streets bustling with people! I guess that's why they call it 'the city that never sleeps.'"

On an icy December 16th, I watched about six hundred people line up at a *Wicked* Cast Recording release event at the Gershwin Theatre. Lines of people snaked through the lobby, waiting to arrive at the table on the landing where Schwartz and all the stars except Kristin (who was home protecting her voice for an evening performance) scrawled their autographs over the cover. More fans shivered outside waiting for their turn. David Stone pointed out to me some teenage girls who were in tears as they met Idina Menzel. Gregory Maguire came from Boston as well and did some signing. It was a happy zoo.

The cast album sales skyrocketed immediately, surpassing the first week sales of every cast album since *Rent*. Within a few weeks it reached the *Billboard* charts. In 2004 it won the Grammy Award for Best Musical Show Album, and in 2006 it went Platinum, having sold over a million copies.

"The Wizard and I"

Did that really just happen?
Have I actually understood?
This weird quirk I've tried
To suppress or hide
Is a talent that could
Help me meet the Wizard
If I make good
So I'll make good...

When I meet the Wizard
Once I prove my worth
And then I meet the Wizard
What I've waited for since-- since birth!
And with all his Wizard wisdom
By my looks, he won't be blinded
Do you think the Wizard is dumb?
Or, like Munchkins, so small-minded?
No! He'll say to me,
"I see who you truly are -
A girl on whom I can rely!"
And that's how we'll begin
The Wizard and I...

Once I'm with the Wizard
My whole life will change
'Cuz once you're with the Wizard
No one thinks you're strange!
No father is not proud of you,
No sister acts ashamed
And all of Oz has to love you
When by the Wizard you're acclaimed
And this gift - or this curse -
I have inside
Maybe at last, I'll know why
As we work hand and hand -
The Wizard and I!

And one day, he'll say to me, "Elphaba,
A girl who is so superior

Shouldn't a girl who's so good inside
Have a matching exterior?
And since folks here to an absurd degree
Seem fixated on your verdigris
Would it be all right by you
If I de-greenify you?"

And though of course
That's not important to me
"All right, why not?" I'll reply
Oh, what a pair we'll be
The Wizard and I...
Yes, what a pair we'll be
The Wizard and...

Unlimited
My future is unlimited
And I've just had a vision
Almost like a prophecy
I know - it sounds truly crazy
And true, the vision's hazy
But I swear, someday there'll be
A celebration throughout Oz
That's all to do with me!

And I'll stand there with the Wizard
Feeling things I've never felt
And though I'd never show it
I'll be so happy, I could melt!
And so it will be
For the rest of my life
And I'll want nothing else
Till I die
Held in such high esteem
When people see me, they will scream
For half of Oz's fav'rite team:
The Wizard
And I!

LYRICS BY STEPHEN SCHWARTZ. USED WITH PERMISSION

GODSPELL SONG STORIES

You've got to stay bright to be the light of the world

GODSPELL

Here are some additional observations and details about songs that may be of interest to *Godspell* fans and actors performing in the show.

Context for the Songs of *Godspell*

On the surface, it may appear that *Godspell* is a structureless hodgepodge except for the last 20 minutes. A closer study reveals a deep structure.

According to Stephen Schwartz, the actual story of *Godspell* is in the subtext, not in the playful revue of parables on the surface. "What really happens in *Godspell* is that ten separate individuals come together and then turn to the audience and attempt to get them to also become a unit—with them."

At another time, he wrote: "The show is really about the formation of a community. That is the event of the show. These troubled strangers arrive in a place and then a person comes, and you can think he's a smart guy or you can think he's the son of God—and around his philosophy they become a community. And then there's a point at which the audience is invited to participate in the community, and then they all go through something together and at a certain point the guy leaves. He says, 'Well, now I'm going and you've got to carry on without me.' The fact that they've become a community allows them to carry on. That's the story of the show, and it doesn't really have to do with whether or not you believe in the divinity of the central character."

Stephen Reinhardt, the original music director, expresses his own interpretation of *Godspell*'s structure in terms of the role of each song. "In *Godspell*," says Reinhardt, "you have a combination of songs that are meant to fulfill a particular moment in the story about why Jesus came. 'Save the People' is his statement of why he came. 'Bless the Lord' is just an expression of joy. 'Day by Day' is a prayer. So some of the songs are situational, and some of the songs are about the heart and the faith journey."

Musical Inspiration for *Godspell*

While the *Godspell* score has endured through the decades, popular music has changed and we may forget the musical context for this vintage 1971 score. I once handed Stephen Schwartz some images of album covers from around 1970 for recordings by James Taylor, Joni Mitchell, Laura Nyro, and Carole King. He sat across a table from me, grinning as though he'd been given pictures of his nearest and dearest relatives. "I *loved* these records. Look at James," he said fondly about Taylor, whom he'd met during their efforts on another musical. "Oh my God. These were big albums."

The following "Creativity Note" details the way Schwartz worked with the music

Herb Braha, David Haskell, and Stephen Nathan clown around in *Godspell*.

A group interview session with Stephen Schwartz about the *Godspell* score. From left: Michael Lavine, Stephen Schwartz, Carol de Giere. (Alex Lacamoire, hidden from view.)

CREATIVITY NOTES

Musical Diving Boards

For Stephen Schwartz, being creative does not mean operating in a vacuum. Naturally he is pleased if melodies spring to his mind unbidden, yet he also loves discovering a touchstone for a new song in the musical groove of someone else's song, whether it's by singer-songwriters like James Taylor, Joni Mitchell, and Carole King, or by Puccini or Beethoven or Bach. Sometimes he intentionally writes in a "pastiche" style. The term is used for works of art that imitate the style of some previous work or period. For example, "Wonderful" from *Wicked* is supposed to sound like it's from L. Frank Baum's era, the early 1900s in America. For writing pastiche or finding musical inspiration, it helps to be exposed to great music.

In 2005, as part of my search for *Godspell*'s musical foundations, I invited Stephen Schwartz to meet with a small group of musicians at the Manhattan apartment of music director Michael Lavine (who may have the largest privately-held, actively-used collection of Broadway-related sheet music). We congregated around Michael's shiny black upright Kawai piano in an alcove created by a floor-to-ceiling bookcase full of songbooks. While Stephen took over the piano bench, Michael pulled a Laura Nyro songbook from his shelves, and in a moment we were all swaying and singing along to "Save the Country," from Nyro's 1969 album *New York Tendaberry*, as Stephen played. He closed his eyes for a moment and whispered, "Oh, she was *so* brilliant," as if he'd just witnessed a stunning performance. "Everything she did was very inspiring for me, but I can point to 'Save the Country' as the specific song that influenced 'Bless the Lord.'" He shifted into his own music for "Bless The Lord," and we could hear some rhythmic and chord structure similarities.

"The point is that this is the first time I'd ever heard that," Schwartz paused to explain. He spread all his fingers into a slightly dissonant suspended chord and pressed the keys with enough force that it sounded like he was playing with an extra hand. "Everybody else would do [he played an ordinary dominant chord]. And then all of a sudden she would do G over A." Not only were Nyro's chords influential, but also her rhythms. "Pop music at the time was about hitting a rhythmic groove and sticking with it. She did really radical things like changing tempo and the feel within songs (such as in "Eli's Comin'")."

Now we understood how Nyro's quirky pop-music model inspired the frequent changes in rhythm that make *Godspell*'s songs so much fun to hear. "Bless the Lord" swings along at an easy beat and then shifts into an energetic frenzy. "All For the Best," "Day by Day," and the "Finale" also shift gears mid song.

Periodically throughout the afternoon, the fifty-seven-year-old songwriter settled on a couch away from the piano as he answered our questions and sipped chai tea. From a theoretical standpoint, he wanted us to understand about borrowing musical ideas, something composers have done for centuries. (For example, many classical composers he had studied at Juilliard wove folk tunes into their pieces.)

"I would define the score for *Godspell* as pop pastiche," Schwartz stated when giving perspective. "At the time, I didn't think of it in those terms, but now I do. I mean *Godspell* is a pop pastiche score, just as *Joseph and the Amazing Technicolor Dreamcoat* and others are. In other words, they use specific pop styles for different numbers that are pretty easily identifiable by the people who made those styles famous. Not every single number in *Godspell* is pop pastiche, but you can really point to numbers and say, 'That's a Laura Nyro number, that's a Supremes number,' and so on.

"It wasn't that I was trying to satirize or make an homage to any given pop artist, but that they were the jumping-off points. Because I was writing the score so quickly, I would put a lyric in front of me and think, well, how do I jump into the pool this time? What's my diving board? And I would pick something. And I'm sure there were ones I picked where I hit my head on the cement, and went back up to the diving board and tried a different entry point."

Artists of all types can benefit from researching style models. Next time you're in a quandary about how to begin your writing or painting or whatever, try finding a new inspirational model—a new diving board for the dip in the pool of inspiration.

of his peers.

Godspell Song Highlights

"Prologue" (Tower of Babel)

Music by Stephen Schwartz
Lyrics source: Quotes from various
philosophers

For the earliest *Godspell*, the prologue opener was a verbal free-for-all conceived by John-Michael Tebelak. "John-Michael was an idea guy," explains Andy Rohrer, the first actor to play Jesus at Carnegie. "He was living in his intellect. He had been studying religion, philosophy, and drama since his early teens. Approaching his master's thesis project, he naturally thought of philosophers."

Tebelak derived the notion of the "Prologue" from the *Book of Genesis,* Chapters 10 and 11—the Tower of Babel representing social discord created by people speaking different languages. He collected quotations from Western philosophers (including contemporary Buckminster Fuller, whose work he loved) and asked his cast to speak them out sequentially and then simultaneously to show chaos in diversity.

This way his show would open with the antithesis of a harmonious community, as a contrast for what was later created by Jesus and the disciples—a transformation that would be theatrically compelling.

Sonia Manzano recalls, "At Carnegie Mellon we read the lines simultaneously, so there was a cacophony of sound with no one listening to each other. Then seconds before a philosophical battle broke out, someone would throw an empty can up on the stage from the back of the house and scream 'F—k you.'"

The desired theatricality was lost on Stephen Schwartz, who saw a version of it at La MaMa. "The cast came out in their little sweatshirts that said Socrates or whatever, they turned on the lamps above them, and they each said these lines. It was really tedious and *reeeal-ly* long."

When the producers hired Schwartz to prepare the score for a full-fledged musical version of the show, the songwriter altered the opening while keeping the concept. "I basically whittled down the speeches so they could all fit within the framework of a piece where eventually all eight parts could be sung simultaneously."

Schwartz wanted this number to contrast with the rock music style of the rest of the show, and therefore composed more of a classic musical theatre piece, accompanied by solo piano. He wrote a slightly different musical and rhythmic style for each singer, ranging from classical to ragtime to assorted musical theatre pastiches, and then layered the pieces together in counterpoint.

"That's one of those things that looks really impressive but it's actually not very hard to do," Schwartz says modestly. "Basically, the chords give you the harmonic structure. And you know it's all going to come together if they are all singing the same chord." He developed a pattern of chords and then wrote melodies within that pattern. At the points where it looked like melodies would clash, he'd just change those particular notes.

A note for directors: Schwartz is emphatic that the "Prologue" be included in every performance of *Godspell*. "If you're doing a show about the formation of a community," he says, "don't you think you have to see what the individuals are like when there is no community?"

"Prepare Ye the Way of the Lord"

Music by Stephen Schwartz
Lyrics source: Matthew 3:3
    also Isaiah 40:3

For the original cast recording and performance, David Haskell learned to play the shofar, the traditional ram's horn used as a call to prayer in Jewish celebrations such as Rosh Hashanah and Yom Kippur.

"David had a terrible time learning how to do it," remembers *Godspell* music director Stephen Reinhardt. But on the cast album David's blast provides the authentic sound at the beginning of this song.

John-Michael's notion for the transition from the "Prologue" to the rest of the show was to have the actor playing John the Baptist enter from the back of the hall. He would blow a loud note on the shofar. John the Baptist would then start walking through the audience singing "Prepare Ye The Way of the Lord" and be joined by the full cast.

The pre-Schwartz *Godspell* included the piece as a chant song accompanied by rock music with a heavy drumbeat and hand clapping frenzy. The words "Prepare ye the" stayed on the same note, "way" rose up a note, and "of the Lord" came back to the original pitch.

In 1971, when Schwartz sat at his piano to write a song with a one-line lyric, he wanted to compose something with melodic interest. "I made it 'Pre-ee-ee' rather than "Pre-pare-ye-the-way," and added a lot of melodic jumps." He worked on it until he found music that could be sung over and over again, music on which he could also build choral harmonies.

When it came time to stage the show, Schwartz and the others prepared a powerful transition moment between the "Prologue" and "Prepare Ye the Way of the Lord." It succeeded in stirring their audiences. First, philosophers appeared in sweatshirts illuminated with white light bulbs, while singing the solo piano-accompanied opening number. Then someone in the band blew a ram's horn, after which the John the Baptist character sang "Preeee…" *a cappella.* Very softly, underneath, organ notes were layered in, and then all of a sudden, the band came in. Schwartz says, "Suddenly there were drums, there was electric guitar, there was a bass, and at that moment all colored lights came on. Literally. '…of the… Lord' was the light cue. The colored lights that were on the sides all came on and suddenly you had color." The moment offered a surge of exciting energy.

"Save the People"

Music by Stephen Schwartz
Lyrics source: Episcopal Hymnal 1940
    no. 496

When Stephen Schwartz listened to Stephen Nathan sing "Save the People" at Café La MaMa, he heard a rock ballad with a sweetness and pace similar to John Lennon's "Imagine," but with more heavy percussion and strong electric organ.

Schwartz wanted to pick up the pace on the song and switch accompaniment to acoustic guitar. "I was trying to combine the feeling of pureness and simplicity in the Jesus character with a melody and accompaniment that gave the song some theatrical energy."

"Day by Day"

Music by Stephen Schwartz
Lyrics source: Episcopal Hymnal 1940
    no. 429

"Day by Day" represented the character Robin's epiphany. Actress Robin Lamont says, "My goal was to try to communicate through the song a sense of 'Aha!' revelation, the first sense of 'Oh, wait a minute, this isn't just fun and games, is it?! I get it! Isn't that right?' And then the pleasure in receiving his acknowledgment that, 'Yes! That's right.'"

Before he wrote the music, Schwartz was handed the lyrics from the Episcopal Hymn, which were written by Richard of Chichester (1197-1253). In the original Carnegie Mellon version, the hymn lyrics were used verbatim, so the song started *"Day by day/Dear Lord, of thee three things I pray."* Schwartz made the rhythmic adjustment: *"Oh, Dear Lord/three things I pray,"* and then continued with, *"To see thee more clearly/Love thee more dearly/Follow thee more nearly/Day by day.*"

Because the single stanza would be repeated over and over, Schwartz wrote music that an audience could pick up after one listening and then sing along. "That's probably why it became a hit," he reflects. "It was deliberately so accessible."

"The harmonic progression is a little unusual," Schwartz explains. "You start in F, then suddenly you're in G for a little while, then you arrive at C major, which happens to be the 5 of F, so you're back to F. So it's a little bit of a circle of fifths journey. Now I can analyze it, but I certainly wasn't thinking of this in any way when I wrote it. I just put the lyric in front of me and started playing along and this is what happened."

After the show opened, the twenty-three-year-old songwriter was questioned about the lyrics. "The publisher Tommy Valando asked me to write more words to it," Schwartz recalled later, "because he thought it had the potential to be a hit, but he felt it could never be a hit with just these six lines." Stephen shrugged and said, "What can I tell you? That's what the song is. If it's not a hit, it's not a hit." "Day by Day" went on to become one of his all-time biggest hits.

Robin Lamont suggests several reasons for the song's success: "I think it's like any hit song. It's memorable in its simplicity. It's

Gilmer leads "Learn Your Lessons Well."

easy to remember, it's easy to hum, and it's easy to sing. It's not a simplistic tune at all. Musically it is complex. But that's Stephen's brilliance; he writes fabulous tunes and that was one of his most fabulous."

"Learn Your Lessons Well"

Music and Lyrics by Stephen Schwartz

Gilmer McCormick was both pleased and terrified to have a song written for her. In college, her plan was to be a non-singing actress and comedienne. But Schwartz thought he could come up with a song for her, even though it was rather last minute.

"Learn Your Lessons Well" wasn't written until early May 1971, about a week before the show opened at the Cherry Lane. Schwartz remembers talking to Tebelak about the time gap between "Day by Day" and the next musical number. "John-Michael, we can't go this long without a song," he suggested. ("So much of writing for the theatre is just instinct," he says. "It's not always an incredibly conscious decision.") Besides, it seemed right that every clown should have a musical number, and Gilmer was the only clown without one.

He remembered Gilmer's childlike approach to her clown character and wrote her a song that would suit a schoolgirl. "Learn Your Lessons Well" became the only song added to the score during rehearsals.

The lyric ideas came out of what was happening in the scene. "The players are enacting the parable of Lazarus. Gilmer says, 'If they don't listen to Moses and the prophets, they ain't going to listen to anybody.' And that was where she had to sing, so it was about you should learn your lessons. It was pretty clearly indicated by the foregoing material."

"Learn Your Lessons Well" was appropriate for her to sing, but that didn't mean it was easy. The late start on the song meant that Gilmer McCormick had four days to learn the number and the staging. She was not a professional singer. "I completely panicked to suddenly have a song with the

tongue twisters that he put in there," she recalls, referring especially to:

I can see a swath of sinners settin' yonder and they're acting like a pack of fools.

Schwartz had tried to make it easier for her by using a lot of lyric alliteration, but she remembers going out on opening night with the words written on her hand so she couldn't forget them.

"Bless the Lord"

Music by Stephen Schwartz
Lyrics source: Episcopal Hymnal 1940
     no. 293 (adaptation of Psalm 103)

The original "Bless the Lord" music for Carnegie was an uptempo blues number. Schwartz felt that this moment of the show needed a clear burst of energy, so he

Everyone joins Joanne to complete the roof-raising musical number "Bless the Lord."

created a song with ever-increasing tempo and excitement.

In addition, he helped the cast work out the musical staging. He remembers, "I would divide the cast into small groups and send them off to work on steps for various sections of the song. Then, helped by former dancer Stephen Reinhardt, we would say things like, 'All the girls do what Joanne is doing for these eight beats, or the boys on the table should do the hand jive movement that Steve Nathan just worked out.' John-Michael added the idea of twirling streamers at the end and we ended up with the high energy, colorful show stopper the show needed at that point."

In the movie version of *Godspell*, Lynne Thigpen powerfully belts "Bless the Lord," with other cast members supporting. She once explained that she liked it "because it's very joyful, it's a very upbeat song. 'Day by Day' is a beautiful, gentle song that gets the audience clapping and singing along. 'Bless the Lord' is the roof raiser."

"All For the Best"

Music and Lyrics by Stephen Schwartz

When Schwartz wrote the music and lyrics of "All For the Best," he wanted audiences to care about Jesus as a character. "To care about a character, he must amuse

and delight you," Schwartz told a reporter. It wasn't enough that he spoke wisely. "A man who does the soft-shoe, tells jokes and cheers people up when they are depressed" would capture their hearts.

He also remembers suggesting to John-Michael Tebelak that Jesus and Judas needed to connect in song and dance to make the show work dramatically. He told him, "Look, we all know he's going to betray him,

Stephen Nathan in the original cast of *Godspell* performs "All For the Best."

but why do we give a damn? There's nothing special about their relationship. If this weren't a story that everybody already knew, and there were these two guys who were doing something together and at the end of the story one of them was going to betray the other, you've got to set up their relationship. So we've got to do a song for them."

Schwartz's music for "All For the Best" harkens back to music of an earlier generation of show music songwriters. In 1957, when nine-year-old Schwartz was beginning training for his chosen career of musical theatre songwriting, the golden age musicals were thriving. While he never saw Irving Berlin's *Call Me Madam*, one of its songs, "You're Just in Love," was a hit at the time. In the Berlin song, two melodies mesh. Schwartz explains: "Someone sings, 'I hear music and there's no one there,' then Ethel Merman sings, 'You don't need analyzing,' and then they sing the two things together. I love it." Similarly, Berlin's "Old Fashioned Wedding" from *Annie Get Your Gun* employs countermelodies.

In 1971, Schwartz decided to pay homage to Irving Berlin when he needed a duet for *Godspell*. With the concept of the two performers and Irving Berlin's countermelody style in mind, Schwartz invented the playful number.

"All Good Gifts"
Music by Stephen Schwartz
Lyrics source: Episcopal Hymnal 1940
    no. 138

Just before the *Godspell* cast sings "All Good Gifts," they enact the parable of the seeds from the Gospel of Mark 4. So there's a natural segue in the song that begins, "We plow the fields, and scatter/The good seed on the land."

The chord relationships for James Taylor's 1970 hit ballad "Fire and Rain," and Elton John's "Your Song," inspired the music Schwartz composed for "All Good Gifts." He was pleased with how it turned out. "The song that struck home the most was 'All Good Gifts.' Musically, I hooked into something very heartfelt for me. It's the *Godspell* song about which I have the most passion."

"Light of the World"
Music by Stephen Schwartz
Lyrics source: Adaptation of
    Matthew 5:13-16

The introduction to "Light of the World" is like a rap song and, although it's not included on the original cast album or the soundtrack, it can be heard on the 2000 off-Broadway and 2001 albums.

The concept of a rap-like presentation in *Godspell* came from Andy Rohrer. Rohrer had attended high school in Chicago and on weekends got to see blues acts, as the blues scene was still lively from the days of Muddy Waters. So in 1970, when Rohrer was preparing to play Jesus at Carnegie Mellon and John-Michael asked for ideas about the "Sermon on the Mount" piece, he remembered Waters' popular R & B hit "Hoochie Coochie Man," with its heavy blues bass. He and another student named Bob Miller goofed around with it. "Bob and I would go da da da dum.... we'd sing it... then I'd put the lyric on top of it."

For the Cherry Lane *Godspell*, Schwartz needed to complete a "Light of the World" piece for Herb, who had virtually no singing skills. (Herb had never intended to sing in musicals, but Tebelak had seen some of his comic performances at school and wanted him in the cast. He was a natural with impersonations; for example, mimicking Bela Lugosi.)

Schwartz wrote it so it could be half spoken, on the order of Rex Harrison's performance of "Why Can't the English?" in *My Fair Lady*, and then all the other singers could join in to make it a song.

Intermission Notes

Although the jam session music played during intermission is not included on a cast album, in live performances there was always something in the air. Schwartz explains, "One of the concepts for *Godspell* for me was that there was no finite moment where you took your intermission; you just leak in and out of it. You couldn't actually say, Oh, this is the end of Act One and this is

the beginning of Act Two, rather that it was sort of all going on, and therefore 'Light of the World' ended with this jam session as the audience was leaving. Meanwhile, the band continued to play and the audience was invited on stage and had wine or grape juice, and again, after intermission, the cast just started to do some version of 'Learn Your Lessons Well' and we sort of leaked out of intermission into the second act." In some cases the cast members who could play musical instruments got drafted to play at intermission. It was all part of creating the *Godspell* community feeling.

"Turn Back, O Man"

Music by Stephen Schwartz
Lyrics source: Episcopal Hymnal 1940
    no. 536

In the pre-Schwartz *Godspell*, Robin Lamont, with her long straight hair and somber expression, turned to the audience and wailed "Turn Back, O Man," a minor key number in the vein of protest songs of the mid 1960s. The piece, with harmony by cast member, Bob Miller, had a strong thrust similar in energy to Schwartz's "Alas For You."

By the time Stephen Schwartz saw the musical and was sorting out what song to give which actor, he allocated "Turn Back,

O Man" to Sonia Manzano.

Schwartz had accompanied old silent films in college and knew how to create an old movie, honky-tonk kind of feel to an accompaniment that might remind audiences of a Mae West-era scenario. He came up with a tune to suit both Manzano's character and her limited vocal range. "It's what I call hootchy-kootchy music," Schwartz says.

For her performance, Manzano would do a fake strip tease after sauntering down the aisle. "I would do this seductive thing of peeling off my stocking, only it wasn't a

Sonia Manzano

stocking, it was a sweat sock. I also wore a stripper's fringed bra, only I wore it outside my dress."

She remembers ad-libbing her asides as part of her performance. When Leonard Bernstein was in the audience, she said seductively, "When you're a Jet, you're a Jet all the way."

About whether sexual innuendos were appropriate in the show, Manzano comments, "I certainly didn't see any reason to ban sexuality. It's part of life."

"Alas For You"

Music by Stephen Schwartz
Lyrics source: Adaptation of
Matthew 23:13-37

"'Alas For You' is a moment of anger and frustration for Jesus, almost despair, and it triggers a lot of the events that follow," Schwartz explains when actors ask about it. "It is meant to be the *Godspell*ian equivalent of the expulsion of the money changers from the temple."

The song was converted from a speech. John-Michael Tebelak's idea, while still working on the show at Carnegie Mellon, was for Jesus to orate a passage from Matthew 23 from the stage. In the first rehearsals of *Godspell* at Carnegie Mellon, Andy Rohrer had to memorize and deliver that monologue. He recalls it with some pain: "It was a horrible long speech that John-Michael insisted on. And that cost me my voice. I said, 'Alas, alas for you, lawyers and Pharisees, hypocrites that you are…' It went on for five minutes! [Other cast members were just sitting around.] It was really bad. That's why I say John-Michael did not have a lot of theatrical chops. He let it sit right there. He somehow thought one voice could carry this five-minute speech to some great oratorical climax. It wasn't possible."

Fortunately, when Schwartz saw the performance in Greenwich Village and met with Tebelak, he said, "I think I can musicalize that." Then he went home and worked it out. "I remember sitting with the Bible and going through that section and turning it into lyrics."

About the music Schwartz says, "'Alas For You,' is very pianistic, very Leonard Bernstein, because of its shifting rhythms. It's the most 'musical theatre' of the songs in the show because it comes out as part of the story, and musically it's not pop."

Schwartz remarked thirty-some years later, "'Alas For You' is also one of the songs that betray my youngness as a lyricist. I would never make a bad pun like 'You cannot escape being devil's food' in an impassioned song like this now."

"By My Side"

Music by Peggy Gordon
Lyrics source: Song by Jay Hamburger

"By My Side" came into the show in early 1971. Peggy Gordon, a member of the original cast at La MaMa (and later at Cherry Lane), wrote the music and brought it in during a rehearsal. Tebelak had asked the actors to start rehearsals with 20 minutes of "Show and Tell." Says Peggy, "That consisted of anything: theatre games, stories, and songs. That is how 'By My Side' got into the show. I played it for Gilmer McCormick, and she said hey, let's bring that in for John-Michael for 'Show and Tell.'" Peggy taught it to Gilmer, who played it on her twelve-string guitar. "After Gilmer learned the song," Peggy continues, "she came up with this gorgeous seminal harmony part, as I worked up all movement to complement the lyrics. We played it for John-Michael, who sat there silently listening. He then immediately said that it should go right in that spot following the stoning scene."

Notes from the song's composer, Peggy Gordon: "Ironically, 'By My Side' was written for a project we were working on in my freshman year at Carnegie Mellon University. It was originally a love song sung by a character named Marigold to her love, Elkin, so, it was called 'Marigold's

Song.' The song's lyricist, Jay Hamburger, was actually the author of the play *Marigold and Elkin*. In the song, Marigold must dare herself not just to declare her love for Elkin, but to commit to go with him on his journey. So when John-Michael decided to put 'By My Side' into that spot in *Godspell*, it somehow seemed to fit the same need.

"It also solved another problem. I didn't know what the comedic clown caricature was for my character yet. When John-Michael put the song in the show, my character fell into place. I chose to play a clown that suffered not just from an exaggerated comedic shyness, but a need to overcome this fearfulness. In other words, after my character survives the attempts to stone her, Jesus says lovingly that he doesn't condemn her. 'You may go. Do not sin again.' She, in that moment, knows that she wants to go with him, wherever he goes—but does she have the courage?" The lyrics seemed suited to telling the story.

"We Beseech Thee"

Music by Stephen Schwartz
Lyrics source: Episcopal Hymnal 1940
no. 229

The Supremes' 1966 chart-topping single, "You Can't Hurry Love," by the songwriting team of Holland-Dozier-Holland, inspired the music for this song.

In the context of *Godspell*'s second act, Schwartz explains, "'We Beseech Thee' is the last unalloyed celebratory moment." Things are taking a turn for the worse when Judas is given money to betray Jesus. However, this song is part of the transition between the playful joy and the downturn of events already set in motion. The composer suggests, "The emotional transition is aided by the fact that Jesus, having recognized that things have begun getting a little dire, has picked up the mood with the sheep and goats parable. And in that parable, he promises his faithful followers 'eternal life.'" Consequently, Jeffrey's character reacts to the happy promise. He sings about love in "We Beseech Thee."

"On the Willows"

Music by Stephen Schwartz
Lyrics source: Adaptation of Psalm 137

Schwartz took stylistic inspiration for "On the Willows" from Tebelak's suggestion that it be "oceanic." The comment triggered the songwriter's memory of an arrangement he'd heard for a Judy Collins piece—an adaptation of a William Butler Yeats poem, "Golden Apples of the Sun." With that in mind, a lilting tune flowed out.

In the musical it is supposed to be sung by the band. Schwartz explains that the song serves as sort of movie-like scoring to the action.

He also has commented about a particular word that has confused people over the years. For the script, the word "lyres," found in the original Psalm, was changed to "lives."

> On the willows there
> We hung up our lives

"The adaptation of the lyric, with the change of words, was suggested by the conceiver and original director of the show, John-Michael Tebelak. I'm not sure I would make the same change today, but the reasoning behind it was that we wanted to be clear it was their entire life that had changed for each of the disciples, and we weren't sure the metaphor of the lyres would be clear enough, particularly since we don't get to the explanatory line about singing the Lord's song in a foreign land until much later in the song."

"Finale"

Music by Stephen Schwartz
Lyrics source: Various

The "Finale" begins, "Oh God, I'm dying." As it continues, some cast members sing "Long live God" while a second group brings in "Prepare ye the way of the Lord" in counterpoint.

Schwartz explains that "long live God" existed in the script. "In the script that I got from John-Michael, which was about thirteen pages long, at the end they sang 'Long live God, long live God, long live God.' There was this one line repeated over and over again and I thought, 'Oh! Well I should do something with that and then have 'Prepare Ye' come in on top of it.' It was just one of those things that suggests itself, because they just seemed similar in their structure."

For the music, the beginning of the scene included an electric guitar riff typical of the period. "It's sort of Vanilla Fudge or Jefferson Airplane or one of those sort of electric guitar dominated groups," Schwartz says. Then it smoothes out and a lullaby-like tune is sung in counterpoint with "Prepare Ye."

At Carnegie Mellon, a revolving red light was switched on to represent the top of a police car, because Jesus had been arrested.

"I remember those lights from when the cops bust you," says Sonia Manzano. "And the Jesus Christ character had a line: 'Oh God, I'm busted.' So that kind of gave the feeling that we all had been caught doing something wrong by the authorities so it was very theatrical that way."

Schwartz thought the lights and the 'Oh God, I'm busted' were way over the top and that they trivialized the crucifixion. "I just said to John-Michael, you can't. That's a really bad idea. And he got it right away."

At the end of the original production, Andy Rohrer as Jesus was carried out the back of the theatre, but the process became refined for later shows. "It's very dangerous," Rohrer recalls. "That was typical of John-Michael. It was out of control. And instead of the very orderly thing that you see in a current production of *Godspell*, part of the intention was that they took me down like a piece of meat. They didn't take me down with respect. They took me down like children would take a body down. So

Lamar Alford (left), David Haskell (right), and others carefully carry Andy Rohrer (center) in a much-refined version of *Godspell*'s "Finale" during the New York run of the show.

they had me under each arm, under each leg while they were singing 'Prepare Ye.' It was more like a body carried out of the battlefield in Vietnam. It had a very different imagery to it. It worked for that production because the production was so out of control. But it was very troubling for the actor. So I was fighting for my life. It's like being in a low budget movie in a bad stunt."

For Cherry Lane, the actors lifted Jesus carefully during the gentle "Long live God" section of the song.

"Beautiful City"

Music and Lyrics by Stephen Schwartz

In many productions of *Godspell*, "Beautiful City" is included right before the Last Supper, but it has also been used as an opening for the second act, and even in place of "long live God" at the end of the show.

Speaking about the original movie version of the song, Schwartz explains, "We had this idea for a song called 'Beautiful City' since the movie was set in a magically emptied out New York. And it was very sort of *Godspell*y and flower child-like, and the cast went skipping through the streets and sang these sweet words. I have to admit I always felt the song was a little too sweet for its own good.

"And then some years later there was to be a one-night benefit production of *Godspell* in South Central Los Angeles, right after the L.A. riots [1991]. It was to include 'Beautiful City' and I suggested that I rewrite the words, because I felt I could come up with something more appropriate for this particular situation."

The new lyrics reflected a more thoughtful, practical approach to rebuilding community in contemporary society. At the same time, they suggested metaphorical construction, or reconstruction, of community spirit, as was the case for the followers of Jesus in *Godspell*.

After the September 11th destruction of the World Trade Center in New York, the song was used in many memorial services and benefit performances.

The *Godspell* Movie

In early 1972, in preparation for shooting a film version of *Godspell*, film director David Greene, Stephen Schwartz, and John-Michael Tebelak traveled to every production of the show, looking for a cast and for performance ideas. Greene selected a cast he felt would work on film.

The actors then faced the challenge of re-creating *Godspell* in a new medium, and, in many cases, playing unfamiliar roles. "They had two Gilmers, two Robins, and two

John-Michael Tebelak and Edgar Lansbury plan a scene for the *Godspell* movie.

Joannes," remembers Gilmer McCormick. She believes this was an immediate drawback for their rehearsal process. Joanne recalls, "Sonia could not do the movie because of her *Sesame Street* commitment and they wanted so much to have Lynne Thigpen in the movie, so I was asked by the producers if I was willing to split the role of Joanne and Sonia. Lynne sang the heck out of 'Bless the Lord' and I could bring a lighter tone to 'Turn Back O Man' (less vampy and more campy)."

Katie Hanley had perfected the Robin role while performing in the stage version of the musical, and felt self-conscious in the Peggy role. (Greene gave Hanley roller skates to wear, which gave her reason to roll in and out of the background and added visual fun for the audience.)

For the song score, Greene felt the high-energy theatricality of "We Beseech Thee" wouldn't translate well in the film medium. Schwartz wrote "Beautiful City" to replace it.

The movie loses some of the excitement of the stage experience. But with New York City as its stage, it allows audiences to view a version of the show in the context of some interesting spots like the Bethesda Fountain in Central Park, Times Square, and even the top of one of the World Trade Center towers.

If Schwartz had his choice, he would have changed the costuming. He once explained, "Because the show was originally produced in the hippie era, and because the director of the *Godspell* movie somewhat misinterpreted the characters as hippie-esque, that misunderstanding has come to haunt stage productions of the show a bit [because some directors took visual cues from the film]. The characters in *Godspell* were never supposed to be hippies. They were supposed to be putting on 'clown' garb to follow the example of the Jesus character as was conceived by *Godspell*'s originator, John-Michael Tebelak, according to the 'Christ as clown' theory propounded by Harvey Cox of the Harvard Divinity School (among others)."

Godspell in South Africa

In 1974, *Godspell* became the first show to break the color barrier in South Africa. Tebelak and Schwartz stipulated that as a condition for receiving performance rights, a production had to maintain a racially integrated cast and be performed before an integrated audience. Schwartz says: "When asked about my proudest moment in show business, I often cite what we were able to accomplish in South Africa—the small but real role we played in breaking the strict policy of apartheid."

The two verses of "Learn Your Lessons Well" have always been divided by dialogue. The director of a potential Broadway revival of *Godspell* asked Stephen Schwartz to musicalize the spoken section, so he wrote out the pages shown here. They are good examples of Schwartz's handwritten musical notation.

Music and Lyrics © Stephen Schwartz. Used with permission.

Stephen and Carole Schwartz, Trevor Nunn and his then-wife (and *The Baker's Wife* star) Sharon Lee Hill, and Joseph Stein at the Schwartz residence in Connecticut for one of their meetings about *The Baker's Wife* revisions.

UPDATES AND NEW PROJECTS

The spark of creation
May it burn forever

CHILDREN OF EDEN

Updates: *Pippin, The Baker's Wife, Captain Louie, Mass, Geppetto & Son, Working.*

New Projects: *Mit Eventyr (My Fairy Tale), Kéramos, Thiruvasakam, Enchanted, My Antonia, Séance on a Wet Afternoon.*

Stephen Schwartz describes himself as an "inveterate futzer." He is "very happy with a blue pencil in my hand for cutting things and rewriting things" while a show is being developed. Catch him years after an original production has closed and he may still be adjusting song lyrics or helping fix the story, as with the countless revisions that he and Joe Stein made to *The Baker's Wife.*

He decided to refine his lyrics when there began to be new productions of Bernstein's *Mass,* and he altered *The Magic Show* for a Canadian film version. When the Music Theatre International licensing agency mentioned they needed family-oriented musicals for large ensembles, he helped adapt his made-for-television film musical *Geppetto* as a stage show, *Geppetto & Son.*

On some occasions a producer or production company invites him to update a piece, as when he and Alan Menken were brought in to expand the film score of *The Hunchback of Notre Dame* for a German stage production, *Der Glöckner von Notre Dame,* or when the producer of the family musical *The Trip* revived it, and it became a longer piece called *Captain Louie.*

As of this writing, a revamped version of *Working* is being tested in a regional theatre with a cast of six.

By the time Schwartz contributed comments for this book, over three decades after *Pippin* opened on Broadway, his perception of his own show's development had altered, as had his advice for directors staging the show. "I was so resistant to a lot of what Bob Fosse did, and now, of course, I'm the protector of his vision." Not only has his perspective on *Pippin* changed, but also the ending has been altered for the licensed version of the musical's script in a way he believes Fosse would have liked.

This "Updates" chapter tracks some of the changes. In addition, the chapter updates readers on Schwartz's projects since 2003.

Revised Versions of Older Shows

Pippin

Pippin is among the shows that Schwartz has revised over the years. The current version includes a revised ending, a return of some of the Leading Player interruptions cut from the original published version, and new lines, new cuts, and new lyric revisions. Schwartz explains: "After *Pippin* opened, when the show was being released for stock and amateur productions, Roger Hirson and I went through the script and de-Fosse-ized it, such as removing many of the Leading Player's interjections. In recent years, I've come to feel that the show is better with them, and we've put the majority of them back in. It's ironic that I've become the champion of Bob's vision. When asked about the revisions I sometimes joke, 'I know somewhere Bob is looking up and laughing.'"

The story of a revised end to the show, known as the "Theo ending," begins about thirty years after *Pippin* first appeared on Broadway. Stephen Schwartz attended a production of the show at a London fringe theatre. Because of British child labor laws, the director had cast a teenager as Theo instead of a younger boy. At the end of the show, Pippin sang his little reprise of "Magic Shows and Miracles," and then Theo began to sing "Corner of the Sky" a cappella. Schwartz explains that because the actor was old enough, it was believable that he was starting his own "Pippin-esque quest." Catherine and Pippin looked on, somewhat in shock. The troupe of players came back in and began focusing on Theo, as if starting the show all over again.

Schwartz loved this ending, and worked with Hirson and Music Theatre International to include it in the revised *Pippin* for the licensed version of the show.

Answering a question on his website about the meaning of this new ending, Schwartz commented: "By taking the spotlight—literally and figuratively—off of Pippin at the end, and putting it onto the emerging consciousness of Theo, I feel that the ending more clearly and theatrically dramatizes the universal human choice each of us must make about our life."

The Baker's Wife

After *The Baker's Wife* shuttered in 1976 before reaching Broadway, Stephen Schwartz decided not to give up on it. At one point he concluded, "I think there are some shows that are essentially misbegotten, and at a certain point the creators realize they're never going to work and abandon them. But that was not the case with *The Baker's Wife*. It was always clear there was a show there; we just hadn't found the way to put it on the stage."

After a recording of solos from the score was released following the closing of the original production, singers began performing many of the songs in cabarets and at auditions. When eminent British director Trevor Nunn heard "Meadowlark," and others from *The Baker's Wife*, time and again during auditions for his London shows, he contacted Schwartz and Stein about a revised production in London.

In the interim, Stephen Schwartz had directed a revival at the York Theatre in New York (1985), trying a stripped-down approach. He openly admits it failed. "We tried to do exactly what all the smart people had been advising, to concentrate on the central love triangle. We cut a lot of the Villagers' material. For instance, the role of the Teacher was eliminated entirely. The Villagers basically came in from time to time, told their jokes, and went away. It was much more focused on the central characters, and it didn't work at all."

Nunn had a different vision. He felt the show was about the village and it needed to be refocused. Schwartz says, "What I call the 'Trevor Nunn Solution' is to make the village itself the protagonist, and to show how the central story works a transformation on this comically petty, small-minded provincial (and Provençal) town."

The reshaped show, though better, became problematically longer. Still, Schwartz believes it almost worked. He explained on the cast album notes, "As new scenes and songs were added and old ones resurrected, as dialogue was revised and lyrics and melodies restructured and rewritten, all under Trevor's clear and consistently inspired guidance, as new French-flavored orchestrations were contributed by David Cullen, as a cast was assembled and design and staging elements added, *The Baker's Wife* Joe and I had seen in our heads fifteen years ago began to emerge."

Nunn staged *The Baker's Wife* in London at the Phoenix Theatre in the West End theatre district. It starred Sharon Lee Hill and Alun Armstrong. While reviewers offered praise, audiences were small and the show closed after only 56 performances. Schwartz explains, "The major thing that was wrong was that it was just too long. There were things we were desperate for Trevor to cut in London and he wouldn't do it."

Nunn comments, "What I saw in the show was the potential for it to be the theatrical equivalent of [the French films] *Jean de Florette* and *Manon des Sources*; teeming with eccentricity, and in many ways a hymn to a lost world of much greater simplicity than our own, but closer to nature and the primal human needs of daily bread and love. So, yes, the life of the village was central, and we had some thrilling rehearsal room improvisations that brought the community to life in richly comic and truthful ways.

"We started the show out of town (actually in my own home town) in a theatre that had a thrust stage pushing out into an amphitheatre style auditorium. It meant the action could spill off the stage and erupt out of the audience in a delightfully inclusive way. Every performance there had a standing ovation, which is not at all a normal response in the English provinces. Nobody ever said the evening was long.

"The West End theatre we moved to was the only one we could get, and it's my view that it was the theatre space that killed us. Everything had to be put back behind a proscenium, and therefore the audience watched without participating. The score held together magnificently and the show was moving and life-loving in its conclusion. But given the 'odd' title (no indication of either romance or comedy) and the somewhat hidden location of the theatre frontage down a small alley, and given the loss of the idea of shared community, we found ourselves casting our sweetness upon the desert air. A triumph out of town had become just another show in the West End."

Yet for the 1989/90 season, the show received a nomination for the Laurence Olivier Award for "Musical of the Year," alongside *Miss Saigon* and others.

Stein and Schwartz continued to rework the show for a production in November of 2002, at Goodspeed's 200-seat Norma Terris Theatre, not too far from Schwartz's Connecticut home. Much of their effort involved trimming the length while carefully retaining Nunn's concept. Finally, the show seemed to work and it enjoyed a frequently sold-out run. Schwartz had collaborated closely with Stein and director Gordon Greenberg. Greenberg went on to direct the show at Paper Mill Playhouse in New Jersey in 2005, where it was tweaked again. At long last, *The Baker's Wife* worked, both for critics and audiences. The show was videotaped for the archives at the New York Center for the Performing Arts so that future directors and performers using the library could access an ideal version.

"I have been thrilled with the Paper Mill production and immensely gratified that the show has finally been finished," Schwartz affirms. "My son Scott asked me what I was going to do with the rest of my life, now that I don't have to work on *The Baker's Wife* anymore."

The revised version is available for licensing through Music Theatre International.

Captain Louie

In 1981, while Schwartz was working with Charles Strouse on *Rags*, he attended a performance of *The Nightingale*, a children's opera piece by Strouse commissioned by the First All Children's Theatre. "I was impressed with the talent and quality," Schwartz says, and he asked Meridee Stein, the show's producer and director, if she would be interested in having him write something for her company. She immediately responded, "Absolutely."

This collaboration marked the beginning of a new stage musical for children that later became known as *Captain Louie*. Its first incarnation, a thirty-five-minute show called *The Trip,* included songs by Schwartz and book by Stein's husband, Anthony Stein. Adapted from Caldecott Award-winning author Ezra Jack Keats' picture book, *The Trip*, the musical presents the story of a young boy, Louie, who escapes into his own imagination as a means of coping with the loneliness he feels from having

The York Theatre cast performs *Captain Louie*.

moved to a new neighborhood. His imaginings are played out on stage as he "flies" in his big red plane back to his old neighborhood to spend the evening with his Halloween-costumed friends. He returns with more courage to make friends in his new neighborhood.

Meridee Stein's troupe of talented and carefully directed child actors performed *The Trip* in New York City in December 1983. The reviews were so positive that the Kennedy Center in Washington, D.C. invited the company to perform the show as the centerpiece for its "Imagination Celebration."

Schwartz believed that to be sustained as a licensable musical, it had to be longer "without it feeling padded." He and Tony Stein added characters and expanded the story until it would work as a longer show, running about an hour.

In 2005 co-producers Meridee Stein, Kurt Peterson and Robert Reich mounted two productions of *Captain Louie*, one at The York Theatre, and another off-Broadway at the Little Shubert. In 2006-2007 the production toured nationally. Ms. Stein directed all of these. Schwartz produced a studio album in which he recorded the nine songs for the PS Classics label.

Meridee Stein comments: "Having somebody like Stephen Schwartz writing for this age range is such a boon to the field of family entertainment. Someone at his level says, 'I want to do this because I care about the future of the American musical theatre, I care about children coming into the theatre, and I'm going to do my best.' People like Stephen and Charles Strouse don't stop doing their best when they write for young people."

Song list: "New Kid in the Neighborhood," "Big Red Plane," "A Welcome for Louie, Shadows," "Trick or Treat," "Looza on the Block," "Spiffin' Up Ziggy's," "Captain Louie," "Home Again," and "Finale."

Bernstein's *Mass*

What Leonard Bernstein called *Mass: A Theatre Piece for Singers, Players and Dancers* became popularly known as "Bernstein's

Mass," with music by Bernstein and additional English lyrics by Stephen Schwartz. It is available both in CD and DVD formats, although neither one includes Schwartz's revised lyrics from 2005.

The recording that includes original cast members with The Norman Scribner Choir and The Berkshire Boy Choir came out on the Sony Music label in 1971. A version performed at the Vatican was preserved on DVD.

Schwartz contributed lyrics to: "A Simple Song," "I Don't Know," "Easy," "Thank You," "The Word of the Lord," "God Said," "Hurry," "World Without End," "I Go On," and "Things Get Broken."

In 2005, for a performance at the Hollywood Bowl, Schwartz revised many of the English lyrics, with the approval and assistance of Leonard Bernstein's daughter, Jamie Bernstein Thomas. Schwartz describes his motivation for the revisions: "The original *Mass* was written very quickly over the summer of 1971. We had a major deadline, as the Kennedy Center was set to open at the beginning of September and *something* had to be up on the stage! Therefore, many of the lyrics were first draft, without time to go back and polish. It only recently occurred to me that I could do just that. My revisions sometimes addressed what I felt was weak or unclear content and sometimes addressed what struck me as clumsy writing. One of the challenging and enjoyable aspects of these revisions is that I was careful not to change a note of music or rhythmic stress, even when the music or rhythm had been written to accommodate the original lyric! In any case, I at least am considerably happier with the revised English texts, and I hope for a recording of this new version."

Geppetto/Geppetto & Son

Geppetto & Son (in progress since 2006) is a revised stage version of the made-for-television movie *Geppetto*, which aired on *The Wonderful World of Disney* in May of 2000 and was later released as a video and DVD, with a soundtrack recorded on the Disney label. David Stern wrote the book, and Stephen Schwartz wrote the music and lyrics.

Storyline: The familiar *Pinocchio* story told from the father's point of view. It includes an amusing take on the Blue Fairy and the villainous Stromboli.

The idea for adapting *Geppetto* as a stage musical came up during discussions with Stephen Schwartz and representatives from Music Theatre International (MTI), who will soon license it to theatre companies offering shows for young audiences. They told Schwartz they needed musicals "with

a minimal number of adults and an infinite number of children." He immediately

David Stern and Stephen Schwartz

Pinocchio (Alex Peterson) turns into a real boy in the first production of Disney's *Geppetto & Son*, mounted at the Coterie Theatre, Kansas City, Missouri, in the summer of 2006. Also pictured: Geppetto (Charles Fugate).

thought *Geppetto* would work well. *Geppetto & Son* songs are by Stephen Schwartz with the exception of two songs from the Disney animated feature *Pinocchio*: "When You Wish Upon a Star," and "I've Got No Strings."

Song list (Schwartz songs):
"Toys," "Empty Heart," "Rise and Shine," "Geppetto and Son," "Bravo Stromboli," "Just Because It's Magic," "Satisfaction Guaranteed," "Pleasure Island," "Since I Gave My Heart Away."

Working

In May 2008, an updated version of *Working*, directed by Gordon Greenberg, was presented at the Asolo Theatre in Sarasota, Florida, and was very well-received. As of this writing, it is next scheduled to play the Old Globe in San Diego in the spring of 2009. This revised version addressed concern that some of the original show's material had become dated since its first presentation in the 1970s, given that the American workplace has changed so dramatically. In addition to cutting some old material, the revised version includes material from the Studs Terkel book that is more relevant to contemporary issues, new interviews conducted by Schwartz and others, plus two new songs by Lin-Manuel Miranda, the talented young songwriter of *In the Heights*.

Songs cut from this new version include "Lovin' Al," "Un Mejor Dia," and Schwartz's own "I'm Just Movin'" (which replaced his "Newsboy" song in later productions).

New Projects

2005: Mit Eventyr (My Fairy Tale)

Commissioned to celebrate the bicentennial of the birth of Denmark's best-known author, Hans Christian Andersen, *Mit Eventyr* includes songs by Stephen Schwartz and others. Adam Price translated Schwartz's lyrics for this musical that was performed in Danish in Copenhagen and elsewhere.

Storyline: Hans Christian Andersen takes a fantastical journey through a world peopled by characters from his own stories. It includes characters and incidents drawn from "The Emperor's Nightingale," "The Ugly Duckling," "The Little Mermaid," "The Snow Queen," "The Princess and the Pea," and "The Shadow," among others.

Song list (Schwartz songs—titles in English):
"Stay With Us," "Fellow Traveler," "On Wings of a Swan," "Come Drown in My Love," "Colloquy," "Save Us," "Can You Imagine That?"

2006 "Kéramos"

"Kéramos" is an *a cappella* choral setting of a poem by Henry Wadsworth Longfellow commissioned by artistic director Daniel Hughes, for The Choral Project, San Jose, California.

Schwartz says, "Longfellow's poem immediately suggested music to me, particularly a constant, circular motion. I made decisions about what verses to include and in what order, based on my own responses to the content and emotion of the poem. I tried to arrive at a structure that had its own natural build and story.

"I was told by friends who speak Greek, when I asked, that 'kéramos' can mean both the 'ceramic' and the 'ceramicist' (or 'potter'). I tended to think of it more as the former, as the clay that is being formed and re-formed by the invisible Potter, be it nature or the universe or God."

The Choral Project recorded Kéramos on their *One is the All* album (Clarion), 2006.

2006 *Thiruvasakam*

Stephen Schwartz contributed English lyrics to a section of *Thiruvasakam,* an adaptation of classic Tamil poetry. *Thiruvasakam in Symphony* is a project of Maestro Ilayaraaja of Tamil Nadu, India, who wrote the music. Agi Music.

2007 Disney's *Enchanted*

The feature film *Enchanted* includes songs by Alan Menken (music) and Stephen Schwartz (lyrics) that help tell the story of Giselle, a traditional Disney animated heroine, who is sent into the gritty live-action world of modern-day New York.

Their songs are designed to evoke different eras of Disney films as well as Giselle's journey. Songs include: "True Love's Kiss," "Happy Working Song," "That's How You Know," "So Close," and "Ever Ever After."

2008 *My Antonia* (in progress)

For the play *My Antonia*, Scott Schwartz adapted the novel of the same title by Willa Cather. Stephen Schwartz wrote the incidental music. Stephen says, "I loved this play so much when I saw it in readings, I exercised my parental prerogative and 'insisted' to Scott that he let me write the incidental music."

2009 *Séance on a Wet Afternoon* (in progress)

Stephen Schwartz has based his first opera on the novel *Séance On A Wet Afternoon* by Mark McShane and the screenplay by Bryan Forbes. Commissioned by Opera Santa Barbara, it is scheduled to premiere in the fall of 2009, directed by Scott Schwartz.

Storyline: A psychological thriller about a medium, Myra Foster, and her doting husband, Bill. Because Myra has never received the recognition she feels her gifts merit, they hatch a plan: They will kidnap the daughter of a local wealthy industrialist and keep her safe while the media frenzy over her abduction builds. When Myra has a "vision" that leads to the successful recovery of the girl and the ransom, her fame will be assured.

Schwartz explains his interest in the story. "It demands the kind of atmospheric moodiness that music can provide, and the two main characters are psychologically complex and compelling, with passionate needs and emotions."

A portrait of Stephen and Scott Schwartz taken during a 2007 workshop for *Séance on a Wet Afternoon* at Schroon Lake, New York.

CREATIVITY NOTES

Creative Discipline and Writer's Block

Question: Would you say that artists need to find a way to manage their creativity, so they can have something actually come out on demand?

Stephen Schwartz: Absolutely. I think that's one of the differences between someone who is an amateur, who wants to be a writer, and someone who actually is a professional writer. Amateurs just write when the spirit moves them, but a professional writer has to learn how to harness his or her creativity in the service of deadlines. Each writer has to develop his or her own process to be able to be creative on demand. But once you learn how to do this, deadlines are your friends. There's something about having a deadline that forces the work to come.

Question: What if you have trouble being creative on demand? What if you get really blocked and you just can't think of what to write?

Stephen Schwartz: I remember one time when I really felt as if I had Writer's Block, that dread thing writers have complained about throughout history. It was on a song for *The Hunchback of Notre Dame*. Nothing was happening and all my little techniques to get things going were not working for me at all. I had a conversation with my friend John Bucchino one evening, complaining about this. I said, "I start to write something down and I realize it's not very good and I walk around and try to think of other ideas and they don't seem very good. So I'm just here with a pile of discarded bad ideas around me."

And John said something very simple but completely brilliant, and I promise you it is the solution to Writer's Block. He said, "Oh, you're just being the Editor too soon." And I realized what he meant was that when we write, it's actually a two-part process. We're constantly unconsciously switching back and forth between being the "Writer" and being the "Editor." The Writer is producing material and the Editor is judging the material and deciding what is going to be kept and what is going to be discarded.

And Writer's Block stems from the Editor showing up too early in the process. I compare the writing process to "pump priming," trying to pump for water. For a while, you just keep pushing the pump handle up and down and nothing seems to be happening, then there is a little trickle of sludge, and then finally comes a flow of the clear water you've been trying to get to. If you start judging so early that you can't get past the "sludge," then you never get anywhere. I have a professional screenwriter friend who deliberately titles his first draft "Shitty First Draft" to give himself permission to write bad material at first. The solution to Writer's Block is to allow yourself to do bad work and to shut the Editor up for a while and let the Writer generate some material that actually can be edited.

CREATIVITY NOTES

Alan Menken Speaks on Creative Blocks and Rewrites

Carol de Giere: So many people have creative blocks and it just sounds, from everything I've heard about you, that you don't have any.

Alan Menken: I don't really have creative blocks if I have the right assignment. I can have *big* creative blocks if I have the wrong assignment. That's not a creative block—that's just a logical block, you know what I mean? If you have the wrong assignment, it doesn't make for a good song. You cannot write a song out of thin air. There's got to be an emotion behind it, a style behind it, tension behind it.

Carol de Giere: Does it frustrate you that, for example, you were writing love songs for Esmerlda and Phoebus, and then someone decided they can't be used?

Alan Menken: Sometimes… momentarily…. Our job as musical dramatists is more to rewrite than to write. The biggest thing we have to do is be constantly willing to embrace the task of rewriting. And those who can't rewrite will not succeed—I can guarantee that.

An *Enchanted* Conversation

There is joy to be claimed in this world
Enchanted

What follows is a slightly edited version of a conversation with Stephen Schwartz recorded on February 15, 2008.

(This is also available as a podcast. See www.defyinggravitythebook.com for the link.)

Carol de Giere: First of all, let's talk about the assignment you and Alan Menken were given and how you conceptually approach writing songs for movies. Was it up to you to discover the ways that songs might advance the story?

Stephen Schwartz: In the case of *Enchanted*, a screenplay existed, a screenplay that had been worked on for many, many drafts by many, many writers until Disney finally came back to the original conceiver and writer Bill Kelly. The screenplay that Alan and I read was not only terrific, but very close to what was actually shot. This wasn't one of those cases where a great deal changed during the filming process, because the screenplay had been extensively worked over by Kevin Lima, the director.

And there were places for songs already built into the screenplay. Kevin and Bill knew that they wanted to open in the animated world with a song ["True Love's Kiss"]. The idea of Giselle cleaning up the apartment and having the vermin come and help her was already in the screenplay ["Happy Working Song"], although I'm not really sure whether they knew that was going to be a song or not.

Definitely with "So Close," the idea for it was not only already in the script, but the title was too. Kevin Lima suggested the title, "So Close," which I really liked because of its multiple meanings.

We added "That's How You Know." That scene was in the script, and maybe there was an idea that it was a musical number, but we added the whole idea of her singing, and Robert being embarrassed about it and asking her not to sing, and gradually all the different people in the park joining in. We added the idea of the steel drum guy who would play along with her, et cetera. That was all something that Alan and I came up with.

And then the last number, "Ever Ever After," which is the voiceover, that was something I felt very strongly about. I kept saying to Kevin, "Look, you have to close this movie musically. You cannot just close in a scene." And ultimately, after a few false starts, we discovered a way to do that.

Carol de Giere: You've mentioned before that there's an evolution to the pastiche aspect that begins with the old Disney song style.

Stephen Schwartz: Classic Disney.

Carol de Giere: Could you explain that?

Stephen Schwartz: It was one of the ideas which sort of emerged—it wasn't that conscious from the very beginning. For a while there was a discussion of whether or not the opening should be an "Alan Menken style" number, like "Belle" from *Beauty and the Beast*.

I felt that we wanted to be in the world of *Snow White*, *Sleeping Beauty*, and *Cinderella*. Alan and I watched those movies and really tried to channel that sensibility, both musically and lyrically. Obviously, we made fun of it a little bit. But basically the idea was to both honor and send up the classic Disney-styled songs.

Carol de Giere: And then you moved forward.

Stephen Schwartz: The second song is also a send-up of a song from *Snow White*. "Happy Working Song" is basically the sensibility of Snow White transported to modern day New York. She's dealing with rats and pigeons and cockroaches, but she's still singing as if they were adorable furry bunnies and little fluffy rabbits and elves and birds, et cetera.

But then the songs started started moving forward in time, stylistically. As Giselle develops as a character and becomes more of a contemporary young woman, the score becomes increasingly contemporary. So "That's How You Know," which is kind of the centerpiece, is more in the style of the 1990s Disney animated features. It's meant to send up "Under the Sea" and "Kiss the Girl" from *The Little Mermaid* and to some extent "Topsy-Turvy" from *The Hunchback of Notre Dame* and the big Disney production numbers that came in with the new golden age of animation that Alan started with Howard Ashman. The Caribbean quality of "That's How You Know" was directly related to the fact that we wanted to have fun with "Under the Sea" a little bit.

And then "So Close" is deliberately meant to evoke the title song of *Beauty and the Beast*. Kevin Lima always planned to use the famous camera move that was built into *Beauty and the Beast,* where they are dancing and the "camera" swirls around them; he wanted to re-create that camera move live. So part of the assignment was to build in a dance section where that camera move could take place.

Finally, at the very end, in "Ever Ever After," we catch up to contemporary animation, where the characters aren't even singing on screen, it's a voice-over.

CAROL DE GIERE: You've talked before about starting with titles and you've mentioned that a couple of them were provided. So I'm curious about the advantage that it gives you to start with a title.

STEPHEN SCHWARTZ: For me, the advantage of starting with a title is it focuses what the song is about. It helps to define for me what the content of the song is, so the lyrics aren't all over the map. I've just found over the years that as I've gained experience as a songwriter, figuring out the title is very helpful.

CAROL DE GIERE: In "That's How You Know," it's interesting that you start out with "How does she know you love her?" and then after a chorus it becomes "That's how you know." Do you remember consciously working with this?

STEPHEN SCHWARTZ: I remember worrying about it. Because I had the title "That's

How You Know," but because of the scene the song was coming out of, the first question had to be "How does *she* know?" And I thought about changing the title to "That's How She Knows" but it's just not as good a title. So I tried to structure the lyric so it could go to the real title, "That's How You Know," without it being too big a speed bump, and I think I was pretty successful in doing that.

CAROL DE GIERE: You've said before that you don't love to write love songs.

STEPHEN SCHWARTZ: No, I don't.

CAROL DE GIERE: So how did "So Close" come out for you?

STEPHEN SCHWARTZ: Kevin really wanted the last line to be "So close and still so far." That created a bit of a problem. The song, which I think works really well in the movie, has a problem as a stand-alone song because it shifts gears in the middle. The whole first part of the song, which ends with "So far we are so close," is one idea. And then at the end of the song, which accompanies a scene where Giselle is now leaving, the idea changes to "So close and still so far." It works for the movie but makes the song have a slightly split personality.

But anyway, the title "So Close" helped to define what the words of the song would be. And I had the idea (which I really had to fight for at one point because Patrick

Dempsey didn't want to sing) that it was imperative that his character sing along at a certain point. And so part of the song was written so the words would reflect exactly what Robert (the Patrick Dempsey character) was feeling at that time, and he would sing that into her ear.

It was a bit of a struggle to get Patrick to do that. And then later on, when I saw Patrick after the movie came out and was doing well, he said to me, "Why didn't I have a song?" I said, "Patrick, it was all we could do to get you to sing those two lines!"

CAROL DE GIERE: Interesting. I wonder if you could talk about "bridge." Let's look at "Happy Working Song." I suppose we would say the bridge is:

> *Oh, how strange a place to be*
> *Till Edward comes for me*
> *My heart is sighing…*

STEPHEN SCHWARTZ: Definitely. That whole section.

CAROL DE GIERE: What's the role of a bridge like that?

STEPHEN SCHWARTZ: Just to talk in general terms, the other term for bridge is the "release." And I think that's the more accurate term. It sort of refreshes the ear. It takes you somewhere different musically and lyrically before you return to the main tune.

Many classic songs are first verse, second verse (that is musically identical to the first verse), then a release that takes you somewhere else, and then a last verse that's like the first verse again.

Of course when the music changes, you want to go someplace lyrically that supports the change of music. In the case of "Happy Working Song," we wanted to catch up with Giselle's story. And so there's a storytelling element to the bridge. It's also satirical of *Beauty and the Beast* because musically it suggests, "I want adventure in the great wide somewhere."

Then for the bridge of "So Close" I basically said to Alan, "We just need to go somewhere else here. And he felt it too. And then he wrote that really beautiful music, and because it was more melancholy, it suggested the lyrics that ultimately wound up there (about facing the faceless days).

CAROL DE GIERE: Lastly, let's talk about writing comic songs like the "Happy Working Song." That's a "wink," I guess, so it's a funny situation.

STEPHEN SCHWARTZ: Well, it's a really funny idea. And full marks to Kevin Lima because it was his conception. Once you have the idea that you're going to do "Whistle While You Work," or whatever they sing in *Snow White* when they're washing the dishes, but you're going to do it with rats, pigeons, etc., then the specifics kind of suggest themselves.

One thing that inspired the song was a television special I saw many years ago with Julie Andrews and Carol Burnett, called *Julie and Carol at Carnegie Hall* (1962). One of the things they did in it was make fun of *The Sound of Music*. They sang a song that satirized "My Favorite Things." It was called "Pigs Feet and Cheese." It was a similar sensibility to "Happy Working Song" in that Julie Andrews sang everything so sweetly, and she would sing lines like "Knitting and tatting and cleaning the barn." I just found that song so hilarious that I remembered

it for forty-five years. And so I thought to do exactly what they did—to take the *Snow White* super sweet sensibility and put a lot of words in there like "toilet" and "vermin." I just tried to think of a lot of ugly words and put them into the song, so she could be singing about smelly socks and things, but with her incredibly sweet attitude. That just seemed really funny to me.

> …*You can do a lot when you've got*
> *Such a happy little tune to hum*
> *While you're sponging up the soapy scum*
> *We adore each filthy chore that we determine*
> *So friends, even though you're vermin*
> *We're a happy working throng…*

In the trophy case at the Schwartz home, an array of awards is flanked by two of Stephen's Oscars.

Several hundred people cram into the ASCAP cafeteria in New York each evening of the workshop; about an equal number appear in the Disney commissary in L.A. There's something exhilarating about listening to insightful comments by esteemed panelists and hearing Stephen Schwartz size up each musical at the end of the evening. The list of past panelists includes such songwriters as Lynn Ahrens, Stephen Flaherty, Sheldon Harnick, and Stephen Sondheim, as well as many directors and producers.

The sessions begin with some behind-the-scenes efforts by Schwartz. Michael Kerker comments, "He spends time with each writing team privately before the workshops, explains the guidelines, and encourages them to listen carefully to the feedback from the panelists, maybe even tape record what's being said so they can listen to it again later. He also helps them understand that panelists aren't always right and to not take everyone's feedback to heart."

During the evening session, as Kerker explains, "he provides both very insightful, specific feedback on the work as well as general feedback on some of the key rules of writing for the musical theatre, which not only benefits the teams presenting, but also is extremely helpful to the many other musical theatre writers who come and audit our workshops."

One participant, who calls himself Doctor Musical, comments, "I have been fortunate enough to attend the workshops both in Los Angeles and New York, and I can assure you that Mr. Schwartz: 1) is incredibly insightful; 2) can zero in with amazing accuracy on what's wrong with a whole piece, a song, a lyric, a song as it relates to the show, what-have-you; 3) is committed to sharing and teaching—he so obviously cares deeply about the past, present and future of musical theater that it's infectious; and 4) has little ego about his own work."

Another participant recalls something that happened when his musical was workshopped. "Stephen stunned the room by saying, 'I know what's giving you problems in your plot and here's how to fix it!' And then, in about four minutes, he outlined specific revisions to help us strengthen the show!"

Schwartz also provides some advice and commentary over the Internet. His own site, www.stephenschwartz.com, has included a question/answer discussion forum since it was founded in 1997. He also agreed to allow some of his writing tips to be posted in the tips section of www.musicalwriters.com.

Schwartz likes to remain open to many of the people with whom he previously established an advisor/advisee relationship.

Composer Brad Ross and his collaborator had their work accepted based on the CD and the script that they submitted. He recalls that Schwartz's feedback was "extremely helpful." Ross has had occasion to call on Stephen Schwartz several times since this ASCAP experience. "Whenever I've had a question, Stephen has always returned my emails. He's wonderfully friendly and supportive. It's meant a lot to me knowing I have a high profile ally in the business who will talk to me and return my queries. Stephen is a personable kind of guy. I think the world of him."

It also helps his advisees that he has a sense of humor about his own work. During one ASCAP workshop I attended, Stephen compared the weakness of the musical being critiqued to a weakness in one of his musicals, *Rags,* which he feels has too many characters and subplots. He helped the writers see how they could focus on the central concerns of the show and cut characters. He got a good laugh from them when he said, "I know this is a tall order, but it's not too late for *you!*"

Stephen Schwartz Reaches Out

In addition to his ASCAP activities, Stephen Schwartz occasionally gives concerts, often with Liz Callaway, or Debbie Gravitte, and Scott Coulter. Spot-

On Entertainment books these "Stephen Schwartz and Friends" concerts: www.spot-onentertainment.

In an interview, Tony Award®-winner, Debbie Gravitte remarked on the signifi-

Stephen Schwartz with award-winning vocalists Liz Callaway, Scott Coulter, and Debbie Gravitte.

cance of Schwartz's activities and attitudes. "When we were first working together, he had a button that he would wear that said 'Just Say No.' It didn't have anything to do with drugs or sex. It had to do with volunteering, because Stephen is one of those people who, when asked to do a benefit, will say, okay sure—that's his nature. He wants to help out people. And at a certain point, with his amount of fame and notoriety, you do have to learn to say no."

Since *Wicked* opened he's been more in demand, and must often say no. But he still sometimes speaks to college classes, or offers master classes during which he reviews students' works in progress, as he has done at Harvard University for several years.

"He gets joy from discovering other talents," Ms. Gravitte observes. "That says a lot, because in show business, basically we all walk around looking over our shoulder, in some ways, meaning, 'Who's that person coming up behind me? Are they going to replace me?' Stephen does not do that. He welcomes the person over his shoulder. He wants to see who's coming, because he's confident enough in what he does and his body of work. The reality is, there is room for everybody."

Among the student writers who benefit from his attention are those at Lovewell

Institute, run by his long-time friend David Spangler, with whom he worked on *The Magic Show*. At Lovewell's summer programs (www.lovewell.org), students ages 13 to 19 develop and perform in original musicals. Schwartz has presented several workshops for them over the years. "Stephen has a great gift to give beyond the musicals he writes," says Spangler. "He's really an educator as well, inspiring kids on the benefits of working on creative projects like musicals."

For those with a musical under development, he recommends finding opportunities for feedback, such as presenting the work in local readings, musical theatre festivals, or workshops such as ASCAP provides. Various opportunities are listed on www.musical-writers.com, which also posts songwriting

Stephen Schwartz speaks about *Wicked* at a public talk in Connecticut.

Schwartz makes a point during a master class at Harvard University.

tips from Schwartz.

"Basically you have to write, and put it out there, and get some kind of response," Schwartz has said in encouragement. "You have to be tough enough, and objective enough, to recognize what needs to be fixed, and also confident enough to recognize what doesn't need to be fixed, and then just keep plugging away."

One of the writers who came through Stephen's ASCAP workshop is Glenn Slater, who went on to collaborate with Alan Menken on the Broadway production of *The Little Mermaid* and other shows. The photo was taken in 1999 when Glenn visited Berlin during rehearsals for *Der Glöckner von Notre Dame*.

MARYANN LOPINTO

Since 1999, Stephen Schwartz has traveled the world in concert with Debbie Gravitte, Scott Coulter and Liz Callaway. They sing songs from *Godspell*, *Wicked*, and many other Schwartz musicals. Scott Coulter remarks, "The concerts are always well received because his music really speaks to people. His music is about finding your place in the world and that is something everyone can relate to. It's so hopeful and uplifting and his melodic lines soar."

Wicked Outline By Stephen Schwartz (September 1998)

In September 1998, after reading Gregory Maguire's novel *Wicked*, Stephen Schwartz developed the following outline as a basis for planning the musical with his colleagues.

ACT ONE

I. OPENING—"No One Loves the Wicked"

Narrated by a figure who appears to be a man, though we can't see his face. The man's face is concealed, a la those revealing info about organized crime figures on news broadcasts—he explains there would be political and personal ramifications for him if his identity were known, because he knows details of the "inside story" of the Wicked Witch of the West.

Today is a joyous day for all Oz because they are celebrating the death of the Witch—the little girl Dorothy has killed her, with the help of her friends the Scarecrow, the Tin Man and the Cowardly Lion, and is bringing back to the glorious Wizard of Oz the witch's broomstick.

Narrator tells us he knows how the Witch came to reach the heights (or depths) of wickedness that have made her death a cause for celebration for the entire land. Some say it began because her father never showed love to her, because he was never sure she was his…

II. BIRTH OF ELPHABA

We flash back to eighteen-some-odd years ago. As the action is narrated in song, we see the beautiful Melena bidding goodbye for the day to her husband, Frex, the Governor of Munchkinland; we see a Travelling Salesman, whose face we never quite see, come by and seduce a fairly willing Melena with the aid of a bottle of intoxicating green elixir; we see Melena turn, and she is visibly pregnant; we see the birth, her husband standing anxiously by; and finally, the horrified reaction—the baby has something wrong with her —she's green!

Music and Lyrics © Stephen Schwartz, Used with permission.

Original handwritten music and lyrics for Elphaba's birth.

III. ELPHABA LEAVES FOR SCHOOL

We meet Elphaba, now a green teenager preparing to leave for college, bidding farewell to her father, Frex, and sister, Nessarose. Her mother, we learn, died giving birth to Nessarose. It is clear that her father prefers the beautiful

Nessarose, who looks very much like her mother. Both Elphaba and Frex are very protective of Nessarose, because she is unable to walk. Elphaba tells her sister she will see her next year when she joins her at school; in the meantime, Elphaba is determined to fit in and make good. Perhaps if she works really hard, someday she will find a way to earn the affection of not only her father, but of all of Oz. ("Good Intentions")

IV. ON THE TRAIN

Elphaba meets Doctor Dillamond, the talking Goat who will be her biology professor. He is kind to her when the other passengers avoid her because of her green skin, and he tells her of his experiments to prove that talking Animals have the same consciousness as Humans.

We also learn something of the political situation in Oz—how the Wonderful Wizard arrived in the capital city some eighteen years or so ago, how the people were so awed by his magic arrival from the air that they helped him overthrow Ozma, and how he financed his public works projects—making the Emerald City, building the Yellow Brick Road to unite the country—by confiscating property owned by the talking Animals. Elphaba likes Doctor Dillamond, but believes the Wonderful Wizard must know what he's doing and has all Oz's best interests at heart.

V. ELPHABA ARRIVES AT SCHOOL

Elphaba and Galinda (beautiful, selfish, spoiled) are made to room together by the school's headmistress, Madame Morrible, despite Galinda's obvious displeasure at the prospect. Elphaba realizes that what she most wants is to be like Galinda.

VI. ORIENTATION DANCE

Galinda and the "popular" girls giggle over a plot: Galinda leaves Elphaba a peaked black hat with a note saying all the girls are wearing hats to the dance and this will go with the black dress Elphaba always wears.

Elphaba shows up at the dance wearing the hat; of course none of the other girls are wearing hats. Everyone laughs at Elphaba, then they pair off to dance. Galinda dances with a tall gangly boy named Boq who is clearly smitten with her. After a moment, Elphaba starts to dance determinedly by herself. Gradually, all stop to watch her.

Then Galinda extricates herself from Boq and comes to tap Elphaba on the shoulder—"May I cut in?" Elphaba and Galinda start to dance together, and soon they are whirling faster and faster, laughing with abandon. In some strange way, they have become friends.

VII. SORCERY CLASSES

Madame Morrible recruits Elphaba and Galinda for her private class for those with special talents for sorcery. Perhaps something Elphaba has done indicates this talent, perhaps one even beyond Madame Morrible's understanding. Madame Morrible explains that they will use their magic to help serve the Wonderful Wizard when they graduate. She teaches them out of a big book of spells, The Grimmerie, which is very hard even for her to understand. For some reason, Elphaba seems to be able to read it easily.

VIII. SUMMER BREAK

Galinda invites Elphaba to come with her, to the North, but Elphaba stays over vacation to help Doctor Dillamond with his experiments, especially since Doctor Dillamond has been reduced from Professor to Lab Assistant by the Wizard's new laws. Galinda doesn't like Doctor Dillamond, who can't even pronounce her name right; he calls her "Glinda." But Elphaba has a personal motive as well—perhaps helping with these experiments is the key to her doing something so good all Oz will love her.

IX. NESSAROSE COMES TO SCHOOL

Nessarose arrives for the second term; she joins the sorcery class, but doesn't have Elphaba's talent (or even Galinda's). Nessarose is smitten with Boq, who, in order to be close to Galinda, helps to carry her around. In secret, she begins working on spells from the Grimmerie to make Boq fall in love with her.

X. ANOTHER NEW ARRIVAL—FIYERO

Fiyero, a handsome young man from the Winkie country, arrives at school. He and Elphaba bond when they save a frightened Lion cub from an experiment in the new biology class, taught by Doctor Dillamond's human replacement (or taught by Madame Morrible as a temporary replacement for Doctor Dillamond?)

We learn Fiyero is already married to a girl from the West (perhaps they even have a child together?) But Fiyero and Elphaba remain friends. He even helps her and Doctor Dillamond.

XI. DOCTOR DILLAMOND'S EXPERIMENT SUCCEEDS

Doctor Dillamond now has scientific evidence that talking Animals and Humans are identical in their Consciousness. Dillamond, Elphaba, and Fiyero celebrate, and as they do, it is clear there is a spark between Fiyero and Elphaba. Madame Morrible interrupts their celebration, Nessarose in tow, with bad news: they must return home; Frex, their father, has been taken ill.

XII. ELPHABA'S FATHER IS DYING

On his deathbed, Frex has gifts for his daughters—When Nessarose opens hers, she discovers a magic pair of shoes that Frex has spent all their inheritance having made for her. They have such power that when she puts them on her feet, she is able to walk!… Elphaba opens her gift—it is the empty green bottle of elixir the Traveling Salesman left behind. Upset, Elphaba asks Frex why he is so much kinder to her sister. But he denies it, saying only, you were always the strong one, you never needed my help." He dies making her promise to "watch out for your sister, always. . ."

XIII. ELPHABA RETURNS TO SCHOOL

Nessarose decides to stay behind and assume the rulership of Munchkinland, since Elphaba doesn't want it. But she returns to school to find a catastrophe in progress: there is a fire in Doctor Dillamond's laboratory. He has been killed and his work destroyed.

XIV. ELPHABA AND GALINDA

Galinda announces she is changing her name to "Glinda" to honor Doctor Dillamond. But Elphaba is not interested in sentimental gestures—she has made a secret extra copy of Doctor Dillamond's formula that she made because she didn't trust Madame Morrible. She tells Galinda to come with her—they are leaving for the Emerald City to present their evidence to the Wonderful Wizard himself.

XV. THE WIZARD'S PALACE

Elphaba and Glinda are brought into the Wizard's presence, a little surprised that it has been so easy to get an audience with him. But he says he has been waiting for them; he has heard much of their progress from his able assistant, Madame Morrible.

Elphaba rashly accuses Madame Morrible of somehow causing Doctor Dillamond's death, and tells the Wizard that once he sees the results of Doctor Dillamond's experiments, she knows he will reconsider his cruel deprivation of the rights of the talking Animals. The Wizard takes the formula—then calmly rips it in two. He explains that where he comes from, this is how all animals are treated and that to do otherwise puts too severe a financial strain on the other citizens of Oz; what he is doing is for the greater good, etc. Perhaps a song for the Wizard: "Sentimental"—how he has never had a family or children of his own, and so he cares for the "true citizens of Oz" as if they were his children.

When Elphaba responds angrily, and Glinda futilely tries to calm her, the Wizard calls in... Madame Morrible.

She tells Elphaba and Glinda that now they are ready to join their powers of sorcery with hers to begin assisting the Wonderful Wizard for the glory of Oz. She says their first task will be giving monkeys, on whom they have been grafting wings, the power of flight; that way the Wizard will be able to have monitors from the air who can report to him about goings-on all over Oz. She has one of the winged monkeys with her. Elphaba furiously refuses.

Using the Grimmerie, Madame Morrible begins to put a spell on Elphaba, so that she will be "good" and help the Wizard. Elphaba appears to succumb... but when Madame Morrible gets close, Elphaba leaps up, snatches away the Grimmerie, and runs out. The Wizard calls his guards to pursue.

XVI. ELPHABA TRAPPED IN THE PALACE

Elphaba barricades herself in a small room, with nothing in it but an old broom leaning against the wall. With the Wizard's guards trying to break down the door and others climbing up a ladder to the window from below, Elphaba desperately riffles through the Grimmerie, looking for a spell to help her escape. She begins to chant... and lo and behold, the old broom comes to life, clumsily at first. Elphaba leaps onto it, and just as the Wizard and his men break down the door, she flies out the window on the broom, the book under her arm, her trademark peaked black hat on her head, laughing wildly as she flies into the sky.

ACT TWO

I. ELPHABA GOES TO NESSAROSE

Elphaba has brought her sister, who is now ruler of Munchkinland, the Grimmerie for safekeeping: "You're the only one I can trust." Elphaba says she is leaving to fight the Wizard. Nessarose: "Everybody in Oz will curse your name." Elphaba: "I don't care anymore." When Elphaba leaves, Nessarose calls in Glinda and Boq, who have been hiding there. "You were right to call me," says Glinda. "I'll figure out a way to help her." Glinda tells Boq to stay with Nessarose while she is gone.

II. ELPHABA LAUNCHES A REBEL ATTACK AGAINST THE PALACE

Elphaba, with the help of a few malcontent talking Animals, launches a raid on the Wizard's palace and frees the Winged Monkeys. In the ensuing melee, Elphaba is captured by a soldier. But the soldier turns out to be Fiyero: "I always did have a knack with disguises." Glinda had confided her fears to him about Elphaba's plans, and he has come to save her. He tells the monkeys to make their way to the West, to his castle at Kiamo Ko.

III. ELPHABA AND FIYERO

They hide out in Fiyero's rooms. A love scene—she says she doesn't care that he is married. Perhaps a song: "As Long as You're Mine." After the song, the Wizard's men break in. Fiyero fights them off long enough for Elphaba to

escape, but for all she knows, Fiyero is captured or perhaps even killed.

IV. ELPHABA RETURNS TO NESSAROSE, SEEKING HELP

When Elphaba reaches Munchkinland, she learns that Nessarose has been using the Grimmerie in her absence and has become so disliked by the Munchkinlanders they are calling her the Wicked Witch of the East. Elphaba discovers what has happened between Nessarose and Boq—unable to make Boq love her rather than Glinda, Nessarose, in a fury, uses the Grimmerie to take his heart out "as he has stolen hers." Elphaba comes upon the scene, and to save Boq, she turns him into a Tin Man who won't need a heart to live. Elphaba and Nessarose have a confrontation and Elphaba takes the Grimmerie and leaves.

V. MEANWHILE, BACK AT THE WIZARD'S PALACE

The Wizard and Madame Morrible; Elphaba's natural abilities are too strong for them to attack her directly, and Madame Morrible's powers have been greatly reduced without the Grimmerie. But she has an idea—she still has some control over the weather; if she summons all her powers…

VI. ELPHABA WITH THE GRIMMERIE

Desperately, she is saying spells to try to save Fiyero, but since she doesn't know what has happened to him, she doesn't know if anything is working. As she sinks into despair, a high wind starts to come up, and Elphaba sees it as a metaphor for what she has brought down upon them all: "Reap the Whirlwind." After the song, a winged monkey arrives with terrible news: the cyclone was carrying a house of some sort, and it has fallen on Nessarose and killed her.

VII. THE WITCH IS DEAD

Not only has Nessarose been killed by a falling house, but the house has contained a little girl and a dog, who are now on their way to see the Wizard. And worst of all, Elphaba arrives to find that Glinda has given the little girl Nessarose's magic shoes.

Elphaba is furious with Glinda and they have a huge fall out—at first Glinda says she gave the girl the shoes because the little girl wanted to get home again so badly and Glinda thought the magic shoes might help her; but finally she admits that she is trying to get Elphaba to give up her sorcery before things get even worse. She says she is doing it out of concern for Elphaba and friendship, but Elphaba is implacable: "You are not my friend anymore. Maybe you never were."

Elphaba flies off.

VIII. HEADING WEST

Elphaba on her broom, accompanied by the winged monkey: She is on her way to Fiyero's castle, Kiamo Ko. She hopes Fiyero's widow will forgive her and give her refuge… but even if she can't stay there, she is in desperate need of forgiveness from somebody.

IX. KIAMO KO

But when Elphaba arrives, Fiyero's widow is in the process of abandoning the castle, taking their child with her and returning to her own family.

She has no time to talk of forgiveness; she is afraid of reprisals from the Wizard. She leaves the castle to Elphaba. And so Elphaba is alone in her castle, accompanied only by her winged monkeys; she has become the Wicked Witch of the West.

X. NARRATOR RETURNS

The Narrator tells us that the next part of the story is a matter of public record: how the little girl, Dorothy, and her three new friends went to the Wizard and were given the assignment to kill the Wicked Witch of the West and bring back her broomstick as proof. The Wizard adds, as an afterthought: "Oh, and you might as well bring the big magic book she has, as well—the Grimmerie, it's called, or something like that." And finally Dorothy and Toto and the intrepid trio found themselves trapped on a rampart of the witch's castle. And now we will see how the Witch added one last sin to her long list: murder.

XI. RAMPART OF THE WITCH'S CASTLE

Elphaba confronts her cornered captives: "Before I kill you, I want to say a few words about ingratitude." She knows nothing of the Scarecrow, she says, but as for the Tin Man and Cowardly Lion, she reminds them how she has saved them both, for the Lion is in fact the cub she and Fiyero rescued long ago. But the two are unimpressed; the Tin Man blames all witches for his state and the Lion feels if he'd had to fight his own way out as a cub, he wouldn't have turned out so Cowardly. So even when Elphaba thought she was helping, she was wicked.

Dorothy, however, doesn't actually wish to kill the witch. She wants only "forgiveness" for killing Elphaba's sister. To Elphaba, this is the cruelest blow of all. She sets her broom alight and tries to burn the Scarecrow; not only does he catch fire, but her magic book, the Grimmerie, also gets set aflame. Elphaba leaps to save the book, right into the way of Dorothy, as she inevitably, famously, throws the bucket of water and melts the Wicked Witch of the West.

XII. "NO ONE MOURNS THE WICKED" Reprise

Once again, we see all Oz celebrating. But this time, we see a little more: we see Glinda, sitting by herself as the celebration goes on outside. She is weeping for her lost friend.

And we see Dorothy and friends returning to the Wizard; they couldn't bring the broom or the magic book, since both were burnt. So instead they have brought another token they found — an empty green bottle of elixir. As the Wizard takes the bottle, all the blood drains from his face: "But surely… this can't be…when I was a young man and had first come to Oz, before I came to the Emerald City, I had one beautiful night…" The bottle falls from his hands as he realizes he has killed his own daughter.

XIII. NARRATOR WRAPS UP

And so, we are told, all the heart had gone out of the Wizard. Angrily, he throws Madame Morrible into prison for her part in the undoing of Elphaba.

And then he departs Oz forever, leaving the Emerald City in the joint rule of Dorothy's three friends, assisted by Glinda. But the Scarecrow, we are told, declined the offer and set off on his own for…

XIV. THE SOUTH

The badlands where nobody goes. We are on a scruffy little farm. And, the Narrator tells us, we have not been misled when we were told that Elphaba's last sin was murder; she murdered… herself! And with this, the Narrator unmasks and we discover a green-skinned woman instead of the man we thought he was: Elphaba has faked her own death. She lives out here with the winged monkeys and the other Talking Animals who find their way here seeking safety. And today, she is expecting one more guest… The Scarecrow arrives. And of course, he is Fiyero, and the spell with which Elphaba saved his life is what turned him into this. "I always did have a knack for disguises," he reminds us. He had gone to Elphaba the night before the confrontation at the castle, as the others slept, and revealed himself; and after their joyous reunion, they worked out the plan by which she could escape the Wizard's vengeance forever. Of course, it has all worked out far better than either of them expected. And as Fiyero slips his arm around Elphaba's waist and they walk off with the Animals, they sing a reprise of "As Long as You're Mine."

Stephen Schwartz plays a song from *Children of Eden* during a discussion of his music.

Schwartz records songs for *Reluctant Pilgrim.*

About Stephen Schwartz's Musical Influences and Style

Dr. Paul R. Laird, Professor of Musicology and Director of Musicology Division, University of Kansas, provides an academic perspective on Stephen Schwartz's music: "A major influence on Stephen Schwartz's early scores for musicals were the singer/songwriters Laura Nyro, James Taylor, and Joni Mitchell, among others, but Schwartz has also acknowledged his great interest in the folk music revival, Motown, and other popular styles. From these various influences, he forged a style of composition that emphasized moving, singable melodies with hints of blues notes, jauntily syncopated rhythms, and subtle melismas that sounded over active, idiomatically-conceived piano parts with distinctive harmonic shadings. Among older theater composers, Leonard Bernstein's music, with its complex meters and compelling use of dissonance, was a special interest for Schwartz. As a young piano student, Schwartz played the music of many classical composers, and cites his special interest in Bach, Beethoven, Debussy, Rachmaninoff, Hindemith, and Bartók, and snatches of their rhythmic and harmonic styles come out in his music as well."

Schwartz reviews sheet music for songs cut from *Children of Eden.*

RECORDINGS

We've got magic to do, just for you
PIPPIN

To collect Stephen Schwartz albums and DVDs is to gather a cornucopia of musical expressions to suit your every mood. This one songwriter's body of work ranges from intimate story songs to grand anthems, from powerfully belted theatrical pop numbers to quiet folk ballads, from American gospel to world music.

Popular pieces like "For Good" from *Wicked*, "When You Believe" from *The Prince of Egypt*, and "In Whatever Time We Have" from *Children of Eden*, are frequently used out of context for weddings, graduations, memorial services, concerts, talent shows, and auditions.

Schwartz songs are always emotionally evocative. Dean Pitchford (songwriter for *Footloose* and *Fame*) comments: "I think Stephen taps into an incredibly deep level. I don't think that he always wears his heart on his sleeve, but there are pieces where you would have to be blind and deaf not to get the emotion. But I also find that the great thing about his work is that it bears repeated listening, and it gets deeper and deeper and richer…His lyric takes you on a journey into the heart of the emotion."

Songs from the following musicals have been recorded on cast albums, studio albums, or soundtracks: *The Baker's Wife, Bernstein's Mass, Captain Louie, Children of Eden, Der Glöckner Von Notre Dame, Enchanted, Geppetto, Godspell, The Hunchback of Notre Dame, The Magic Show, Personals, Pippin, Pocahontas, The Prince of Egypt, Rags, Wicked,* and *Working.*

In addition to cast albums, Stephen Schwartz has released two "singer/songwriter" CDs: *Reluctant Pilgrim* and *Uncharted Territory.* While they contain three songs from his shows and movies, they are mostly original songs, including collaborations with John Bucchino, Mary Fahl, Steven Lutvak, Alan Menken, Dean Pitchford, and Lindy Robbins. A compilation CD, *The Stephen Schwartz Album,* features Schwartz songs from a variety of musicals.

DVDs are available for: *Enchanted, Geppetto, Godspell, The Hunchback of Notre Dame, The Magic Show, Pippin, Pocahontas, The Prince of Egypt,* and *Working.*

To purchase these recordings or read more about them, please visit these websites:

www.DefyingGravityTheBook.com
www.MusicalSchwartz.com
www.StephenSchwartz.com

CREATIVITY NOTE

Interviewing— A Technique for Songwriting

Stephen Schwartz first used interviewing as a technique for developing one of his signature songs, "Forgiveness' Embrace," and he subsequently employed it to develop two other songs on the *Uncharted Territory* CD and others since, including "For Good" from *Wicked*.

"Forgiveness' Embrace" grew out of a project with Broadway singer Cass Morgan, who helped develop *Pump Boys and Dinettes* and had starred in an early *Children of Eden* production. Schwartz says, "Cass had been putting together an autobiographical one-woman show. She and I had known each other a long time, so she asked me to write the closing song for her. I saw a reading of the show as it existed then, so I kind of knew what it was about. I went with a yellow pad of paper and interviewed Cass at her house. She talked about her ideas and feelings while I took notes. Then I went home and used those notes as the basis for a song. I also tried to find where what she was saying coincided with things that I felt (I told her I was going to do this) so that I could write something that was both appropriate for her show and something I could sing as well. It turned out to be a really good way to write a song."

"Forgiveness' Embrace"

I have served a full life sentence
As a prisoner of my past
As a victim of a victim of a victim
Seems my parents' parents' parents
Left traps that held me fast
And they still catch me even when I think I've
   licked 'em
Well, I have blamed them, I have fought them
But I never understood
All they really did is did the best they could

Is there a way to rise above
If I look at them with love
Though I look at them full honest in the face?
Can I make my peace at last
With the pieces of my past
And enfold them in forgiveness' embrace?
And enfold them in forgiveness' embrace

I forgive my poor flawed parents
For the things they could not be
I forgive my valiant lovers
For not completing me

And the hardest thing of all now
I forgive myself the sin
Of not being all I planned
And all I thought I should have been
But there's an alchemy in time
Transforms each grief and loss and scar
Into the precious stuff of who we are

And there's a way to rise above
If I look at them with love
Though I don't deny that harm has taken place
I can make my peace at last
With the pieces of my past
And enfold them in forgiveness' embrace

Some call it wisdom and some just call it grace
When we make our peace at last
With the pieces of the past
And enfold them in forgiveness' embrace
And enfold them
I will enfold them
Now I enfold them
In forgiveness' embrace.

NOTES

About the notes: I primarily based *Defying Gravity* on original source material rather than previously published comments. I drew from transcripts made from my phone, email, or in-person interviews with Stephen Schwartz, or with writers, producers, designers, and cast members for the musicals. I conducted these interviews between 2000 and 2008. The notes below list published sources first. These are followed by the names of interviewees who provided the remaining quotes in the chapters. A few Stephen Schwartz quotes originated from previously published comments but have been adapted and authorized for use in this book.

OVERTURE

1 "'Cause getting your dreams…" Stephen Schwartz, "Thank Goodness" song lyric from *Wicked*.

CHAPTER 1

5 "With a talent…" Stephen Schwartz, "The Wizard and I" song lyric from *Wicked*.

8 "…how do you…" Suskin, *Opening Night on Broadway*, 612.

The remaining quotations are from the author's interviews with William ("Billy") Gronfein, Ralph Sammis, Sheila Schwartz, and Stephen Schwartz.

CHAPTER 2

15 "Morning glow…" Stephen Schwartz, "Morning Glow" song lyric from *Pippin*.

15 "In terms of liberation…" Aswad, "It's An Art: Reflections on a Life in Song."

21 "[Strauss] was reading through…" Attinson, "'Pippin, Pippin' Called Best Collaborative Effort," 1.

21 "That sounds wonderful…" A Stephen Schwartz comment as remembered by David Spangler, Spangler.

22 "Since March 6…""S'nS Prepares for Annual Spring Show," 9.

22 "Keeping with the…" Ibid.

29 "What I really want…" Goldberg, *Wild Mind*, 73.

The remaining quotations are from the author's interviews with Colette Bablon, Nina Faso, Bill Gronfein, Larry Miller, Kay Morgan, Sheila Schwartz, Stan Schwartz, Stephen Schwartz, and David Spangler.

CHAPTER 3

31 "Let's go down…" Stephen Schwartz, "Dancing Through Life" song lyric from *Wicked*.

31 "Show business is…" Wilker, "Stephen Schwartz: Musical Theater's True Believer."

37 "I was 21…" Aswad. "It's An Art: Reflections on a Life in Song."

38 "a three-octave range…" Sontag, "POP/JAZZ; An Enigma Wrapped in Songs."

39 "What the composer…" Green, *The World of Musical Comedy*, 360

The remaining quotations are from the author's interviews or correspondence with Joanne Jonas, Sheila Schwartz, Stan Schwartz, Stephen Schwartz, Carole Schwartz, and David Spangler.

CHAPTER 4

43 "You are the light…" Stephen Schwartz, "Light of the World" song lyric from *Godspell*.

45 "…an old priest came out…" Barker, "Dramatics Interview, John-Michael Tebelak and Stephen Schwartz: a candid conversation with the visionary creators of 'Godspell.'

46 "I held a rehearsal…" Miller, "Singing about Jesus, sighing over Shangri-La," 121.

46 "All right, tonight…" John-Michael Tebelak as remembered by Andy Rohrer. Rohrer interview by the author.

The remaining quotations are from the author's interviews with Colette Bablon, Nina Faso, Leon Katz, Edgar Lansbury, Sonia Manzano, Stephen Reinhardt, Andy Rohrer, and Stephen Schwartz.

CHAPTER 5

55 "You guessed!…" Stephen Schwartz, "All for the Best" song lyric from *Godspell*.

60 "I don't know how…" John-Michael Tebelak as remembered by Nina Faso. Faso interview by the author.

62 "I was quite trepidatious…" Stephen Schwartz interview by Ashley Griffin, with continuing quotes mixed from that interview and unpublished comments by Schwartz written in Shirley Bernstein's memory after she passed away.

63 "No matter what…" Stephen Schwartz as remembered by Carole Schwartz in correspondence with the author.

65 "The creation of…" Carl Jung, posted on http://www.quotationspage.com/quote/27093.html

65 "Enthusiasm (from the Greek…" Cameron, *The Artist's Way*, 153.

65 "Through spontaneity we…" Viola Spolin. http://www.answers.com/topic/viola-spolin?cat=entertainment

The remaining quotations are from the author's interviews with Nina Faso, Peggy Gordon, Joanne Jonas, Edgar Lansbury, Sonia Manzano, Gilmer McCormick, Stephen Nathan, Stephen Reinhardt, and Stephen Schwartz.

CHAPTER 6

67 "So let your light…" Stephen Schwartz, "Light of the World," song lyrics from Godspell.

70 "Is there anything…" Burton, *Leonard Bernstein*, 400.

71 "Terribly depressed…" Burton, *Leonard Bernstein*, 403.

72 "As for the critical reactions…" Coe, "The 'Mass': A Simple Song, Complex People."

74 "I can't think of anything…" Stephen Schwartz. http://www.StephenSchwartz.com forum.

75 David Merrick details are from Kissell, *David Merrick: The Abominable Showman*.

76 "Kathy, I'm lost," Paul Simon. "America."

76 "I feel an emptiness…" Unpublished script for *Pippin* from Stephen Schwartz's collection.

The remaining quotations are from the author's interviews or correspondence with Peggy Gordon, Roger O. Hirson, Joanne Jonas, Robin Lamont, Edgar Lansbury, Gilmer McCormick, and Stephen Schwartz.

CHAPTER 7

81 "I wanted magic…" Stephen Schwartz, "Finale," song lyric from *Pippin*.

81 "That's when Stephen…" Ostrow, *Present at the Creation*, 64.

82 "This is our last…" Roger O. Hirson conversation as remembered by Stephen Schwartz in an interview by the author.

85 "our most mysterious…" unpublished *Pippin* script from Stephen Schwartz's collection.

88 "We need someone…" Shurtleff, *Audition*, 171

88 "For the first time…" Ibid.

90 "Either I get…" Ostrow, *Present at the Creation*, 66.

91 "Fosse didn't miss…" Rosenfeld. "Remembering All That Fosse."

91 "In a profession…" Gussow. "A Tip of the Hat to Bob Fosse."

92 "Very little of what…" Watt, *New York Daily News*, September 8, 1972.

94 "I'd worked on that…" Townsend, "He's made a million but missed his mark," 3.

95 "My issue with…" Stephen Schwartz. Stephenschwartz.com discussion forum.

96 "This one looks…" "Pippin," *Variety*, September 27, 1972.

96 ""Last night's premiere…" Coe, " 'Pippin': A Rare Welcome Original."

97 "The Bob Fosse…" Doctorow, "Tap-Dancer Among the Literati"

98 "feeble." Barnes, "Theater: Musical 'Pippin at Imperial."

98 "*Pippin* is almost…" Kerr, "REVIEW: It's a Lovely Way to Do a Show."

98 "passable." "Pippin" *Variety*, October 25, 1972.

98 "awkward and amateurish charm." Simon, "Pippin," 84.

99 "Who cared what…" "V.J. Gillespie, email correspondence with the author, 2002.

99 [Schwartz's] score was… Peter Filichia, email correspondence with the author, 2002.

The remaining quotations are from the author's interviews or correspondence with Dean Pitchford, John Rubinstein, David Spangler, and Stephen Schwartz.

CHAPTER 8

107 "'Cause there's one thing…" Stephen Schwartz, "Up To His Old Tricks" lyric from *The Magic Show*.

107 "The music [of Spellbound]…" Marvin Krauss. Interview by John Harrison for *Spellbound*.

108 "Edgar and Joe…" Stephen Schwartz as remembered by David Spangler.

114 "And still it has…" Gottfried reprinted in Suskin, *More Opening Nights*.

The following quotes were taken from interviews by John Harrison for *Spellbound: The Wonder-filled Life of Doug Henning*. "The thing that was so appealing…" "Doug was incredibly…" "We deliberately wanted…." "Doug was also extraordinarily deft…" "The rabbit sort of…" "My picture of Doug…" "We felt that The Magic Show…"

The remaining quotations are from the author's interviews or correspondence with Nina Faso, Edgar Lansbury Stephen Reinhardt, Stephen Schwartz, David Spangler, and Dale Soules.

115 "As a kid…." Stephen Schwartz. Stephenschwartz.com discussion forum.

CHAPTER 9

121 "And then one day…" Stephen Schwartz, "Chanson" lyrics from The Baker's Wife

121 "I lived in France…" Schwartz, "Author Chat."

121 "Well, I have this…" Neil Simon as remembered by Stephen Schwartz, author's interview with Schwartz.

128 "Everything he touches turns to ink." Kissell, *David Merrick*, 22.

132 "delicate, bittersweet approach" "The Baker's Wife," *Variety*, 123.

138 "catch the personality…" Stephen Schwartz, Liner notes for *The Baker's Wife* Original London Cast, Jay Records, 1989.

The remaining quotations are from the author's interviews or correspondence with Robert Billig, Darlene Conley, Carole Demas, Josh Ellis, Kurt Peterson, Teri Ralston, Stephen Schwartz, Joseph Stein, and Bruce Yeko.

CHAPTER 10

145 "Hey somebody, won' cha…" Stephen Schwartz, "All the Livelong Day" lyric from *Working*.

145 You'll never feel the same about your job again! Broadway Advertisement for *Working*.

146 "It's something to run…" Terkel, *Working*. 39.

147 "I was attracted…" Terkel. Album notes for *Working*, Columbia. 1978.

149 "I worked in…" "Terkel, *Working*, 589.

156 "To be a waitress…" Terkel, *Working*, 297.

160 "In the preface to…" Stephen Schwartz, handwritten notes to cast members, 1978, from the collection of Steven Boockvor.

161 "I'm just sitting…" Cross, "Terkel Finally Gets Onstage," 18.

161 "Taking pride in…" Ibid.

164 "It's a long evening…" Christiansen, "A 'Working' that teeters near triumph."

164 "The most irritating difficulty…" Syse, "'Working' Should Work."

168 "Ambivalence here we…" Barnes, " 'Working' musical falls flat."

168 "An intelligent musical…" Gottfried, "Working," 24.

The remaining quotations are from the author's interviews or correspondence with Susan Birkenhead, Steven and Denise Boockvor, Craig Carnelia, Nina Faso, Zelda Fichandler, Micki Grant, David Patrick Kelly, Robin Lamont, Matt Landers, Irwin Meyer, Stephen Reinhardt, Stephen Schwartz, Lynne Thigpen.

CHAPTER 11

The quotations are from the author's interviews or correspondence with Steven and Denise Boockvor, Nina Faso, Stephen Reinhardt, and Stephen Schwartz.

183 "…I thought I would…" Stephen Schwartz in an email to the author at a discouraging moment in 2002.

CHAPTER 12

193 "It's difficult not…" Viagas, "Rags: A new B'way musical portrays the immigrant experience," 19.

193 ""Because of the…" Russo, "Tailoring 'Rags' For Broadway."

196 "I tried to clarify…" Holden, "How the Curtain Came Down on the Dream of 'Rags.'"

196 "I tried to clarify..." Russo, "Tailoring 'Rags' For Broadway."

196 "I don't know..." "However, after the..." "Don't let the show close..." Leon, "Rags: A Musical About the Jewish Immigrant Experience."

197 "Part of the problem..." Kissell. "Rags," *Women's Wear Daily.*

The remaining quotations are from the author's interviews with: Josh Ellis, Madeline Gilford, Stephen Schwartz, Joseph Stein, Bob Strauss, and Charles Strouse.

CHAPTER 13

206 "...brought up in a..." Campbell, "Joseph Campbell and the Power of Myth."

216 "British Equity backed..." Ellis, "You Mean God Isn't English?"

217 "well-meaning, indecisive..." Peter. Review. January 13, 1991.

217 "In the beginning..." Paton. Review. January 9, 1991.

217 "...this is yet..." Koenig. Review. January 16, 1991.

221 "It might be tempting..." Partin, Review. December, 1991

222 ...it's an affecting show..." Gladden, "'Children of Eden,' A Stylish, Entertaining Look at Genesis," November 30, 1991.

222 "...one of the most..." Filichia, "A Musical Paradise."

223 "Showing our writing..." Cameron, *The Right to Write,* 177.

The remaining quotations are from the author's interviews with John Caird, Charles Lisanby, Ken Page, Stephen Schwartz, and Ernie Zulia.

CHAPTER 14

229 "What I love..." Stephen Schwartz, "Just Around the Riverbend" lyric from *Pocahontas.*

237 "Composer Alan Menken..." Hodgins, "The Hunchback of Notre Dame."

237 "...the Alan Menken-Stephen..." Glieberman, "Movies: Towering Achievement, Disney Reaches New Heights with 'The Hunchback of Notre Dame.'"

237 "Some children are..." Baumgarten, "The Hunchback of Notre Dame."

The remaining quotations are from the author's interviews with Kevin Bannerman, Philip LaZebnik, Alan Menken, Peter Schneider, Stephen Schwartz.

CHAPTER 15

249 "No life can..." Stephen Schwartz, "Through Heaven's Eyes," lyric from *The Prince of Egypt.*

257 "We started doing..." Goldmark. "Doing the Lord's Work: Finding Inspiration in 'The Prince of Egypt.'"

The remaining quotations are from the author's interviews or correspondence with Brenda Chapman, Steven Hickner, Philip Lazebnik, and Stephen Schwartz.

CHAPTER 16

279 "And the Oscar..." Quincy Jones. 68th Academy Awards ceremony, March, 1996.

The remaining quotations are from the author's interviews or correspondence with John Bucchino, Gregory Maguire, and Stephen Schwartz.

CHAPTER 17

283 "Elphaba found the..." Maguire, *Wicked,* 77.

The remaining quotations are from the author's interviews with Stephen Schwartz, as well as his original 1998 outline.

CHAPTER 18

The quotations are from the author's interviews with Winnie Holzman, Gregory Maguire, Marc Platt, and Stephen Schwartz.

CHAPTER 19

299 "Begin at the beginning..." Carroll, *Alices Adventures in Wonderland,* 1865.

The remaining quotations are from the author's interviews with Winnie Holzman, Gregory Maguire, Marc Platt, and Stephen Schwartz.

CHAPTER 20

The quotations are from the author's interviews with Stephen Schwartz.

CHAPTER 21

308 "Galinda didn't see..." Maguire, *Wicked,* 64.

309 "who have problems..." Winnie Holzman, Interview by Robert J. Elisberg. Verified by correspondence with Winnie Holzman.

The remaining quotations are from the author's interviews with John Bucchino, Winnie Holzman, and Stephen Schwartz.

CHAPTER 22

318 "I had to harken..." Flatow, "Behind the Rainbow."

The remaining quotations are from the author's interviews with Raul Esparza, Stephen Oremus, Marc Platt, Stephen Schwartz.

CHAPTER 23

321 "extremely clever idea..." Schwartz, "Update."

322 "I am sitting..." Schwartz, "Update."

The remaining quotations are from the author's interviews with Winnie Holzman, Idina Menzel, and Stephen Schwartz.

CHAPTER 24

334 "She's a comic..." Wong, "The Leading Men: World Wide Wicked."

334 "I wish that..." Gans, "DIVA TALK: A Chat with Kristin Chenoweth PLUS Diva NEWS!"

342 "I stayed as far..." Gregory Maguire. Interviewed by Lori Halloran, KQED producer, and witnessed by the author. San Francisco. June 10, 2003.

345 "We're especially happy..." Marc Platt, from the author's notes from the reading.

346 "We learned a..." Stephen Schwartz, "Update," *The Schwartz Scene.*

The remaining quotations are from the author's interviews or correspondence with John Bucchino, Michael Cole, Idina Menzel, Bruce Kimmel, Joe Mantello, Gregory Maguire, Jayd McCarty, Idina Menzel, Stephen Schwartz, and David Stone.

CHAPTER 25

348 "I like Fiyero..." Carter & Fiona Comley, "Wicked Interviews – Adam Garcia and Helen Dallimore."

350 "He's sort of..." Wong, "The Leading Men: World Wide Wicked."

356 "I would like..." Schwartz, "Update."

359 "Writing is like..." Doctorow, In "Writers at Work."

The remaining quotations are from the author's interviews or correspondence with Winnie Holzman, Joe Mantello, and Stephen Schwartz

CHAPTER 26

368 "The song 'Defying Gravity'…" William Brohn, In an interview formerly posted on Decca Broadway's website (No longer available).

373 "I'm sitting here…" Schwartz, "Update."

374 "Well, this is…" Dean Pitchford as remembered by Stephen Schwartz in interview with the author.

375 "As I begin…" Schwartz, "Update."

The remaining quotations are from the author's interviews or correspondence with Michael Cole, Nick Francone, Susan Hilferty, Winnie Holzman, Joe Mantello, Gregory Maguire, Idina Menzel, Marc Platt, Edward Pierce, Stephen Schwartz, and David Stone

CHAPTER 27

394 "Their primary choice…" Hurwitt, ""Every witch way: Spellbinding 'Wicked' a charming vision of Oz, but is a few bricks shy of a road."

394 "'Wicked' is a smart…" Craig. "Musical's wicked good."

394 "Gluey, banal sentiment…" Harvey, Review. *Variety*, summer 2003.

398 "I have this Errol…" Wong, "The Leading Men: World Wide Wicked."

The remaining quotations are from the author's interviews or correspondence with Winnie Holzman, Joe Mantello, Idina Menzel, Stephen Oremus, Marge Schwartz, Stephen Schwartz, and David Stone.

CHAPTER 28

Quotations are from the author's interviews or correspondence with Joe Mantello, Marc Platt, Marge Schwartz, Stephen Schwartz, and David Stone.

CHAPTER 29

419 "…Mr. Schwartz's generically…" Brantley, "'WICKED' There's Trouble in Emerald City."

419 "There are Sondheimesque…" Winer, "Bewitched and Bothered, Too."

419 "…nothing really jells…" Kissel, "It's such a 'Wicked' waste of talent."

419 "The merits of Stephen…" Feingold, "Green Witch, Mean Time."

419 "Schwartz… has produced…" Barnes, "Review."

419 "The show's twenty-two songs…" Lahr, "Bitches and Witches."

The remaining quotations are from the author's interviews or correspondence with John Bucchino, Michael Cole, Susan Hilferty, Winnie Holzman, Joe Mantello, Idina Menzel, John Moses, Marc Platt, Stephen Schwartz, and David Stone.

CHAPTER 30

The quotations are from the author's interview with Stephen Schwartz.

EXTRAS

In addition to the author's journal entries, the additional Extras material was drawn from interviews with John Angier, Robert Cronin, Robert Billig, Michael Cole, Danny Kosarin, Debbie Gravitte, Paul Laird, Philip LaZebnik, Andrew Lippa, Michael Kerker, Peggy Kern, Brad Ross, Stephen Schwartz, David Stern, Meridee Stein, Anthony Stein.

The comment by Stephen Sondheim on page 496 was originally published in the program for a Stephen Schwartz tribute, and approved by Mr. Sondheim for publication in this book.

The comments by Michael Kerker are from an interview with Kerker by Shawn McCarthy.

We offer apologies for any inadvertent omissions. Any omissions brought to our attention will be remedied in future editions. To contact the author, with comments or questions, visit: http://defyinggravitythebook.com

Selected Bibliography

Theatre and Film Books

Burton, Humphrey. *Leonard Bernstein*. New York: Doubleday, 1994.

Cote, David. *Wicked: The Grimmerie: A Behind-the-Scenes Look at the Hit Broadway Musical*. New York. Hyperion, 2005.

Filichia, Peter. *Let's Put On A Musical*, revised second edition. New York: Back Stage Books, 2007.

Flinn, Denny Martin. *Little Musicals for Little Theatres: A Reference Guide for Musicals That Don't Need Chandeliers or Helicopters to Succeed*. New York: Limelight Editions, 2005.

Goldman, William. *The Season: A Candid Look at Broadway*. New York: Limelight Editions, 1969.

Gottfried, Martin. *All His Jazz: The Life and Death of Bob Fosse*. New York: Da Capo Press, 1998.

Green, Stanley. *The World of Musical Comedy: the story of the American musical stage as told through the careers of its foremost composers and lyricists*. 4th Edition. New York: DaCapo, 1984.

Grubb, Kevin Boyd, *Razzle Dazzle: The Life and Work of Bob Fosse*. New York: St. Martin's Press, 1989.

Guernsey, Otis L. *Broadway Song and Story: Playwrights/Lyricists/Composers Discuss Their Hits*. New York: Dodd Mead, 1986.

Harrison, John. *Spellbound: The Wonder-filled Life of Doug Henning*. New York: Box Office Books, 2008.

Jones, John Bush. *Our Musicals, Ourselves: A Social History of the American Musical Theater*, Lebanon, NH: Brandeis University Press, 2004.

Jones, Tom. *Making Musicals*. New York: Limelight Editions, 1998.

Kasha, Al, and Joel Hirschhorn. *Notes on Broadway: Intimate Conversations with Broadway's Greatest Songwriters*. New York: Simon and Schuster, 1985.

Kissel, Howard. *David Merrick: The Abominable Showman*. New York: Applause Books, 1993.

Mandelbaum, Ken. *Not Since Carrie: 40 Years of Broadway Flops*. New York: St. Martin's Press, 1991.

Miller, Scott. *From Assassins to West Side Story: The Director's Guide to Musical Theatre*. Portsmouth, NH: Heinemann Drama, 1996.

Ostrow, Stuart. *Present at the Creation, Leaping in the Dark, and Going Against the Grain*. New York: Applause Theatre and Cinema Books, 2006.

Rebello, Stephen. *The Art of Pocahontas*. New York: Hyperion Books, 1995.

Shurtleff, Michael. *Audition: Everything An Actor Needs to Know to Get the Part*. New York: Walker and Company, 1978.

Schwartz, Stephen. *Through Heaven's Eyes: Prince of Egypt Deluxe Storybook*. New York: Dutton Juvenile, 1998.

Solomon, Charles. *The Prince of Egypt*. New York: Harry N. Abrams, 1998.

Steyn, Mark. *Broadway Babies Say Goodnight: Musicals Then and Now*. New York: Routledge, 1999.

Strouse, Charles. *Put on a Happy Face*. New York: Sterling Publishing, 2008.

Suskin, Steven. *Opening Night on Broadway: A Critical Quotebook of the Golden Era of the Musical Theatre, Oklahoma! (1943 to Fiddler on the Roof)*. New York: Schirmer Books, 1990.

Suskin, Steven. *More Opening Nights on Broadway: A Critical Quotebook of the Musical Theatre from 1965 through 1981*. New York: Schirmer Books, 1997.

Adaptation Sources

Giano, Jean. *Blue Boy*, Translated by Katherine A. Clarke. New York: Perseus Publishing, 2000. [*The Baker's Wife* film was adapted from this book.]

Hugo, Victor. *The Hunchback of Notre Dame* (various publishers and translations).

Maguire, Gregory. *Wicked: The Life and Times of the Wicked Witch of the West*. New York: Regan Books, 1995.

Pagnol, Marcel (director). *The Baker's Wife*. Interama Video Classics, 1938.

Terkel, Studs. *Working: People Talk About What They Do All Day and How They Feel About What They Do*. New York: New Press, 1974.

Creativity and Writing Books

Cameron, Julia with Mark Bryan. *The Artist's Way*. New York: Tarcher/Putnam, 1992.

Cameron, Julia. *The Right to Write*. New York: Tarcher/Putnam, 1998.

Cox, Harvey. *The Feast of Fools*. Cambridge: Harvard University Press, 1969.

Doctorow, E.L. In *Writers at Work*, Eighth Series, ed. George Plimpton, 1988.

Goldberg, Natalie. *Wild Mind: Living the Writer's Life*. New York: Bantam, 1990.

McKee, Robert. *Story*. New York: Harper Collins, 1997.

Maisel, Eric. *Fearless Creating: A Step-by-Step Guide To Starting and Completing Your Work of Art*. New York: Tarcher/Putnam, 1995.

Schwartz, Stephen. *The Perfect Peach*. New York: Little, Brown & Company, 1977.

Tharp, Twyla. *The Creative Habit: Learn It and Use It For Life*. New York: Simon and Schuster, 2003.

Articles and Websites

See http://www.defyinggravitythebook.com for links to further relevant information.

Aswad, Jem. "It's An Art: Reflections on a Life in Song." Stephen Schwartz interview, http://www.ascap.com/filmtv/schwartz.html

Sue Attinson, "'Pippin, Pippin' Called Best Collaborative Effort," *Carnegie Tech Tartan*, April 26, 1967.

Baumgarten, Marjorie. "The Hunchback of Notre Dame," *The Austin Chronicle Movie Guide*. June 21, 1996.

Barker, Thomas A. "Dramatics Interview, John-Michael Tebelak and Stephen Schwartz: a candid conversation with the visionary creators of 'Godspell,'" *Dramatics Magazine*, January, 1975.

Barnes, Clive. "Review," *New York Post*, October 31, 2003.

Barnes, Clive. "Theater: Musical 'Pippin' at Imperial," *New York Times*, October 24, 1972.

Barnes, Clive. "'Working' musical falls flat," *New York Post*, May 28, 1978.

Brantley, Ben. "'WICKED' There's Trouble in Emerald City," *New York Times*, October 31, 2003.

Campbell, Joseph. "Joseph Campbell and the Power of Myth," (1988 TV mini-series documentary for Public Broadcasting Service), Bill Moyers interviews with Joseph Campbell. Mystic Fire Video (DVD version) 2001.

Carter, Mandy & Fiona Comley, "Wicked Interviews—Adam Garcia and Helen Dallimore," *MyVillage.com West End*, January 4, 2007.

Christiansen, Richard. "A 'Working' that teeters near triumph," *Chicago Daily News*, January 6, 1978.

Craig, Pat. "Musical's wicked good," *The Contra Costa Times*, June 12, 2003.

Coe, Richard L. "The 'Mass': A Simple Song, Complex People," *The Washington Post*, September 18, 1971.

Coe, Richard L. "'Pippin': A Rare Welcome Original," *The Washington Post*, September 21, 1972.

Cross, Robert. "Terkel Finally Gets Onstage," *Chicago Tribune Magazine*, June 1, 1978.

E. L. Doctorow, "Tap-Dancer Among the Literati," *New York Times*, October 4, 1987.

Ellis, David. "You Mean God Isn't English?" *Time Magazine*, October 1, 1990.

Feingold, Michael. "Green Witch, Mean Time," *The Village Voice*, November 5–11, 2003.

Flatow, Sheryl. "Behind the Rainbow," *Playbill*, October 17, 2003. http://www.playbill.com/features/article/82232.html

Filichia, Peter. "A Musical Paradise," *New Jersey Star Ledger*, November 11, 1997.

Gans, Andrew. "DIVA TALK: A Chat with Kristin Chenoweth PLUS Diva NEWS!" *Playbill.com*, October 11, 2002. http://www.playbill.com/celebritybuzz/article/76268.html

Glieberman, Owen. "Movies: Towering Achievement, Disney Reaches New Heights with 'The Hunchback of Notre Dame,'" *Entertainment Weekly*, 1995.

Gladden, Chris. "'Children of Eden,' A Stylish, Entertaining Look at Genesis." *The Roanoke Times*, November 30, 1991.

Goldmark, Daniel. "Doing the Lord's Work: Finding Inspiration in 'The Prince of Egypt,'" *Film Score Monthly*, Volume 3, number 10.

Gottfried, Martin. "Working," *Saturday Review*, July 8, 1978.

Gussow, Mel. "A Tip of the Hat to Bob Fosse," *New York Times*, October 4, 1987.

Harvey, Dennis. Review, *Variety*, Summer 2003.

Hodgins, Paul. "The Hunchback of Notre Dame," *The Orange County Register*, June 23, 1995.

Holden, Stephen. "How the Curtain Came Down on the Dream of 'Rags.'" *New York Times*, September 21, 1986.

Hurwitt, Robert. "Every witch way: Spellbinding 'Wicked' a charming vision of Oz, but is a few bricks shy of a road," *San Francisco Chronicle*, June 12, 2003.

Kerr, Walter. "REVIEW: It's a Lovely Way to Do a Show," *New York Times*, October 29, 1972.

Kissell, Howard. "Rags," *Women's Wear Daily*, August, 1986.

Kissel, Howard. "It's such a 'Wicked'waste of talent," *New York Daily News*, October 31, 2003.

Koenig, Rhonda. Review. *Punch*, January 16, 1991.

Lahr, John. "Bitches and Witches," *New Yorker*, November 10, 2003.

Leon, Masha. "Rags: A Musical About the Jewish Immigrant Experience." *The Forward*, September 5, 1986.

Miller, Edwin. "Singing about Jesus, sighing over Shangri-La," *Seventeen Magazine*, 1973.

Paton, Maureen. Review. *Daily Express*, January 9, 1991.

Partin, Bruce L. "Children of Eden," *Southern Stages Theatre Magazine*, December, 1991.

Peter, John. Review, *Sunday Times*, January 13, 1991.

Rosenfeld, Paul. "Remembering All That Fosse," *Los Angeles Times*, October 11, 1987.

Russo, Vito. "Tailoring 'Rags' For Broadway," *Newsday*, August 17, 1986.

Schwartz, Stephen. Discussion threads. http://www.StephenSchwartz.com forum.

Schwartz, Stephen. "Author Chat, for *The Baker's Wife*. From a newsletter posted on http://www.MTIshows.com

Schwartz, Stephen. "Update," *The Schwartz Scene*, an website ezine/newsletter for subscribers, from http://www.musicalschwartz.com.

Simon, John. "Pippin, *New York*, November 6, 1972.

Sontag, Deborah, "POP/JAZZ; An Enigma Wrapped in Songs," *New York Times*, October 26, 1997.

Syse, Glenna. "'Working' Should Work," *Chicago Sun Times*, January 6, 1978.

Townsend, Richard. "He's made a million but missed his mark," *Sunday News*, May 2, 1976.

Watt, Doug. *New York Daily News*, September 8, 1972.

Wilker, Lawrence J. "Stephen Schwartz: Musical Theater's True Believer," Stephen Schwartz interview by Kennedy Center President Lawrence J. Wilker. *Playback Magazine*, August 2000.

Winer, Linda. "Bewitched and Bothered, Too," *Newsday*, October 31, 2003.

Wong, Wayman. "The Leading Men: World Wide Wicked," *Playbill.com* November 1, 2003. http://www.playbill.com/news/article/82515.html

"Pippin," *Variety*, September 27, 1972.

"Pippin," *Variety*, October 25, 1972.

"S'nS Prepares for Annual Spring Show," *Carnegie Tech Tartan*, April 5th, 1967.

"The Baker's Wife," *Variety*, May 12, 1976.

LICENSING INFORMATION FOR THE MUSICALS

A note from Stephen Schwartz about *Wicked* licensing:

"I don't expect stock-and-amateur licensing rights to *Wicked* to become available for some time, since they are generally not made available until after the Broadway production has closed, but they will eventually be handled by Music Theatre International."

Music Theatre International

Music Theatre International is the official licensing agency for *The Baker's Wife, Captain Louie, Children of Eden, Geppetto & Son, Godspell Jr., Pippin,* and *Working.* MTI is one of two companies that officially license *Godspell.* The company provides a detailed descriptions, casting requirements, and support materials for the shows that are currently available from them. Visit:

www.mtishows.com/

North America
Music Theatre International
421 West 54th Street, New York, NY 10019
Tel: (212) 541-4684   Fax: (212) 397-4684
Licensing@MTIshows.com
International licensing: www.mtishows.com/contact.asp

Theatre Maximus

Theatre Maximus has licensed *Godspell* since 1972. The Web site includes a Spanish language *Godspell* forum. Contact: Theatre Maximus, 1650 Broadway Suite 601, New York, NY 10019, 212-765-5913. Email: Godspell_The_Musical@Godspell-TheMusical.com

The Rodgers and Hammerstein Organization

The Rodgers and Hammerstein Organization licenses *Rags.* www.rnh.com

1065 Avenue Of The Americas; Suite 2400
New York, NY 10018-2506
Tel: (212) 541-6600   Fax: (212) 586-6155

Samuel French, Inc.

Samuel French, Inc. licenses *Personnals.*

Samuel French, Inc.
45 West 25th Street - Dept.W,   New York, NY 10010
Tel: (212) 206-8990   Fax: (212) 206-1429
www.samuelfrench.com/

Licensing information for CDs, Lyrics, Etc.

To include a Stephen Schwartz song on your own CD, to reprint lyrics, etc., refer to information on www.stephenschwartz.com/contact2.htm or
www.stephenschwartz.com/licensing.htm

MARTHA SWOPE

Leading Player (Ben Vereen) and other Players open *Pippin* with a magical lighting effect.
Stage directions for this effect:

"The hands are illuminated by a light curtain consisting of ungelled floodlights focused directly upwards mounted on the stage floor which keeps the stage in virtual darkness so that the writhing hands exist in a strange, macabre limbo."

Pippin is one of many Schwartz musicals licenced by Music Theatre International.

ACKNOWLEDGMENTS AND CREDITS

Thank you! Hundreds of wonderful people contributed their ideas, stories, and time to make this book possible. I am deeply grateful to each one of them.

For Interviews and Correspondence

I wish to thank John Angier, Colette Bablon, Kevin Bannerman, John Barr, Andrew Barrett, Shoshana Bean, Bob Billig, Susan Birkenhead, Stephen Boockvor, Denise Boockvor, Herbie Braha, John Bucchino, Craig Carnelia, Brenda Chapman, Kristin Chenoweth, Michael Cole, Darlene Conley, Scott Coulter, Carole Demas, Michael Edwards, Raul Esparza, Laurie Faso, Nina Faso, Peter Filichia, Aramond Francone, David Friedman, Alyse Gilbert, Madeline Gilford, Peggy Gordon, Micki Grant, Debbie Gravitte, Gordon Greenberg, Billy (William) Gronfein, Katie Hanley, John Harrison, Steven Hickner, Susan Hilferty, Roger O. Hirson, Winnie Holzman, Joanne Jonas, Leon Katz, Peggy Kern, Bruce Kimmel, Danny Kosarin, David Koyle, Alex Lacamoire, Robin Lamont, Edgar Lansbury, Philip LaZebnik, Andrew Lippa, Charles Lisanby, Patti LuPone, Gregory Maguire, Joe Mantello, Sonia Manzano, Mary Maziotti, Jayd McCarty, Gilmer McCormick, Tim McDonald, Alan Menken, Idina Menzel, Irwin Meyer, Lawrence Miller, Cass Morgan, Katherine Morgan, John Moses, Stephen Nathan, Kerry O'Malley, Stephen Oremus, Kurt Peterson, Edward Pierce, Dean Pitchford, Marc Platt, Louise Quick, Teri Ralston, Andy Rohrer, Brad Ross, Frances Ruffele, John Rubinstein, Ralph Sammis, Peter Schneider, Carole Schwartz, Marge Schwartz, Jessica Schwartz, Scott Schwartz, Sheila Schwartz, Stanley Schwartz, Stephen Sondheim, David Spanger, Anthony Stein, Joseph Stein, Meridee Stein, David Stern, David Stone, Robert Straus, Ron Strauss, Charles Strouse, Lynn Thigpen, Bruce Yeko, David Zippel, Ernie Zulia.

I offer special thanks to Stephen Schwartz for his courage in allowing his artistic life to be the subject of a book, for his time for interviews, for his kindness to me and my husband, and for his patience and endurance in advising me.

For Editorial Support and Feedback

I will always be grateful to Michael Cole for initiating me into the inner workings of Stephen Schwartz's world, introducing me to the New York City area, providing correspondence support, and being a constant guide and friend. I also thank Eric Brown and Nina Faso for their moral support along the way, as well as assistance with the book's content.

I thank my editing and feedback teams. Developmental Editing: Eric Brown and Bob Vieira. Additional editing and feedback: Minda Bernstein, Eric Brown, Barbara Cuvier, Joel Freedman, Peter Furia, Jean Horend, Morgan LaVere, Bettie Laven, Linda Massie, Ellen Metropole, Shawn McCarthy, Jim Phillips, Sheila Schultz, and Bob Vieira.

Musicians and musicologists providing suggestions: Eric Brown, Paul Laird, Steve Parsons, Bob Vieira, and Glenn Weiss.

I couldn't have completed this book without help from dozens of theatre aficionados and friends who provided feedback on drafts or background information. They are too numerous to thank, but among them I wish to list Scott and Janet Cain, Gary Chaterand, Nina Combs, Michael Coolen, Richard Connema, Scott Coulter, Tom Freeman and family, Ashley Griffin, Tony Gonzalez, Noel and Joy Katz, Chris Kuczewski, Jane Knox, Michael Lavine, Bob Levy, Kerry Long, Jim Miller, James McGrath Morris, Justin Paul, Duane Poole, Lynne Robinson, David Roth, Anthony Santelmo Jr., Jason Sherry, William Squier, Lisamarie Testasecca, Glenn Weiss, Steve White, and Sara Wright.

For Additional Support

Additional professional support: Jonathan Kirsch, Nancy Rose, Charmaine Ferenczi, as well as Susannah Greenberg, Mahesh Grossman, John Kremer, and Angela Vieira. Also the UPS Store and Staples copy staff of Ridgefield and Danbury, Connecticut.

A special thanks to the brilliant design team of Terence de Giere, Margo Mooney, and V. Paul Smith Jr.

This book would not have been possible without the constant support of my wonderful husband, Terry de Giere, who shared the journey, processed all the photographs, provided photos of his own, helped proofread, served as my tech support guy, cooked a lot of meals, and so much more. I'm grateful to my family for being there: Evelyn, Pat, Jack, Mariella, Sally, Leslie, Bob, Ann, Nathan, Aaron, and Kyle. I deeply appreciate the steady companionship in Connecticut of Terry and Bernie Nevas without whom I could not have accomplished this task.

I wish to thank my writing teachers: Susan Albert, Julia Cameron, Natalie Goldberg, Jim Karpen, Tony Lawlor, Robert McKee, Mary Carroll Moore, Robert Oates Jr., Craig Pearson, Stephen Schneider, Stephen Schwartz, Lori Soderlind, and William Zinzer. I'm especially grateful to my ninth grade English teacher, Mark Parish, and my eleventh grade English teacher, Mrs. Rowling, who started me on the path.

My Online "Friends": Many thanks go to contributors to theatre message boards including StephenSchwartz.com and All That Chat on TalkinBroadway.com, and to the many people who have emailed me comments and questions.

Lyrics and Publications Permissions

"America"
Copyright © 1968 Paul Simon.
Used by permission of the Publisher: Paul Simon Music.

"Colors of the Wind"
"Just Around the Riverbend"
From Walt Disney's POCAHONTAS
Music by Alan Menken
Lyrics by Stephen Schwartz
© 1995 Wonderland Music Company, Inc. and Walt Disney Music Company
All Rights Reserved. Used by Permission.

"Ever Ever After," "Happy Working Song"
From Walt Disney Pictures' ENCHANTED
Music by Alan Menken
Lyrics by Stephen Schwartz
© 2007 Wonderland Music Company, Inc. and Walt Disney Music Company
All Rights Reserved. Used by Permission.

ILLUSTRATION CREDITS

The illustrations in this book are reproduced by permission of the following:

Academy of Motion Picture Arts and Sciences: Copyright © Academy of Motion Picture Arts and Sciences, pages 227, 271

American Playhouse/WGBH Educational Foundation: Courtesy of the American Playhouse/WGBH Educational Foundation, page 180

Berliner Studio/BEImages: page 286

Jacob Belcher: page 495

Jim Borgman: Jim Borgman © 2006 Cincinnati Enquirer. Reprinted with permission of UNIVERSAL PRESS SYNDICATE. All rights reserved. page 423

Michael Cole: pages 451, 495

Carol de Giere: pages 14, 41, 54, 204, 338, 393, 432, 479, 485, 500

Terence de Giere: pages 14, 41, 137, 233, 434, 488, 497, 510, 510

Eastman Kodak Company: Courtesy of the Eastman Kodak Company, page 276

Nina Faso: pages 152, 162, 297, 468

Thomas England: pages 144, 159, 164, 165, 165

Bruce Glikas: Bruce Glickas/Broadway.com, pages 335, 418

Gerry Goodstein: pages 226, 226

Tristram Kenton: page 348

Marianne Kilroy: page 485

Robin Lamont: pages 45, 171

Joan Lauren: © Joan Lauren www.joanlauren.com, page viii

Michael Le Poer Trench: pages 204, 206, 216, 217, 225,

Mariann Lopinto: pages 499, 502

Joan Marcus: Book Cover (photograph of Eden Espinosa in *Wicked*), pages 269, 293, 294, 300, 310, 312, 320, 328, 332 352, 355, 360, 365, 366, 379, 380, 381, 386, 400, 412, 422, 424, 425

Joseph Marzullo: pages 418, 432

Charles Moore: Charles Moore / Black Star page 475

Scott Mullin: Book Cover (Photograph of Stephen Schwartz)

Andy Newman: ©1998 by Andy Newman page 286

Playbill: PLAYBILL® All rights reserved. pages 36, 68, 97, 115, 166, 197, 417

William "PoPsie" Randolph: Photo by William "PoPsie" Randolph © 2008 Michael Randolph www.PoPsiePhotos.com PoPsiephotos@att.net, pages 3, 66

Carol Rosegg: © Carol Rosegg, page 483

Jessica Schwartz: pages 199, 433, 510

Stephen Schwartz: pages 181, 182, 237, 239, 240, 240, 241, 241, 278, 278, 324, 353, 370, 476, 477, 503

V Paul Smith Jr: pages 292, 432

Ben Strothmann: Photo: Ben Strothman/BroadwayWorld.com, page 421

Martha Swope: © Martha Swope Book Cover (Ben Vereen in *Pippin*, and Doug Henning in *The Magic Show*), pages 54, 58, 64, 80, 82, 89, 101, 102, 103, 104, 105, 106, 114, 116, 116, 117, 123, 130, 136, 137, 141, 149, 186, 195, 195, 195, 195, 464, 465, 466, 473, 519

Take Home Tunes: Courtesy Bruce Yeko/Take Home Tunes, page 139

Theatre Maximus: Book Cover (*Godspell* Logo, original artwork by David Byrd)

Glenn Weiss: page 458

Van Williams: © Van Williams, page 80

The remaining photographs are from the private collections of:

Herb Braha: page 458

Michael Cole: page 374

Micki Grant: page 161

Nina Faso: pages 19, 69, 69

Robin Lamont: page 42

Phillip LaZebnik: page 233

Gilmer McCormick: page 66

Katherine Morgan: page18

Kurt Peterson: pages 120, 141

Carole and Stephen Schwartz: pages 12, 14, 23, 23, 24, 25, 25, 33, 40, 40, 62, 69, 73, 73, 119, 170 172, 172, 174, 186, 200, 201, 202, 203, 218, 218, 218, 228, 237, 248, 258, 264, 266, 276, 277, 277, 347, 374, 392, 434, 440, 478, 496, 501

Jessica Schwartz: page 329

Sheila and Stanley Schwartz: pages 4, 4, 7, 9

Dale Soules: page 113

David Spangler: page 30

Public Domain: William Wallace Denslow, page 270

While every effort has been made to trace copyright holders and obtain permission, we offer apologies for any instances in which this was not possible and for any inadvertent omissions. Any omissions brought to our attention will be remedied, and credit will be adjusted in future editions.

INDEX

Page numbers in *italics* refer to illustrations.

I n July 2008, Wicked *passed* Pippin *and* The Magic Show *in number of continuous performances on Broadway. All three have run over 1900 performances, making Stephen Schwartz the only songwriter in Broadway history with three shows that have reached this milestone.*